R U S S I A

W O M E N

C U L T U R E

EDITED BY

 HELENA GOSCILO AND

BETH HOLMGREN

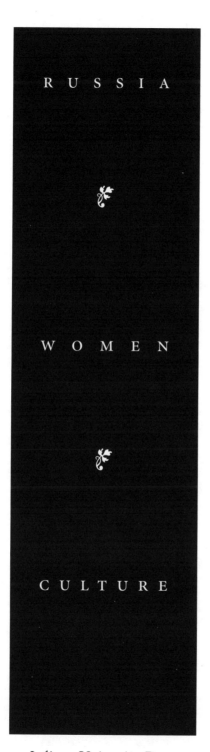

RUSSIA

WOMEN

CULTURE

Indiana University Press

Bloomington • *Indianapolis*

The paper used in this publication meets the minimum
requirements of American National Standard for
Information Sciences—Permanence of Paper for Printed
Library Materials, ANSI Z39.48-1984.

Manufactured in the United States

Library of Congress Cataloging-in-Publication Data

Russia—women—culture / edited by Helena Goscilo and Beth Holmgren.
   p. cm.
  Includes index.
  ISBN 0-253-33019-X (cl : alk. paper). — ISBN 0-253-21044-5 (pa :
alk. paper)
   1. Russia—Civilization—1801–1917. 2. Soviet Union—
Civilization. 3. Women—Russia. 4. Women—Soviet Union.
I Goscilo, Helena, date .   II. Holmgren, Beth, date .
DK189.2.R87   1996
947'.07—dc20   95–38295
1 2 3 4 5 01 00 99 98 97 96

For Mama, aka Lola von Wagner,
for the inestimable gift of an enchanted
childhood.   HG

For our "incomparable" Jess, who fills
our home with joy.   BH

CONTENTS

INTRODUCTION

RUSSIAN WOMEN'S STUDIES, much like other late-twentieth-century studies of obscured subjects, is a field that has developed myopically, resembling a well-intentioned but rather haphazard rescue mission to the alleged margins of Russian culture and society. To a large extent, the field itself formed in response to the myopia of others—of Russianists long blinded to the significance of gender in their material, of feminist scholars who had eyes only for the experience and models of first-world and third-world women. Those of us who signed on this expedition have tended to huddle together in the familiar confines of our own disciplines and to see what we have been trained to see. We literary scholars, for instance, not only struggled along behind more intrepid parties of historians and political scientists, but also focused first on women already present in the extant canon, highbrow artists or public figures spotlighted by a male-dominated critical establishment; we have been less discerning in establishing alternative "sight lines" for analysis and evaluation.[1] While we can take heart from our expedition's rapid growth (the last decade has witnessed a mini-boom in publications on Russian women), we must admit that any truly comprehensive exploration (evidenced by such recent works as the *Dictionary of Russian Women Writers* [1994]) is just getting underway.[2] As our searchlight plays fitfully over the terrain, we are still struggling to expand and adjust our vision.

This book represents our effort to widen the lens—to project a more interdisciplinary, systematically inclusive view of women in Russian culture. Drawing on the latest, least myopic scholarship in (Western) women's studies and cultural studies, we picture the entity of Russian culture as an amorphous, intricate, many-layered and much-lived-in place, a rambling house of countless private and public rooms, with limitless street access, instead of the proverbial museum of cultural monuments.[3] In our perception, all the spaces of this house are vital to the making of Russian culture: the boudoir, bath, linen closet, kitchen, pantry, garden, and even the overdecorated parlor are invested with the same creative potential as the poet's garret and the "master's" book-lined library. And everywhere women are at work in it. Indeed, just as Dostoevsky taught us to heed the mumblings from the basement, so the women situated elsewhere in the house can alert us to the significance of its myriad corners and diverse utterances. In our view of Russian culture, women are never *behind*, but always *on* the scene.

Moreover, our anthology does not so much deviate from as extend certain artistic and critical practices in Russian culture. Far more elaborately than their Western counterparts, Russian artists have worried the connection between life and art in their conduct and works. For much of the nineteenth century, most conceived of culture, and wielded it, as a kind of social service. By the end of the century, some approached the very act of living as an artistic project.[4] Russian scholars have reinforced these notions of an applied or lived art with their scrupulous mapping of a "poetics of everyday behavior"; in the Russian case, the formalism-structuralism continuum progressed *toward* an analytical appreciation of the daily and mundane.[5] Given this emphasis, Russian studies has overlapped considerably with the evolving field of cultural studies, which aims to textualize and historicize concrete experience of everyday life.[6] Yet the Russianist conception of culture remains more limited than the all-encompassing model proposed by cultural studies, especially with regard to those spheres and interactions mainly involving women. In other words, Russian scholarship may scrutinize the (male) poet "at home," but it definitely overlooks the (female) cook in the kitchen.[7]

In order to provide a truly informed tour of this house and its inhabitants, our anthology enlists contributors who subscribe to this more extensive cultural purview and combine in their analysis the different foci and investigative methods of their disciplines (history, literature, art).

Their essays analyze women's creativity of every type (product, performance, collaborative exchange) in every space. Creative sites range from bathhouse to ballroom: from Nancy Condee's historical musings on women's baths and Mary B. Kelly's description of the ritual textiles of peasant women to Helena Goscilo's deciphering of nineteenth-century women's fashion and Stephanie Sandler's ruminations on women, men, and social dance. Darra Goldstein relishes the creative powers that Russian women have traditionally exercised in the kitchen and the larder. Through their complementary survey of Russian salon hostesses in the nineteenth and twentieth centuries, Lina Bernstein and Beth Holmgren usher us into more formal (or at least more publicly oriented) rooms. Gitta Hammarberg, in turn, illuminates the products of the salon—the domestic albums kept, inspired, and shaped by women. Resolutely crossing the threshold from private to public, Nadya Peterson traces how Russian women creatively infused various notions of personal and domestic cleanliness into their daily regimen in prison and camps. And essays by Ol'ga Vainshtein and by Nadezhda Azhgikhina and Goscilo explore women's habits of dress and pursuit of beauty in a Soviet/post-Soviet variant of this space, restructured into communal apartments, beauty salons, hairdressing parlors, and shopping queues.

As our house plan implies, we have designed this collection to dismantle any hierarchy of cultural categories. In keeping with another basic tenet of cultural studies, the essays here challenge the conventional separation and stratification of Russian culture into highbrow, traditional, and popular. Just as we propose a nondiscriminatory tour of the upstairs and downstairs rooms, so we mount a joint display of the varied artifacts within. On the one hand, our conflation of categories partially parallels trends specific to Russian society; in some ways, the Russian critical establishment, as compared to Western academia, proved to be less rigid in creating and maintaining a cultural canon. In the modern period especially, the highbrow love affair with folk culture (mirroring the intelligentsia's moral crisis and therefore tinged with guilt and envy) periodically "de-classed" the boundary between highbrow and traditional. Alison Hilton's essay on women's cultivation of the applied arts in fin-de-siècle Russia extensively documents the ready highbrow embrace of "handicrafts." On the other hand, the scholarship here counters a longstanding premise of antagonism between Russian highbrow and consumer cultures, an attitude presumably exacerbated by the intelligentsia's cultural dominance and the lack of a significantly numerous bourgeoisie. In her analysis of the life and work of romance singer Anastasiia Vial'tseva, Louise McReynolds argues that this artist paradigm reflects new possibilities in middlebrow culture at the turn of the century. Focusing on the same historical period, Holmgren demonstrates the calculated synthesis of highbrow and middlebrow in the burgeoning mass-circulation press and book trade. Whatever boundary these essays question, however, they are linked by the same fundamental supposition: that women, through their social experience and individual ingenuity, figure as crucial agents and sites of cultural mediation. In our collective readings, Russian women, far more than Russian men, both effect and represent the extraordinary variety and vitality of their culture.

Although our anthology attempts an inclusive view of women in the house of Russian culture, we are only too conscious of the many corners left unexplored—women in more traditional religious roles; women's participation in sports culture; female celebrities and celebrity-making in the Soviet era, to name just a few. In leaving off, therefore, we can only urge others to take up the exploration. Our tour cannot reproduce a panorama of the whole, but we hope it will furnish the first stages of a collaborative enterprise, intimating the extensive territory to be surveyed, and enticing others to probe further on, closer up, and with ever sharper sight.

We have grouped the contents according to categories that are contingent—as are all taxonomies—and intended to spotlight differences rather than similarities among the essays. By contrast, the inclusion of individual essays in any given group unavoidably emphasizes their common denominator. Several essays could fit as well under rubrics other than those we have assigned: Hammarberg's reading of the domestic album teases out its performativity; Peterson's analysis of cleanliness during Stalinism addresses issues of class and body hygiene as well as domestication; and almost all of the essays featured in this volume highlight Russian women's acts of creative license that seem to transcend or cut across class boundaries.

Several motifs inevitably but fortuitously reticulate throughout the volume, as do references to such works as Evgeniia Ginzburg's prison memoirs, Pushkin's *Eugene Onegin*, and Anatolii Rubinov's study *The Intimate Life of Moscow*. In general, the contributors' extensive use of literary texts reflects less their own attachment to literature than the extraordinary status it enjoyed in Russian and Soviet culture. If the essays by Goldstein and Sandler turn to fiction for corroboration or illustration of social phenomena, that far from naive "appeal to fictional authority" stems from an awareness of the extensive interplay between literature and life that Irina Paperno's study of Chernyshevsky documents in such compelling detail.[8] As the essays by Vainshtein and by Azhgikhina and Goscilo demonstrate, myth and fantasy figured much more prominently in Soviet journalism than in Soviet fiction.

We thank our contributors for their collegiality, readiness to revise, and patience with the "double burden" of two editors separated by many miles, though united by shared standards as well as regular communication. Janet Rabinowitch has our gratitude for believing in the value of this project from its inception, as do our respective institutions, the University of North Carolina at Chapel Hill and the University of Pittsburgh, for funding travel connected with the volume.

The most profound pleasure in this collaborative venture came from my co-editor, whose humor, intelligence, and generosity turned labor into laughter. For this she has my loving thanks (H.G.).

The admiration is mutual: My deepest gratitude goes to *my* co-editor, who shouldered the joint responsibilities of editing and translating with characteristic industry, skill, and verve, and who proved a true friend indeed to her colleague-turned-mama. I also thank my husband, Mark, for his loving support and my daughter, Jessye, for her inspirational presence (B.H.).

Notes

1. Russian historians and political scientists who pioneered the first monographs in the field of Russian women's studies include Barbara Engel, Gail Lapidus, David Ransel, and Richard Stites in the United States, and Mary Buckley and Linda Edmondson in England. An excellent example of scholars' collective work in this vein is *Russia's Women: Accommodation, Resistance, Transformation*, ed. Barbara Evans Clements, Barbara Alpern Engel, and Christine D. Worobec (Berkeley/Los Angeles/Oxford: U of California P, 1991).

2. This mini-boom includes such recent anthologies of essays as *The Fruits of Her Plume: Essays on Contemporary Russian Women's Culture*, ed. Helena Goscilo (Armonk/London: M. E. Sharpe, 1993); *Sexuality and the Body in Russian Culture*, ed. Jane Costlow, Stephanie Sandler, and Judith Vowles (Stanford: Stanford UP, 1994); and *Women in Russian Literature*, ed. Toby W. Clyman and Diana Greene (Westport/London: Greenwood P, 1994). The *Dictionary of Russian Women Writers*, ed. Marina Ledkovsky, Charlotte Rosenthal, and Mary Zirin (Westport/London: Greenwood P, 1994), provides information on a wide array of women writers, including both highbrow and popular.

3. The interdisciplinary approach of our anthology echoes general trends in ethnic, cultural, and women's studies. As Jon Cruz and Justin Lewis remark in their introduction to *Viewing, Reading, Listening: Audiences and Cultural Reception* (Boulder/San Francisco/Oxford: Westview P, 1994): "the scramble for interdisciplinarity is symptomatic of a crisis in the politics of knowledge after poststructuralism. . . . The newer disciplines (such as ethnic studies and women's studies) . . . have, at least in part, been created out of this interdisciplinary focus on representation" (2).

4. For an analysis of the latter phenomenon, see the recent collection of essays titled *Creating Life: The Aesthetic Utopia of Russian Modernism*, ed. Irina Paperno and Joan Delaney Grossman (Stanford: Stanford UP, 1994).

5. For examples of this kind of structuralist criticism (and its later development), see *The Semiotics of Russian Cultural History*, intro. by Boris Gasparov, ed. Alexander D. Nakhimovsky and Alice Stone Nakhimovsky (Ithaca/London: Cornell UP, 1985), and Irina Paperno, *Chernyshevsky and the Age of Realism: A Study of the Semiotics of Behavior* (Stanford: Stanford UP, 1988).

6. Simon During posits this feature in his introduction to *The Cultural Studies Reader* (London/New York: Routledge, 1993), 25.

7. Rare exceptions to this rule include the popular journalist Anatolii Rubinov, who for decades investigated such officially ignored venues as Russian women's hair parlors, prostitutes' "beats," and toilets, and the renowned scholar Iurii Lotman, who has analyzed the role of dolls, women's dress, and tea drinking in Russian culture no less assiduously than he has analyzed recherché aspects of the literary canon. Both would feel at home in our house, although they doubtless would enter by different doors. See, for instance, Anatolii Rubinov, *Intimnaia zhizn' Moskvy* (Moscow: Ekonomika, 1991), which examines, *inter alia*, the lives of prostitutes, men's baths, women's hair and beauty parlors, and cemeteries. See also Iu. M. Lotman, *Izbrannye stat'i*, 3 vols. (Tallin: "Alleksandra," 1992–93).

8. See Paperno, *Chernyshevsky and the Age of Realism*.

PART I

BODY WORKS

THE SECOND FANTASY MOTHER, OR ALL BATHS ARE WOMEN'S BATHS

Nancy Condee

Introduction: The Unreal *Bania*

THE BATHHOUSE, OR *BANIA* IN RUSSIAN,[1] is a vast topic. The specific focus of discussion here is the women's contemporary, urban *bania*, not the so-called "real *bania*" of the peasant countryside or the distant past. Like so much in Russia that is real, this real *bania* exists primarily in the imagination of the deracinated inhabitant as an amalgam of imperfectly recollected types: the village *bania*, the family bania, the so-called black (or unvented) *bania*, the white (or vented) *bania*.

I relegate all these to the periphery of my discussion, along with the elite, closed *bania* (pre-Soviet, Soviet, or post-Soviet). The centrality here of the urban *bania*—a public, single-sex, commercial, and communal space—has less to do with some posited norm of the social sciences than with an interest in the "unreal" *bania*—i.e., the one grounded in the lived experience of most urban Russians. I preface my analysis with a brief historical excursus.

The Church, the Baths, and the Foreigner Narrator

The Russian public baths have been a topic of bemused commentary since the eleventh-century legend which tells of the Apostle Andrew's visit, back in Rus' in pre-Christian times, to the areas stretching from Kiev to Novgorod:

> I saw with wonder the Slavic land as I traveled through it. I saw wooden baths, and how they heat them red-hot, and undress, and are naked, and anoint themselves with tallow, and take upon themselves a young twig

switch, and beat themselves, beating themselves to the point that they barely escape alive, and pour cold water over themselves, and so are revived. And so they do every day, being in no way tormented by it, though they torment themselves; and in this way they carry out their washing and not their torment.[2]

This familiar passage from the *Tale of Bygone Years* (Povest' vremennykh let) is in fact the second of two utterances made by Andrew concerning his travels through Rus'. His first, made at the sight of the future Kiev, predicted that a city would rise, shining with "many churches" (*tserkvi mnogi*). Having blessed the hills of the future Kiev, erected a cross, and offered a prayer to God, Andrew proceeds to the future Novgorod, where he surveys the bathhouse scene described in the passage above.

Much of the resonance between these two episodes derives from the inversion of roles played by Andrew and the local populace. In Kiev, the sacred Andrew conjures up a spectacle of the future ("many churches"), when the local populace will cease to be outsiders and will join Orthodoxy, the communal, universal faith. In Novgorod, the local populace, engaged in its secular bathing rituals, presents the outsider Andrew with a spectacle of the present ("wooden bathhouses"), marked by communal practice and national particularity. Andrew is the marveling foreigner ("I saw with wonder . . ."), as appreciative and untutored about Rus'ian bathhouse culture as the future Kievan converts would (allegedly) be about Christianity in later sections of the *Tale* (Dmitriev 72, 73).[3]

The visit of the Apostle Andrew is one of Russia's central myths of legitimation, invoked over the centuries to shore up Russia's claim to lawful stewardship (inherited from Rome and Byzantium) of the Orthodox faith. It is of no small cultural import that Andrew travels through the Kiev and Novgorod regions on his way *back* to Rome, the original locus of Orthodox Christianity. In this account (and henceforth for centuries), baths serve as an identifying "tag" of Russian-ness, a site for the playing out of national identity, textually tied with churches. The church and the baths are buildings that share specifics of likeness and unlikeness. Their respective geographic loci in the Primary Chronicle—Kiev in the south and Novgorod in the north—form the twin pillars of Russian culture. The sacred site of the universal faith is materialized in Kievan churches; the secular site of national particularity is materialized in Novgorod baths. Twins and opposites, they have been central to defining the boundaries between heaven and earth, between the soul and the body, dividing and redividing the territory, exchanging features, and modeling ideals of spiritual and physical purity. This is suggested in some of the more familiar bath proverbs, juxtaposing church and bath, body and soul within a single cultural system:

> Fast on Wednesdays; go to the bathhouse on Saturdays.
> (*Postnichai po sredam, khodi v baniu po subbotam.*)

> The soul loves coolness; the flesh loves the bathhouse.
> (*Dusha liubit prokhladu, a plot'—baniu.*)

> Steam breaks no bones; it won't drive the soul away.
> (*Par kostei ne lomit, von dushi ne gonit.*)

> The bathhouse is not like fasting; it has no prohibitions.
> (*Bania ne zagoven'e—na nee net zapretov.*)

Contrary to the wisdom of the last proverb, of course, many prohibitions have historically existed concerning the use of the bathhouse. Most of these are specifically religious prohibitions, forbidding, for example, the preparation of the bathhouse oven on Sunday. In this fashion, the church has served in some respects as an abstract model governing the baths, whereas the baths have provided a kind of "applied spirituality," a secular pathway to purity, using the vehicle of the body. Thus, the very custom of observing "bath day" (*bannyi den'*) on Saturday, the original sabbath, suggests that the bathhouse occupies the status of a kind of alternate temple:

> Observe Saturday [the Sabbath Day]: go to the bathhouse.
> (*Pomni den' subbotnyi—idi v baniu.*)

> Saturday [the Sabbath Day] is Bath Day.
> (*Den' subbotnyi—bannyi den'.*)

This alternate temple, as we have seen, predates the dominant religion; it is in fact a site of enduring pagan religiosity. Elements of this pagan religiosity flicker through much of Russian Christianized culture. The expletive "Go to the bathhouse!" (*Idi v baniu!*) as an alternative expression to the Christian "Go to the devil!" (*Idi k chertu!*) or the vulgar "Fuck off!" (*Idi na khui,* literally "Go to the prick!") sends the addressee to the bathhouse as a kind of "pagan negative space" (Prokhorov).[4]

Within this secular temple, the twig broom or *venik*[5] serves, first, as the most specific instrument of national identity by which observers such as Andrew have identified Rus'ians bathing ("[they] take upon themselves a young twig switch . . . "). Second, within the existing dualism of church and bath, the *venik* serves as the secular cross. The studied devotion with which the *venik* is to be assembled—from the north side of the young birch, by the full moon in early June, ten days after Trinity (*Troitsa*), and so forth[6]—suggests precisely the cultic significance that the *venik* is capable of bearing, as well as its explicit interconnection with the church calendar. It is also, incidentally, another example of the baths' conceptual subordination to the church.

This cultic significance is, of course, voluntary. It can easily be profaned by the fool who buys a *venik* at the bathhouse door rather than gathering it and drying it carefully in the shade of the dark, cool attic, thus preserving the unmediated connection between God's world and the body. In buying an "anonymous" *venik* at the bathhouse door, the bathhouse fool is no different from the Christian fool who buys a paper icon at the church door: both are tainted by characterizing features of the city—convenience, randomness, and the exchange of coins at the holy site. The one suggests a slipshod approach to spiritual salvation, the other a slipshod approach to physical reconstitution.

The legend of Andrew's visit is noteworthy not only as an early description of Russian baths as a site that is narratively linked with holiness and national identity. The gaze of the outsider, the foreigner or non-Slav (in this instance, Andrew), is a common position from which the Russian baths have been contemplated. While in the *Tale of Bygone Years* all three elements—the event, the foreigner, and the utterance—may indeed be legendary, this *mise en scène* remains a dominanat model for future descriptions of the Russian baths: the marveling outsider and the self-absorbed and (in the outsider's account, at least) self-abusive native. The baths were to become, in A. G. Cross's words, a "compulsory subject for comment from all who visited Russia in whatever capacity . . . into the reign of Peter" (39), most notably included in descriptions by Giles Fletcher and Adam Olearius (Berry and Crummey; Baron).

Of course, the baths had no dearth of native observers either, but this genre must be distinguished from that written by the foreign traveler, the transient figure condemned to write travelogue while the native writes autobiography. The two genres share common features, but a key difference is the kind of narrative authority brought to the act of narration. The native narrator speaks from a wealth of experience, using fixed epithets that underscore expert knowledge ("inveterate" [*zavziatyi*], "experienced" [*byvalyi*], "thorough" [*zapravskii*], "with a long length of service" [*so stazhem*]) (Feoktistov; Galitskii; Giliarovskii; Polevichek; Rubinov; Seimuk). These same turns of phrase are those most often used to describe hunters, mushroom pickers, or other amateur, devoted enthusiasts.

The foreign narrator, on the other hand, describes the bathing spectacle as an isolated event to a posited reader who is also the foreign outsider. The native instructs; the foreigner recounts.[7] The implicit terms of these genres, therefore, dictate that this article be written in the tradition of the marveling foreigner, always insufficiently tutored in the subtleties of the *bania*, empowered largely by right of apostolic succession to appreciate its spectacle. Although my experience with the Russian municipal baths may be vast and deep, this is not a credible claim to narrative authority, which is grounded instead in three qualifications: foreign blood, a wonder at spectacle, and a perpetually *incomplete* knowledge.

All Baths Are Women's Baths

While peasant culture under specific conditions might intermingle the sexes (long a part of the appeal of the bathhouse), the urban, commercial baths in our century have generally observed a putative isolation of the sexes. This isolation is, of course, continually breached, yet the conditions of its breaching are highly differentiated. They include the assignment (for a variety of reasons) of bathhouse personnel to baths of the opposite sex; the illicit admission of members of the opposite sex for amorous liaisons; and visual trespass—attempts to peer into the baths of the opposite sex from whatever angle and under any conditions of personal hazard that might afford a glimpse.

Since the historical, scholarly, and artistic literature on bathhouse culture is written almost exclusively by men,[8] the gender roles of sexual incursion are assigned with a kind of deadening predictability: smuggled visitors tend to be women; peeping toms tend to be men.[9] Thus, the norm of bathhouse literature is the self-observing male community, while deviance is that same male community in tenuous contact (administrative, amatory, or specular) with the female. Nowhere do we find extensive verbal descriptions of the "other norm," so to speak: the women's side of the tile wall. Even the Moscow journalist-historian Giliarovskii speaks of the women's baths only briefly and in passing.

But they are not, therefore, wholly uncharted territory. Extensive representation of women bathing can be found in visual texts: wood-carvings (*lubki*) and late-eighteenth-century copper engravings from the Akhmet'ev factory depict the women's baths; Mikhail Kozlovskii's *Russian Baths* (1778) and Emel'ian Korneev's *Le bain russe* (1812) both portray men and women bathing together; Kuz'ma Petrov-Vodkin's famous *Morning: Women Bathing* (1917) and Boris Kustodiev's *Russian Venus* (1926) both show female bathing.

Yet in these works the female nude is an object of contemplation more or less in accordance with the traditions of Western European easel painting.[10] Thus, the visual text has negotiated a cultural logic—or "pretext," if you will—for displaying the female nude in the process of bathing where the verbal text has not. In so doing, however, the painter-engraver lays no claim to expertise or wealth of experience in the women's baths other than as painter-engraver; instead, he becomes the marveling outsider, a foreign traveler through the land of the women's baths. His work shares the quality of voyeurism inherent in the genre of travelogue. He is the chronicler of difference: While his own men's baths promise the disappearance or blurring of social difference, his preoccupation with the women's baths is the documentation of sexual difference.

And so the male has historically been granted conditional entrance to the women's baths (constructed abstractly as a permissible topic), provided that he draws but does not write. The female is permitted unconditional entrance to the women's baths (constructed concretely as mundane chore), but must neither draw nor write. At the very least, she historically has not done so.

Why does the Russian woman go to the public bathhouse? It could be argued that the reasons are as varied as (and essentially no different from) those often cited by her male counterpart. She may go out of necessity: no facilities at home, broken facilities; facilities under repair or closed down for cleaning. She may go because of a perceived professional need: For dancers and actresses, as for male boxers, jockeys, and riders, the baths have long constituted a routine therapy of weight control, as well as muscle, bone, and cardiovascular maintenance. She may go for better health; for relaxation; out of habit, most often from years of living in a communal apartment. Indeed, for all the ways in which the peasant *bania* may have shaped behavior in the municipal *bania*, the communal apartment has surely shaped that performance in at least as many ways. The bathhouse reconstitutes the communal privacy of the apartment in its naked bodies, washing "unobserved" for all to see. In both these related spaces—the communal apartment and the *bania*—the capacity to navigate in silence through communal space while carrying out one's own rituals of survival is a cherished skill. But still they are not equals: The bathhouse is merely the ablutionary outbuilding of socialism.

What does the woman do in the bathhouse? The routine tasks include washing with a synthetic or linden scrubber (*mochalka*); the application of heat and its regulation (with headgear, pelvic wraps, dousing, and so forth); the heightening of physical sensation, usually by thrashing with the *venik*; and some kind of inter- and post-steam leisure. None of these tasks differs substantially from those performed in the men's section.[11]

Yet motivation and routine do not exhaust the categories of potential similarities and contrast. Judging from the oral, written, and cinematic accounts that constitute Russian men's bathhouse culture (the best known of which are Giliarovskii, Riazanov, and Zoshchenko),[12] I gather that the principal appeals of the bath—hygienics aside—include the opportunity for organized or spontaneous male camaraderie; for the contemplation of (or escape from the contemplation of) an important issue; and for a range of pleasures other than sex. In addition to washing, steaming, and thrashing, these pleasures might include alcoholic or non-alcoholic beverages, food, card playing, and, on occasion and only for the special few, brawling. This panorama of pleasure is specifically marked (indeed, perhaps made possible) by the absence of female intercession. Thus, while one of the traditional mythic allures of the male baths is the possibility of heterosexual sex, the wealth of pleasure (including physical pain) concentrated in the male bathhouse more often displaces the female sex organ, assigning it (briefly, blessedly) to the periphery of physical sensation. This displacement has less to do with the kinds of motivations or routines enumerated above than with an elusive state of consciousness attainable only under specific conditions, principally including the presence of good steam, good company, good beer, and good dried fish (*vobla*).

Could the same be said for women's bathhouse culture? Is the *bania* a place where women come not only to wash, but for camaraderie, contemplation, and a range of physical sensations that temporarily relegates the male sex organ to the periphery, assuming that Russian women's culture hadn't placed it there already? Washing, yes; comaraderie, perhaps (though not necessarily); contemplation, yes. As for the other, it is, of course, a deeply personal question that each must answer for herself, because to speak about the *bania* at all is simultaneously to conjure up a cultural canon and to speak from the innermost place in the heart.

Before we get to the heart, let us address the bathhouse canon, an abbreviated list of which is included in the Works Cited. The canon could be said to divide up into two kinds of texts. First are the named texts—i.e., by specific cultural producers, such as Giliarovskii or Riazanov. Insofar as these tend to represent the urban, municipal men's section, the women figure only as peripheral characters: Zoshchenko's female bathhouse administrator (the "Kursk anomaly" [*kurskaia anomaliia*] [2: 215; see also Rubinov 251–99]) or the anonymous woman bather, illicitly viewed by the male spectator (Rostotskii; Rubinov; Tot).

The second group in the bathhouse canon are the unnamed or anonymous texts: proverbs, riddles, incantations, superstitions, prohibitions, cus-

ns, and fortune-telling activities surrounding the *bania*. The constitu-
elements of this latter category tend to be unnamed both in the
sense that the texts have no author and in the sense that they tend not to
name either male or female.[13] Instead, they tend to focus on the bath, the
venik, the steam, or the act of bathing. Surely this is due not only to customary Russian reticence to speak about the body, but also in part to the
fact that peasant, small-town culture, and even suburban culture, did not
traditionally delineate a bathing space permanently and exclusively reserved for men or women. The very notion of a women's section is thus
a relatively modern concept of an urban, industrialized Russia.

While the men's section might freely contemplate its reflected image
in both named and unnamed texts, the women's section experiences
these texts somewhat differently. In the named texts, the woman is peripheral; in the unnamed texts, she is (at most) implied, or perhaps androgynous. Thus, the cultural constitution of the women's section is an
ephemeral phenomenon, largely consisting of aural recollection: the received wisdom of peasant proverb, urban oral folklore, family history, or
personal memory.

The relative absence of texts within a traditionally conceived canon
leaves any story of the women's baths inaudible, except as a voice of
memory recounting it as a journey backward to a distant place, an original self, most often located in childhood or in the countryside. This
voice of memory is audible in the men's section as well, but it competes
alongside an established genre of bathhouse literature, film, and other
cultural texts.

Thus, in a sense, on two counts it might be convincingly argued that
women's bathhouse culture does not exist: first, the similarity of men's
and women's motivations and tasks; second, the absence of named texts
(either by women about women or *even* by men about women) constituting a tradition of representation. And so our analysis might end, were
it not for the peculiar and inescapable centrality of proverbs and
memory (perhaps even more than the named cultural canon) to the
topic itself, because to speak from the innermost place of the heart (for
either sex) is to draw on this pool of proverbs and memories, to make
the journey to an inner place of mystic origins.[14]

It is perhaps not so surprising, therefore, to discover that the unnamed
texts often, implicitly or explicitly, identify the *bania* (like the motherland
[*rodina-mat'*]) as an instantiation of maternity:

> The bathhouse is the very mother who bore us.
> (*Bania—mat' rodnaia.*)

The bathhouse is our second mother.
(*Bania—mat' vtoraia.*)

The association of the bathhouse with powerful, motherlike forces has its origins, of course, in the Russian pagan goddesses of fate (*rozhanitsy*), whose temple in pre-Christian times was indeed the bathhouse. As fate goddesses, the *rozhanitsy* oversaw bathhouse rituals of curing, sorcery, and fortune-telling. A number of these rituals have survived both the Christian and the communist onslaughts and serve as a parallel culture to each of these other two fantasy systems, sometimes cast in opposition to them, sometimes seen as a harmless and quaint anachronism (Hubbs 14–15; Efimenko 104; Vahros 199–200). Among the surviving elements of these rituals is the custom, which varies from region to region, of performing a washing and gift ritual with the midwife, usually in the bathhouse within three days of a baby's birth. The gifts often include soap, money, and some sort of cloth, such as a towel, a handkerchief, calico for sleeves, a jacket, or simply yards of cloth (Listova 131–33; Martynov 263).

Indeed, insofar as the *bania* traditionally served the Russian all life long, from birth in the bathhouse, to the marriage eve, to the ailments of old age—was noted by Byzantine historian Prokopius as early as the sixth century (Galitskii 7)—it is, perhaps, "natural" that the *bania* should be identified as the mother, the locus of family health, the provider in time of need, the ultimate rescue:

Vania got well; the bathhouse helped him.
(*Vylechilsia Vania—pomogla emu bania.*)

The bathhouse is the family's health.
(*Bania—zdorov'e sem'i.*)

The bathhouse steams you; the bathhouse gives you health.
(*Bania parit—zdorov'e darit.*)

If not for the bathhouse, we all would perish.
(*Koli ne bania, vse b my propali.*)

Further, within this metaphoric world of gender relations, the *bania* is differentiated from the *venik* not as mother versus father, but as mother versus patriarch:

Within the bath, the *venik* is the lord.
(*V bane—venik gospodin.*)

Within the bath, the *venik* is the boss.
(*V bane—venik nabol'shii.*)

The *venik* in the bath is everyone's leader.
(*Venik v bane—vsem nachal'nik.*)
The *venik* in the bath is senior even to the tsar.
(*Venik v bane i tsaria starshe.*)

When the bathhouse culture is viewed through these mystic opticals, then, it consists of a large, maternal woman with a little patriarch inside her: one provides; the other leads.[15]

This odd dyad is further mirrored in the relationship between the bathhouse oven (*pechka*) and the poker (*kocherga*), which is used to move around the burning logs:

In the bath, the *venik* is master; in the oven, the poker.
(*V bane venik—khoziain, v pechi—kocherga.*)

Thus, if we may return to the earlier question of whether the woman entering the *bania* is, in any sense, setting aside the man—or, for that matter, whether the man entering the *bania* is indeed setting aside the woman—we find that the question is more complex than it first appears. More accurately, the sexes are ensured an escape from their day-to-day interaction, which regularly becomes burdensome and demanding, and are allowed to reconstitute themselves in the communal isolation of the second mother. What this isolation accomplishes, among other tasks, is the symbolic reordering of gender relations *under the sign of the mother* in a physically nurturing and emotionally less chaotic fashion. Indeed, cast in this light, much of the debauch of the male *bania* in legend and fantasy[16] might be seen as a wishful sullying of the mother, a breaking of the incest taboo.

The symbolic breaking of the incest taboo extends beyond sexuality to other kinds of behavior, such as drinking and smoking, of which Mother would not approve. Taken together, those behaviors constitute the very oxymoronic nature of the men's *bania*—oxymoronic in the sense that the male sits inside Mother as he performs those transgressive behaviors (whether in fantasy, legend, or fact). She is both present and not present, seeing and blind. The bath within her is a place of both celibacy and license, a place that heals alcoholic intemperance and provides an uninterrupted opportunity to drink. It is a place of healthy pursuits, after which the first cigarette is a real joy. In this act of self-contradiction, the men's baths resemble the railway carriage of Russian culture, from Lev Tolstoi's *Kreuzer Sonata* (Kreitserova sonata) to Venedikt Erofeev's *Moscow-Petushki* (Moskva-Petushki): a *mise en scène* for self-revelation and self-deception.

While this oxymoronic quality may be situated in the men's behavior, it may also be projected onto the woman-bath herself as a filthy location for the rituals of cleanliness ("The commercial bath washes us all, but she herself is dirty" [*Torgovaia bania vsekh moet, a sama griaznaia*]). The profane delight of the proverb "Tobacco and taverns; babes and baths—all the same kind of fun" (*Tabak da kabak, baba da bania—odna zabava*) achieves its illicit corruption of the baths by including them at the end of its list of traditional male bodily sins.[17]

It is precisely within this "maternalized" arena of gender reconstitution that differences between the men's section and the women's section of the municipal public baths must be sought. A false posing of the question from the outset leads to a simple search for points of difference between the sections (although these, of course, exist). Instead, the existing differences are subsumed within a system that posits the maternalized space as offering unconditional love; as helping her symbolic child come clean physically and spiritually (nowadays, even psychologically); as providing a space where the symbolic child (whipped by the patriarch) can arrive at the "naked truth" [*pravda golaia*].

An example of this "coming clean" could be seen in Boris Yeltsin's account of how, in a Moscow bathhouse in 1989, he realizes that he is no longer a Communist (a narrative with hagiographic overtones reminiscent of the conversion topos in certain Russian vitae). His change of world view, as he himself describes it, takes place not just anywhere, but within the warm body of the bathhouse (a more appropriate site of conversion for the admitted nonbeliever such as Yeltsin than the church would be). Yeltsin's conversion in the bathhouse assures the implied reader of its authenticity, its native legitimacy within the historical development of Mother Russia: he sits inside the second mother and emerges a born-again non-Communist.

Another, no doubt equally fictive, example might be found in Aleksandr Askol'dov's film *Commissar* (Kommisar) (completed 1967; released 1987), based on a short story by Vasilii Grossman. The film opens with the Red Army capture of the town of Berdichev during the Russian Civil War (1918–20). Klavdiia Vavilova, the eponymous Commissar, utters the first spoken word of the film when she climbs off her horse and orders the bathhouse prepared for her ("Bath!"). Here, following a cultural logic that extends backward to pagan times, the bathhouse serves as the appropriate symbolic place where Klavdiia Vavilova comes to terms with her change of fate from a Red Army commissar to an expectant mother. She emerges from the bathhouse reborn a pregnant woman.

FIG 1.1. Mozhaisk Baths,
Moscow, 1994.

Fig 1.2. Boris Kustodiev,
Russian Venus (1925–26).

Fig 1.3. Rochdale Baths, Moscow, 1994.

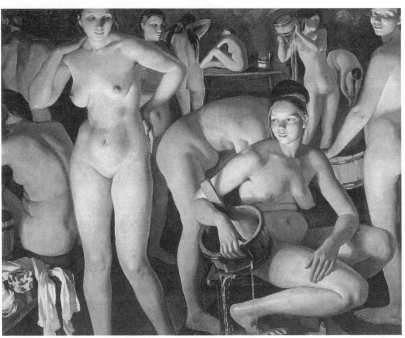

FIG 1.4. Zinaida Serebriakova, *The Bath-house* (1913).

FIG 1.5. Seleznev Baths, Moscow, 1994.

FIG 1.6. Sochi Baths
#1 (Vivacity Baths),
1994. List of services.

FIG 1.7. Niura and Katia
exit the Vivacity Baths.
Sochi, 1994.

This notion of *bania* as a metaphor for a radical sorting out or clarifi-
cation of human relations reverberates throughout Russian culture, from
underworld jargon—where *bania* means, among other things, "interro-
gation" (*dopros*), and "dry bath" (*sukhaia bania*) is essentially a "frisk"
(*obysk*) (Baldaev 24, 238)—to colloquialisms ("to give a bath") [*zadat'
baniu*] means "to reprimand"), to Maiakovskii's famous metaphor of the
bania as akin to a utopian revolutionary machine, sorting out its own.

Thus, while this essay will begrudgingly address the specific differences between the men's and women's baths, this modest task is at odds
with the philosophical orientation of the essay, wherein all baths are
women's baths (*bania—eto my*). This apparent gender megalomania is
not intended as a passing comment or a prefatory remark, but rather as
an orientation that affects all aspects of the topic at hand. As the history
of urbanization, for example, plays itself out across the public baths, that
history is marked by an evolution from the extended peasant family sitting inside the big mother—a kind of real-life stacking doll (*ma-
treshka*)—to a random, anonymous, and transient group of individual
men or women sitting inside the big mother. In each case, the big
mother's tasks and the ways she is described are very different.

Clearly, I am not suggesting that men frequent the baths as *women's baths*, but rather that they flee the "false" world of gender relations for a twofold comfort: first, for all-male company promising unconditional acceptance (hence, the strict, if somewhat subjective, prohibition in longstanding men's bath groups against admitting "assholes" [*mudaki*]); and second, for the "true"—i.e., idealized—world of gender relations reconstituted by sitting inside the mother herself.

The megalomania suggested here and in the title of this essay likewise does not imply an extrapatriarchal space, either for the *bania* or for any other instantiation of motherhood, such as the motherland. Russia has only ever been a patriarchal society. Yet patriarchy (as well as its manifestations in womanhood, the family, and all aspects of intimate life) has been constructed very differently in a society with no extended, sustained experience of capitalism. The *bania* is one area in which that "different patriarchy" is played out, specifically in its construction of the "all-powerful" mother who (not surprisingly) does everything, cures all, and provides the necessary incubator for male action.

Self-Consumption: A Big Difference

The list of services available to women in the *bania* is long and complex, attending to different parts of the female body, with words of Latin derivation: pedicure, manicure, solarium, epilation, cosmetics, massage, masks, and, of course, the hairdresser. Not all services listed are simultaneously available, or available at all, or have ever been available in the history of the particular bathhouse displaying the list. But the list is nevertheless displayed, which is the main thing,[18] and in some of the more expensive public bathhouses, such as the Sandunov Baths or the Krasnaia Presnia Baths, where the personnel now wear specially designed uniforms, one might reasonably expect to be able to make an advance reservation for any of the above services most of the time.

In addition to the services (real or imaginary) offered by any particular *bania*, the women clientele routinely bring their own accouterments: headgear (anything from a chic ski cap to an old plastic shopping bag), pelvic wraps, *veniki*, wooden boards to sit on in the steam room, special brushes to remove the old skin, and jars of body ointments (creams, salves, rubs, and so forth). Some of these anointments may be manufactured, of Russian or of Western origin, but most often (and most suitably) they are homemade.

The most common form of anointment combines an abrasive with a fatty or sticky base: coffee grounds, for example, may be combined with mayonnaise; corn meal with egg white; salt with sour cream, honey, farmer's cheese (*tvorog*), or buttermilk (*kefir*) to strip away old skin and (ostensibly) nurture the new skin. Stale black bread is another such abrasive, either alone or mixed in a cream base.

A second category of self-anointment is the facial mask. Depending on one's supposed condition, this might be a mixture of mustard and oil, oat flour and egg white, mashed potatoes and egg yolk, wheat flour and whey, mashed strawberries and cream, tea compresses, or simply a good strong pickle marinade.

Other parts of the body, too, have their own anointments: calluses are attended to by the liquid given off from baked onions; hair roots are strengthened by the liquid given off when the *venik* is steeped in boiling water in a tub. But gradually this enumeration leads into the more distant fields of herbal medicine, massage, aromatherapy, and other kinds of "hydro-hygienics," such as ice bathing and other means of shocking, tempering (*zakalivanie*), or purging the body.

It is in this ritual of self-anoinment, repetitive rinsing, and re-anointment that we can find a signal point of difference from the men's section, where self-anointment is perfunctory or nonexistent as a part of the larger bathing ritual. While it is, of course, a difference of degree rather than one of kind, it is nevertheless a difference of curious magnitude, because it demonstrates most visibly the conceptual fusion of cosmetic and curative that differentiates the women's section from the other. Self-anointment is therapeutic for both the chronically ill *and* the chronically ugly: Its purpose is to mend, to restore, to balance, to compensate, to soothe. While the curative and cosmetic unctions, so to speak, are distinguishable from each other, they do not exist independently of each other: mint leaves are best for wrinkles; cabbage leaves are best for headaches.

As in the men's section, older layers of the body are stripped away, the pores are opened and closed, the blood circulation is reactivated, and the body is tempered by alternating states of heat and cold. But what is simultaneously most curious about and most typical of self-anointment in the women's section might be described as the shedding of clothes and the donning of provisions, for the woman literally wears on her body the very foodstuffs (mayonnaise, coffee, salt, eggs) that she herself routinely buys as family provender. She performs an act of consecration on herself; she becomes the holy body, the sacred host (or hostess, if you will) of the ceremony.

The significance of this self-consecration becomes clearer in light of the fact that the bathhouse is a site where the woman carries out, however much in a different performative fashion, most of the tasks she would normally fulfill at home—from the airing and sweeping out of the steam room; to the (largely symbolic) rinsing of the benches, tubs, and steam room walls; to the washing of the body and the children (traditionally the laundry as well)[19]—but with one notable exception: she cooks no meal. Instead, she herself becomes the culinary performance, whereby the body, in various combinations and with varying ingredients, is washed, rinsed, dried, prepared (with grease, spices, herbs, or marinades), steamed, and served. At that moment she is simultaneously sacred, healthy, and beautiful.

The women's baths, then, are a site where the rites of female purity are enacted as the physical manifestation of other forms of purity (spiritual, sexual, psychological). The household is reconstituted within this arena of symbolic celibacy, using the vehicle of the female body and including a period of obligatory inert leisure before returning to the outside world. Bathing is secular worship, wherein pleasure is closely linked to duty and ritual and whereby the debauch of the men's baths (if only in legend and fantasy) has no place.

And what of the men's section? According to the lists of services, it is usually possible in the men's section to have a massage, to have one's calluses cut back, and to get a haircut—a rather limited repertoire of services. The cosmetics of the body described earlier—ointments, masks, etc.—are virtually absent. While the men's section may observe certain gender-marked practices concerning the *venik*[20] or the choice of herbs used in the steam room,[21] the donning of groceries is not a routine stage in the process of male bathing. Thus, a curious dichotomy obtains. Two rare and tenuously related acts, virtually unknown in the domestic space, take place: The women engage in a culinary performance of self-consecration, and the men feed themselves.

Historical Closure: The False *Venik*

Later in the *Tale of Bygone Years*, sometime after Andrew's visit in the entry under the year 6453 (or 945 by our system of reckoning), Ol'ga, the putative grandmother of Rus'ian Orthodoxy, avenges the death of her husband Igor', Grand Prince of Kiev, in several episodes. In one such episode, she cunningly invites the "most distinguished men" (*luchshikh muzhei*) of the enemy Derevlian tribe, who had murdered her husband, to visit and escort her to wed their own Derevlian Prince Mal:

> Ol'ga ordered the arriving Derevlians to prepare the bathhouse, saying to them thus: "Wash yourselves thoroughly, then come to me." And the

Derevlians fired up the bathhouse, entered it, and began to wash themselves; and the bathhouse was locked behind them, and Ol'ga ordered that the door itself be set alight, and they all burnt up. (Dmitriev 42, 43)

As should be evident by now, the Derevlians' fatal mistake in this episode was the assumption that the bathhouse was a safe space where they, now as men rather than as warriors, could restore themselves. In fact, it was *not* a safe space; it was a Rus'ian space, and, moreover, it was *Ol'ga's* Rus'ian space. Just as they had invaded Rus' and destroyed its Kievan patriarch, Grand Price Igor', so did the Rus' widow wreak her revenge, slaughtering the Derevlian foreigner—the false patriarch—in the very temple belonging to the fate goddesses.

If we mistakenly conceive of bathers as autonomous individuals rather than as subjects subsumed in a larger symbolic space, the paradigm (motherland = Ol'ga = *bania* vs. foreign enemy = Derevlian = false *venik*) is overlooked. It is only when we acknowledge that Rus' has always already been both Holy Rus' (the church, constituted as a largely male realm) and Mother Rus' (the baths, constituted as a symbolic female realm) that Ol'ga's bathhouse revenge takes on the significance that is its due.

The Derevlians did not mistake the Rus'ian baths for the Derevlian baths (this was already clear); they mistook the woman's (*sing.*) baths for the men's (*pl.*) baths. Had the Derevlians spoken the language of symbols—or, rather, had they spoken the language of symbols necessary for the perpetuation of Russian maternity myths—they would have known better than to have ventured into Ol'ga's bathhouse. Instead, they spoke the language of their own symbolic universe, and they perished. Their misperception of Ol'ga as booty, as defeated widow, rather than as the incarnate yet unconquered Rus' is closely linked to their misperception of *bania* as a safe zone rather than as the symbolic woman's lair. As a result, Mother Russia consumes them as surely as she will later consume all the other false *veniki* (Dmitrii, Napoleon, Hitler, etc.).

Of course, it will be argued that the Ol'ga story is in no way typical, that indeed it has survived as an anomaly, an uncommon story of widowhood and leadership. All this is true; and, had Igor' survived, no amount of cunning, fictive or otherwise, could have coaxed the Derevlians into the Rus'ian baths. But it is precisely as anomaly that the legend is permitted to reveal the underlying symbolic message: The only reason the Derevlians dared attempt possession of the motherland, the woman, or the bath was that Igor', the true *venik*, was gone; the motherland/widow/bath stood empty. But, the legend warns, woe to the Derevlian who sees this as victory. The motherland wreaks her revenge through her most intense physical articulation, the bathhouse, the second mother.

Perhaps this intimacy of mother, motherland, and bath explains some of the public anger surrounding the modern-day closures of bathhouses, as well as their sale and conversion into more lucrative downtown space (Gavrilin; Gladnev; Jones). What is at stake is not merely profit or power, but the very material substance of Russia. It is the city's version of a painful question: Who will own Mother Russia?

If original property rights are to be returned in the newly free Russia, then of course it would be the *rozhanitsy*, the ancient pagan fate goddesses, who would become major property owners in the downtown real-estate market. They, at least, might preserve the temple, keeping the remaining baths from the fate of the Danilov Baths, sold for 20 million rubles (Gavrilin), or the Central Baths, now converted to the restaurant Arcadia (Gladnev).

The mammoth foolishness and tragedy of the Communist era were epitomized in the demolition of the Cathedral of Christ the Savior and the construction in its place of the Moscow Open Air Pools. This twentieth-century version of ancient tension between the church and the baths already marks a demotion of the baths, with their rich spiritual symbolism, to the brazen and debased modernity of the secular swimming pool. The petty foolishness and tragedy of the post-Communist era are epitomized in the closing of the hundred-year-old Central Baths and its conversion into a restaurant. One can only hope that lurking somewhere deep in the pantry among the honey pots, mayonnaise jars, and saltcellars, the *rozhanitsy* are plotting their return.

Notes

Research for this essay was supported by a grant from the International Research and Exchanges Board, with funds provided by the U.S. Department of State (Title VIII) and the National Endowment for the Humanities. I would also like to thank the following colleagues and friends who generously offered citations of, experience about, and camaraderie in the bathhouse: Nadezhda Azhgikhina, Valerii Baburin, Boris Bagariatskii, Alena Bakshitskaia, David Birnbaum, Katerina Clark, Dan Field, Vivian Foley, Igor' Gol'din, Helena Goscilo, Leonid Gurevich, Mark Lipovetskii, Inna Murav'eva, Vladimir Padunov, Aleksandr Prokhorov, Inna Serova, Helena Trochimenko, Dmitrii Urnov, and my bath instructor Liudmila Nikolaevna, whose last name I do not know. None of the above-named organizations or people is responsible for the views expressed.

1. This essay tends to use several terms interchangeably: "bathhouse," "baths," and *bania*, the last of these being the Russian word for "bath." While one might quibble about specific etymological differences among these terms, I will spare the reader my thoughts on the subject. What I have in mind in all three cases is an area for bathing consisting of three parts: the changing room (*predbannik* or *razdevalka*); the washing room (*myl'nia*); and the steam room (*paril'nia* or *parilka*).

This steam room is different from a Western steam room, such as one might find attached to a gymnasium or sports club. The Russian version is a small room with (ideally) wooden benches or shelves, heated by a built-in stove containing wood or (more often nowadays) metal logs. When small ladles of water, beer, or fermented brew (*kvas*) are thrown on these logs, the resultant sharp rise in the room's humidity, invisible to the eye but nurturing to the flesh, is referred to as "steam" (*par*).

For an excellent general description of the Russian bathhouse (both traditional and contemporary), see Gerhart 8–10.

2. Dmitriev 30, 31. An interesting mistranslation of this last clause ("in this way carry out their washing, and *not* their torment" [emphasis mine]) appears in Samuel H. Cross's translation: "They make of the act *not a mere washing, but a veritable torment*" (*Zenkovsky* 47). While Cross's mistake is presumably unintentional, I cannot help but wonder if this mistranslation does not reveal a foreigner's rebellious skepticism about the accuracy of the original "document" in portraying the foreigner's viewpoint.

3. It has been convincingly argued (Vernadsky 309) and counter-argued (Kabanov 134–37) that this passage is in fact a kind of collective mocking by southern chroniclers in Kiev, where steaming was less frequently practiced, of their northern, Novgorod relatives, among whom the practice was well established. Seen in this light, Andrew's comments become part of the larger Great Russian-Ukrainian (*katsap-khokhol*) rivalry. The authenticity of this original authorial intention is less relevant here, where the concern instead is Andrew's putative description, upon returning to Rome, of what the Rus'ians were like as a people. Here and elsewhere, I am less interested in the "pure text" than in the accumulation of meanings and their arrangement in the late twentieth century. By extension, I am less interested in the "eternal" curative powers of birch bathbrooms (*veniki*) (see note 5) than I am in their organizing significance at the specific moment when modernity, medical science, and the female body interconnect. Much of the bathhouse ritual, in my view, enacts anxiety about the demands that modernity makes upon a culture ill equipped to meet those demands.

4. On sorcerers who go to the bathhouse during the holy days celebrated by Christians in church, see Lotman and Uspenskij 9.

5. A term that will be unfamiliar to the non-specialist reader is *venik*, a bundle of small branches (usually oak, birch, nettle, or eucalyptus) bound

together broom-fashion, with which the steam-room bather whips or thrashes herself and/or her cohorts, usually during the second or third session in the steam room. This whipping is intended to facilitate circulation, to bring the blood vessels closer to the surface, to remove dead skin, and to stimulate the entire body. Because there is no comfortable English translation of the term *venik*, I will use the Russian throughout. For further information, see Gerhart 9.

6. This is assuming that the spring has not been particularly rainy. If the ground has remained damp for some time, the *venik* should be gathered slightly later and, preferably, farther up the hillside, where the runoff won't have made the twigs and leaves so pulpy.

7. Nor does this exhaust the possibilities. Aleksandr Pushkin's 1829 description in *A Journey to Arzrum*, for example, of the Tiflis baths (still extant, although now renamed the Blue Baths) suggests a further variation: the foreign *Russian* traveler marveling at the native bathing practices of an alien land (2: 498–99).

8. For an exception to this general rule, see Ivanova-Anninskaia and also Mishchenko. British playwright Nell Dunn's play *Steaming* is a rare example of this theme in western European culture. Her play was rescripted for Joseph Losey's 1986 film of the same title.

9. A rare exception could be found in the anecdote (apparently of Italian origin) about a young student who managed to get himself into the women's baths. See Anonymous.

10. Among well-known western European examples of women's baths, either in isolation or with the opposite sex, are Jean-Dominique Ingres's last major Neoclassicist work, *The Turkish Bath* (1862); Jean-Baptiste Le Prince's *Bain public* (1768); sixteenth-century woodcuts by Hans Beham; Dürer's *The Women's Bath* (1496); Girard's engraving *A Day in the Life of a Courtesan*; L. Surugue's engraving from L. B. Pater's 1741 *Le Plaisir de l'Été*; Giedion's painting *The Russian Bath*; as well as numerous advertisements from the United States and Britain demonstrating the superiority of a particular tub that uses the visual aid of a naked woman (Cross; Wright). There also exists a "mixed tradition" of western European paintings of the Russian baths, including Geoffroy's engraving of P. I.'s (*Ivanov's?*) *Les Bains russes* (1845), Michel-François Damame-Demartrais's *Le Bain russe* (1813), and Gérard de la Barthe's *Vid Serebrenicheskikh ban' i okrestnostei ikh v Moskve* (1799) (Cross 55–57).

11. I speak of the men's baths, of course, as a double outsider (foreign female), relying only on a set of cultural mediations largely produced by men about men. The women easel painters have yet to set up their gear in the men's section.

12. To this list, I would add short texts, episodes, or mentions passim in Aleksandr Askol'dov, Anton Chekhov, Fedor Dostoevskii, Aleksandr Fadeev, Viacheslav Feoktistov, Igor' Irten'ev, Michail Isakovskii, Nikolai Karamzin, V. I. Lebedev-Kumach, Nikolai Nekrasov, Vladimir Papernyi, Ivan Pushchin,

Aleksandr Pushkin, Evgenii Rein, Panteleimon Romanov, Vasilii Shukshin, Vladimir Soloukhin, I. T. Spasskii, Aleksandr Tkachev, Tomasz Tot, Aleksandr Tvardovskii, and Vladimir Vysotskii. See Works Cited.

13. The occasional gender-marked exceptions ("Van'ka got well; the bathhouse helped him" [*Vylechilsia Vania, pomogla emu bania*]) tend to identify the male bather. There are, however, a number of surviving peasant bathhouse superstitions and fortune-telling practices specifically designed to determine an unmarried girl's future husband. According to one of these, she is to put a bared part of her body (probably the breast) into the slightly opened bathhouse door and invite the bathhouse spirit to touch it. If the phantom hand is furry, the future husband will be rich; if the hand is cold, the husband will be poor; if the hand is calloused or rough, the husband will be strong-tempered (Zabylinyi 27). This kind of fortune-telling could be seen as a surviving example of the cult of the fate goddesses (*rozhanitsy*), which will be discussed later in this essay.

14. Cf. Aleksandr Tkachev on the process of steaming and dousing in cold water: "We returned at first to our childhood, then to the childhood of humanity, and finally we became incorporeal angels, swarming in the cool ether." Cf. also Vysotskii: "It is almost a return to original birth" (1981c, 325).

15. The *venik*, the signal instrument within the encapsulated world of the *bania* ("without the *venik*, a *bania* is not a *bania*" [*bez venika bania—ne bania*]), sometimes supplants in the *bania* the place occupied by money in the world outside the *bania*. A number of proverbs ("In the bathhouse, the *venik* is worth more than money" [*v bane venik—dorozhe deneg*]) thus assert the status of the *venik* as the bathhouse's superior "legal tender," a crucial object in managing the micro-world of the *bania*. The *Tale of Bygone Years* confirms this in its own fashion, recounting how tribal payment in birch *veniki* was a common form of tribute (Galitskii 5).

Indeed, the *venik* as a kind of "convertible currency" fulfills multiple important functions in the routine of the bathhouse. In additon to whipping the bather, it may be used as a fan whirled overhead to stir up and equalize the temperature of the steam in the steam room. It may serve as a ready-made seat on which to sit in the steam room. It provides impromptu head covering in the steam room for the ill-prepared few who were foolish enough to come to the *bania* without a hat. When soaked in boiling water, the *venik* renders a liquid ostensibly beneficial to the hair. That same liquid may be splashed on the walls or into the oven of the steam room for added fragrance and good health. Finally, when the steaming session is over, an old *venik* may be used to sweep out the steam room and prepare it for the next session.

16. See, for example, Andrei Murash's verses, wherein the sense of debauch is intensified by a double taboo: sex in contiguity with the Party. For readers who do not know Russian, it should be kept in mind that "Bolshevik" also connotes "that which is bigger"—i.e., an erect phallus:

> In the bath, the dames are bulky.
> But they're whining, sad and sulky.
> Then the Communists come quick,
> Each one with his Bolshevik.

> V bane babon'ki miasisty
> Iznyvali ot toski.
> Vdrug zakhodiat kommunisty
> I u vsekh bol'sheviki.

17. The men's baths, then, have a volatile, unstable quality to them because they are the crossroads where holy pleasure and carnal pleasure intersect, where celibacy is constantly in danger of sero-converting into debauch. It is perhaps not surprising, given the previous list of sins (tobacco, liquor, and women), that illicit property (both stealing and being stolen from) also figures among the standard narratives of the men's bathhouse. Here the visitors voluntarily shed themselves of all worldly possessions, yet fear most that their property may be stolen, a catastrophe that would hinder their passage backward to the adult world of materiality. We find this most familiarly in three stories by Zoshchenko, all enacting anxiety about material possessions: "Bath" (Bania), in which the narrator loses the bathhouse tag for his things; "Story of the Baths and Their Clientele" (Rasskaz o baniakh i ikh posetiteliakh), whose narrator loses his coat; and "In the Baths" (V bane), in which a character comes to the baths carrying a huge bundle of money.

18. A separate essay should be written about bathhouse signs, explicating their prohibitions, customs, and rules of etiquette. One of which I am particularly fond is the sign in the Mozhaisk Baths that reads: "Civil War Veterans [1918–20] get pedicures without standing in line." This sign, in some inchoate way I cannot entirely define, is the true spirit of socialism, with all its internal contradictions cheerfully exposed.

19. Most bathhouses nowadays no longer permit washing laundry. Only poor or working-class baths, such as the Rochdale Baths (until their permanent closing "for repairs"), have allowed this practice to continue.

20. Choosing among the varying "medical" qualities of *veniki* is a highly refined skill: oak, which is normally a "man's *venik*," has a strong bacterial action; it counteracts the rise in arterial pressure that occurs in the steam room and calms the nervous system after exercise. For women, however, oak cures greasy skin, rendering it more translucent and elastic. Birch, which may be used for men or women, cleans the skin, heals scratches, and widens bronchial tubes. Birch *veniki* used by women relieve muscle aches and regulate moods. Linden *veniki* are good for headaches of either sex, especially headaches associated with colds. Mountain ash stimulates internal bodily rhythms. Juniper disinfects the air; it is crucial to fighting bronchitis, laryngitis, and influenza. It also combats neuralgia, radiculitis, and spinal pain. Long hair rinsed in tea or (better yet) the water in which any *venik* has been soaking will grow stronger at its roots and will break less easily.

21. Appropriate restorative herbs, flowers, and roots for men include licorice root and sage; for women, immortelle, sweet clover, mint, and lavender. The intermixing of "male" herbs with "female" ones is not harmful; in fact, in moderation it restores balance and harmony to the organism.

Works Cited

Anonymous. 1992. "Ital'ianskii anekdot epokhi vozrozhdeniia: novella o shkoliare, kotoryi probralsia v zhenskie bani, gde byl razoblachen, no poluchil bol'she chem ozhidal." *Russkaia bania* 3: 5.

———. 1994. "Russkaia bania." *Vechernii N'iu Iork,* 9 May, 12.

Askol'dov, Aleksandr, dir. 1967/1987. *Kommisar.* With Nonna Mordiukova, Rolan Bykov, and Raisa Nedashkovskaia. Gor'kii Studio/Mosfil'm.

Balabanov, Aleksei, dir. 1994. *Zamok.* With Nikolai Stotskii, Svetlana Pis'michenko, and Anbar Libabov. 2 P and K Studio/Lenfil'm.

Baldaev, D. S.; B. K. Belko; and I. M. Isupova, comps. 1992. *Slovar' tiuremno-lagerno-blatnogo zhargona: rechevoi i graficheskii portret sovetskoi tiur'my.* Moscow: Kraia Moskvy.

Baron, S. H., ed. and trans. 1967. *The Travels of Olearius in Seventeenth-Century Russia.* Stanford: Stanford UP.

Berman, Jonathan, dir. 1986. *The Shvitz.* London: Klezmatics.

Berry, L. E., and R. O. Crummey, ed. 1968. *Rude and Barbarous Kingdom: Russia in the Accounts of Sixteenth-Century English Voyagers.* Madison: U of Wisconsin P.

Brokgauz", F. A., and I. A. Efron. 1891. "Bania." In *Entsiklopedicheskii slovar',* ed. I. E. Andreevskii, vol. 3, 17–22. Saint Petersburg: Efron.

Chekhov, A. P. 1983 "V bane." In *Polnoe sobranie sochinenii i pisem v tridtsati tomakh,* 30 vols., vol. 3, 178–86. Moscow: Nauka.

Cross, A. G. 1991. "The Russian *Banya* in the Descriptions of Foreign Travellers and in the Depictions of Foreign and Russian Artists." In *Oxford Slavonic Papers,* ed. I. P. Foote, G. S. Smith, and G. C. Stone, n.s. 24. Oxford: Clarendon.

Dal', V. 1984. *Poslovitsy russkogo naroda v dvukh tomakh.* Moscow: Khudozhestvennaia literatura.

Dmitriev, L. A., and D. S. Likhachev, ed. 1969. *Izbornik: Sbornik proizvedenii literatury drevnei Rusi.* Edited by L. A. Dmitriev and D. S. Likhachev. Moscow: Khudozhestvennaia literatura.

Dostoevskii, F. M. 1972–1988. "Zapiski iz mertvogo doma." In *Polnoe sobranie sochinenii v tridstati tomakh,* 30 vols., vol. 4, 96–99. Leningrad: Nauka.

Dunn, Nell. 1981. *Steaming.* Ambergate, Derbyshire: Amber Lane Press.

Efimenko, P. S. 1877. "Materialy po etnografii russkogo naseleniia Arkhangel'skoi gubernii." In *Izvestiia obshchestva liubitelei estestvoznaniia, antropologii i etnografii pri imp. Moskovskom universitete,* vol. 30, *Trudy etnograficheskogo otd.,* book 5, part 1. Moscow.

Fadeev, Aleksandr. 1959. *Poslednii iz Udege. Sobranie sochinenii v piati tomakh.* 5 vols. Vol. 1, pp. 151–634. Moscow: Khudozhestvennaia literatura.

Feoktistov, Viacheslav. 1993. "Zakladyvali baniu na usad'be." *Russkaia bania* 2: 1.

Galitskii, Aleksei. 1991. *Bania parit—zdorov'e darit.* Moscow: Panorama.

Gavrilin, Lev. 1992. Interview. "Sanduny, vy moi, sanduny . . ." *Russkaia bania* 1: 2.

Gerhart, Genevra. 1974. *The Russian's World: Life and Language.* San Diego: Harcourt Brace Jovanovich.

Giliarovskii, Vladimir. 1983. *Moskva i moskvichi.* Moscow: Moskovskii rabochii.

Gladnev, N. 1993. "V igre da v bane vse ravny?" *Russkaia bania* 2: 2.

Hubbs, Joanna. 1988. *Mother Russia: The Feminine Myth in Russian Culture.* Bloomington: Indiana UP.

Irten'ev, Igor'. 1990. "Sluchai vozle bani." In *Vertikal'nyi srez*, 38–39. Moscow: Sovetskii pisatel'.

Iutkevich, S. I., and A. G. Karanovich, dir. 1962. *Bania.*

Ivanova-Anninskaia, Aleksandra N. "Subbota—bab'ia rabota." In *Dom v Leont'evskom: Rodoslovnaia*, unpublished manuscript, 107–113.

Jones, Sherry, prod. 1994. *Frontline: The Struggle for Russia.* PBS. WQED, Pittsburgh. 3 May.

Kabanov, V. 1986. "Khorosha russkaia bania." *Nauka i zhizn'* 12: 134–47.

Karavayev, Vladimir. 1994. "Temples of Health." *Moscow Magazine* 2, no. 27: 65–67.

Khamidov, Tolib, dir. 1991. *Identifikatsiia zhelanii.* Tadzhikfil'm.

Kol'gunenko, Inna. 1992 "I muzhchiny—u vashikh nog." *Russkaia bania* 2: 2.

Listova, T. A. 1992. "Russian Rituals, Customs, and Beliefs Associated with the Midwife (1850–1930)." In *Russian Traditional Culture: Religion, Gender, and Customary Law*, ed. Marjorie Mandelstam Balzer, 122–45. Armonk, N.Y.: M. E. Sharpe.

Losey, Joseph, dir. 1986. *Steaming.* With Vanessa Redgrave, Sarah Miles, and Diana Dors. New World Pictures.

Lotman, Ju. M., and B. A. Uspenskij. 1984. "The Role of Dual Models in the Dynamics of Russian Culture (Up to the End of the Eighteenth Century)." Trans. N. F. C. Owen. In *The Semiotics of Russian Culture*, ed. Ann Shukman, 3–35. Ann Arbor: Michigan Slavic Contributions (11).

Maiakovskii, V. V. 1965. *Bania. Sochineniia v trekh tomakh.* 3 vols. Vol. 3, 524–72. Moscow: Khudozhestvennaia literatura.

Martynov, S. V. 1905. *Pechorskii krai.* St. Petersburg: n.p.

Mishchenko, V. 1993. "Nad Suroi." *Russkaia bania* 3: 3.

Murash, Andrei. "V bane babon'ki miasisty." Written on a napkin by someone I met at a party.

Nekrasov, N. A. 1959. *Sochineniia v trekh tomakh.* 3 vols. Vol. 3., 73–303. Moscow: GIKhL.

Papernyi, Vladimir. 1991. "V Kistenevskoi bane." *Moskovskii nabliudatel' 5: 41–43.*

Polevichek, G. I. 1992. V baniu za zdorov'em. Moscow: Informatsionno-Vnedrencheskii Tsentr "Marketing."

Prokhorov, Aleksandr. 1994. Electronic mail message. UNIX. 19 May.

Pushkin, Aleksandr. 1968a. *Kapitanskaia dochka. Izbrannye proizvedeniia.* 2 vols. Vol. 2, Moscow: Khudozhestvennai a literatura. 379–483.

————. 1968b. "Puteshestvie v Arzrum vo vremia pokhoda 1829 goda." Ibid., 484–525.

————. 1986c. "Ruslan i Liudmila." Ibid., vol. 1, 275–343.

Rein, Evgenii. 1994. "Bannyi den', ili smert' Marata." *Ogonek* 1: 28.

Riazanov, El'dar, dir. 1975. *Ironiia sud'by, ili s legkim parom!* With Andrei Miagkov, Barbara Bryl'ska, and Iurii Iakovlev. Mosfil'm.

Romanov, Panteleimon. 1984. "Terpelivyi narod." In *Detstvo: povest', rasskazy,* 180–83. Tula: Priokskoe knizhnoe izdatel'stvo.

Rostotskii, Stanislav, dir. 1972. *A zori zdes' tikhie. . . .* Mosfil'm.

Rubinov, Anatolii. 1991. "Muzhchiny v bane." In *Intimnaia zhizn' Moskvy,* 251–99. Moscow: Ekonomika.

Schmidt, Chris, dir. 1990. *Bania.* Zerkalo/Boston.

Seimuk, A. A. 1991. *Sukhvozdushnaia bania, sauna.* Dnepropetrovsk: Redotdel oblastnogo upravleniia po pechati.

Sevela, Efraim. 1993. *Muzhskoi razgovor v russkoi bane.* Moscow: Panorama.

Shukshin, Vasilii. 1975a. "Alesha Beskonvoinyi." In *Izbrannye proizvedeniia v dvukh tomakh,* 2 vols., vol. 1, 318–31. Moscow: Molodaia gvardiia, 1975.

————. 1975b. "Kalina krasnaia." Ibid., vol. 1, 417–92.

Sobolev, A. I. 1983. *Russkie poslovitsy i pogovorki.* Moscow: Sovetskaia Rossiia.

Soloukhin, Vladimir. 1992. "Kolia, nazad!" *Russkaia bania* 3: 4–5.

Spasskii, I. T. 1835. "Kratkii ocherk vrachebnogo otnosheniia k russkoi bane." *Drug zdorov'ia.*

Tkachev, Aleksandr. 1992. "Istopi mne ban'ku po-chernomu." *Russkaia bania* 2: 2.

Tot, Tomasz, dir. 1993. *Deti chugunnykh bogov.* With Evgenii Sidikhin, Aleksandr Kaliagin, and Iurii Iakovlev. Kur'er/Mosfil'm.

Tvardovskii, Aleksandr. 1966. *Vasilii Terkin. Voennaia lirika.* Moscow: Voennoe izdatel'stvo Ministerstva oborony SSSR. 7–202.

Uspenskij, B. A. 1984. "Tsar and Pretender: *Samozvanchestvo* or Holy Imposture in Russia as a Cultural-Historical Phenomenon." Translated by David Budgen. In *The Semiotics of Russian Culture,* ed. Ann Shukman, 259–92. Ann Arbor: Michigan Slavic Contributions (11).

Vahros, I. 1966. "Zur Geschichte und Folklore der grossrussischen Sauna." *Folklore Fellows Communications* 82, no. 197: 199–200.

Vernadsky, George. 1973. *Kievan Russia.* New Haven: Yale UP.

Vigarello, Georges. 1988. *Concepts of Cleanliness: Changing Attitudes in France since the Middle Ages.* Translated by Jean Birrell. Cambridge: Cambridge UP.

Vysotskii, Vladimir. 1981a. "Ban'ka po-belomu." In *Pesni i stikhi,* 2 vols. vol. 1, ed. Boris Berest, 59–61. New York: Literaturnoe zarubezh'e.

————. 1981b. "Ban'ka po-chernomu." Ibid., 304.

————. 1981c. "Blagodat' ili blagosloven'e (Ballada o bane)." Ibid., 325–26.

Wright, Lawrence. 1960. *Clean and Decent:The Fascinating History of the Bathroom and the Water Closet*. New York: Viking.

Yeltsin, Boris. 1994. *The Struggle for Russia*. New York: Times.

Zabylinyi, M. 1992. *Russkii narod: ego obychai, obriady, predaniia, sueveriia i poeziia*. Reprintnoe vosproizvedenie izdaniia 1880 goda. Moscow: Avtor.

Zenkovsky, Serge A., ed. 1974. *Medieval Russia's Epics, Chronicles, and Tales*. Rev. and enlarged ed. New York: Dutton.

Zoshchenko, Mikhail. 1978a. "Bania." In *Izbrannoe v dvukh tomakh*, 2 vols., vol. 1, 107–109. Leningrad: Khudozhestvennaia literatura.

———. 1978b. "Rasskaz o baniakh i ikh posetiteliakh." Ibid., vol. 2, 214–21.

2

KEEPING A-BREAST OF THE
WAIST-LAND: WOMEN'S FASHION
IN EARLY-NINETEENTH-
CENTURY RUSSIA

Helena Goscilo

La Mode est la déesse des apparances.
—Stéphane Mallarmé

For me, the naked and the nude
(By lexicographers construed
As synonyms that should express
The same deficiency of dress
Or shelter) stand as wide apart
As love from lies, as truth from art.
—Robert Graves

Fashion at Large

Defining the Indefinable

THE GREATEST CIVILIZING EVENT in European history was the introduction of trousers. Or so claimed Hippolyte Taine, who otherwise enjoyed a reputation for common sense (Broby-Johansen 177). In a comparably maximal, if blasphemously ironic, vein Ralph Waldo Emerson maintained, "The sense of being perfectly well-dressed gives a feeling of inward tranquillity which religion is powerless to bestow."[1] And, more recently, James Laver imperiled Britishers' vaunted reputation for understatement by declaring fashion "the mirror of our soul"[2] (Wills and Midgley 11). While such pronouncements attest that in the West clothes talk inspires hyperbole, only an ignoramus would gainsay fashion's incalculable significance as both creator and carrier of cultural values. Whatever their specific areas of divergence, all Western commentators on fashion concur that fashion points to something other than itself, that it not only is, but also *means*. Moving eastward, we find Russians making the same fundamental point, as attested by Iurii Lotman's formulation, which also adverts to the elements of spectatorship/voyeurism and communal prohibition on which fashion is predicated:

> Fashion is always semiotic. Inclusion in fashion is the continuous process of transforming the insignificant into the significant. The semioticity of fashion manifests itself specifically in the fact that it always presupposes an observer. [. . .] Like all other forms of conduct residing behind the everyday norm, fashion presupposes an experimental testing of the boundaries of the permissible.[3] (Lotman 1922, 126, 128)

Merely replacing Lotman's sign with symbol yields Cecil Beaton's definition of fashion as "the symbol which describes the subtle and often hidden forces which shape our society—political, economic, psychological . . . the search for the absolute by man [*sic*], who is only able to create the ephemeral" (Wills and Midgley 1973, 11). In fact, fashion also reflects race, class, gender, and social institutions such as theater, sports, and sundry recreations.[4] For instance, horseback riding and the hunt in eighteenth-century England gradually popularized breeches and top-boots as everyday wear; without the current exercise mania in the United States, lycra, spandex, latex, jogging outfits, and $100 sneakers would not have become the casual dress of choice for millions of Americans. Fashion, in other words, responds to and inescapably impinges upon even the lives of those indifferent to it, for "clothes never shut up. They gabble on endlessly, making their intentional and unintentional points" (Brownmiller 81).

Trends in fashion continue to modify our assumptions about where clothing ought to end and the body to begin[5]—or, to put it differently, the body itself is a contingency that may be aestheticized and/or commodified to display coveted items and to signal social status (Finkelstein 4–5). Fashion privileges image over character and mutability over permanence. If, as Lotman and Beaton propose, fashion bespeaks values and thus urges interpretation, particularly eloquent aspects of fashion include faithful adherence to, or restructuring of, basic body shapes; display and concealment; practicality and frivolity; stress on the vertical or horizontal axis; lifting and dropping of lines (neckline, hemline, etc.); shifts in presumed erogenous zones;[6] and sexual differentiation.[7] These are all grounded in the ever-changing, gendered, ideal image created by a plexus of sociopolitical, economic, and aesthetic forces—in short, by the dominant ethos of a given culture at a given moment and by modification of, or rebellion against, it. Whereas the instinct of imitation and the power of endurance decide the durability of a given fashion (Fischel and von Boehn 115), the desire for uniqueness and novelty catalyzes innovation.

Gender and Fashion: Dowdy or Dandy

During the last two centuries or so, women's fashions have undergone more (and more radical) changes than men's attire and have attracted appreciably greater attention. Consensus among analysts of fashion pinpoints the end of the eighteenth century as the time when "men made the great renunciation," relinquishing to women the task of negotiating the balance between modesty and exhibitionism through clothes—a task facilitated by the West's visual sexualization of the female body.[8]

Yet in the eighteenth century, when sumptuous dress was primarily a prerogative of class rather than gender, men's fascination with fashion rivaled women's (Bell 23–24). Moreover, the cult of the dandy during the Regency period in England (1811–20) was a purely male phenomenon, whose foremost representative illustrated the limitless power of unrelenting affectation when combined with succinctness, hygiene, and Hessian boots. George (Beau) Brummel achieved international renown and subsequently passed into myth by programmatically elevating sartorial style to a religious art. As Prince Hermann von Pückler-Muskau observed, "Brummell once ruled an entire generation through the cut of his coat" (McDowell 82). Throughout his reign as divine despot, adult males' social reputations hinged on the Ultimate Arbiter's approval or disapproval of their cravats. Skeptics who question whether maintaining a faultlessly attired look is a worthwhile life goal should remember that "the dandy made his first, impeccable bow in the uneasy atmosphere of shifting perspectives and sinking values that followed the French Revolution" (Moers 17). If clothes serve the double purpose of self-protection and self-assertion (Laver 1937, 379), Brummell's demeanor of untouchable sartorial superiority protected him from close physical and emotional contact and asserted his exclusiveness *beyond* class.[9] As the sovereign authority on taste, Brummell could dictate to the corpulent Prince Regent himself, whose subordination to the Beau's decrees on fashion enhanced the reputation of both. Dandyism provided a public identity for the disaffected aristocrat and for the bourgeois with pretensions to aristocratic society (Moers 122), partly by proclaiming—to invoke Veblen's concept—its practitioners' conspicuous leisure.

When dandyism migrated to France in the 1820s, it bred an Anglomania that prompted the French, contrary to their venerable tradition of linguistic chauvinism, to adopt English names for "stylish" goods—*lavender vater, plom-cake,* and *muffling* (just as the Exclusives in England had superciliously warded off intruders by incorporating French into the cant favored by *their* set).[10] Edward Bulwer's *Pelham* (1828), the dandy's "how to" manual disguised as a novel, not only captivated the susceptible imagination of Benjamin Disraeli, but enchanted French high society, intensified the Russian vogue for dandyism introduced in the 1810s,[11] and inspired Aleksandr Pushkin to embark on his *Russian Pelham*.[12] Yet in the course of the nineteenth century fashion increasingly became identified with women, and by the mid-nineteenth century men's wear, though subject to modified variation, generally settled into the familiar, inexpressive lines that persisted until the 1980s.

As Laver, an astute veteran of fashion analysis, has observed, in periods of marked male domination the clothes of the two sexes are maximally differentiated (Laver 1969, 184, 264). It is no accident that the Bible, for instance, mandates a sex-distinctive dress code (Brownmiller 81), nor that during the upsurge of feminist activity in the 1970s and 1980s, male fashions started to appropriate features formerly associated chiefly or exclusively with women's style: jewelry (especially chains and earrings), perfume, permed or long hair, exposure of various bodily parts, etc.[13] Few periods corroborate Laver's *aperçu* more vividly than the nineteenth century in Europe, in the course of which male wear underwent an evolution dictated by the twin principles of comfort and unfettered movement, while women's dress moved inexorably in the opposite direction—from enticingly lightweight apparel to constraining, multilayered wrappings that immobilized women into useless social ornaments (Cumming 55).

Russian Women's Fashion

Within the framework of that era, the focus of my essay falls on women's formal wear in Russia from the 1800s to the 1830s. Since formal garb by definition presupposes visual consumption by all the members of an "audience" whom the wearer encounters in such "closed" settings as the ballroom, theater, opera house, and the like, it unavoidably transforms the body into a maximally social, supremely public entity. Occasions "requiring" formal clothes place the body "on show"—hence the heightened emotions that typically accompany the selection of a ball gown or an evening dress, whose wearer "sees" and "is seen" in a ritual that blurs the boundaries between exhibition and exhibitionism. What interests me above all in Russian women's "dressy" dress during the early nineteenth century is the potential for individual self-expression, freedom of physical movement, and pleasure in vestimentary play and experimentation that could be exploited by female practitioners of fashion's exacting art.

France as Premier Source for *le dernier cri*

The major arbiters of style from 1800 to 1820 were primarily Paris and, during the Anglomania that followed Napoleon's retreat from Russia in 1812, London.[14] These foreign trend-setters determined fashion not only in Russia but in the entire Western world; their tastes were disseminated internationally through the fashion plates that, thanks to Jacques Esnauts and Michel Rapilly, came into existence in the 1770s (almost immediately accelerating the pace of change in fashion),[15] as well as through the detailed updates on the latest vogues in Paris and London. Both appeared regularly in such Russian journals as *Paris Fashions* (Parizhskie mody), *Ladies' Journal* (Damskii zhurnal), *Galatea* (Galateia), *Moscow Telegraph* (Moskovskii telegraf), *Moscow Observer* (Moskovskii nabliudatel'), and a host of other publications.[16] The specialized journal devoted entirely to women's dress available in Russia during this period, however, was the French *Journal des dames et des modes* (1797–1838/39), recognized throughout Europe as the codifier of fashion (Lotman 1983, 276).[17] Modes announced by this and similar periodicals were often interpreted in exact detail by such contemporary artists as Boilly, Gérard, Garneray, Danloux, and David, renowned for their costumary accuracy (Boucher 343). Throughout these decades, in fact, the symbiosis between styles in fashion, on the one hand, and such visual art forms as painting and sculpture, on the other, reached unprecedented heights. Classical statues and paintings of mythological figures (especially Psyche and Galatea) inspired trends in women's dress, while portraits of the era's most elegant and influential society ladies verged on fashion plates and sometimes seem indistinguishable from them. All were objects of pleasurable aesthetic contemplation.

For all intents and purposes, Russian clothing among the upper classes meant French or English fashion. To describe modish female and male attire of the time was impossible without resorting to French terminology. For instance, an item in the *Moscow Telegraph* on the vogue for satin ribbons details, in Russian, their use as trim for hats worn casually—"*za prosto*"; but either to ensure complete understanding on the part of its readership or to authenticate the information, the author translates the key term "za prosto" into French ("*en négligé*") (1828, no. 1, p. 2). Just as French was the language of social intercourse among educated Russians, so French style functioned as the elitist "sign system" providing a gauge of their sartorial sophistication. Those aristocrats who could afford to do so, in fact, ordered clothing for special occasions from Paris, as confirmed in memoirs, correspondence, and literature.[18] Those less fortunate fell back on the expertise of Lomanov, G-zha Ol'ga,

Brizak, and Ivanova, Russian costumiers famed for their craft along
French lines (Kaminskaia 102). Furthermore, the Russian vogue for
things French was enhanced by a steady stream of French visitors and
dwellers, such as the acclaimed portraitist Elisabeth Vigée-Lebrun, who
during her extended residence in St. Petersburg (1785–1801) painted
the Russian imperial family and achieved a fame that rendered superfluous any explanatory footnote on Pushkin's passing reference to her work
in "Queen of Spades" (Pikovaia dama, 1833).

When Less Offers More: Neoclassical Minimalism of the 1800s

The early 1800s saw the elevation of Napoleon and the waistline.[19]
Whatever his defeat(s) in the military sphere, Napoleon triumphed glo-
riously in the world of *haute couture*. Immediately before and during his
consolidation of power into Empire (1804–14), fashion emphasized the
vertical line and a "classical" look. The Empire style in female dresses, in
effect, continued the semi-licentious Neoclassicism of the Directoire
period (1790–1800) that imitated Greek statues. The mimicry during
that turbulent decade constituted an attempt at self-legitimation via a
rejection of absolutism's gorgeous trappings[20] and a revival of Hellenic
republican ideals—largely through association with an authoritative aesthetics harnessed to a "democratic" sociopolitical philosophy (Tortora
and Eubank 211). Flimsy draped material, preferably white so as to
evoke marble, flowed in a straight, soft fall to the floor, creating an
effect of delicacy echoed in the fashionable pallor aided by rice powder
that was obligatory in the evenings (Broby-Johansen 178; Ryndin 96).
Startlingly low cut and high waisted, with the minimal bodice closely
fitted, these décolleté gowns with short or arm-hugging sleeves (or
none) revealed in fleshly duplicate the globe virtually conquered by the
heavily uniformed Napoleon (see fig. 2.1).

Like the Corsican conqueror, the waist had migrated northward, to
"support" and showcase the exposed mountainous terrain[21]—what
McDowell in all seriousness calls "the twin peaks of passion" (11)—that
so obsessed the eighteenth century. Under this sheer, light robe of (optimally) white or pastel Indian muslin or calico,[22] women wore only a
chemise instead of the formerly mandatory corsets, and sometimes pink
or white tights that stimulated imaginations by simulating skin. Just as
the fine arts of this period took "noble simplicity" as their ideal, so
female fashion cultivated "natural" undress, in accord with the Classical
veneration of nudity (Robinson 439). As often happens, in this instance
fantasy colluded with practicality, for the popularity of muslin and calico
stemmed not only from a disavowal of monarchical luxury, but also from

2.1. L. Boilly's painting *The Point of Convention* (late 18th century) dramatizes, in near-caricature, the contrast between the multilayered male costume, appropriate for a cold climate, and the exiguous female garb, more fitting for the tropics.

the financial constraints that complicated the procurement of silks, velvets, and laces during a time when those industries suffered from the political upheaval in France (Evans 83). In an increasingly mechanized world, costume was coming to depend increasingly on economic factors (Boucher 334).

To reveal what might inadvertently be concealed by this diaphanous garb, women reportedly used to dampen their dresses, causing them to cling to their bodies in imitation of the Greek garments represented in antique statues (Laver 1969, 152).[23] According to one account, "so many people caught severe colds and pneumonia from going around soaked to the skin that after a number of deaths had occurred the [British] government intervened, declaring it illegal [!] to wear soaked clothing" (Bigelow 156). Among the female population in France, the number of deaths during the decade of Neoclassical minimalism exceeded the death toll for the preceding forty years (*Damskie mody* 17). During this Mammary Era, the fabled Russian beauty of Alexander I's reign, Tiufiakina, is reputed to have perished in precisely this manner, on the chilly altar of *haute couture* (Vigel' 178; Kirsanova 266).

The "barely dressed" look of the accurately labeled *robes en chemise*—public dress that evoked the private, intimate image of a skimpy night-dress, of undergarments—was accentuated by the footwear, which consisted of light slippers without heels, usually in pastel.[24] Not coincidentally, the observable distinction between morning dresses, daytime dresses, and evening gowns verged on nil[25]—as typically occurs during periods of liberalism (see fig. 2.2).

Echoing the sentiments of N. Karamzin's "On the Light Dress of Fashionable Beauties in the Nineteenth Century,"[26] F. F. Vigel', an eagle-eyed and waspish-tongued Russian memoirist of the period, lamented

Fig 2.2. François Gérard's famous portrait of Mme Récamier (1802) epitomizes the style of the period.

Russia's automatic aping of French fashion, according to which "women all want[ed] to appear as ancient statues descended from their pedestals." To that end, "without any fear of the dreadful winter, they were dressed in semi-transparent dresses that closely embraced their supple waists and faithfully traced their lovely forms; indeed it seemed that light-winged Psyches were flitting on the parquet floor" (Vigel' 177–78). Aleksandr Herzen waxed even more sardonic about Russia's wholesale adoption of the Mediterranean-based French style: "During the tortures of Russia's freezing weather, Paris, with the indifference of a surgeon, has been dressing our ladies as marble statues in gauze and lace, from which our aristocratic ladies are perishing in the thousands, like autumnal flies. And by the number of untimely graves, Paris can determine the number of fool women in Russia" (Gertsen 420; Kirsanova 266). Doctors in France cautioned women to abandon a dress style better suited to the balmier climate of Greece, but the advice fell on deaf ears there and abroad (*Damskie mody* 17), for the suggestive conflation of vaporous and carnal proved irresistible to women intent on forging a memorable social persona by visual means. Vladimir Borovikovskii's portrait of Skobeeva splendidly captures the "poetic" yet nipple-revealing flimsiness of this style, the unbitten apple in her hand intimating the as yet unexplored paradisaical rewards of "virginity on the verge"[27] (see fig. 2.3).

The beguiling pseudo-ethereal mode was registered in sundry literary texts treating this period: for instance, the girlish heroine of Evdokiia Rostopchina's "Rank and Money" (Chiny i den'gi, 1838) attends a ball "in a white transparent dress, which twined [. . .] lightly about her."[28] Transparent white, reportedly codified by Gérard's painting of Psyche (Brooke and Laver 346),[29] in fact, was the "flavor" of the age; it evoked and exploited soulful virginity while advertising physical endowments that implicitly invited men to sample its untouched promise (see fig. 2.4).

Fig 2.3. Vladimir Borovikovskii's portrait of Skobeeva (late 18th century), in which the placement and shape of the apple emphasize the semi-exposed breasts.

Moralists frowned on balls not only because dancing—particularly the controversial waltz—brought women's bodies into intimate contact with men's in a regular rhythm evocative of sexual intercourse, but also because even more than normally the formal gowns of this period pa-

FIG 2.4. Borovikovskii's portrait of E. N. Arsen'eva, painted in the second half of the 1790s, repeats the pose and the apple/breast parallel.

raded women's flesh, and particularly the bosom, before strangers' eyes.[30] Aleksandra Smirnova in her memoirs recalls a ball hosted by Eliza Khitrovo, who wore a "white dress, very décolleté; her plump little shoulders climbed out of her dress." Khitrovo's near-nakedness allegedly prompted Pushkin, then in attendance, to compose the sly verses "Liza now is sampling / The Austrian gala's fare, / Though not as sweet as formerly, / She remains just as bare" (Smirnova 174–75).[31] (See fig. 2.5)

The English *Lady's Monthly Museum* for June 1802 and March 1803 records contemporary disapproval, on both medical and moral grounds, of this "female demi-nudity . . . the close, all white, shroud looking, ghostly chemise undress of the ladies, who seem to glide like spectres"; for "a party of high-bred young ladies, who were dressed or rather undressed in all the nakedness of the mode [. . .] it really was as much hazard of health, as it was trespass against modesty, to come into public *en chemise*, as if they were just out of their beds" (Bradfield 86). Life seeped into art, as a "feverish, bleached kind of Nordic eroticism" infected the British Neoclassic (near-)nudes, with pronounced breasts and buttocks showing through clinging fabric, in the era's paintings (Hollander 118). Vestimentary minimalism verged on nihilism, and Mme Tallien, who with Mme Récamier led the social set dubbed *Les Merveilleueses*, enhanced her fame when she reportedly attended a ball in a dress weighing, together with her accessories, approximately five ounces (Broby-Johansen 177).[32] Small wonder that contemporaries nicknamed her Notre Dame de Thermidor (Hansen 142).

This minimalist vogue projected a highly ambivalent image of woman, an ambivalence Fred Davis and others justifiably consider typical of fashion (Davis 81–99): on the one hand, fragile, beautiful to contemplate—to be pedestaled, like statuary—she represented the "high

FIG 2.5. This fashion plate, reproduced in Russia, shows a more "modest" version of the *robe en chemise*.

ideals" with which the long, slender fingers is synonymous (an association carried to an extreme, for example, by El Greco). In this context the raised waistline that elongated the legs participated in symbolic idealization or at least abstraction, by departing from natural body lines. The semi-naked breasts and the analogy with intimate apparel, on the other hand, tended to place this statuary (mentally) in the bedroom—hardly the locus of contemplative idealization, for there the male

Pygmalion could bring his quasi-marmoreal Galatea to lusty life.
Moreover, the "dangerously unfeminine" freedom from physical restriction in such flimsy attire intimated a parallel freedom from moral strictures,[33] implicitly negated, however, by the white or pastel hues that
symbolized innocence, and contradicted by the "quintessentially feminine" titillation of the attire's scantiness (Brownmiller 96). The mixed
messages are neatly encapsulated in the *fichu*—the gossamer scarf in a
contrasting color that attracted attention to the breasts it was ostensibly
intended to conceal (Broby-Johansen 177; Mackrell 28). As the then
common, disillusion-steeped term *fichu menteur* ("fibbing scarf") de-
notes, the riveting gauze material was an alluring *trompe l'oeil*, designed
to create the illusion of more substantial endowments around the bust
than was actually the case (Mackrell 26). So the erotic/chaste dialectic
characteristic of women's fashion played itself out quite visibly in the
semi-screened exposure of the female form. (see fig. 2.6.)

Accessories as Creativity and Control

A kindred paradox during this era of bare coverage was the unprecedented vogue for shawls and stoles. Quite apart from other considera-
tions, they fulfilled the practical function of keeping semi-naked women
warm.[34] The scanty dresses of the 1800s supposedly occasioned an epi-
demic of illnesses (Black et al. 68) and, for that matter, may have accounted quite naturally for some of the pallor that hardier women,
cursed by greater stamina, were forced to cultivate artificially. On a less
overtly pragmatic level, a woman's skill in draping and wielding her shawl
was an index of her sophistication or seductiveness.[35] Graceful movement, cleverly draped shawls, and elegantly manipulated trains (which, if
worn, were suspended from a ribbon below the breasts) allowed women
self-expression through poses and gestures that evoked the plasticity of
sculpture and the harmony of dance (Hansen 142). Vigée-Lebrun, in fact,
boasted of her ability to beautify the women whose portraits she painted
by her artful positioning of the large scarves that anticipated shawls
(Mackrell 26). Female agency had free rein here, for strategic deployment
of a shawl could both *accentuate* various parts and lines and *control* visual
access to the body from one moment to the next. In other words, shawl-
wearers had the Saloméic potential of making men lose their heads (with
apologies to John the Baptist),[36] even as they protected themselves from
the health hazards of postrevolutionary fashion.

Whether carried in the hand or over the arm, or arranged as contrasting background for the white dress, the shawl as accessory played a key

FIG 2.6. A fashion plate showing the semi-screened body and the eye-catching "ornament" that draws the eyes to the breasts.

aesthetic role in women's physical self-presentation (Hansen 143). When war posed increasing dangers to Eastern trade routes and threatened the availability of Kashmir (in French, Cashmere) shawls, the insatiable demand for French and Scottish imitations boosted the economies of both countries (Black et al. 75). Ultimately, however, the nation to make the most invaluable and lasting contribution to the shawl industry was Russia. It not only learned to manufacture its domestic variant of the cashmere shawl in the factories of Merlina, Kolokol'tsov, and Eliseeva, but also eventually revolutionized French production by pioneering the versatile shawl that had two identical sides instead of a right and wrong side (Kirsanova 265).

Because pockets in dresses that threatened to evaporate at any second were, at the very least, impractical, this decade witnessed the emergence of the little bag dubbed the reticule or ridicule (Bradfield 91–92). Whether the latter name alluded to its impracticality or to women's penchant for cramming it full of personal effects remains unclear. Its diminutive size and whimsical appearance suggested decoration,[37] but actually disguised designers' skill in elevating felt necessity to apparent frivolity: In that sense, the reticule reified in miniature the essence of fashion's art. According to reticule etiquette as mandated by *La Belle Assemblée* in 1808, no lady of fashion appeared in public without a reticule, which contained "her handkerchief, fan, card money and essence bottle" (Alexander 50). With time, the reticule expanded substantially, to hold candy and other edibles, as evidenced in the fourth chapter of Mariia Zhukova's *Summer House on the Peterhof Road* (Dacha na petergofskoi doroge, 1845) (Kirsanova 196–97).

Fans, formerly of daunting dimensions, now shrank to more manageable size, and their deployment, like that of the shawl, gave a measure of a woman's worldliness and charm, thereby affording her the chance to assert her individual personality. At least one representative of that era, Mme de Genlis, associated the shrinkage in fan size with a corresponding growth in female self-confidence: "Previously when we blushed so frequently, and wished to hide our embarrassment and timidity, we used a large fan. Now we seldom blush and no longer feel timid. There is no longer any inclination to hide oneself [;] therefore, the fan has become smaller" (Broby-Johansen 178). Indeed, it is difficult to find a period antedating the twentieth century when women hid themselves so little. Yet to suggest that the fan's sole function consisted of covering visible signs of women's outraged innocence would be the height of ingenuousness. For the fan belonged to that arsenal of expressive props—along with such accessories as the shawl, the glove, the handkerchief, and the locket—that enabled women to act out sundry roles and construct a persona on the public stage of social gatherings. Mme de Staël, in fact, believed that no ornament among worldly women's paraphernalia could match its versatility and "produce so great an effect" (Flory 52–53). Depending on how she fanned herself, a woman could express languidness, fastidiousness, impatience, or a vast spectrum of other emotions. Joseph Addison, the editor of the *Spectator*, compared women's fans to men's swords, claiming that the female "weapon" sometimes performs more "executions," and through the "infinite variety of motions" at its disposal can convey a correspondingly rich variety of feelings and moods (Flory 33–34).[38]

Moreover, a fan played an inestimable role in the game of coquetry: Skill in handling it could transform its movements into a private code between lovers and (far less likely) spouses. With the aid of a fan, a woman could entertain a very public yet discreet rapport with a man initiated into the intricacies of its manipulation. Although some scholars ascribe fan communication to the repertoire of party games (Alexander 46), others deem it a bona fide language of at least implicit—and at most illicit—romance. In the sign system of fans recorded in America, for example, rapid fanning reportedly meant "I am engaged," slow fanning "I am married"; opening and shutting the fan signaled "You are cruel," while drawing it across the cheek constituted a declaration of love, and so forth (Shafer 233).[39] The saliency of the fan in the language of coquetry may be inferred from Louisa May Alcott's matter-of-fact reference in *Little Women* (1868) to Meg as "flirting her fan" in response to a young man's attentions (Aldrich 1). Fans vouchsafed women the rare opportunity to control at least one form of language, whereas fanless men could merely observe, interpret, and react, without initiating any fan-communicated *badinage*.

While facilitating flirtation, fans could also betray a woman's real or imagined indiscretions, as Oscar Wilde's play *Lady Windermere's Fan* some decades later illustrates. The likelihood of forgetting or inadvertently dropping a fan, of course, is much greater if its dimensions are modest while its owner is not. Apart from its potential as a means of silent communication, the chief importance of the fan ultimately was its participation in the erotic dialectic of concealment/exposure that marks women's attire.[40] A journal of 1794, in fact, expressed lyrical admiration for various beauties who artfully deployed their fans to "unwittingly" wreak a "pleasing disorder" in their *fichu* and their hair (Ryndin I, 16). Fan movement therefore enabled women to capitalize on the piquancy of clothing "disarranged by violence or mistake" (Hollander 185) through orchestrating such "mistakes."

The Grecian (and later Roman) mania also dictated simplified hairstyles, with the hair arranged in flat ringlets about the face or worn in a simple knot from which a few ringlets or tendrils were allowed to escape. Coiffures bore such names as *à la Sappho, à la Venus,* and *à la Caracalla*, openly adverting to the taste for Greek, Roman, and Oriental fashions (de Courtais 96). Yet the self-conscious quest for simplicity and naturalness *à la grecque* seemed at odds with the feathers, especially plumes of ostrich feathers (*aigrettes*), that women stuck in their hair, even in the daytime (Laver 1969, 153). This taste for opulence doubtless stemmed from Napoleon's passion for ostentatious luxury and his preference for imperial Rome over democratic Greece once he firmly ensconced himself in "legitimate" power—hence the revival of ancient Roman architecture in such monuments as the Arc de Triomphe. Certainly the widespread influence on fashion of both the French Revolution and Napoleon's achievements manifested itself quite transparently in favored hairstyles and headgear. For example, the popular short curly cut for women called *la victime* alluded to the practical habit of shearing hair on victims en route to the guillotine, while *à la Titus* referred to the cropped hair depicted on statues of Roman men, after whom Napoleon molded his public persona (Tortora and Eubank 215).[41] Both sexes sported coiffures *à la Titus*, as illustrated by David's famous portrait of Mme Récamier, in which her ultra-short "masculine" hairstyle unproblematically complements the radically "feminine" *robe en chemise* semi-covering her form (see fig. 2.7). This gender-blending of styles exteriorizes their wearer's supreme confidence in her intellectual prowess (the "masculine head") and her sexual appeal (the "feminine body"), while more broadly implying the wide range of possibilities for women's self-presentation that characterized the 1800s.

Turbans came into vogue during the Orientalism that followed Napoleon's Egyptian expedition (1798–99), as did Egyptian motifs on the borders of gowns (Broby-Johansen 177). In Russia, the turban's popularity endured to mid-century, although it peaked after the visit in 1812 of Germaine de Staël, who favored it as headgear.[42] Russian women wore turbans to balls and concerts, on official visits, and for portraits, and *how* they wound them about their heads likewise demonstrated their taste—or lack of it. That is why the *Moscow Telegraph* (1825) counseled female readers to entrust the arrangement of their turbans only to the artists (*artisty*) responsible for their coiffures (Kirsanova 138–41). Agrafena Zakrevskaia (1800–79)—the "bronze Venus" on whom E. Baratynskii modeled the heroine of his "Ball" (1828) (Chizhova 162–63) and who

Fig 2.7. Mme Récamier, hair dressed *à la Titus*, as painted by Jacques-Louis David.

served as the possible prototype for Nina Voronskaia in Pushkin's *Eugene Onegin* (chap. 8)—reportedly wore a light blue turban fastened with large diamonds, which, as Lotman rightly argues, would be vulgar by the unostentatious, self-assured taste of the novel's (finally) sophisticated heroine Tat'iana (Lotman 1983, 587). Like all accessories of the period, headgear afforded women a public forum for displaying their aesthetic sense and powers of visual seductiveness.

Improving on Nature: Romanticism Gone to Waist

The "lightness" and ambiguity of women's dress during the tumultuous first two decades of the nineteenth century, then, allowed for rare comfort and mobility, playfulness, and a degree of sexual self-expression. The 1820s, after Napoleon's demise[43] and Beau Brummell's fall from grace,[44] ushered in a paradigm shift. The horizontal axis supplanted the vertical axis of the preceding decades as, sometime between 1820 and 1822, the female waist rediscovered its natural location. Pseudo-natural (Neoclassical) yielded to genuinely artificial (Romantic) as waistlines dropped and corsets and bustles returned. Tight-lacing squeezed the waist into waspish slightness, its forced diminutiveness emphasized by belts decorated with an eye-catching ornament.[45] The Romantic look, as it was called, demanded a fundamental redistribution of focus so as to make the waist—minimized in the service of ethereality—the epicenter of the female body.[46] Thus extant portraits (e.g., by A. Briullov or V. Gau) of Pushkin's wife, Natal'ia Goncharova, famous for her spectacular figure, spotlight her miniature waist,[47] which by the mid-1820s represented every fashionable woman's dream in Russia (Ryndin 12) (see fig. 2.8).

In Mikhail Lermontov's story "Kniazhna Meri" the romantic Princess Mary possesses a waist that is unusually "voluptuous and supple" (*sladostrastnoi i gibkoi*, 79). In Nikolai Gogol's *Dead Souls* (Mertvye dushi, 1837), the waists of the townsladies, who entertain romantic fantasies about Chichikov, are "tightly laced and most agreeably shaped" (*talii byli obtianuty i imeli samye krepkie i priiatnye dlia glaz formy*, 169).[48] And Ivan Goncharov's *A Common Story* (Obyknovennaia istoriia, 1846) endows Tafaeva, a parody of the romantic ideal, with an "airy waist" (*vozdushnoi taliei*, 201). The romantic female *topoi* of facial delicacy, minute and fragile hands and feet, and above all slender waist, which collectively denoted aristocratic debility, offered visible proof of women's estrangement from all aspects of "vulgarly productive labor" (Harrison 35).[49] The premium on ethereal daintiness spiraled predictably into the cult of invalidism, which ultimately envisioned femininity itself as a disease.[50]

At the close of the 1830s, designers shrank the waist further through elongation: The waistline was dropped even lower in front, forming a

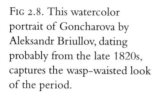

Fɪɢ 2.8. This watercolor portrait of Goncharova by Aleksandr Briullov, dating probably from the late 1820s, captures the wasp-waisted look of the period.

point that directed the eye to what euphemism has dubbed the core of a woman's (presumably sexual) being. That signpost arrowing downward tantalized in a context of prohibition, however, for the "core" remained an unattainable goal, safely enveloped in distancing layers of petticoats and skirts that hid the "immodest, ungodly and sinful" potential of the "bifurcated woman" (Brownmiller 83). Pushkin's risqué *Count Nulin* (Graf Nulin, 1825) anticipated the suggestive visual invitation issued by the dropped waistline, as indicated by the exchange between the provincial Natal'ia Pavlovna and the count, recently returned from Paris: "How high are waists now?" "More than lowish, / Almost to . . . this point, more or less."[51] Typical for Pushkin, the frisson of sexual allusion is achieved through the eloquently unspoken (" . . . "), a verbal analogue for the flirtatious fichu. (See fig. 2.9.)

To attain the hourglass effect, skirts and sleeves (*gigot* or leg-of-mutton) puffed out dramatically, the latter cut so as to radically restrict arm movement, the former weighted at the bottom by flounces, frills, and even bands of fur (Laver 1969, 163). Heavier, more substantial materials, such as velvet and satin, replaced muslin and calico. That process had begun in France during Napoleon's reign and at his behest, the new sumptuous attire calculated not only to parade the court's recovered resplendence and stability, but also to revive the domestic fashion-related industries (e.g., lace, silk, brocade) whose demise had impoverished regions economically dependent on large-scale demand for luxury fabrics (Bigelow 168).

At its most exaggerated, the female form now approximated two stacked isosceles triangles, their apexes meeting at the waistline. The es-

FIG 2.9. A later portrait of Goncharova by Vol'demar Gau, which demonstrates the dropped V waistline.

sentially geometric effect was softened by adornments that blurred lines.[52] A plethora of feathers, bows, ribbons, artificial flowers, gold chains, pearls, and other precious stones tacked onto dresses and headgear transformed women's appearance into a combination of aviary, maypole, and Christmas ornament (see fig. 2.10).[53] With Gothic and Rococo style dominating fashion, furniture, and architecture, overabundant decoration became commonplace, and taste irrelevant. Just as interior decoration in the mid–1830s passed from the cabinetmaker to the upholsterer, who concealed the basic lines of furniture with upholstery, fringes, and tassels, so the heavy materials, laces, ruffles, and ribbons of the increasingly mass-produced "latest" mode disguised the female form (Hansen 146). By mid-

century, when bulky solidity visibly announced moral and economic respectability, women's figures were no less upholstered than their sofas.

Hairstyles also acquired extraordinary complexity as loops or plaits of
false hair enhanced women's own tresses (Tortora and Eubank 223).
Hats—trimmed with a mass of colorful flowers, ribbons, and feathers—
mushroomed to such dimensions that an unobstructed view of the stage
at the theater, where hats were worn, became a rarity, and parasols could
only be carried, not used (Laver 1969, 164). A diarist of the period complained that at dinner table the hats of his companions prevented him
from seeing his own plate (ibid., 165). Indeed, caricaturists of the age
ridiculed this afflatus by showing hats so huge that they served as umbrellas. While turbans continued to be worn,[54] berets became the new
rage, enabling Pushkin, with his keen eye for changing styles, to intimate
laconically Tat'iana Larina's newly acquired worldliness through her
"raspberry beret" ("v malinovom berete," *Eugene Onegin* [8.VII]).[55] More
than half a page in N. Polevoi's *Moscow Telegraph* (1828) describes in mi-

FIG 2.10. Imported
into Russia, this
example of the latest
Parisian fashion
eloquently conveys
the slide into
grotesque excess
during the late
1820s.

nutest detail the then wildly popular "Arlesian beret." And in 1836 Lermontov, as was his wont, borrowed from Pushkin, to place Tat'iana's beret on a society lady in his unfinished novel *Princess Ligovskaia* (Kniaginiia Ligovskaia, chap. IV).[56]

In addition to carrying fans and reticules, women were extravagantly beribboned, armed with bouquets of flowers, and hung with several pounds of jewelry in the form of "lockets, crosses, gold bracelets, mosaic and cameo brooches and gold chains supporting little bottles of perfume" (Laver 1969, 168). In short, the late 1820s and 1830s exemplified the Liberace or Liz Taylor notion of chic (see fig. 2.11). As perishable confection, the "fashionable woman" resembled an overdecorated torte (Brownmiller 87). The rejection of luxury that had accompanied revolutionary fervor was slowly ceding to a renewed appreciation for external signs of affluence unchecked by good taste. As the century progressed, women increasingly became an ambulatory index of their fathers' or husbands' socioeconomic status, their bodies functioning as advertisements of bourgeois prosperity and conspicuous consumption—illustrating what Veblen called the great economic law of wa(i)sted effort. Women's burdensome attire underscored gender difference by proclaiming simultaneously their dissocation from productive labor and the success of their male counterparts in precisely that arena.

Weighted Ladies in Waiting: Portable Property as Marital Investment

Whereas the unstable 1800s had allowed women relative freedom of mental and physical movement, the heavy petticoats and corsets, plus the increasingly voluminous skirts that by the 1840s made walking through doorways an inordinately complicated enterprise, restricted their mobility in all senses. Psychological inhibition dictated by an anxiously guarded moralism was continuous with bodily containment. It is no coincidence, therefore, that the steel skeleton of the crinoline[57] that in Russia and elsewhere triumphed during the 1850s—the acme of patriarchal institutionalization—resembled a cage (see fig. 2.12).[58] While endangering women's health and constraining their physical activity, the crinoline galvanized (!) the steel industry, which had to produce sufficient wires for the crinoline frames.[59] Once the size of the crinolines became associated with social hierarchy, they grew to fantastic proportions. As one critic wryly notes, a large ballroom full of crinolines resembled an encampment (Broby-Johansen 188). The logistics of accommodating the billowing waves of skirt limited the number of women who could be invited to balls and parties, and forced theater managers to space seats more widely (Ryndin III, 7) (see fig. 2.13). A symbol of women's unapproachability and fertility, the crinoline—

FIG 2.11. The most moderate look in women's dress recorded in the late 1830s or early 1840s.

which corresponded in English architecture to "the overloaded ginger-bread facade in the heyday of Victorianism" (Robinson 439)—asserted the primacy of family values (Laver 1969/1979, 184). Quite literally, the bulk and weight of women's dresses ensured their near-immobility, curbing any temptation to flight or flightiness.[60] The natural shape of the female body that had been so visible in the 1800s—according to the Classical principle that dress should reveal the body's beauty—became an inaccessible (and possibly shameful) mystery, buried and locked away under the countless layers of corset, petticoats, metal, and yards upon yards of skirts that imprisoned it. How women's bodies ultimately escaped from that confinement is another story. . . .

Whether the peekaboo nature of women's flimsy garb during the first two decades of the nineteenth century may really be equated with a "truly revolutionary nudity," as some commentators (Hollander 118)

FIG 2.12. This grim figure seems imprisoned by the metal bars purported to enhance her "femininity."

have contended, is debatable. What does seem certain, however, is that this period of sociopolitical upheaval, economic chaos, morally questionable values, and frenetically changing tastes offered privileged women considerable latitude in defining their social persona through clothes. Literally and metaphorically uncorseted, they could utilize formal social gatherings as risky but exhilarating theaters for enacting roles aided by a costume whose very minimalism intensified the significance of every detail. While prosaically functioning as conventional accessories, the obligatory shawl and fan were key tools for female agency: they enabled women appearing in public to equivocate, to articulate various selves through wordless rhetoric, to exercise options as they calibrated spectators' perception of their bodies. In adopting the feminine ideal of a materialized (and sexualized) Psyche, the era embraced an aesthetic of paradox and ambiguity that, within certain parameters, proved encouragingly receptive to women's self-fashioning. Men such as Karamzin, Vigel', and Herzen condemned what from an observer's distance they generally viewed as Russian women's undiscriminating imitation of French styles, failing to appreciate the degree to which individual

Fig 2.13. A daunting clutch of crinolines, typical for mid–century.

women fluent in the language of clothes could transform impersonal discourse (*langue*) into personal statement (*parole*). Or perhaps this vocal masculine derision sprang from the tacit, nervous realization that female evening dress of this era threatened the mythical male virtue of sexual self-restraint by giving women more, and more public, power over men's desires and behavior than made them comfortable. Ostensible concern that women might catch cold perhaps masked genuine alarm that men grew heated. Whatever the case, by permitting women's bodies to breathe freely and their movements and gestures to "speak," the tantalizing *robes en chemise* and the accessories that accompanied them could legitimately be called one of women's most rewarding socio-psychological investments.

Notes

My warmest thanks to Bozenna Goscilo, Beth Holmgren, and Ol'ga Vainshtein for reading and responding to an earlier draft of this essay; to Sergei Kibal'nik of Pushkinskii Dom, Elena Aleksandrovna Usova of Literaturnyi muzei im. Pushkina, and Elena Trofimova for helping me obtain pertinent illustrations and other materials; to Raisa M. Kirsanova for generously sharing the fruits of her research with me; and to the Russian and East European Center at the University of Pittsburgh, which subsidized my research in Russia for this essay.

1. Quoted in Wills and Christopher 1993, 46.

2. Laver, *Taste* chap. 22.

3. Unsurprisingly, Lotman's comments on fashion overlap substantially with Roland Barthes's in his *Système de la mode* (Paris: Seuil, 1967), translated as *The Fashion System* (New York: Hill and Wang, 1983). For a Russian analysis of American fashion, see Vainshtein.

4. For a short but fascinating sketch of how sport influenced British fashion in the 1880s, see Laver 1969, 202–206.

5. Polhemus 174.

6. For instance, in the early 1930s, according to Laver, as ultra-short skirts gave way to backless dresses, the emphasis moved from the legs to the back (Laver 1969, 241–42).

7. On the ambivalence of dress, particularly women's, see Davis.

8. Laver, who echoes Flügel's theory of men's "renunciation," maintains that "the sexuality of the female body is more diffused than that of the male, and as it is habitually covered up the exposure of any one part of it focuses the erotic attention, conscious or unconscious, and makes for seductiveness" (Laver 1937; reprinted in Wills and Midgley 382). Yet, I would argue, the distinction between the role of the body owner and that of the viewer is crucial. Laver is not anticipating Luce Irigaray's contention that *women* have multiple areas of sexual stimulation, but that *men* associate various areas of women's body with their *own* sexual excitement. The (primarily male) viewer has been trained to eroticize the female form, whereas only recently has the male body become subject to a kindred kind of eroticization. Taking the heterosexual female viewer into account in Laver's scenario, I would argue that if exposure of habitually covered body parts in daily attire were the determining criterion of seductiveness, then every inch of virtually every part of the male body—which has been under wraps for centuries—should prove unbearably seductive. Irigaray's riposte to Laver's contention might be the question, "Whose lips are speaking here?" (Irigaray).

9. As Moers rightly points out, "In the social sphere the dandy's refinement is exclusivism; in the purely physical it is hyper-sensitivity" (20). McDowell stresses the sexuality of dandies' attire, noting that "Regency and early Victorian breeches were very tight. [. . .] They outlined the legs and the genitals in a calculated and provocative way" (52). Such emphases accord with one of McDowell's central theses, that "sex and clothing are inextricably linked" (11).

10. For a fine study of dandyism, see Ellen Moers. Moers follows the practice of some historians in dating the Regency period as 1800–1830, but admits that doing so requires a rather imprecise concept of Regency unmodified by

the fact that George served as the Regent for his ailing father only in the second decade of the century. Moers 39, 41.

11. In Russia, dandyism took the form of a cultivated negligence in dress and a self-assured superciliousness in manner that bordered on rudeness. Pushkin's notorious flouting of decorum in the theater and his sartorial idiosyncrasies exemplify the Russian version of dandyism. On this, see Lotman 1983, 124–25, and Driver.

12. For a thoughtful discussion of Pushkin's dandyism and the vogue of the dandy in Russia, see Driver 77–135.

13. See, for instance, the current "hunk" commercial for Coke and the "Damsel in Distress" advertisement for Brut, which feature women growing hot when men strip off their shirts to bare their muscled chests. See also recent issues of *GQ*, and especially the extraordinary special spring issue of *Esquire Gentleman* (1994).

14. Brownmiller correctly observes that London, "the somber city of banking and mercantile commerce with its cautious, responsible tailors of Savile Row," drew men, while women "cast their covetous eyes toward Paris, the thrillingly wicked citadel of romance and art, with its [. . .] fanciful dressmakers and ingenious corseteries" (88).

15. On the origins and development of the fashion plate, see Holland, and Fischel and von Boehn. Holland emphasizes the fact that the first magazine to issue fashion plates with any regularity was not French but English: *The Lady's Magazine*, which started in 1770 (Holland 52). Yet fashion plates, like everything connected with clothes styles, were consistently associated with France: The most renowned artists to produce fashion plates (e.g., the Colin sisters, Héloise Leloir, and Gavarni) were French, and even British publications carrying fashion news and illustrations bore French names, as demonstrated by John Bell's British monthly, *La Belle Assemblée* (1806–68).

16. French diffusion of fashion had started somewhat earlier. For instance, Rose Bertin, dressmaker to Marie Antoinette, opened a dressmaking establishment in the Rue St Honoré called the Grand Mogol, from which each month she sent little dolls dressed in the latest fashion to various foreign courts, Russian among them (Brenninkmeyer 266).

17. Founded by an ex-Oratorian priest, Pierre de La Mésangère, the periodical provides an unrivaled inventory of fashions from June 1797 to the late 1830s, when it folded. See Mackrell 40–41.

18. See, for instance, Karolina Pavlova's *A Double Life* (Dvoinaia zhizn', 1848), where the heroine Cecily for her birthday receives two dresses, and a "charming lace scarf" ordered from Paris (chap. 4). For a fascinating account of sumptuary laws that regulated various nations' modes of dress to ward off importation of fashions from abroad as well as to distinguish courtiers and aristocrats from the bourgeoisie, see Herman Freudenberger, "Fashion, Sumptuary Laws, and Business," Wills and Midgley 137–46.

19. Studies of fashion cycles in women's dresses by Jane Richardson and A. L. Kroeber, as well as by Agnes Young, have hypothesized a stable cyclical pattern in their design. According to Richardson, each cycle lasts approximately a hundred years and contains three sequential phases: a bell or full-skirt phase, followed by a back-fullness phase, replaced by a tubular or sheath phase. Young argues for a shorter cycle. For a balanced elaboration and modification of this theory, see Carman.

Since my primary focus here is on women's evening dress and I exclude all mention of streetwear such as jackets, coats, etc., it is worth noting parenthetically that Napoleon's military campaigns actualized the army's influence on women's dress, specifically on the tall crowns of hats, braid for trimming on spencers, use of specific colors to signal political allegiances, and so forth. See Fischel and von Boehn 91. Napoleon's role in female fashion was immense, from the violets (his favorite flower) women wore to indicate their political leanings, to the headgear that reflected his Eastern campaigns. See Evans 95 and Brooke and Laver 360.

20. As various critics have noted, during the French Terror anyone wearing rich clothes courted danger. See Brooke and Laver 334.

21. This dislocation of the waistline led a wit to compose the lines "Shepherds, I have lost my waist; / Have ye seen my body" (Black et al. 72).

22. In Russia, the material almost identical to muslin was called *kiseia*. See Kirsanova 115–17.

23. Men also suffered from the wetting mania, dampening their breeches so as to make them cling more suggestively to the thighs—and other strategic regions, presumably. Bigelow 156.

24. In the late 1790s and into the 1800s, women wore sandals, in keeping with the Classical look. See Black et al. 74.

25. Lotman points out that in Russia women's morning wear during this era was synonymous with "undress," and "dressing" meant donning garments in which one could be seen by non-intimates. Lotman 1983, 231.

26. Citing modesty as women's outstanding trait since time immemorial, Karamzin lamented the potential damage wrought by the period's "semi-paradisial zephyric dress" (*poluraiskaia zefirnaia odezhda*) on their irreproachable reputations. Karamzin 304.

27. The portrait, housed in the Russian Museum in St. Petersburg (and reproduced in Rice 219), has much in common with his portrait of E. N. Arsen'eva in the late 1790s.

28. In Russian, "beloe, prozrachnoe plat'e, kotoroe legko obvivalos' okolo nee" (Iakushin 78). See also A. F. Vel'tman, *Serdtse i dumka* (1838), part I, chapter IX.

29. Just as portraits of the period now provide valuable clues to the styles of the late eighteenth and early nineteenth centuries, in their time they helped to promote some of those styles. The countless references to Psyche in com-

mentaries on women's diaphanous garb of this era both consciously and sub-
liminally evoke Gérard's then-famous painting.

30. In his remarkable study, signally titled *From the Ballroom to Hell*, T. A.
Faulkner graphically traces the "long, sweet and purely sensual pleasure" experienced by the woman (presumably Psyche) "in the vile embrace of the Apollo
of the evening" as she sinfully waltzes her way to hell. Faulkner 14–16. For a
splendid account of ballroom dancing in America and contemporary responses
to the various dance forms, see Aldrich. For reactions to the waltz, see Aldrich
154–56.

31. The original Russian reads: "Nynche Liza *en* gala / U avstriiskogo
posla, / Ne poprzhnemu mila! / No poprezhnemu gola." Pushkin's authorship of
these lines, which represent half of the poem, has not been authenticated
(Smirnova 408). For a different version of the lyric, which, however, preserves
the same two lines that close the Smirnova version, see the memoirs of V. A.
Sollogub, quoted in N. I. Brodskii, *Literaturnye salony i kruzhki* (Moscow/
Leningrad:Academia, 1930), 222.

32. As Boucher points out, during the Directoire, dancing and spectacles
were the sovereign amusements. Carnival disguises and, in 1802, masks were au-
thorized in the streets. Boucher 338.

33. In fact, some critics couple the two freedoms. See, for instance, Black et
al. 72.

34. As Laver remarks, "Perhaps at no period between primitive times and
the 1920s had women worn so little as they wore in the early years of the nineteenth century" (1969, 155).

35. Laver points out that the shawl formed an essential part of every
woman's wardrobe, and the ability to wear a shawl gracefully "was considered
the mark of the fashionable lady" (155). On the provenance and manufacture of
shawls, see Laver 1969, 155.

36. Indeed, dancing with a shawl was the ultimate test of a woman's grace
and stylishness. Lady Emma Hamilton (portrayed as a dancing Bacchante in an
engraving by Thomas Piroli [1794]) mesmerized audiences at the British
Embassy with her dance performances with kashmir/cashmere shawls, setting
an example that expanded into a shawl mania. See Mackrell 33–36. For more
details, and for the relevance of this phenomenon to Mme Marmeladova's
prickly pride in her girlhood experience in shawl-dancing (Dostoevskii's *Crime
and Punishment*), see Kirsanova 267–68.

37. Evans refers to the reticule as "commodious," but its size increased only
later (Evans 84). During the first quarter of the nineteenth century, reticules
could not comfortably accommodate much more than a handkerchief, a purse,
and a couple of small items. See Alexander 52–53.

38. For a detailed survey of the composition, look, and function of fans, see
Nancy Armstrong, *A Collector's History of Fans* (New York: Clarkson N. Potter,
1974).

39. For more examples, see Shafer. In fact, Shafer analyzes the semiotics of "handkerchief flirtations," "glove flirtations," and "parasol flirtations," as well as "fan flirtations." Shafer 231–34.

40. On the psychology of fans, see Laver 1953 and Langner 324–25.

41. Lotman notes that by 1812, hairstyles à la Titus had been replaced among modish Russians by the English cropped cut, and that the "artists" (*artisty*) initiated into the mysteries of shearing one's locks accordingly charged high prices for their artistry. Lotman 1983, 124.

42. Pushkin's unfinished novel *Roslavlev* commemorates that visit, but provides no information about the French author's attire except that Moscow's fashionable world perceived her as "a fat, fifty-year-old woman not dressed according to her years."

43. Exiled to Elba in 1814, Napoleon suffered decisive defeat the following year at the Battle of Waterloo.

44. Brummell's legendary powers as arbiter of fashion spanned the Regency period (1811–1820) in England. In 1819 he fled to the Continent to escape his creditors.

45. As McDowell somewhat anachronistically maintains, "Tight-lacing and corsetry have always been central to bondage games. Even the Victorians openly accepted their erotic quality" (17). Yet the bondage of the contemporary S/M female practitioner and the constraints imposed upon corseted women in the eighteenth and nineteenth centuries differ dramatically. Female participants in "bondage games" engage in service consciously and with the awareness that it constitutes a "game," which can hardly be said of their predecessors.

46. The association between Romance and a tiny female waist not only influences hopeful young women's diets in American society, but also rules the descriptions of heroines in Harlequin Romances. A "set scene" of the genre has the hero span the heroine's waist with his hands, an action that seems to demonstrate that she "fits" him and possibly implies that other, more intimate parts of their bodies would make an equally "good fit."

47. See the copious references to her debut at the ball where Pushkin first saw her ("v belom vozdushnom plat'e") and to her figure ("s basnoslovno tonkoi tal'ei"). Beliaev 12, 32.

48. For an excellent study of costume in Russian literature, see Kirsanova.

49. As Langner rightly argues, extremes of fashion typically made women physically useless for work. The styles he cites include the sixteenth-century farthingale, the *grand pannier* of 1777, *la Bétise* with side panniers of 1785, and the crinoline of the mid-nineteenth century. Langner 284.

50. See Barbara Ehrenreich and Deirdre English, *For Her Own Good* (New York/London: Doubleday, Anchor Books, 1978), especially 101–40; Martha Vicinus, ed., *Suffer and Be Still* (Bloomington: Indiana UP, 1972).

51. In the original Russian: "Kak tal'i nosiat?" "Ochen' nizko. / Pochti do . . . vot po etikh por." See *Pushkin Threefold*, trans. Walter Arndt (New York: E. P.

Dutton and Co., 1972), 93. These lines are cited, by no accident, in Petr Vail''s recent review, "Around the Waist" (Vokrug talii), of the 1994 exhibit mounted by the Metropolian Museum of Art in New York devoted to the waist in fashion and life (!). See *Panorama* 680 (April 26, 1994): 37. My thanks to Volodia Padunov for supplying the review.

52. Although it is an axiom in fashion circles that geometric shapes form the basis of all dressmaking (see Brenninkmeyer 295), some styles attempt to disguise, others to spotlight, the geometric principles at work. The constructivist style in Russia vividly demonstrates the fundamental role of geometric pattern in clothesmaking.

53. Throughout the 1820s and the 1830s, the *Moscow Telegraph* carried detailed descriptions of shifts in Parisian fashion, usually reported in French, then in Russian. See the journal, especially for the period 1825–31. Analogous information in *Ladies' Journal* (Damskii zhurnal) for the same period was sketchier and conveyed in Russian.

54. While most specialists in fashion trace the turban to Napoleon's Eastern campaign, Fischel maintains that it was imported to the Continent from England, where it had been introduced by Indian nabobs (Fischel and von Boehn 121).

55. On Tat'iana's beret, see Nabokov 3: 181–83.

56. Headgear throughout the nineteenth century signaled political sympathies. For example, the impractically wide-brimmed Bolivar worn by Pushkin and his protagonist Eugene Onegin in the first chapter of the eponymous novel indicated support for Simón Bolívar's liberationist movement in Latin America. On the astounding variety of political statements via Russian hat styles throughout the nineteenth century, see Kirsanova 50–52.

On details regarding the changing tastes in headgear during the nineteenth century, see Clark 15–43.

57. The term derives from *crin*, "horsehair," rolls of which were stuffed in the underskirt as a scaffolding for women's dress.

58. Veblen's theory that the consistent physical discomfort of civilized women's fashion illustrates their economic dependence on men—their role as men's chattel—is perhaps best borne out by the crinoline. On this, see Harrison 35–36.

59. The crinoline is reputed to have been the brainchild of Charles Worth, the English *parvenu* who dictated style for decades in the mid-nineteenth century. Worth (born 1825) overcame his seedy origins quite rapidly and in 1845 (some sources cite 1850) left London for Paris, where he eventually became the court designer to Empress Eugénie. He exploited his position as imperial dressmaker to aggrandize the status of his profession, tipping the social balance between customer and clothes purveyor in the latter's favor through his arrogant condescension toward his clients (McDowell 147).

60. Such "woman-clothes," as one critic put it, "made it difficult for her [woman] to wander far from the camp fire and the children" (Langner 52).

Davenport aptly observes that "the body and the spirit became immobilized, sheathed and protected, drooping, helpless, and meek: colors muted" (Davenport 795).

Works Cited

Aldrich, Elizabeth. 1991. *From the Ballroom to Hell: Grace and Folly in Nineteenth-Century Dance*. Evanston: Northwestern UP.

Alexander, Hélène. 1984. *Fans*. London: B. T. Batsford.

Beliaev, M. D. 1993. *Natal'ia Nikolaevna Pushkina v portretakh i otzyvakh sovremennikov*. St. Petersburg: Opyty.

Bell, Quentin. 1976. *On Human Finery*. London: Hogarth.

Bigelow, Marybelle S. 1970. *Fashion in History: Apparel in the Western World*. Minneapolis: Burgess.

Black, J. Anderson; Madge Garland; and Frances Kennett. 1975/1980. *A History of Fashion*. New York: Orbis.

Boucher, François. 1967. *20,000 Years of Fashion: The History of Costume and Personal Adornment*. New York: Harry N. Abrams.

Bradfield, Nancy. 1968/1975. *Costume in Detail: Women's Dress, 1730–1930*. Boston: Plays.

Brenninkmeyer, Ingrid. 1973. "The Diffusion of Fashion." In Wills and Midgley 259–302.

Broby-Johansen, R. 1968. *Body and Clothes: An Illustrated History of Costume*. New York: Reinhold.

Brooke, Iris, and James Laver. 1937. *English Costume from the Fourteenth through the Nineteenth Century*. New York: Macmillan.

Brownmiller, Susan. 1984. *Femininity*. New York: Fawcett Columbine.

Carman, James M. 1973. "The Fate of Fashion Cycles in our Modern Society." In Wills and Midgley 125–36.

Chizhova, I. B. 1993 *"Dushi volshebnoe svetilo. . . . "* St. Petersburg: Logos.

Clark, Fiona. 1982. *Hats*. London: B. T. Batsford.

Cumming, Valerie. 1982. *Gloves*. London: B. T. Batsford.

Davenport, Millia. 1948. *The Book of Costume*. Vol. 2. New York: Crown Publishers.

Davis, Fred. 1992. *Fashion, Culture, and Identity*. Chicago: U of Chicago P.

de Courtais, Georgine. 1973/1986. *Women's Headdress and Hairstyles*. London: B. T. Batsford.

Driver, Sam. 1989. *Pushkin: Literature and Social Ideas*. New York: Columbia UP.

Evans, Mary. 1930/1938. *Costume throughout the Ages*. Philadelphia: Lippincott.

Faulkner, T. A. 1892. *From the Ballroom to Hell*. Chicago: Henry.

Finkelstein, Joanne. 1991. *The Fashioned Self*. Philadelphia: Temple UP.

Fischel, Oskar, and Max von Boehn. 1927. *Modes and Manners of the Nineteenth Century*. Vol. 2. London, New York: J. M. Dent and Sons; E. P. Dutton.

Flory, M. A. 1895. *A Book about Fans*. New York: Macmillan.

Gertsen, A. I. 1953. *Sostav russkogo obshchestva*. In *Polnoe sobranie sochinenii v 30 tt*, vol. 2. Moscow.

Gogol', N. V. 1959. *Sobranie sochinenii v 6 tt*. Vol. 5 Moscow: Khud. lit.

Goncharov, I. A. 1972. *Obyknovennaia istoriia*. Moscow: Khud. lit.

Hansen, Henny Harald. 1956/1962. *Costume Cavalcade*. London: Methuen.

Harrison, Fraser. 1977. *The Dark Angel: Aspects of Victorian Sexuality*. New York: Universe Books.

Holland, Vyvyan. 1955. *Hand-Coloured Fashion Plates, 1770–1899*. London: n. p.

Hollander, Anne. 1975/1993. *Seeing through Clothes*. Berkeley: U of California P.

Iakushin, N. I., ed. 1991. *Serdtsa chutkogo prozren'em. . . .* Moscow: Sov. Rossiia.

Irigaray, Luce. 1985. "When Our Lips Speak Together." In *This Sex Which Is Not One*, 205–18. Ithaca: Cornell UP.

Kaminskaia, N. M. 1977. *Istoriia kostiuma*. Moscow: Legkaia industriia.

Karamzin, N. 1803–1804. *Sochineniia Karamzina*. Vol. 7. Moscow.

Kirsanova, R. M. 1989. *Kostium—veshch' i obraz v russkoi literature XIX veka*. Moscow: "Kniga."

Langner, Lawrence. 1959. *The Importance of Wearing Clothes*. New York: Hastings House.

Laver, James. 1937. *Taste and Fashion*. London: George G. Harrap and Co.

———.1953. *Clothes*. New York: n.p.

———. 1969/1979. *A Concise History of Costume*. Norwich: Jarrold and Sons.

Lermontov, Iu. M. 1965. *Sobranie sochinenii v 4 tt*. Vol. 4. Moscow: Khud. lit.

Lotman, Iu. M. 1922. *Kul'tura i vzryv*. Moscow: "Gnozis"/"Progress."

———. 1983. *Roman A. S. Pushkina "Evgenii Onegin." Kommentarii*. Leningrad: Prosveshchenie.

Mackrell, Alice. 1986. *Shawls, Stoles and Scarves*. London: B. T. Batsford.

McDowell, Colin. 1992. *Dressed to Kill: Sex Power and Clothes*. London: Hutchinson.

Moers, Ellen. 1960/1978. *The Dandy: Brummell to Beerbohm*. Lincoln: U of Nebraska P.

Polhemus, Ted, ed. 1978. *The Body Reader: Social Aspects of the Human Body*. New York: Pantheon Books.

Pushkin, Aleksandr. 1964. Translated and edited by Vladimir Nabokov. *Eugene Onegin*. 4 vols. New York: Bollingen Foundation.

Rice, Tamara Talbot. 1963. *A Concise History of Russian Art*. New York: Frederick A. Praeger.

Robinson, Dwight E. 1973. "Fashion Theory and Production Design." In Wills and Midgley 433–50.

Ryndin, V. F., ed. 1963. *Russkii kostium 1750–1830*. 5 vols. Vol. 1, Moscow, 1960; Vol. 3, Moscow.

Shafer, Daniel R. 1877. *Secrets of Life Unveiled; or Book of Fate*. St. Louis: Shafer.

Smirnova, A. O. 1929. *Zapiski, dnevnik, vospominaniia, pis'ma*. Ed. M. A. Tsiavlovskii. Moscow: Federatsiia.

Tortora, Phyllis, and Keith Eubank. 1989/1990. *A Survey of Historic Costume.* New York: Fairchild Publications.

Vainshtein, Ol'ga. 1993. "Odezhda kak smysl: ideologemy sovremennoi mody." *Inostrannaia literatura* 7: 224–32.

Vigel', F. F. 1928. *Zapiski.* Vol. 1. Moscow.

Wills, Gordon, and Martin Christopher. 1973. "What Do We Know about Fashion Dynamics." In Wills and Midgley 11–24.

———. 1993. "Does Fashion Matter?" *New York Times Magazine*, October 24.

Wills, Gordon, and David Midgley, eds. 1973. *Fashion Marketing: An Anthology of Viewpoints and Perspectives.* London: George Allen and Unwin.

Damskie mody XIX veka. St. Petersburg: A. S. Suvorin, 1899.

Damskii zhurnal. 1823–31.

Galateia. 1826–28.

Moskovskii telegraf. 1825–33.

FEMALE FASHION, SOVIET STYLE: BODIES OF IDEOLOGY

Ol'ga Vainshtein
Translated by Helena Goscilo

> Our fashion, if examined closely, is also singular. It seems to be regular fashion, yet at the same time it's not fashion at all, but something else. We have fashion and yet we don't.
>
> —K. Kantor[1]

SOVIET FASHION IS LIKE the Cheshire cat: The scholar is left with a vague smile when the object has already dissolved in air. Philosophical arguments obviously don't work in the face of this phenomenon, as the above epigraph illustrates. Journalists' attempts to describe typical Russian wear normally begin with a juxtaposition of contrasts: "They are all simple Russian folk, wearing neither Persian lamb nor polar fox, and not driving Mercedes, but you can't make sense of what they were dressed in: zippered jackets, mittens, old caps with earflaps, and carrying shabby briefcases" (Murav'eva 11). The expression "you can't make sense of" is highly typical—what follows is the author's list of perfectly concrete items, but they, paradoxically, don't add up, don't cohere. Soviet dress, in short, seems to have lacked coherence and meaning, and so eludes customary symbolic rubrics.

My essay examines women's dress, women's bodies, and the ideology of fashion in Russia during the last few decades. Following Roland Barthes's concept of dress as cultural sign, I focus on two of its aspects: on the signified as that which people really wear in their everyday lives, and on the signifier as the rhetorical discourse of fashion (Barthes 1967, 239–47).[2] The women's magazines *Woman Worker* (Rabotnitsa) and *Peasant Woman* (Krest'ianka) of the first half of the 1960s serve as the basic primary material for my analysis, since they set the standard for "typical" Soviet women's wear from the 1960s to perestroika.

The 1960s were one of the liveliest and most dynamic periods in the history of Soviet fashion: owing to Khrushchev's Thaw, with its comparative receptivity to the West, this decade witnessed the emergence of the "cool dresser" (*stiliaga*). Familiar to every reader of Vasilii Aksenov's novels, the *stiliaga* was living proof of just how significant fashion statements were for the West-oriented segment of Russia's young male population. The *stiliaga* favored narrow, straight-leg pants or "pipers" (*briuki-dudochki*), pointed shoes, a Hawaiian shirt, sunglasses, and a bandana around his neck; he wore his hair short, was in love with jazz, and danced the "twist" and the "shake." The female version of the *stiliaga* was the ingenue, characterized by a childlike hairstyle, a round turndown collar, a slight décolleté, a naive gaze (achieved by outlining the eyes to make them round and wide), light pastel hues in makeup, a miniskirt, clothes that outlined the figure, and the mannerisms of a capricious child (Kriuchkova 248). In many respects, quite obviously, this image corresponded to the tendencies dominating Western fashion of the time, exemplified by the British model Twiggy.

In Russia during this period there were no shortages of everyday items perfectly fine in quality, such as coats, suits, and skirts, available at prices that were simply too high for most people. Some categories were well represented, including traditionally inexpensive and quality stitch-embroidered linen and cotton wear: dresses, *khalaty* (housecoats/robes), blouses, shifts, and aprons. Nonetheless, Soviet textile production did not afford Russians the possibility of choosing fashionable clothing. The limited assortment in stores made countless duplications in outfits inevitable. You often could find two or three women on any trolleybus wearing identical dresses. The panicky fear of meeting one's double played a perceptible role in the psychology of purchasing clothes and selecting their style. Many women preferred to have their outfits sewn by tailors or to knit their own woolen items so as to avoid these dreaded duplications. A famous incident long discussed in the press and in conversations occurred at a reception during the Moscow Film Festival in 1961. Elizabeth Taylor and Gina Lollobrigida turned up in identical dresses! Taylor's greeting, "Hello, sister!" thereafter became the standard response to coincidences of this type.

A particularly heightened awareness of individual differences in dress
arose in reaction to the "discipline" imposed by social dicta upon one's
physical appearance. A unitary aesthetic derived from the ideology of
collective "leveling" codified public behavior, concepts of propriety, and
thoroughly normative notions about beauty. For instance, precisely
specified rules about color coordination regulated people's attire. Entire
generations were raised on the ironclad maxims "Pink suits blondes,"
"Red can't be worn with green, nor blue with orange" (R 1960, 4). At
school, in the classroom, it was explained that an outfit had to adhere to
the law of "three colors," and if a fourth color intruded, then the wearer
was guilty of an impermissible liberty and sheer bad taste. A single-tone
range was considered the best solution: ideally, a woman had to be able
to coordinate a matching outfit and accessories. Heaven forbid that she
combine black shoes and a brown handbag! Contrasting combinations
(apart from black and white) were discouraged. (See fig. 3.1.)

Changes of clothing were regulated just as precisely, and the tone of
instruction was just as authoritative: "Upon coming home, one must
change one's clothes, and one shouldn't walk around town in industrial

FIG 3.1 Accessorizing as
unobtrusively as possible
(R 1962, 1963).

[working] clothes" (R 1960, 6). Why was it so important to the Soviet regime that everyone change clothes at the same time, as one "man," so to speak? Most likely because vestimentary specificity had great significance for official surveillance over the individual: clothes had to correspond to place, time, and function; each person had to be clearly classified, and ideally she had to represent her place in some group, whether it was based on age, gender, or social standing. As Foucault notes, "The distribution according to ranks or grade has a double role: it marks the gaps, hierarchizes qualities, skills and aptitudes; but it also punishes and rewards. [. . .] [T]his classification was visible to all in the form of slight variations in uniform" (Foucault 1977, 183).

Soviet citizens' changes of clothing from the sixties to the mid-eighties were regulated by a series of binary oppositions: home/work, day/evening, holiday/weekday.[3] The same system of clearly marked oppositions governed women's lives, demanding that they effect quick and skillful reincarnations depending on the circumstances: "During the day she wears a dark dress, suit, or sweater, thick stockings, and boots; her overall appearance is businesslike, sporty, and dynamic. In the evening, however, she's femininity itself: a soft, blurred silhouette, folds, flowers, glittering embroidery" (R 1963, 8). According to this scheme, a woman had to cardinally alter her image, metamorphosing into a capable worker one moment, and a seductress the next.

In practice, however, lived experience undermined the metamorphoses urged by official discourse, for what free time existed was spent on such everyday problems as buying groceries and taking care of family needs. Within the family unit, women's fundamental role was that of housewife, and through a lengthy process of historical selection, the most eloquent, inimitable items in a Soviet woman's wardrobe became a *khalat* for housework and a nondescript coat for standing in lines.

"The coat for standing in lines" underwent multiple modifications, but its essence changed very little; it was and remains the "armor" that women don when they go out to hunt for provisions. This armor must protect its owner from bad weather, constant shoving, and excessive curiosity. In the last decade the most popular version was a dark, water-resistant coat made of nylon or similar material typically used for raincoats (e.g., Bologna) that fit snugly and solidly around the body. It was inevitably accompanied by a knit cap or a mohair beret (which was periodically combed so as to look good) and a canvas bag with solid handles. "Huntresses" (or scavengers!) recognized each other by these trappings, and if one of them noticed something of interest in another one's bag, she immediately asked where her fellow huntress had bought it. The usefulness of the coat for standing in line is indisputable: it doesn't show dirt, the slippery texture of its material allows one to break a trail through a crowd, the warm lining protects one from the cold, while its impermeability protects one from the rain, and its snap fasteners or, more commonly, zipper eliminates the risk of losing a button in the battle to acquire provisions. It's not surprising that this type of coat may be found in the closets of most middle-aged and older women responsible for shopping for the family.

At the beginning of the 1990s, when the Russian market was inundated with goods from Turkey and southeastern Asia, the classic Soviet shopper's coat lost its purity of line. Decorative variations with stitching design, appliqués on the back, bouffe sleeves, and other extravagant touches appeared. These mutations, however, didn't appear out of nowhere, for Soviet fashion historically "embellished" working clothes (see fig. 3.2). For example, magazines regularly advertised "color padded jackets trimmed in fur and braid. They're recommended for women whose

FIG 3.2. Embellished
working clothes
(S 1957).

1. Телогрейка цветная, отделанная искусственным мехом и тесьмой. Рекомендуется женщинам, работа которых связана с пребыванием на открытом воздухе.

2. Пальто прямого покроя из хлопчатобумажной пропитанной ткани, воротник из искусственного меха, подкладка из набивного сатина; понизу отделано защипками, пуго-

work requires spending time outdoors." In the twenties L. Popova and V. Stepanova developed variations on "working clothes" and "overalls" in a Constructivist style, which represented a genuine innovation in the history of costume (Bowlt 213). Their models, however, weren't produced—not because of any technical problems but because they were rejected by the workers for whom they were intended. Working women accustomed to brightly colored designs and "cheerful" trims expressed a desire for more imagination than the "overly simple" geometric models of the Constructivists offered (Strizhenova 98–102).

Such desires on the part of working women, prompted by the tradition of prerevolutionary factory and middle-class attire, evidently caused Soviet designers numerous headaches. Indeed, "embellished" work clothes represented an attempt at just such a compromise in taste between functional and "dressy." However, judging by the wealth of didactic admonitions in magazines, women stubbornly continued "to get dressed up" for work. "I don't think you have to dress in a monotonous and boring style, but there are certain norms for a working dress," the artist-designer E. Semenova attempted to enlighten the working masses. "Brocade, velvet, kapron, and lace linen are all fabrics unsuitable for a working dress" (*R* 1963, 8).

The woman who "dressed up" frequently became the object of angry social criticism:

> You happen to go into an office on business and among the *modestly* dressed women you can't help but instantly notice someone in a revealing dress of patterned silk brocade, with earrings in her ears, glittering beads around her neck, and three bracelets on her wrists. Heavy makeup and a complicated formal hairstyle complete her getup. Such an outfit is out of place during working hours; it doesn't correspond to the setting, and, besides, it doesn't inspire confidence in the efficiency of its wearer. (*R* 1963, 8)

During the sixties a woman wouldn't be expelled from the party or the Komsomol for such an outfit, but the anti-bourgeois sentiment of such criticism was quite evident.

Being "dressed up" at work, apart from everything else, violated the above-described rules of the dress code that differentiated between work and home, morning and evening. A woman who confused her vestimentary roles rejected the metamorphosis demanded of her and was guilty, in a sense, of a Freudian slip. In so doing she not only raised doubts about her efficiency, but was suspected of sexual looseness, for she'd been specifically cautioned: "It's not acceptable to wear dresses that are very revealing or of a decidedly transparent material such as kapron to work [the headline of this article was also most eloquent: 'Please watch yourselves!']" (*R* 1960, 6).

Concepts of beauty and chic were inseparable from an outfit's generic appropriateness: "If clothes don't correspond to their function, they look unattractive. To sit at a typewriter in a ball gown and glittering jewelry is as absurd as attending a ball in a worker's overalls" (*R* 1965, 7). The ideology of beauty during this era demanded that an outfit be entirely functional. The normative specificity of the fashionable ideal corresponded on an aesthetic level to the classicist concept of style as appropriateness and propriety.[4]

The canon of Soviet fashion was based on two key formulas: "simple and attractive" and "modest and attractive." Simplicity and modesty constituted the ideology of beauty informing socialist bourgeois fashion. The epithets "comfortable," "understated," "practical," and "severe" also entered this conceptual field, but they were less programmatic. Modesty seems to have served as an absolute imperative of appearance, manners, and dress of the fashionable woman of the sixties: "Everyday hairstyles, like one's outfits, should be marked by modesty" (*R* 1962, 1). Modesty was also touted in advertising; the editors of *Peasant Woman* (Krest'ianka), for instance, featured photographs from a Czech fashion magazine because "the fashions are modest and comfortable" (1961, 5). Predictably, then, any and all extravagances were instantly branded as "immodest": Chunky metal chains were considered immodest, as were miniskirts and long, loose hair.

Equally essential for those concerned with being fashionable was "a sense of measure." In reply to an inquiry about fashionable accessories from a young reader, the editors of *Woman Worker* (Rabotnitsa) responded, "Jewelry? Yes, but not in excess" (1959, 12). Moderation was similarly invoked in criticisms of the *stiliagi*: "Having no sense of measure, they do everything in excess: for example, since short dresses are in fashion, they wear them above the knee; narrow pants are in fashion, so they have narrow straight-leg pants sewn for them" (*K* 1963, 12). A sense of measure acted as the fashion plate's conscience, that interiorized voice of decorum, of the norm, and thus, according to the logic outlined above, also as the guarantor of beauty and taste: "When adding . . . jewelry to one's outfit, one shouldn't forget a sense of measure—the prerequisite for good taste" (*R* 1959, 12).

Soviet fashion adopted and urged "moderation," "simplicity," and "modesty" as the supreme aesthetic criteria for three reasons. First, through inertia, the ascetic ideals that had characterized the first decade of Soviet rule had not yet lost their hold. Second, light industry in the fifties had barely recovered from the economic ruin of World War II. Third, "modesty" was encouraged in the framework of an ideology of collectivism—discipline demanded that one not stand out from the masses. In this context the epithet "modest" fit into another series of synonyms: "serious," "dependable," "honest," and even "party-minded."

The social nature of such "modesty" may be clarified with the aid of J. C. Bologne's theoretical differentiation. In his study titled *Histoire de la pudeur*, he posits a distinction between "pudeur," as the individual's sense of shame, and "décence," as the norm of social decency (14). Soviet "modesty" is, of course, "décence." According to Bologne, the dialectic of shame presupposes an inner conflict between various levels of consciousness: between emotion and reason, the Id and the Superego (in Freud's definitions), the fleshly/earthly and the divine (16). Accordingly, the category of "moderation" in Soviet fashion is invoked to mediate between the imperative of modesty and personal taste, which, as experience shows, leads women steadily away from the puritan aesthetic of physical appearance.

To examine more closely the phenomenon of "dressing up," which I've alluded to several times: We frequently encounter the chicly dressed woman in the history of Russian fashion. She not only figures as the heroine of feuilletons, but is also unquestionably a type we know in real life. Her image since the 1980s is that of a woman in evening makeup, with gold jewelry, dressed vividly and richly, with a preference for fur, real leather, clothes from famous Western fashion houses with designer labels intended to catch the eye—in short, she exhibits "conspicuous consumption," to use Veblen's term. Her clothes and grooming have been chosen according to the principle of "you can never overdo it"; the overall image gives the impression of abundant luxury, which in popular parlance is called "a style of excess."

On closer examination, however, we discover something peculiar about this image: the combination of an expensive dress and cheap shoes, an abundance of lurex, inexpertly bleached hair, and a discrepancy between the cut and the material. But the chief thing is the absence of casualness in appearance, of freedom and relaxation; on the contrary, one senses a forcedness and tension. "The style of excess" excludes the device of understatement in appearance, the rhetorical figures of omission and negation, and any variants of alternative fashion or nonconformism.

"The style of excess" in various modifications is a stable idiolect in the history of Soviet clothes, which may be explained not only by the compensatory mechanisms and women's subversion of the principles of

ascetic modesty imposed on them. It would be most simple to characterize the impulse to "dress up" as an attempt at bourgeois chic with
inadequate means; then at least it would be easy to interpret the dressed-
up look through the worker-peasant government's rudimentary, instinc-
tive class fear of the bourgeoisie. However, both the social and the
psychological genesis of "the style of excess" is more complex—these
clothes, after all, parade not so much wealth per se as "a condensed
image" of wealth. Its sources may be located, for instance, in the phili-
stinism of Russian middle-class wear and in the festive outfits of prerevolutionary factory workers:

> It was the custom to have one's formal wear and one's Sunday clothes
> sewn by tailors who offered styles extraordinarily overburdened by trims.
> This was explained first of all by the fact that all the findings—the stiffen-
> ing in the bodice [it was sewn into dresses for special occasions], the tulle,
> lace, ribbons, trim [beika], ruches, and so forth—were sewn on by the
> seamstresses of their own accord, and they charged extra for these embel-
> lishments. Frequently a dress made from a simple patterned material—
> satin, cotton with nap [bumazeia], or regular cotton—was sewn in a style
> that was intended for an expensive fabric in one color, which gave it a pe-
> culiarly middle-class stamp. (Ryndin 38–39)

The sociology of clothes offers more general reasons that explain this
unconquerable passion for cheap chic. As many scholars have shown,
the basic algorithm for the dissemination of fashion moves from the top
down, as the lower classes strive to appropriate the status-marked symbolism of the upper classes (Lipovetsky 29–80; König; Descamps). In
proportion to this process, different substitutions and distortions occur
(such as the replacement of one fabric with another in our example),
not least of which is a worsening in the quality of work (the finish on
seams, the trim, the cut), which, one can assume, was better in the
hands of prerevolutionary tailors than in Soviet factories. But what remains unchanged are the efforts of the poorer classes to express their
social expectations through clothes. As Alison Lurie has noted, social
status is manifested even in the style of children's clothing: children
from working-class families often are dressed more pretentiously than
their counterparts from rich families, who can "afford" to dress "unobtrusively" (152).

The simplest case of "dressing up" occurs when one has the financial
means, but no knowledge of the ideological language of fashion. This is
precisely the situation with Russia's contemporary nouveau riche,
the groups of New Russians that have appeared after perestroika. The

historical prototype of the dressed-up spouse of a successful businessman is the Russian merchant wife:

> On rich but insufficiently cultured merchant wives the expensive clothes ordered from the best Parisian, London, or Viennese firms lost their elegance. This happened not only because they didn't know how to wear them, but also because they wore an excess of rich jewelry (a diamond brooch or a multi-strand necklace of large pearls together with a regular daytime dress, even a summer frock) and some adornment or other that they'd added for greater embellishment. . . . Intent [. . .] only on outdoing those around them in the richness and dressiness of their attire, these women chose the most fashionable and complicated cuts, without taking their appearance into account . . . and they'd give orders to have more expensive trim sewn on—guipure, lace, beads, fringes, and so forth. Together with such a dress, which lacked harmony of line, color, and finish, some merchant wives wore ultra-modish shoes . . . others, not wishing to feel constrained, would wear woolen-fabric or morocco-leather shoes with a slight heel, with elastic bands on the sides or laces of the type worn by workers. These shoes didn't prevent the merchant wife from wearing a hat on the crown of which was mounted a heap of jewelry, and a fashionable cape, or from carrying a bright silk parasol with a ruffle and bow, a gold lorgnette (to appear refined), and, without fail, a reticule most frequently covered with pearls. (Ryndin 5, 47)

The 1990s version of the Russian merchant wife typically wears a leather coat, sunglasses with tortoiseshell frames, a Rolex watch, and high-heeled Gabor shoes. The general effect remains essentially the same: the woman is transformed into a showcase of disconnected things that completely bury the female body under them. What is foregrounded is the intrinsic value of the various items in her outfit, as well as the dissonance of her selection.

In the sixties and seventies this mixing of incompatibles was further heightened by the virtual impossibility of acquiring good Western clothes, which were radically fetishized. But even clothes domestically produced from expensive materials demanded special care, and from time to time magazines carried rather peculiar instructions on how to treat and wear clothes: "A smart dress suit in black velveteen. A spare skirt so that the flaps can be folded back when one sits down, since velvet wears out from constant wear" (R 1960, 9). Careful treatment of an expensive material here merges with a sort of naive pornography, as if the female body simply didn't exist in the system of cultural signs.

A unique symbol of the suppressed lower bodily strata in clothes is the simple black skirt—an obligatory item in the wardrobe of every

Russian woman. A straight, severe black skirt was considered absolutely indispensable, for it helped to solve the problem of assembling an outfit: You could wear the same skirt forever, merely changing blouses and sweaters. Moreover, it is universally believed that a black skirt slenderizes the hips, which explains its popularity especially among plump women. Girls who wore a black uniform in school merely exchanged it for standardized dark skirts when they reached adulthood.

In the context of Russia in the '60s and '70s, the black color and severe style excluded the customary associations with bohemia, chic, and intellectualism attributed to black clothing in European dress.[5] The Soviet black skirt ideally answered the above-mentioned requirements of, "simple and attractive" and "modest and attractive." The programmatic "modesty" of such skirts fulfilled a double function: On the one hand, it was the ideological antipode to "dressing up"; on the other, it worked as an anti-inflammatory, according to James Laver's observation that "the modesty of clothes is called upon to dampen sexual ardor" (9). The absolute attachment of women of all ages and classes to standard skirts may be read as a graphic illustration of the notoriously absurd claim by a Russian woman that "we have no sex"[6]—which, with its "democratic" implications made explicit, would read as "we all have no sex, and in that respect we're all equal." (See fig. 3.3.)

The black skirt divides the silhouette in half, directing the viewer's gaze to the top half of the figure. It forms a "blind spot" of sorts in the silhouette. Such a politics of the gaze is a characteristic symptom of the incomplete presence of the female body in culture, of a constant play of exclusion and inclusion around forbidden zones. (See fig. 3.4.) Indeed, the whole history of fashion confirms the presence of such a principle, for each epoch accentuates a particular part of the female body: the breasts during the eighteenth century, for instance, or the shoulders during the Victorian era. Marginalized parts of the body escape from one's field of vision, become almost invisible (Steele).

In practice, what is the determining factor in the body image of the fashionable Russian woman during the 1960s and '70s? "The head and legs" was the confident answer supplied by the experienced designer Natal'ia Orskaia,[7] who has worked for many years in the famous old House of Models on Kuznetskii Most. What makes her response paradoxical is that the body as such—the middle part of the figure and the basic object of the designer's efforts—turns out to be completely unrelated to women's beauty. The fragmentation of the silhouette thus reaches its apogee: the center drops out, and only the edges or extremities— "the head and the legs"—remain.

FIG 3.3. The multi-use ubiquitous black skirt (*R* 1963, 1965).

This dialectic is confirmed by the evolution of the stage image of the popular singer Alla Pugacheva, whom many Russians reportedly consider the most attractive woman in the country.[8] In the early phases of her stage career, Pugacheva established as her physical trademark the luxurious mass of long, loose curly hair that cleverly turned attention away from the plump body she hid under a shapeless tunic. When she later lost weight and began wearing miniskirts, the audience focus shifted to her shapely legs.

For the typical girl, nice legs ensured that at least young fellows at dances would notice her. Accordingly, shoes had a special significance for fashion-conscious Soviet girls. Acquiring good shoes, however, normally presented considerable difficulty, as one may deduce from the description of a major character in I. Grekova's novel *The Department* (Kafedra), set in the 1970s: "Stella [. . .] was what's called stylish, and wore fashionable clothes and, more important, shoes. On that occasion she was wearing

FIG 3.4. Erotic
subtexts created by
hand placement
(*R* 1960).

high platform shoes and constantly kept inspecting her snakelike foot,
which she thrust out sideways from under the table" (Grekova 9).

That the "head and feet" formula does indeed reflect what Russian
women today, as earlier, deem primary in physical self-presentation may
be illustrated by the following simple and well-known fact: If a Russian
woman needs to look chic no matter what the cost, she will not go to
an atelier or a store selling ready-made dresses, but will head directly to a
hairdresser's. Hairdressing salons have flourished during every period of
Soviet history; moreover, they have functioned as social salons, trading
points, and information offices. (See Azhgikhina and Goscilo below.) For

many women a hairdresser's was the one place where they could genuinely relax and chat while at the same time getting groomed (Rubinov 300–350). "A hairstyle can really transform a face!" *Woman Worker* rhapsodized. "And not only the face. The walk can change too, become lighter, more graceful, and even the most *modest* dress can look more dressy. In a word, an attractive hairstyle works miracles" (1965, 5, emphasis added). A new hairdo, then, served as a metonymy for beauty and for an overall concern with one's appearance—which probably explains most Russian women's fanatical preoccupation with their hairdos. No one in Russia considers it strange that women adjust their hair at every opportunity, for in doing so they are merely taking advantage of one of the liberties sanctioned by the society's convention of permitting people to attend to their grooming in public.

Indeed, on the Moscow subway one often observes both women and men carefully combing their hair as they stare at their reflections in the dark-glass window. To see women calmly applying makeup in public places is likewise common. Whereas in other countries it is accepted practice to confine one's grooming to the bathroom, Russian women have no qualms about using as a makeup mirror any surface that reflects their image, whether it be a shiny car or a powder compact. When she enters a house, the first thing a Russian woman will seek is something in which to inspect how she looks. Hence the large mirror normally found in the corridors of most apartments or in the lobbies of official buildings that attracts passersby like a magnet.[9]

"The mirror stage" (in the literal, not Lacanian, sense) not only is essential for purely pragmatic reasons (for example, people wear headgear several months out of the year), but also has a basis in ritual. It is a sign of entering social space where one must be "in uniform." The more one's work requires public contact and generates potential nervous tension, the more one tends to "mask" one's individual self through the protective devices of makeup, uniform, etc. Receptionists, salesgirls, and those constantly dealing with customers tend to apply makeup more heavily, as Terence McLaughlin and others have noted (McLaughlin 4).

El'dar Riazanov's film *A Romance at Work* contains a revealing episode: the working day begins with all the female employees putting on makeup to the sound of bravura music. Just how deeply rooted and universal this tradition is in Russia may be inferred from an item that appeared in *Woman Worker* in 1965: "Upon arriving at work, women sometimes start creating a hairdo, or else they come with curlers in their hair. All of this should be done at home. . . . One also shouldn't file one's nails, paint one's lips, or powder one's face in the presence of one's co-workers" (1965, 7). In Riazanov's film, as in life, women patently do exactly the opposite, their automatic narcissism triumphing over the stale conventional imperative that private and public spheres be strictly differentiated.

The reasons for such a disregard of convention must be sought at the deepest levels of the collective psychology that is especially vividly expressed among women who constantly work together. Sitting in the same room for eight hours in a row, they form a general collective body, and the ritual of applying makeup as a group is merely the most innocent manifestation of this familial intimacy: "Comrades" usually are in the know as regards all the details of everyone's health and personal life. It is also common practice among fellow workers to criticize one another aloud or, on the contrary, to compliment one another on their outfits or appearance.

This tradition of public commentary, which reflects the communal mode of life, has exerted a much more vital influence on people's conduct than have any manuals of good manners or formal rhetoric. The viewpoint of "one's own" group has played a decisive role in individual choices of style. The normative discourse of social discussions of clothes created a situation of total surveillance. Not only colleagues at work but also neighbors and teachers at school could be the mouthpiece of "public opinion," as could old ladies sitting on a courtyard bench or even chance fellow travelers on the subway or tram. And in cases of controversy, the disputants would appeal to the judgment of the press:

> The editors have received a letter from one of our female readers. She's thirty years old. Although she has three children and works on a kolkhoz, she nevertheless finds time to take care of her appearance, to keep up with fashion. She wears a sheath dress and short hair. Yet the women in her village make fun of her, call her a *stiliaga*. (R 1963, 12)[10]

One can well imagine how many caustic barbs this village fashion plate had to put up with! Her case evidences how even the mildest deviations from convention instantly rendered a person an outsider.

Plump women particularly occupied a special place in the ideological space of beauty. They were marked as a deviation from the norm and served as the object of all kinds of instructions, often with a moralistic cast. In the world of fashion, they functioned as the classic scapegoat and marginal figure. A characteristic example of dogmatic orders on how plump women should dress is the following:

> Plump women should be especially careful about their choices [in dress]. They ruin the impression they make if their clothes have something ex-

cessive. Styles for plump women should have trims and buttons along the vertical axis and the neckline should be elongated. Suits with straight skirts, blouses not tucked into the waistband, and flat sewn-on pockets are designed for plump women. It looks unattractive when a *small plump* woman wears a skirt that's too short, heels that are too high, and a very tall hairdo. When choosing fabrics, *plump older* women should select a small, dense, and conventional decorative pattern. (*R* 1965, 7, emphasis added)

As we can see, according to designers, the plump woman had to direct her efforts at hiding her indecently ample figure, at visually elongating its proportions, camouflaging her waist, and in general not drawing excessive attention to herself with bright colors and trims or a bold decorative pattern. Like literary censors monitoring all deviations from the Socialist Realism canon, designers treated a woman's plump body with suspicion, for such a body clearly could not be contained within the frame of Soviet measurements and standards, and its Rabelaisian proportions undermined the image of a strict heroine of labor or an athletic Komsomol member.

Moreover, incredibly detailed recommendations existed regarding precisely what a plump woman could allow herself to wear and what she had to avoid. Magazines contained advice about specific types of fabric appropriate for women with "the problem," as, for instance, "a dress made of woolen crepe . . . in a muted tone with a velvet trim" (*R* 1963, 12); about the permissible range of colors, in which black and dark tones predominated, for they "slim" the figure; about the cut and choice of various components: blouses without pocket flaps and yokes, with large buttons; jackets without a belt; a silhouette that accentuated the shoulders, so that the hips would look narrower. Plump women, in fact, were under total surveillance and felt the relentlessly vigilant eye of the other fixed on them—the other identified with the normative discourse of power, in Foucault's terms. Such a situation inevitably evoked a sense of guilt in the plump woman for her failure to integrate herself into the norm, and it bred an inferiority complex. (See fig. 3.5.)

Not only clothes, but other bodily spheres, such as makeup, gestures, and walk, were similarly regulated. Certain hairstyles were "prohibited": "Very plump women with a round face are advised not to cut their hair short. A lavish hairstyle doesn't suit them either, for it seems to widen a face that's round to begin with." A. Vainer, the hairdresser who made that pronouncement, doesn't specify what hairstyles actually suit plump customers, apparently in the conviction that nothing could redeem their appearance (*R* 1960, 5).

FIG 3.5. Fashions for
plump women
(*R* 1963) and
caricatures of them
(*R* 1960).

Magazines from the 1960s suggest that Soviet society invariably associated women's plumpness with two other parameters: shortness of height
and advanced age. These elements combined to create a summary negative image of a short plump woman getting on in years, the antipode
to the stylish ideal of the "tall, young, shapely girl." It is no accident that
in the passage cited above, the epithets "short and plump" and "plump
and getting on in years" are paired: They are virtually synonyms that
metonymically conjure up one and the same subject. If one ignores this
semantic equivalence, then many of the statements on fashion defy com-
prehension and read like literature bordering on the absurd:

Justly Offended

"Participants in the conference reproached the artists for not thinking
much about plump women: Dressing is more difficult for them than for
thin and shapely women. The models offered for the young generation
also take only tall, nicely shaped figures into account. Yet there are young

girls who aren't tall and who are aren't thin at all. How are they to dress? Surely they don't have to wear dresses that are recommended for older women?" comrade Mikhtiakhidinova, a worker at a sewing factory, asked the artists. (*R* 1960, 7)

According to this logic, if a girl is short and plump, she automatically joins the ranks of the middle-aged or older, and the possibility that tall plump women or thin older women exist is rejected a priori. Such a notion is considered incredible even from the viewpoint of the "opportunistically" inclined worker Mikhtiakhidinova, who allows the seditious thought that nature actually permits the existence of young women who are short and "not thin at all."

Thus the rather crude and cruel system of oppositions—"short/tall," "plump/thin," "middle-aged/young"—organically discriminates against size, height, and age. Commentaries on style in fashion magazines frequently stipulated with authoritative strictness "recommended only for young and shapely women" or "only up to size 52" (American size 18 [H. G.]). If intended for women who were plump and no longer young, the outfit usually would be characterized as "comfortable," "practical," but almost never "elegant" or "dressy."

Typically, plump models in illustrations accompanying fashion commentary are shown with eyes downcast, presumably because they are embarrassed by their plumpness. Their modest, thoughtful expression contrasts with the normative, standard figures of slender models (see fig. 3.6). Occasionally a plump model is depicted surrounded by her shapely coworkers, who seem to regard her with irritation and an element of ridicule. In middle-aged women the downcast glance has an additional motivation: Their lowered gaze frequently is directed at the children standing beside them, the grouping unavoidably suggesting the image of a grandmother (see fig. 3.7).

For Soviet fashion of the seventies and eighties, the "grandmother" did not exist, either as an ideological image or as a concrete consumer. In a symbolic sense, she was "invisible," creating the effect of a significant absence, a zero morpheme of sorts. Barthes in his discussion of "the racism of youth" in fashion explains this phenomenon as a fear of death: "The social repression of the old body . . . the regressive nature of clothes adapted to old age. It's all part of this kind of generalized erasure of death that marks our society in a rather tragic way" (1982, 653). Such an explanation of the symbolic elimination of images of old age from social consciousness is particularly illuminating when applied to Soviet ideology, whose system for decades cultivated the heroics of "the young

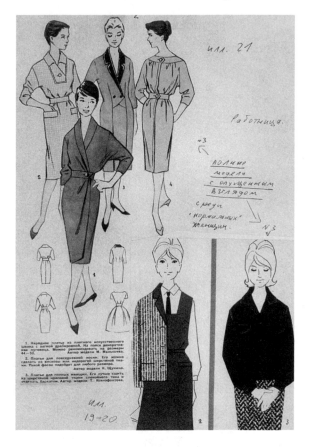

Fig 3.6. Plump models with bashfully lowered eyes, their slimmer colleagues eyeing them askance.

builders of communism" and mummified its leader as an emblem of corporeal immortality.

Proceeding from this concept, Barthes interprets social hostility to plumpness as follows: "The thin body becomes assimilated into the young body. Thinness is reliable evidence of youth.... The desire to get thinner—that is, to maintain one's body in a state of mythic youth, is in fact to dream of immortality" (1982, 653). During the 1970s, the period of stagnation, decaying socialism, and gerontocracy, one of the oblique indications of a political "freeze" was the gradual disappearance from stores of fashions created for the older, plump segment of the population. If in the sixties designers still strived to "correct" awkward female figures with the aid of loose clothes that had an elongated silhouette, in the decade that followed, society seemed to "forget" this category of people, acting as though it didn't exist. A well-known designer, Slava Zaitsev, complained that he frequently prepared special collections pre-

FIG 3.7. The grand-
mother image of older
plump women.

cisely for this group of clients, but only models up to size 48 [American
size 14, H. G.] were accepted for production.

As is to be expected, the inferiority complex of plump women grew
according to the degree of their social ostracism: In this period "Japanese" and "Hollywood" diets became extremely popular, and magazines
tirelessly published an endless stream of "magical" new formulas for
losing weight. The entire phenomenon in turn provided a fashionable
topic for discussions in various circles.

The exclusion of plumpness from the sphere of the normative
spawned new tendencies in the way people bought and wore clothes.
Plump women started acquiring outfits a size smaller than they needed,

not only because it was difficult to find the right size in the stores, but also because they psychologically refused to accept their own bodies, to acknowledge them as their own. A soft, loose-flowing silhouette and light colors practically disappeared, which, apart from anything else, meant that the traditional look of national dress forms such as the sarafan was relegated to the past.

The loose cut of the Russian sarafan ideally suited the generous Slavic figure, and light hues in combination with a colorful design lent it a uniquely dressy look. In its reduced form, the sarafan has been preserved as a sleeveless dark blue or black close-fitting dress, under which are worn various kinds of blouses: This was the classic outfit for women teachers and office personnel.

During these years only one type of garment for plump women survived and even flourished—the *khalat* (housecoat/robe)—and it deserves special commentary. The *khalat* enjoys universal usage in Soviet society. A woman may wear it at home from morning till night as she goes about her housework. Although historically the *khalat* served as a morning dress and in its aristocratic version (the peignoir) could even be elegant, Russian reality drastically transformed its essence, significantly weakening the appeal it had derived from literary associations—of lazy relaxation, the couch, a cup of morning coffee, profound Oblomovitis.[11]

The *khalat* simply became a working uniform in the home—one that plump women especially liked for its free and comfortable style, its lack of restriction. No matter what difficulties and shortages existed, Soviet manufacturing went on producing *khalaty* in large sizes and the most diverse (sometimes insane) color combinations, in order to encourage women's enthusiasm for domestic work.

The *khalat* was considered an "irreplaceable" garment: women wore a flannel *khalat* in the winter, a cotton one in the summer; to wear a *khalat* when receiving close friends was quite acceptable; it was possible simply to throw a coat over one's *khalat* before running down to the nearest grocery for a few things without incurring neighbors' disapproval; and, finally, a woman always took her *khalat* when going on a trip, to wear on the train or in a hotel; this way she could not only feel at home but also protect her good clothes during travel.

The ever-present *khalat* played a dual role in the life of a plump woman. On the one hand, its comfortable cut helped her to hide from the Other's censorious gaze and to redeem her eternal sense of guilt through her usefulness. A *khalat* was perceived as a natural attribute of domesticity, which rendered a plump woman's body socially acceptable.

A new *khalat* with flowers and ruffles plus slippers with pompons constituted the standard image of the ideal housewife and even the symbol of
coziness, which historically was sanctioned, moreover, by the traditions
of middle-class (philistine) dress. On the other hand, staying at home in
a *khalat* for prolonged stretches of time gradually weaned a woman away
from the habit of socializing, and any social event or visit to the theater
doomed the owner of the *khalat* to the tortures of wondering, "What
should I wear?"

In a more general sense the need to leave the warm, protective family
circle and plunge, appropriately dressed, into the large, alarming world
outside could be seen as a metaphor of initiation—of a transition from
childhood to responsible adulthood. This female "rite of passage" with
its attendant "test" is connected here with looking in the mirror. (See
fig. 3.8.) As she gazes into the mirror while taking off her *khalat* before
leaving the house, the plump woman is trying on not so much her dress
as the glances of her acquaintances.[12] Her prolonged hesitation stems
from her transition into a new space or dimension, where the empowered voice of the Other speaks, pointing out the "defects" of her figure.
If in this dialogue the Other proves stronger, then a woman may spend
her entire life in her *khalat*, trapped in her unresolved problems.[13]

The original function of the *khalat* was that of "transitional" clothing
worn between morning, when one gets out of bed, and daytime, when
one may have a task that requires leaving the house. Constantly wearing
a *khalat* at home may be viewed as prolonging the hiatus between childhood and adulthood. That is why the *khalat* is one of the Soviet
woman's most symbolically significant garments, a realized metaphor for
her fear of life's trials and her infantile state of limbo as all genuine pleasures and all genuine sufferings pass her by.

Additionally, the *khalat* has a sexual aspect. A woman in a *khalat* is actually only half-dressed, her nakedness barely screened, everything held
in place by only a few buttons (in the morning women often slip the
khalat on over their naked bodies, and any panties they wear may show
through). This garb creates a notorious image of female weakness and
vulnerability vis-à-vis men. Maguelonne Toussaint-Samat maintains in
this regard:

> A dress or robe, like a woman, is open from below. So the Western
> woman, unprotected by the iron gates of the harem, is susceptible to rape,
> which compels her to exercise caution. So a dress or robe is in fact the
> garment that has kept woman in her place in society. It has kept her aloof
> from all activity (economics, sports . . .) other than motherhood. (376)

FIG 3.8. Sarafans for the generous Russian figure (*R* 1971) and mirror checking (*R* 1960).

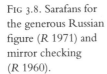

Her remarks are especially applicable to the case in question, for the *khalat* is a dress which, apart from anything else, opens easily in the front.

A woman who spends entire days in her *khalat* in the kitchen most likely will wear an apron on top of the *khalat*—also an emblematically defensive garment, not unlike a widened variant of the Soviet Eve's hip fillet. It is hardly coincidental that in the various illustrations of Soviet women in a *khalat* or an apron, the position of their hands suggests that they are shielding their genitals (see fig. 3.9).

Yet the Soviet *khalat* is hardly steeped in connotations of sexual seductiveness. It sooner projects an aura of active, bustling motherhood. More frequently than not, the *khalat* would get dirty from repeated daily use, and its messy appearance could hardly entice men to engage in am-

FIG 3.9. Variations on the *khalat*, with hands repeatedly placed at genital level (R 1961, 1962, 1963, 1965).

orous advances. On the contrary, a housewife's slovenliness and her lack of interest in dressing properly and prettily at home just for her family reduced her sex appeal in her husband's eyes, just as a man's appeal was diminished in his wife's eyes if he went around the house for years in slippers that were full of holes and sweatpants that bagged at the knees. Whereas the European peignoir was capable of serving a self-assured lady's erotic ends, the Soviet *khalat* in most cases functioned as a sign of women's problematic relationship to their own bodies and of long-standing, unacknowledged conflicts in their unconscious.

A telling example of the neglect/guilt/lovelessness/bodily girth paradigm may be found in an unusually powerful story by Elena Tarasova

titled "The Woman Who Doesn't Remember Evil." The plump heroine from whose perspective the story unfolds sits alone in a *khalat* in the
kitchen on her birthday, baking a pie that she ultimately burns, in
the process burning her hands on the hot frying pan. Her only friend—
the neighbors' daughter—never shows up as promised, but the story
underscores the fact that despite all of her own problems and isolation,
the protagonist with no memory for evil regularly visits and brings food
to her mother, who is a major source of her considerable sufferings.[14]

The catastrophic perception of her own body by Tarasova's protagonist is fairly typical for many Soviet women. The unstable social situation, uncertainty about the immediate and distant future, the un-
predictable availability or total absence of goods in stores, as well as
uncertain prices in recent years—all these have bred the habit of neurotic overeating "just in case." Practically every household as a rule hoarded
extra supplies of food that wouldn't spoil over a long period of time,
such as grain, macaroni, and potatoes. The need to obtain and then use
up these huge reserves, the absence of a culture of healthy nutrition, the
Russian tradition of endless tea drinking along with sweet things—
all this drove women into the vicious cycle of a love/hate relationship to
food. Hence the popular joke: "'What are the Soviet woman's two basic
concerns?' 'How to get food and how to lose weight.'"

One may trace parallel psychological models in women's relationship
to food. Since clothes as a category of goods were always more expensive than comestibles, the fetishistic respect for them was even stronger.
Families with a decent income bought a lot of dressy clothes so as to
maintain their status. Poor families made do with cheap Soviet goods
and also sewed and knitted their clothes, often very skillfully. But in both
poor and well-to-do families, no one ever threw out clothing, and in
many apartments whole mountains of old clothes accumulated.[15] These
musty storepiles (*zagashniki*), kept in spare closets, attics, trunks, or, most
frequently, in summer homes, had the same underlying psychological
causes as neurotic overeating. On the one hand they materialized unarticulated complexes and fundamental fears, yet on the other hand they
constituted a graphic archive of familial memory, a form of power that
parents could exert over their children. The mother who doesn't "let
go" of her adult/plump daughter in a sense foists off upon her her own
wardrobe, tastes, and views on life. The fact that children often shared a
single apartment with their parents resulted in many clothes' becoming
"communal," "everybody's," and people would take turns wearing them.
So it is unsurprising that in a Soviet's wardrobe one could readily find

items from various periods and in various styles, which created the effect of incoherence mentioned at the outset of this essay.

At times, however, fashion itself seemed to encourage "family" traditions in clothes. This tendency from the Soviet period persists to this day: In the winter of 1993–94, Muscovites lost their heads, so to speak, to a new fashion that swept the city. The entire female population, as if by divine edict, started wearing warm, fluffy caps made from mohair resembling hoods that came to a sharp point at the back of the head. These hoodlike caps were sold literally everywhere you turned, the original Chinese version costing six to seven thousand rubles in November, while the Russian imitation went for half that much. The most popular shade was dark violet or green, and one could buy gloves to match. The hoodlike cap effectively protected the neck and ears from the cold, and in the subway, bus, or tram you could easily push it back like a turndown collar. Both girls and women wore them without any regard for age differences. In fact, one often saw a mother and daughter in identical hoodlike caps. This erasure of distinctions enabled girls to participate in "adult" fashion, while mature women, conversely, resembled children muffled up against the elements by protective parents who didn't want them to catch a chill.

This obvious infantilization of the woman's image underscored her weakness and vulnerability: A child's hoodlike cap indirectly appealed to the feelings of the "strong" sex by drawing attention to the woman-girl's lack of independence, her inability to "warm" herself, her need to be taken care of and protected. As J. Flügel has remarked, by buttoning up and drawing their garments closely around them, people protect themselves "against the general unfriendliness of the world as a whole; or [seek . . .] reassurance against the lack of love" (Flügel 77). So such a hermetic sealing off, quite apart from ensuring warmth (this wasn't the first bitterly cold Moscow winter, after all), probably also provided psychological security. In the severe winter of 1993–94, marked by the October attempt at a takeover, Zhirinovskii's success in the elections, and a permanent rise in prices, the mass popularity of the mohair hoodlike cap is completely understandable. The cap enabled a sense of inner comfort, creating the illusion of a closed, warm family circle, out of which necessity forced the infantile woman to emerge briefly into the cold, hostile world.

If, as I contend here, Soviet women's fashions reflect the zigzags in the country's ideology, what items of women's wear would be exhibited in a future museum of Soviet civilization? Among its precious collections the museum undoubtedly would display the coat for standing in lines, the *khalat*, the black skirt, and the hoodlike cap. But will the visitor to the museum even for a second be able to feel how the women who wore these clothes—whether plump or thin, young or old, rich or poor, strong or weak, cheerful or gloomy—really lived? If s/he has difficulty imagining their lives, s/he could do worse than consult the bored middle-aged woman who doubtless will be guarding the museum collection.

Notes

For the sake of simplicity, all citations in the text from the *Woman Worker* (Rabotnitsa) and the *Peasant Woman* (Krest'ianka) are identified in parentheses as *R* and *K*, respectively, followed by year of publication and number of issue. Unless indicated otherwise, all footnotes belong to O. Vainshtein. French texts of which there is no standard English-language version have been translated by H.G.

1. Kantor 141.

2. Chapter 17, which in the English edition may be found on pp. 235–45.

3. Only in the last few years has the disciplining of external appearance weakened, and in public one increasingly sees people dressed in violation of formal principles: for instance, the combination of jeans plus jacket has gained currency only recently. Other novelties include the unfastened coat, not wearing a hat in winter, eating on the go, listening to music—all the earmarks of a demonstratively casual style.

4. Classicism, with its strict division into high, middle, and low styles, by no means contradicted the poetics of Socialist Realism; one could even say that it constituted a secret substratum of it. The very notion that art ought to subordinate itself to clear-cut rules that receive confirmation from outside superbly justified the specifically regulatory nature of official esthetics.

5. The black skirt was the only possible Soviet parallel with Coco Chanel's famous "little black dress," and was permitted solely by virtue of its democratic overtones.

6. This claim, made by a Russian participant in one of the Soviet-American TV shows intended to build "bridges" between the two countries, subsequently became an oft-quoted joke.

7. During an interview with me (O.V.).

8. A joke circulating in the early eighties was reproduced in a tellingly headlined article on Brezhnev. Intended for an encyclopedia of the future: "A minor political figure in the era of Alla Pugacheva" ("Melkii politicheskii deiatel' epokhi Ally Pugachevoi").

9. Few people use this mirror to check the whole body, however. The most characteristic behavior is to get up close to the mirror and examine the

face and hair. In his classic study "The Mirror Stage," Jacques Lacan argues that the earliest phase of a subject's self-identification is accompanied by alienation and, consequently, by the fragmentation of the image of one's own body. "Une image morcelée du corps" evidences the dramatic tension between the inner and outer world of personality, the notorious impossibility of accepting oneself fully as one is, which ineluctably leads one to a symbolic reduction (93–94).

G. Lipovetsky maintains: "Masculine narcissism is more synthetic than analytical. By contrast, in women the cult of self is structurally fragmented, the image that she has of her own body rarely being whole: the analytical gaze prevails over the synthetic" (160–61).

10. This letter obviously placed the editors in a difficult position. The class sympathies of the *Woman Worker* must have been on the side of the village worker, the mother heroine who, however, turned out to have adopted an ideologically alien fashion, that of the *stiliaga* (cool dresser). The art specialist's response to the author of the letter is a small masterpiece of verbal tightrope walking.

11. A term coined by the nineteenth-century critic Nikolai Dobroliubov in the article "What Is Oblomovitis?", which designates the ineffectual sloth and passivity of the eponymous protagonist of Ivan Goncharov's novel *Oblomov* (1859).

12. As Hollander notes, "People look at their clothes in mirrors to see how they fit into the common visual scheme or indeed to make themselves fit in. . . . Visual expectation is what makes the reflected image take on a certain kind of pictorial style when it is perceived" (417).

13. A memorable instance of just such a case is the character portrayed by Yvonne Mitchell in the British film of the 1950s signally titled *Woman in a Dressing Gown*. The Cuban film by Marisol Trujillo *Woman in Front of the Mirror* (1983) uses the mirror as a key symbol in the woman's traditional conflict precisely between domestic and professional life (H. G.).

14. Kim Chernin in her study of women's food consumption has concluded that in many cases symptoms of overeating and bulimia are a sign of difficulties in negotiating rites of passage, in an unsolved Electra complex. One of the symptoms of this disorder is infantilism—the daughter's emotional and practical dependence on her mother. Extrapolating from the work of Melanie Klein, Chernin explains the origins of the stable complex "mother-food-guilt-aggression" in terms of the moment of the infant's suckling/biting at the maternal breast: The overeating and the reflex of regurgitation appear as retribution for the symbolic cannibalism; they are the sadomasochistic rejection of one's own "guilty" body.

15. Saving an enormous pile of old unfashionable clothing at home, of course, has historical-social causes. The older generation can still recall the deprivations and poverty of the war years, while the younger generation was raised during the shortages (*defitsit*) of the Brezhnev era and the precept of taking the maximum possible of whatever was available when it *was* available. The fears of

the older generation proved warranted, for now many older people actually do live in poverty if no one helps them materially. Musty storepiles (*zagashniki*) also kept growing because the 1970s witnessed the gradual disappearance of the people who used to collect old stuff and would make the rounds of the court-yards shouting, "Used clothes?" A more or less normal circulation of clothes ex-isted only in the sphere of children's wear: The long-established tradition continued of passing down everything outgrown by a given child to younger siblings or to friends or neighbors with children.

Works Cited

Barthes, Roland, 1967. *Système de la mode*. Paris: Seuil.

———. 1982. "Encore le corps." *Critique* 38, no. 423/424: 645–54.

———. 1983. *The Fashion System*. Translated by Matthew Ward and Richard Howard. New York: Hill and Wang.

Bologne, J. C. 1986. *Histoire de la pudeur*. Paris: Olivier Orban.

Bowlt, John E. 1985. "Constructivism and Early Soviet Fashion Design." In *Bolshevik Culture*, ed. A. Gleason, P. Penez, and R. Stites, 203–19. Bloom-ington: Indiana UP.

Chernin, Kim. 1986. *The Hungry Self: Women, Eating, and Identity*. London: Virago Press.

Descamps, M. A. 1979. *La psychosociologie de la mode*. Paris: P.U.F.

Flügel, J. C. 1971. *The Psychology of Clothes*. New York: International UP.

Foucault, Michel. 1977. *Surveiller et punir*. Paris: Gallimard, 1975.

———. *Discipline and Punish*. Translated by Alan Sheridan. New York: Pantheon Books.

Grekova, I. 1980. *Kafedra*. Moscow: Sovetskii pisatel'.

Hollander, A. 1993. *Seeing through Clothes*. Berkeley: U of California P.

Kantor, K. M. 1973. "Moda kak stil' zhizni." In *Moda: za i protiv*. Moscow: Iskusstvo.

König, R. 1969. *Sociologie de la mode*. Paris: Petite bibliothèque Payot.

Kriuchkova, V. A. 1973. "Moda kak forma potrebleniia." In *Moda: za i protiv*. Moscow: Iskusstvo.

Lacan, Jacques. 1966. *Ecrits*, I. Paris: Seuil.

———. 1977. *Ecrits*. Edited by Alan Sheridan. New York: Norton.

Laver, James. 1969. *Modesty in Dress*. London: Heinemann.

Lipovetsky, G. 1987. *L'empire de l'éphemère*. Paris: Gallimard.

Lurie, Alison. 1981. *The Language of Clothes*. New York: Random House.

McLaughlin, Terence. 1972. *The Gilded Lily*. London: Cassell.

Murav'eva, I. 1994. "Komnata s vidom na proshloe." *Russkaia mysl'* 3 February.

Rubinov, A. 1991. *Intimnaia zhizn' Moskvy*. Moscow: Ekonomika.

Ryndin, V., ed. 1972. *Russkii kostium 1750–1917*. 5 vols. Vol. 5, with text by E. Berman and E. Kurbatova. Moscow.

Steele, V. 1985. *Fashion and Eroticism: Ideals of Feminine Beauty.* New York: Oxford UP.

Strizhenova, T. A. 1972. *Iz istorii sovetskogo kostiuma, 1917–1945.* Moscow: Iskusstvo.

Tarasova, Elena. 1990. "Ne pomniashchaia zla." In *Ne pomniashchaia zla: Novaia zhenskaia proza*, ed. L. Vaneeva, 189–216. Moscow: Moskovskii rabochii.

Toussaint-Samat, Maguelonne. 1990. *Histoire technique et moral du vêtement.* Moscow: Bordas.

Veblen, Theodore. 1912. *The Theory of the Leisure Class.* New York: Macmillan.

4

GETTING UNDER THEIR SKIN:
THE BEAUTY SALON IN RUSSIAN
WOMEN'S LIVES

Nadezhda Azhgikhina and Helena Goscilo

The beauty that addresses itself to the eye is only the spell of the moment; the eye of the body is not always the eye of the soul.

—George Sand

The only means of living in beauty consists in avoiding the thousand and one daily annoyances which interfere with an existence in the full ideal.

—Mata Hari

Beauty for some provides escape.

—Aldous Huxley

Cosmetics and Politics

VIKTOR EROFEEV'S NOVEL *Russian Beauty* (Russkaia krasavitsa, 1990, trans. 1992), conceived as a broad canvas depicting an entire epoch, met with scant success in Russia, despite the author's extraordinarily aggressive advertising campaign on its behalf.[1] The work left Russian critics and readers unstirred, not only because it addressed itself primarily to an audience abroad, as some hostile commentators maintained (validly, to an extent), nor only because its *enfant terrible* author, following the classic motto of the French literature he so admires ("Emma Bovary—c'est moi!"), ventriloquized through the heroine's persona his own purely male complexes and problems. Perhaps its failure on home ground may best be explained by Erofeev's not having taken into account (or deemed it necessary to do so) the Russian reader's traditional hierarchy of values, which accords pride of place not to beauty, but to the "rich inner content" of a protagonist's soul. Russian readers always prefer to witness not the predicament of a beautiful woman who suffers for profound if ill-defined reasons, but the story of the ordinary Cinderella who suddenly becomes beautiful and finds Prince Charming (optimally, on the last page).

This national scale of priorities explains the colossal success of Vladimir Kunin's novella *Intergirl* (Interdevochka, 1988), which has no pretensions whatever to Literature, unfolding, instead, the "touching story" of a young foreign-currency prostitute who has the "good fortune" to marry a highly successful middle-aged Swedish businessman. It is telling that the actress chosen for the leading role in Petr Todorovskii's popular film (1989) based on the novella was Elena Iakovleva, who, unlike *Pretty Woman*'s Julia Roberts, but like Kunin's pleasant-faced heroine Tania, is attractive enough, but hardly a stunning beauty.

Since Kunin takes Arthur Hailey as his model, his narrative, unlike Erofeev's, abounds in particularized descriptions of and references to products and services essential to the protagonist's profession—famous brand-name and ordinary lipstick, blusher, beauty salons that transform girls' faces, and so forth (Kunin 8, 11, 69, 77). These realia, painfully familiar to every Russian woman yet rarely incorporated into (especially male authors') literary texts,[2] decidedly enhanced the appeal of *Intergirl* for a broad range of female readers.[3] Of course, the novella treats a specific category of women—prostitutes—but the details about beauty procedures are accurate (Kunin interviewed more than two hundred prostitutes while writing his novella) and comprehensible to all women, regardless of their moral principles and sphere of professional activity. Another reason for readers' sympathy and understanding is that in Soviet and post-Soviet Russia the attitude to one's appearance—to one's hairstyle, makeup, and contour of eyebrows—has never been merely a woman's personal affair, but has always revealed something larger: a worldview, a relationship to one's environment and to the prevailing ideology as a whole.

Russian's perception of women's physical appearance was shaped from the outset by concepts from mass literature, many of which were refined in the fiery crucible of Soviet high school "literary" discussions, to emerge as inflexible clichés. Students educated in the Soviet system can hardly forget the tedious classes on Lev Tolstoi's *War and Peace* (Voina i mir) belaboring *ad nauseam* the two polarized female images that proved so convenient for the binarism of Soviet gender ideology: the cold, worldly society queen Hélène Kuragina-Bezukhova, whose sculptured beauty was demonized as a shell for her evil soul, and the unbeautiful but charming, spiritually and emotionally irresistible Natasha Rostova. Female images populating works of classic Russian literature

from Pushkin to Bunin include vivid, memorable women with an attractive exterior, but almost no "knockout beauties." Their inner wealth,
the admirableness of their character and manner, are primary; authors
emphasize their aesthetic "incorrectness," their lack of correspondence
to universally acknowledged standards of beauty posited by various
epochs. In that sense, Russian culture from the nineteenth century onward embraced the Romantic, not the Classical, feminine aesthetic ideal
by valorizing anomaly over perfect harmony.

Russian literature has always been cognizant of its self-appointed
function as a battlefield for conflicting tendencies: Western and Eastern,
democratic and conservative, sacred and profane, etc. This dualism likewise organized the female images generated by and presiding over Russian culture: One, dictated by the "educated, worldly" segment of society,
is the philosophically overdetermined image that derives from the ideals
of the German Romantics, who were extraordinarily popular in Russia,
while the second is rooted in popular national values. This opposition
finds fullest reflection in N. Chernyshevskii's novel *What Is to Be Done?*
(Chto delat'?, 1863), where the two heroes, Lopukhov and Kirsanov, discuss Vera Pavlovna's appearance and conclude that from the viewpoint of
"sophisticated society," which extols small-boned, pale-faced, and physically delicate women, Vera Pavlovna is not beautiful. But from the viewpoint of homegrown populist aesthetics (which Chernyshevskii
privileged), her beauty is indisputable and lasting: "She's got a broad
chest, so there's no danger of tuberculosis." The ideologically freighted
contrast between "sophisticated and worldly" and "down-home natural"
versions of beauty interweaves like a red thread throughout Russian literature and through critical discussions at the end of the nineteenth and
the beginning of the twentieth centuries—as evidenced in the symbolic
opposition of Sofiia and Varvara in Andrei Belyi's novel *Petersburg* (1911).

This habit of ideological/aesthetic binarism existed not only in literature, but also in life. Ivan Turgenev's caustically malicious portrait of the
slovenly and unfeminine Kukshina in *Fathers and Sons* (Ottsy i deti, 1862)
successfully captured a tendency widespread among the populists, nihilists, and supporters of various proliferating groups and circles: the rising
revolutionary subculture's championship of the ideal of the "natural
woman"—devoid of cosmetics and coquetry, and indifferent to elaborate
hairstyles. A *sui generis* culture was developing at the very core of "alternative" anti-bourgeois movements. Its echoes sound in Sofiia Kovalev-
skaia's writings, in the correspondence of exiled Socialist Revolutionary
women, female avant-gardists, and other socialists. These women (and
those men of a revolutionary bent who advocated gender equality) be-

lieved that women's liberation manifested itself partly in casting off a slavish dependence on the vagaries of fashion, on expensive hairpins and other accessories, as well as on the services of the hairdresser. The new standard of female beauty that emerged within this culture eventually grew as despotic as the traditional image of bourgeois femininity. As the above-mentioned correspondence reveals, "progressive" women harshly criticized those female friends who elected to dye their hair, pluck their brows, and paint their lips. Such frivolities were strictly frowned upon according to the new, revolutionary standard of neatness, simplicity, cleanliness, and severity.

Two styles of female beauty—polarized ideals subsuming a complex of values and qualities—thus became sedimented in people's subconscious. That dualism continued to flourish in Soviet society for decades. Memoirs from the 1910s and 1920s documenting the postrevolutionary and NEP periods readily reveal the indivisibility of attitudes toward women's hairstyles and makeup, on the one hand, and their authors' ideology and aesthetic aspirations, on the other. If the adherents to Symbolism traditionally sang paeans to women whose appearance— achieved with powder, makeup, and recherché coiffures—smacked of theatricality, then the Acmeists (who "overcame" Symbolism) were largely indifferent to that look,[4] while the representatives of left-wing art abhorred it. All of Vladimir Maiakovskii's poems about women and his scornful reference to "woman smearing herself" express his highly publicized contempt for everything bourgeois[5]—with the sole, obsessive exception of Lily Brik, who even in her late eighties elaborately penciled her eyebrows and dyed her long braid unideologically red.[6]

A ubiquitous cliché in Soviet life and literature became the eloquent opposition of the overly made up NEPwoman and the Komsomolka with short hair and unpainted face. I. Il'f' and E. Petrov's satirical novel *The Twelve Chairs* (Dvenadtsat' stul'ev, 1928) vividly captures this contrast in Madame Gritsatsueva and the cannibal Ellochka, on the one hand, and, on the other, the modest vegetarian from the communal dormitory. That synchronic polarization receives diachronic treatment in N. Ostrovskii's epochal work *How the Steel Was Tempered* (Kak zakalialas' stal', 1932–34), which couches the "spiritual growth" of Taia, Pavel Korchagin's last beloved, as a shift away from a preoccupation with her looks, fostered by her pretty-bourgeois family, to a simplicity and modesty that she attains after meeting the ideologically exemplary hero. Indeed, the symbol of the 1920s and '30s became the painter Aleksandr Deineka's "Girl with an Oar" (Devushka s vesloi), a short-haired athlete inspired by the dream of building a great future. In her singleminded pursuit of this goal, not only eyebrow pencil but even "unnecessarily" long hair proved an impediment. Seriousness, in other words, was synonymous with disdain for appearance,[7] and cropped locks signaled "the activist," "the doer." Fascinatingly, that image of purposefulness and sanitized physical energy echoes Charlotte Perkins Gilman's feminist utopian novel *Herland* (1915), where everyone in the athletic, happy, all-female society wears her hair short, "some few inches at most . . . all light and *clean* and *freshlooking*" (Brownmiller 65, emphasis added). Whereas shorn hair on women signaled orthodox Soviet values, in the American context, conversely, it challenged mainstream assumptions about gender differentiation. And Gilman's public insistence that the convention of long hair on women merely serves to institutionalize the masculine-feminine polarity caused hair to become a topic of public debate and impassioned controversy in the newspapers during the 1920s.[8] Thus short hair carried subversive sociopolitical implications in America, but in Soviet Russia indicated compliance with the official Soviet image of womanhood.

All of these instances illustrate the degree to which the Soviet ideological machine invaded people's private lives and dictated even the "correct" form of female beauty—one most advantageous for the regime, since it allied political probity with the womanly ideal of modesty, severity, and simplicity touted by the radicals of the nineteenth century. This campaign was initiated by the "leader of the peoples" himself. Anatolii Rybakov's novels *Thirty-five and Other Years* (Tridtsat' piat' i drugie gody) and *Children of the Arbat* (Deti Arbata) record Stalin's irritation with women from "the higher rungs of power" who prized cosmetics and perfume. According to a document Rybakov cites, on one memorable occasion Stalin became infuriated with a relative of Nadezhda Aliluieva's who presented her with French perfume from a trip abroad. An authority on feminine iconicity, as on all else, Stalin declared that "a woman should smell of freshness" and nothing but; all cosmetic "tricks" were the unhealthy inventions of the West, which presumably turned to artificial aids so as to camouflage the unpalatable. Whether implicitly or overtly, this moralized scenario equated makeup with cover-up, transforming mascara into a waterproof Watergate. In a country short of consumer goods, of course, the valorization of the lack of cosmetics illustrated how effectively Stalin could make a virtue of apparent necessity—and need.

Thus in Stalin's time cosmetics became politicized; orthodoxy came well-scrubbed, whereas decadence wore paint. As Boris D'iakov's *Tale of Past Experience* (Povest' o perezhitom, 1966) testifies, young women who resorted to such enhancements during Stalinism were condemned for "kowtowing to Western fashions and perfume." Such incidents inevitably prompted, on the one hand, a fear of showing excessive interest in "the art of being beautiful," and, on the other, a passionate desire to master that art.

The post-Stalin era witnessed similar tendencies: Soviet schools promulgated the ideal of the "modest girl without makeup," sporting either unstyled short hair or a braid—no other hairstyle would do. Marina Bernatskaia's novella *Serafima, My Angel* (Serafima, angel moi, 1992) superbly recreates this binarized world. Even today many women recall with a shudder the humiliating inspections during class when teachers would carefully examine the older girls' faces in an effort to detect traces of lipstick or mascara, and in front of a classful of witnesses they would force those guilty of such ideological infractions to wash their faces and rub off the makeup. Modesty required visual corroboration not only in class, but also at school parties, dances, and other social events: Girls with perms or striking makeup could always expect punishment. Such prohibitions, of course, only intensified girls' desire to use makeup outside of school, even if only for the sake of protest. In the 1960s and '70s, girls would form spontaneous collectives, to spend hours experimenting with various kinds of makeup (which, incidentally, was not easy to procure in those decades), as they tried on first one face then another, in search of the "right self," uncompromised by official dictates.

Curiously, despite these strict ideological pressures, the Soviet Union tolerated both hair parlors and perfume stores. Moreover, families of the *nomenklatura* had access to "closed" establishments that sold imported products and to "closed" beauty salons in which they could leaf through Western magazines advertising the latest hairstyles, which the average Soviet citizen never saw. In a number of memorable cases the political machine defended home-produced cosmetics and services, as, for instance, during the 1970s, when stagnation was in full bloom. As shortages in imported eye shadow, lipstick, perfume, and brassieres created kilometer-long lines of hopeful customers outside the stores Wanda, Leinzig, and Belgrade, the Russian press released an avalanche of articles about the harmfulness of foreign cosmetics. Creams from England, France, and Germany (even from "democratic" Poland and Hungary) were faulted for damaging the skin and poisoning the organism with chemical additives, in contrast to "healthy" Russian creams, lipsticks, and soaps. While credulous readers actually believed these claims about the superiority of domestic beauty products, the majority reacted skeptically, for the press was simultaneously launching a campaign against such purportedly "harmful" items as coffee, butter, and meat—all of which by happy coincidence also had disappeared from the shelves of Russian stores.[9] Russian women's response to this transparent device was swift and simple: Lines stretched ever longer as women left work on the pretext of sickness, so as to buy blusher, for which they stood waiting several hours; the black market in cosmetics flourished; and at every workplace women spent a significant part of the working day discussing cosmetics and how to purchase them.

During the period of stagnation, the acquisition of cosmetics became an important basic part of Soviet women's lives; conversations conducted in lines outside the perfume store fulfilled a key role in their emotional well-being; and a visit to the hair parlor constituted the supreme moment of women's self-expression, even when, as often happened, they were forced to wait for hours unless they had the necessary "pull" with the specific hairdresser who for double the price would take them out of turn.[10]

At the same time, information about cosmetic products, beauty salons, and stores hardly existed in the mass media. Moreover, the infrequent books on the topic (basically, translations from Polish) were virtually unobtainable and circulated only according to special lists among the political elite or else kept getting sold and resold at three times their price without being openly advertised. To speak of beauty procedures and care of one's face was considered indecent among the serious mass media, and the rare items that did appear (largely recipes for face masks and massage) were published primarily in such women's magazines as the *Woman Worker* (Rabotnitsa) and *Peasant Woman* (Krest'ianka). What little information circulated did so orally, passed on from one friend to another. These circumstances transformed hair parlors and beauty salons into unique sources of information.

The Poetics and Prosaics of Hair

Soviet women's lives without hair parlors resemble cocktail parties without double martinis—devoid of sinful pleasure and the hazy glow of temporary self-oblivion. Analysts of culture rightly contend that hair is the most malleable and versatile feature of the body, serving as "raw material" for personal statements and as an indicator of class, sexuality, age, race, and fashion (Perutz 69; Brownmiller 57). Hair can be cut or grown, curled or straightened, thickened or thinned, stiffened or made limp, lacquered or powdered, dyed or stripped of color, shaped, ornamented, and, of course, simulated by hairpieces and wigs. More than any other part of the body it can drastically alter a person's general appearance (see the essay by Vainshtein in this volume). Perhaps that explains why in the twentieth century beauty experts have accorded it more attention than at any other time (McLaughlin 145). "Throughout history and geography," as one optimist would have it, "individuals have been concerned with what's on their head only slightly *less* [*sic*] than with what's in it" (Perutz 72, emphasis added). Whatever the shifts in fashion, a hardy Western tradition allies long hair with female sexuality (women's so-called "crowning glory"), and, consequently, short hair with mannishness, lesbianism, or lack of sexual energy and appeal (Perutz 74). Indeed, Stalin's campaign against long, loose tresses for Soviet women (like the Catholic decree for nuns) was clearly intended to dampen their sexual allure and simultaneously to encourage the sublimation of their libidinal drives into productive labor at work and reproduction in a spirit of familial ardor at home. Women who allowed their hair to grow long had to discipline and minimize its aura of lushness by braiding, which visually de-eroticized women through analogy with the pigtailed schoolgirl.

In the decade following Stalin's death, women's hairstyles suddenly became a topic of discussion and debate in the press (Rubinov 303). The chemical permanent and hair dye, which became popular respectively in 1959 and the early 1960s, not only revolutionized hair parlors (Rubinov 318, 320) but rescued women from the inevitability of the uniform "communal" look that trapped them within a single generalized image. While the counsel on hairstyle selection directed at readers of women's magazines in the 1960s adhered to a normative aesthetic and adopted a solemn, didactic tone, the illustrations accompanying the dogmatic texts nonetheless implicitly sanctioned efforts to cultivate physical attractiveness and provided models for doing so (see fig. 4.1). Yet options consisted of variations on what was basically a single conservative theme: moderately short hair arranged neatly and "modestly," never falling below the shoulders or cut dramatically close to the scalp. To Western eyes, the individual differences in detail (e.g., waves versus curls, wisps versus bangs) dissolved in the overall sameness of such hairdos, which cautiously eschewed all connotations of eroticism, windswept casualness, cultivated neglect, and gender ambiguity, so as to tame and domesticate women's "crowning glory" (see fig. 4.2).

A comparison of American and Russian grooming practices involving hair underscores the significance of culture-specific elements for interpretation of what superficially resembles identical social behavior. Whereas for American women raised in the shadow of the beauty myth a short hairdo may symbolize jettisoning the psychological manacles of

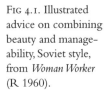

FIG 4.1. Illustrated advice on combining beauty and manageability, Soviet style, from *Woman Worker* (R 1960).

misogynistic stereotypes within their culture, for their Soviet counterparts it may sooner evidence conformity, compliance with imposed norms. Similarly, whereas American feminists consider women's "obligatory" elimination of body hair as part of society's machinery of oppressive sexual differentiation, precisely the *absence* of such gender-specific conventions in Soviet Russia reflects the unisex orientation of Stalinist ideology. Removing underarm and leg hair has never been a part of Soviet women's hygienic or beautifying regimen, a fact that, in light of the country's chronic shortage of shaving supplies, may well have saved many a marriage otherwise doomed to disintegration in battles over razors.

The real revolution in women's relationship to hair, as in other aspects of Russia's subculture, came with perestroika and intensified with de-Sovietization. As Western images permeated a basically monolithic formula of gendered beauty, the aesthetics of paucity (short hair) ceded to diversity, the commodification of women's bodies fostering an aesthetics

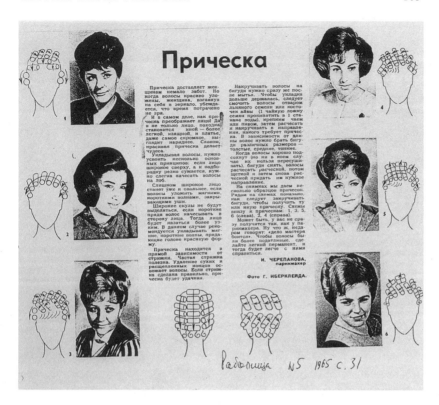

FIG 4.2. Five years later, hairstyles hardly evoked images of the wild and the reckless (*R* 1965).

of plenitude (unfettered long hair), particularly in those public spaces that exploit young women's sexuality. Today in Moscow the spectrum of hairstyles, lengths, and colors especially among the younger generation compares with that in the West. For the first time in many decades, one even encounters the alluring "siren" image of abundant, freely cascading hair anathematized during Stalinism and popularized in late-1970s America by Farrah Fawcett in *Charlie's Angels*.

Manufacturing Nature and Wearing Food: Paucity versus Plenitude

Whereas "natural" as the first and final criterion of female beauty was the rallying point of Stalin's repressive gender aesthetics from the 1930s to the mid-1950s, ironically enough, in the United States of the 1960s it was the radically anti-establishment element that reinvented and touted a kindred aesthetic. The rejection by 1960s youth of the "culture" that had plunged America into the mayhem of Vietnam stimulated a renewed appreciation for "nature." As flower power and health gurus such as the protojogger James Fixx and the cuisine queen Adele Davis (who ruled by yogurt, spinach, and granola) flourished, politically liberal and disaffected women intent on recapturing an "authenticity lost" placed their faith and dollars in the "natural look" and "natural cosmetics."[11] The Woodstock generation shed not only clothes and conventional cleaning rituals, but also those trappings of civilization that emphasized gender distinctions. Unisex clothes came into fashion. Women forsook brassieres, depilatory devices, and makeup rife with chemicals. Men, as the original musical and, subsequently, Milos Forman's nostalgic cult film *Hair* (1979) richly illustrate, articulated their nonconformity through realized metaphor: They let their hair down by growing it long, luxurious, and undisciplined. Products and procedures typically enlisted to exaggerate superficial differentiation of gender suffered a blow.[12] So the "naturalness" that Stalinism imposed on women in Soviet Russia as evidence of political orthodoxy served an opposite purpose in the United States. Women (mostly educated liberals) eagerly abrogated artifice in protest *against* the establishment, and that "naturalness" even seeped into the aesthetics of more mainstream cosmetics firms and beauty specialists. Summarizing the revolution in makeup in the mid-1950s, Mary Quant announced: "Make-up—old style is out. It is used as expertly as ever but it is not designed to show. The ideal now is to look as though you have baby skin untouched by cosmetics" (McLaughlin 141).

In today's America the naturalness that earlier was inseparable from resistance to mainstream ideology sooner symptomatizes political correctness—the current broad-based opposition to chemicals, cholesterol, animal experimentation, and destruction of the environment. Cosmetic giants such as Revlon and Elizabeth Arden have co-opted flower child images by incorporating the discourse (or buzzwords) of "nature" into the texts of their beauty ads, if not the ingredients into their products. For such "experts" in beauty, the illusion of minimalism—supplied at exorbitant prices—is the ideal (or at least advertised) goal. As a rule, the more skillfully cosmetics cover their traces while achieving their effect, the more expensive and exclusive their marketing.[13] That partly explains why, when post-Stalin Russia opened its doors wider to the blandishments of artifice, women's tastes in makeup seemed to favor an overly enthusiastic and visible application, whereas the problem actually consisted of poor-quality goods that lacked subtle tones. What Western ob-

servers noticed, therefore, suggested a heavy hand with primary colors—
fire-engine red lipstick and crimson nail polish, lurid blue eyeshadow,
and mercilessly black eyeliner and mascara. Perfumes such as the notorious Red Moscow (Krasnaia Moskva) were potent enough to anesthetize
a herd of buffalo, and the henna in Russian hair dyes produced heads of
brassy yellow or orange-red tresses that could stop a line of speeding
traffic. Products capable of creating discreet effects belonged to the realm
of myth (i.e., abroad).

Whereas in the West successful marketing of manufactured beauty
aids had effectively curtailed the nineteenth-century tradition of preparing cosmetics in the home, official condemnation of the glamorous
look, coupled with the ineffectualness of the Soviet cosmetic industry,
deprived Russian women of genuine choices. With foreign makeup pro-
hibitively priced and beyond reach, and domestic products scarce, inferior, and standardized, women resorted to "natural" home expedients
recommended by women's magazines: Comestibles such as grains, eggs,
honey, butter, milk, vinegar, fruit, and vegetables constituted the chief ingredients of their recipes for beautification, particularly of the skin and
hair. At least three Russian women of my acquaintance have shared with
me (H.G.) their private ("infallible") method of revitalizing their skin by
smearing it with a paste that blends oatmeal with water. Approximately
half of a recent book titled *Cosmetics* (Kosmetika, 1994) lists home con-
coctions—creams, masks, and cocktails—for improving the skin. Face
masks consisting of, for example, (1) egg yolk, honey, and butter or
(2) cabbage leaves and whipped egg whites or (3) sour cream, cottage
cheese, and salt indicate that Russian women not only ate their food but
also wore it for the sake of beauty.[14] Unlike in America, however, recourse to such aids sprang not from the political or medical conviction
that "natural is best," but from the practical recognition that food provisions, while rarely plentiful, could be found more readily and cheaply
than reliable factory-produced (i.e., foreign) cosmetics. A dearth of
practicable alternatives, then, motivated Russians' preservation of the
nineteenth-century traditions that the West had lost and only in recent
years has begun recuperating in (com)modified form.

Such was the situation until perestroika, which reoriented Russians'
lifestyle in virtually all aspects, completely reversing what until then had
been accepted practice. According to the unwritten law of the new
era—"everything that formerly was forbidden must be wonderful"—the
mass media started filling in "blank spots" with a vengeance. As a consequence, not only formulas for face care, but also beauty advice and advertisements for beauty salons proliferated. The ideal of the ideologically

committed woman indifferent to all but modesty and neatness in her appearance ceded to a new image: the fashion-conscious woman who devoted practically all her free time to her looks, a point to which we shall return later.

Why Is It Necessary to Be Beautiful?

In keeping with the post-perestroika enthusiasm for introducing readers to the latest items from the West, in 1993 the "women's issue" of the journal *Foreign Literature* (Inostrannaia literatura) published an extract from Naomi Wolf's popular *Beauty Myth* (1991). Although the piece did not provoke much discussion, in a small number of relatively narrow circles (especially among the literary and literature-connected intelligentsia, which avidly consumes any new information that reaches Russia), reaction to the publication was quite lively, and for the most part negative.[15] In large measure, readers took issue with Wolf's polemic against the traditional (and, for many, absolute) concept of women's beauty as a higher value. Wolf contends that men have a vested interest in propagating the relentless cult of female beauty, grounded in their desire for complete economic and political control over the "fairer sex." The majority of Russians interpreted Wolf's solution to male political repression of women (through techniques that consistently deflect their energies to their looks) as necessitating women's voluntary rejection of all aspirations to beauty. Reductive as that reading may be, it was facilitated by the style and form Wolf favored—that of art propaganda (*agitka*), a political mode startlingly reminiscent of Bolshevick proclamations in early-twentieth-century Russia. Since the Soviet intelligentsia in its entirety was intellectually weaned on this genre in the educational system's obligatory course on the history of the Soviet Communist Party, the style and formulation of Wolf's ideas caused Russians to read the extract published in *Foreign Literature* as a typical Party article, its categorical tone inevitably provoking resistance.

Such a reaction was instructive in many ways and provides an explanation for the phenomenon that many Western commentators find puzzling: namely, why to this day the post-Soviet democratic intelligentsia does not embrace feminism. Anyone analyzing the majority of anti-feminist articles appearing in the mass press, from *Moscow Komsomol Member* (Moskovskii komsomolets) to *The Capital* (Stolitsa), cannot help but notice that the authors (mostly women, incidentally) focus specifically on feminism's criticism of the "beauty myth." These articles conceive of feminists as some sort of monsters, determined to combat anything redolent of female attractiveness, to prohibit other women from dressing stylishly, using makeup, and wearing fashionable hairdos, and men from opening doors for them. Russian critics view these prohibitions as an encroachment on what little area of "comfort" Russian woman finally have begun enjoying in the last few years. Essays, interviews, and other items dealing with feminism rarely move beyond a discussion of these elements; the major concepts of feminism and the significance of its agenda are reduced to a hairdo, lipstick, and a wish to work in coal mines. A memorable and pertinent moment in my own personal experience (N.A.) occurred during a recent radio program in Moscow about women in the United States. The first question directed at me as a participant was: Is it true that all American feminists are unattractive, never visit the hairdresser's, have no children, and hate men?[16] Listeners were clearly disappointed by my answer in the negative, for it did not fit the widespread stereotype. Many democrats, including women, perceive feminism as a form of party-mindedness (*partiinost'*),[17] and over the last couple of years Russians have developed a strong immunity to anything smacking of party-mindedness. A democrat of my acquaintance, in fact, informed me that "feminism is Nazism," their common ground purportedly being an active, even aggressive, defense of a given position. That the most extreme symbolic act of early radical feminism entailed burning brassieres—as opposed to others' live bodies—apparently is an irrelevant detail.

All this bespeaks the surrealistic consciousness of post-Soviet Russians of both sexes. It also suggests that anyone discussing the beauty myth on Russian soil should optimally know something about this soil.[18] In this instance the specifics of the Russian situation that elude commentators operating in a standard Western framework involve the significance of Russian women's concern for their physical appearance. For many years a preoccupation with enhancing their looks was virtually Russian women's sole means of self-expression, a demonstration of their possible independence from the bleak deprivations of everyday life, an unsuccessful marriage, dissatisfaction with the job, politics, and much else. The possibility of altering their physical selves offered women a form of psychological self-defense and compensation; beauty salons and hair parlors therefore functioned as oases of independence in an arid realm of toil, subjugation, and failure. Refreshed and energized by those moments "outside of time," women could plunge back into their customary round of work, worry, financial problems, child-rearing, and so forth.

Women in Soviet Russia strived to be beautiful not only for men, and not only because men demanded that they do so (male pressure being a point often iterated by Western feminists), but because they wished to prove to themselves that, despite the grueling demands of Soviet life, they "still looked pretty good."[19] They used cosmetics and tried out new hairstyles less for their husbands and lovers than for themselves. Cosmeticians' and hairdressers' observations confirm as much, as do surveys among women who work in exclusively female collectives, with nary a man to appreciate hairdos and makeup jobs. Patients checking into a women's hospital always take their cosmetics bags; and women prisoners not only apply makeup and get perms, but take both procedures very seriously. Evgeniia Ginzburg in her prison memoirs (*Journey into the Whirlwind* and *Within the Whirlwind* [Krutoi marshrut, 1967–79]) repeatedly mentions how even after the last in a series of body searches, female prisoners found ways of smuggling lipsticks and combs into their cells, driven by the need to maintain their "womanhood"—i.e., their only possible freedom under the circumstances—so as to survive (see Peterson's essay below). Vasilii Grossman's *Life and Fate* (Zhizn' i sud'ba, written in 1960 but not published until 1980) shows how in the gulag women from simple families managed to maintain a decent level of grooming, unlike those from the intelligentsia, who let themselves go. In war conditions, at the front, where death threatened every second, women attempted to curl their hair and grow it long, regardless of the absence of any amenities, and those who had known poverty and discomfort from childhood fared appreciably better in sustaining morale through regimen. All of these behaviors suggest that for Russian women "being beautiful" means combating adversity, challenging life's trials, staying in good shape, and hoping (and actively working) to succeed. Paradoxically, then, cosmetics and other forms of grooming associated with superficiality and coquettishness may, in specific circumstances, be the outer signs of a lifesaving adherence to discipline. They may constitute part of a regimen that bolsters the psyche instead of betraying a weak dependence on group approval. Routine imposes an external order that ultimately not only paints the literal face but strengthens the metaphorical spine.

The significance of Russian women's commitment to self-beautification is a topic studied by the psychologist-cosmetician Galina Selivanova, the sole professional in Moscow to successfully combine these two specializations. The results of her work are extraordinary: After several sessions with her, women suffering from severe nervous disorders leave physically and psychologically renewed. Selivanova believes that their problems consist of profound complexes, and inasmuch as outer appearance is inextricably linked to one's inner world, the beauty salon that transforms their looks simultaneously helps women acquire self-confidence. However temporarily, the visible reconstitutes their sense of the invisible. In perceiving their enhanced external selves, they credit the possibility of solving their internal dilemmas. In this enabling environment, pig fat and similar cosmetic ingredients function as "articles of faith," as a means of instilling hope.

Having worked as a consultant for young women who participate in beauty contests, Selivanova concludes that Russian women differ from their Western counterparts in both their basic indifference to their physical appearance and their exaggerated readiness for self-abnegation. These traits lead to various complexes (or, perhaps, symptomatize them). The gender-marked space of the beauty salon helps women perceive themselves with different eyes, enables them to "make corrections," to contemplate other selves.

So far Selivanova's office (which in its modest appearance duplicates hundreds of similar neuropathologists' offices, except for the beauty salon that adjoins it) is the only establishment of its kind in Moscow. The last few years, however, have witnessed a marked growth in the city's beauty salons, which, despite their high prices, attract a steadily expanding clientele. So it is likely that Selivanova's synthetic approach to women's psycho-physical needs will catch on and result in additional salons-*cum*-offices.

Russian women have always frequented hair parlors and beauty salons as one might visit a psychiatrist (almost nonexistent under the Soviets), a church, a club, or a friend. Because the rigors of Soviet life essentially deprived women of leisure time, a visit to the hair parlor or beauty salon acquired the aura of a special event; an illicit escape from ceaseless duties, the visit afforded relaxation among other women and a respite, however brief and illusory, from coping with endless obligations and problems. In that regard an appointment at the beauty parlor or hairdresser's parallels the consumption of a Harlequin Romance, which similarly caters to women's pleasure by providing a fantasy that compensates for, instead of reconciling them to, the unbeautiful, unromantic aspects of their everyday existence.[20]

Soviet hairdressers used to enjoy a special and wide-ranging relationship with their regular clients. In addition to being entrusted with all kinds of confidences, they dispensed advice, lent money, helped to arrange a purchase, find a good gynecologist or pediatrician, and obtain a medication; they would listen to a confession, cheer their clients up, and ply them with restorative tea. Virtually all beauty salons observed the custom of tea sessions at which the cosmetician and the women s/he attended would drink tea while the client's face mask dried or her steambath was prepared, or simply because both wanted a break. Fully grasping the importance of that moment, experienced cosmeticians strived to appoint their salons in a style reminiscent of a fairy-tale illustration.[21] They created a world of sparkling mirrors and wondrous aromas, starched robes, creams, beautiful flacons, and items that almost always were sold on the premises (unofficially, of course), and as soon as any woman accustomed to the fumes in her cramped kitchen, children's shouts, and run-down apartment walls stepped over the threshold, she felt herself entering another world. In this new, exotic world she became beautiful, with jet-black brows, glowing skin, and a fantasy hairdo; here she could talk about anything and everything, and almost always about love. The endless conversations in a hair parlor or beauty salon were an essential component of the urban woman's subculture, which developed its own language, its approach to popular art, politics, and much else. Democracy ruled here, for in this environment the wife of a political leader and an office secretary were equals, and age played no role. This micro-world helped a woman to enrich her existence by discovering new facets in it; here female solidarity unexpectedly but visibly materialized in primordial form.

Hairdressers were ultimately psychologists and occasionally wheeler-dealers as well as artists. Many of them played the role of the neighborhood black-market "godfather"—or "godmother"—although there were well-known cases of their selfless concern for the children of their friends, especially those arrested for bribes, embezzlement, and other "economic" crimes. The hair parlor often was a version of a large communal family, where some form of not quite legal business, such as the sale of cars, clothes, and jewelry, would percolate. These were all variants of Soviet alternate life during the stagnation era.

Unfortunately, this sphere of life found scant reflection in contemporary literature, apart from I. Grekova's *The Ladies' Hairdresser* (Damskii master, 1963) and N. Baranskaia's *A Week Like Any Other* (Nedelia kak nedelia, 1969). The latter contains a startlingly simple and seemingly naive yet verisimilar scene in which the heroine rushes to the hair parlor and emerges reborn, overcome with a sense of happiness that culminates with her husband's uncharacteristic sexual arousal at her "young girl" appearance (27, 34). Today's practitioners of "new women's prose," by contrast, have bypassed hair parlors; their heroines have no time for them. Their lives, loves, and misfortunes occur outside the glittering walls of beauty salons.

After Perestroika

The post-perestroika Russian's view of the world has not grown less illusory. On the contrary, if anything, new surrealistic concepts have merely combined with the old ones, as illustrated by the prevailing current notions of "beauty." Formerly, beauty was conceived as abstract and elevated in nature, predicated above all on harmony. Such an understanding of beauty may be found in Dostoevskii, who declared that beauty would save the world; in Chekhov, who likewise observed that everything should be beautiful in a human being; in Zabolotskii and others. Within women's subculture, concern with physical appearance either fulfilled a largely compensatory function or sometimes was lacking altogether. Indeed, within certain milieux, such as alternative art groups and dissident circles, women demonstratively neglected their looks and a hairdresser's services.

After perestroika everything changed, as with mounting frequency surfaces began substituting for essentials. If previously the attempt to create an impact through one's looks was a means of self-expression or a form of *épatage*, and the desire to publish something about the beauty of hair required contravening what was officially accepted in the press, then after perestroika an extravagant exterior operated first and foremost as an advertisement, and publications about services such as beauty salons and hair parlors had a direct line to the market and business. Today, serious publications of any tendency, from the newspaper *Pravda* to the *Businessman's Daily* (Kommersant deili), carry items about hairdresser and hairstylist competitions, about the season's new hairstyles and the art of makeup. They likewise give information about new domestic and imported products from cosmetic firms. Almost half the pages of the old-style women's magazines, such as *Woman Worker* and *Peasant Woman*, not only are devoted to discussions about the art of making oneself beautiful, but also ascribe ever-increasing importance to that aspect of life. New publications of the *Little Lady* (Sudarushka) and *Women's World* (Mir zhenshchiny) type focus on fashion and makeup news, alongside simple advice and guidelines from sexologists, while an endless array of ads for face masks and ways of coloring hair at home bombard female readers. Newspaper stands now sell the publication of the Moscow beauty salon Enchantress (Volshebnitsa), one issue of which contained various tips from E. Lakhova, the president's adviser on women's issues. Lakhova recommended that women spend more time in the kitchen (in the interests of femininity), tend to their appearance, and invest more time and energy in sex, which, she gravely announced, is an important activity (presumably not in the kitchen, however). This counsel, which apparently exhausted her agenda for women, accords completely with the spirit of publications intended for "poor women." Meanwhile, for "rich women," targeted by the expensive journal *She* (Ona), a series of fashionable hairstyles at the hands of fashionable stylists supplies the answer to their problems. Chic hairstyles and high-priced cosmetics from L'Oréal, Christian Dior, and Estée Lauder, in fact, have inundated the city, promoted daily in magazine ads and television commercials. In short, the transition to a market economy has made cosmetics and "the latest" hairstyles a key part of the market, which is geared primarily to the New Russians—that segment of the population which can afford those products and services financially inaccessible to the majority.

What recourse does the average person who wishes to make herself more attractive have now? She may peruse the directory *All of Moscow* (Vsia Moskva) or such ad newspapers as *From Hand to Hand* (Iz ruk v ruki) and decide which she prefers: one of the ultra-expensive and ultra-fashionable hair salons (e.g., the transparently named Enchantress and Sourceress [Charodeika])—small, private establishments with an impressive reputation, where between various beautifying procedures women drink coffee and visit the small shop of consumer goods. A salon of this new sort purveys a large number of services, from a pedicure to a body massage. The alternative is the standard, familiar hair parlor on lease, which, incidentally, provides perfectly adequate services at inexpensive rates. One's choice depends on taste, money, and time. Some customers favor the calm and experienced personnel of hair parlors housed in large hotels, into which entrance was impossible earlier, whereas now one need only walk off the street into the hotel Rossiia or Belgrade and buy any service that the parlor provides. The new emporia of large salons no longer have the small-scale, cozy, intimate atmosphere that ruled during the stagnation period, and the female employees are predominantly young, ambitious, and not given to intensive socializing, sympathy, and the readiness to hear someone else's confidences. Yet Russian women's need to speak and be heard is enormous. Where can it be adequately realized in post-perestroika's hustler-filled Moscow?

To define specific tendencies in today's dominant image of the "soignée beautiful woman" in Russia is difficult, for pluralism has ushered in multiple images as varied and random as all of current Russian life. If formerly Russian women chose their idols from among popular film and stage actresses (e.g., Mireille Mathieu, Elizabeth Taylor, Claudia Cardinale), today no comparable universally acclaimed embodiment of beauty reigns supreme. Many women—and that includes TV personalities and actresses—therefore give free rein to their own imagination and, like Madonna in the West, engage in calculated but unconstrained experimentation. Not all succeed in forging an individualized and striking appearance, although some, such as the popular stage entertainers Alena Apina and Laima Vaikule, follow their own tastes and intuitions in elaborating their hairdos and style of makeup, programmatically eschewing all imitation (see fig. 4.3).

A recent development in Russia that manifestly affects women's innovations in this area is the frank sexualization of hair care and grooming. Commercials and ads now broadcast such truisms as "Hair is a sexual concept," a device that exemplifies the pervasive sexualization of advertising and mass culture in Russia of the 1990s. This trend found its apotheosis in the contest organized by the popular newspaper *Moscow Komsomol Member* (Moskovskii komsomolets) for Miss Hair, which followed analogous competitions for Miss Bust, Miss Legs, and Miss Erotic.[22] Tellingly, all the contestants for Miss Hair chose to appear on stage sporting only seductive smiles and bikini briefs, as if to corroborate advertising's proclamation that hair is, indeed, a key part of sexuality (see fig. 4.4).

What Price Beauty? Repackaging the Oldest Profession

The market mentality and the new, sexualized cult of beauty in Russia have bred a fierce competitiveness and widened the divide between generations of women. Within the new economy, female youth and beauty have become salable commodities in disguised and overt form. Careers in modeling, movies, and prostitution constitute the New Age Dream for women under thirty, who also have become exportable products as exotic or docile brides for Western males seeking "personal happiness" through cyberspace and the international postal system. Binational romance predictably matches middle-aged American men with considerably younger Russian females through so-called "correspondence clubs"—e.g., Scanna International in New York, International Correspondence Agency in Florida. Hundreds of pretty young hopefuls enroll for training sessions intended to enhance their prospects of marriage to affluent foreigners (primarily pot-bellied businessmen), who purchase future brides through these profit-making organizations. In 1993 one such agency reported a waiting list of seven thousand Russian women eager to sample *amour* American style via the post-perestroika marriage market. In 1994, the woman-oriented newspaper *Women's*

FIG 4.3. Among the proliferating new paradigms of desirability, the Barbie Doll look, exemplified by a contestant in the Miss Hair competition in Moscow 1993.

Affairs (Zhenskie dela) carried an ad by the agency Intermatchmaker (Intersvakha) encouraging "dear ladies" (*milye damy*) to submit their photographs and thirty thousand rubles ($15) in the hopes of snagging an American spouse (6 [1994]:22).[23] This international traffic in legalized prostitution masquerading as conjugal bliss is confined, predictably, to nubile females whose endowments seem chiefly physical. Advertisements of vacancies in jobs that normally require minimal office skills, such as typing and filing, unabashedly stipulate youth and beauty as the chief requisites for applicants. A typical want ad for a secretarial position specifies "Not older than 25; striking appearance, long legs compulsory"; young women working at joint ventures serve primarily as sexual lures, relying on their looks to garner contracts for the firm.[24] With women constituting 80 percent of the unemployed in Moscow and St. Petersburg,[25] the monetary awards of selling one's "beauty" have enticed an increasing number of women into prostitution, competitions of the Miss Bust and Miss Erotic variety, pornographic modeling, and what is eu-

FIG 4.4.
Today's
almost-Lady
Godiva, a
participant in
the Miss Hair
competition
of 1994.

phemistically labeled "hostessing" and "performance" at casinos and nightclubs (see fig. 4.5).

These options are closed to middle-aged women and pensioners—precisely those categories within the female population that sought refuge and rejuvenation in the Soviet-style hair parlors and beauty salons of the sixties and seventies. As a recent headline in *Newsweek* proclaimed, there is "No Market for Grannies" in the brave new world of post-Soviet Russia.[26] Whereas Western feminists have long noted that American society practices gendered age discrimination by respecting older men as "distinguished" but denigrating or ignoring women "past the age of beauty,"[27] in Russia the process of gendered devaluation started only with de-Sovietization. Under the Soviet system of conservative hierarchical structures, which privileged traditions and the past, age represented a

FIG 4.5. Flashing
flesh in the 1993
Miss Bust contest
in Moscow.

degree of authority. As the self-appointed but unchallenged guardians of Soviet morality, older women uninhibitedly passed judgment on how young women—even strangers casually encountered on the street or in the subway—should dress and groom themselves.[28] The transition to a market economy and the attendant commodification of female bodies have completely disempowered this social group. Economic and ideological differences between women who sacrificed "frivolous" desires so as to "build Communism," on the one hand, and their offspring, who came to maturity during perestroika, on the other, have split "mothers and daughters" (as well as "fathers and sons") into mutually alienated and sometimes antagonistic camps. Although Kunin's admonitory *Intergirl* sentimentalizes his prostitute heroine's attachment to mother and homeland, it nevertheless accurately conveys the unbridgeable gulf separating the conventional Soviet concept of women's bodies as sites of labor and transcendence and the current commodification of those bodies into attractively packaged marketable items (Kunin 21–22).[29] In Kunin's scenario, that gulf ultimately dooms both mother and daughter. Although it is premature to assess its consequences for Russian society, the discrepancy in generational values and mores unquestionably has contributed to the perceptible erosion of familial relations.

In post-perestroika Russia, as before, the world of hair salons, makeup, and body presentation remains for many a form of alternate existence, a parallel world. Life is brutally difficult for thousands of women, who cannot frequent a beauty salon every week, and so continue their old habit of painstakingly saving money so as to visit "their own" hairdresser. The only difference, perhaps, is that in today's uncertain conditions such forays vouchsafe less joy than in the past, even though they may smack of what a bygone era elevated to the status of "forbidden pleasures."

Notes

We thank Josif Bakshtein and Ol'ga Vainshtein for transmitting and lending us materials crucial for this article, Mark Shteinbok for supplying the photographs, and the Center for Russian and East European Studies at the University of Pittsburgh for funding the travel that facilitated our collaboration.

We include in our bibliography those magazines and newspapers that we perused on a regular basis so as to identify general tendencies. Hence the absence of references to specific issues and items within them.

1. Many bought it—the run of 100,000 copies reportedly sold out in two days (Köchel 19)—fewer probably read it, and virtually no one waxed enthusiastic about it. A kindred fate met the novel's publication in the United States, and the *Times Literary Supplement* review buried it quietly, British style (Hughes 17).

2. Since women's prose reflects women's real-life experience to a much greater degree, it contains appreciably more data about women's techniques of beautification. See Zekulin 36–37.

3. On the ideological treatment of these products in *Intergirl*, see Goscilo 10–12.

4. The dazzling exception, of course, is Anna Akhmatova (see Holmgren's essay on salons in this volume).

5. See, for example, his poems "Parisian Woman" (Parizhanka, 1929) and "Beauties" (Krasavitsy, 1929), Maiakovskii 590–94.

6. For a frank, unhagiographic portrait of Lily Brik in her old age, see Proffer 79–89.

7. In the meantime, by 1926 American women reportedly were spending $5 million a day on beautification (Vinikas 59).

8. On Gilman's address on this topic, see Brownmiller 65–66.

9. The point is not whether these products are actually unhealthy, but that the government conveniently happened to "discover" their deleterious properties just when they vanished from Soviet stores.

10. I. Grekova's novella *Ladies' Hairdresser* (Damskii master) faithfully describes a typical scene in a hair parlor. In general her fiction conveys a palpable sense of the mundane specifics and the texture of Soviet women's everyday lives (*byt*).

11. On the fallacy of assuming that natural cosmetics avoid chemical processes and big business practices, see McLaughlin 142–43.

12. An industry source in the mid-1920s in America estimated that 90 percent of women over the age of eighteen used face powder, 71 percent used perfume, and 55 percent used rouge (Vinikas 59).

13. In order to appreciate the financial profits and social prestige commanded by "high-class" beauty businesswomen, one has only to look at the success story of Estée Lauder, ingenuously titled exactly that in her self-congratulatory autobiography. See Lauder.

14. Fascinatingly, the volume (in a run of 5,000 copies) provides tips for men also, supplementing these items with strict (and, in the current Russian klondike context, quite fantastic) rules of civilized conduct. For instance, the authors urge tolerance, punctuality (!), attentive silence while others are speaking (!!), and similar courtesies that seem included precisely because they run counter to the "norms" of Russian behavior as I have witnessed it during the last twenty years (H.G.).

15. A tragic incident that occurred in connection with that publication increased interest in the piece: After a heated discussion of the extract with the literary commentator Irina Sandomirskaia, the young critic V. Kuz'minskii attempted to commit suicide. The article as such was not the direct motive, of course, but it functioned as a catalyst for his personal drama. See Sandomirskaia and Kuzminskii.

16. Norman Mailer and Camille Paglia would have answered in the affirmative, approving, moreover, both the presuppositions motivating such a query and its specific formulation (H.G.).

17. For a discussion of this misperception, see the recent article on women's prose by the playwright Mariia Arbatova.

18. This issue was discussed at a round table organized by the Journalists' Association in the spring of 1994, devoted to another American article: Ann Snitow's piece on feminism in Eastern Europe. Snitow's unfamiliarity with "the soil" and the realia of the countries she analyzed resulted in a lack of understanding and occasionally proved more pernicious than illuminating.

19. So the Soviet case seems to counter Charles Darwin's and many Western commentators' conviction that the purpose of beauty is "to attract a mate and, thus, assure the perpetuation of the species" (Baker 11).

20. On the role of Harlequin Romances, which entered the Russian book market in 1992, see Ann B. Snitow, "Mass Market Romance: Pornography for Women Is Different," *Radical History Review* 20 (1979): 141–61; Beatrice Faust, *Women, Sex, and Pornography* (New York: Macmillan, 1980); Janice Radway, *Reading the Romance* (Chapel Hill: U of North Carolina P, 1984); Tania Modleski, *Loving with a Vengeance* (New York: Methuen, 1982/1984), 35–58.

21. Although some beauty salons modeled their decor on illustrations from Western magazines, that was not the main tendency.

22. The birth of such competitions as Miss Russia and Miss Moscow was prompted by the country's extensive post-perestroika contacts with the West, and above all the United States, where the perennial quest for the (money-making) ideal of female pulchritude led to the Miss America pageant, instituted in 1921. See Vinikas 53.

23. The newspaper, edited by Liubov' Panova, started publication in early 1994, with a run of 250,000 copies, now increased to 450,000. Its contents focus on scandals, beauty tips, and sex (ads for massages and "pleasure" are a staple). Naked female bodies not only have appeared on the covers of all six issues published so far, but also are scattered throughout the paper's twenty-four pages.

24. For a more detailed examination of how Russia's new business etiquette mainstreams pornographic values, see "To Be Young and Pretty in Moscow," *U.S. News & World Report*, 56.

25. According to one source, "women largely in the 45 to 50 age bracket account for 79.4 percent of all the jobless" (*Women's Discussion Club*, May 1993, 4).

26. For a brief but astute glance at the fate of Russia's older women, see *Newsweek*, 37.

27. See, for instance, the chapter titled "Fading Flowers" in Baker 149–74, Greer 280–362, and Friedan passim.

28. Soviet Russians accepted without protest the "right" of this constabulary to monitor young women's appearance—to criticize strangers' skirts as too short, makeup as unsuitable, and so forth. On a research trip to Moscow in the mid-1980s, in fact, I was asked by a Soviet policeman not to sit sunning myself, legs exposed just past the knee, on the steps at the Moskva River. He was the self-confessed emissary of four "grannies" parked on a nearby bench, *their* legs spread so wide as to expose their underwear. A passing Galahad's defense of my right to show leg, on aesthetic grounds, carried no argument with the policeman, and certainly not with the grannies (H.G.).

29. For an analysis of *Intergirl* as a signal text of perestroika, see Goscilo 10–12. An ironic, literarily more satisfying dramatization of the new generation gap may be found in Galina Shcherbakova, "The Three 'Loves' of Masha Peredreevna" (Tri "liubvi" Mashi Peredreevnoi), translated in *Women's View*, *Glas* 3 (1992): 94–147.

Works Cited

Arbatova, Mariia. "Partiinaia organizatsiia i partiinaia literatura." *Literaturnye novosti* (March 8, 1994): 2.

Baker, Nancy C. 1984. *The Beauty Trap: Exploring Woman's Greatest Obsession.* New York: Franklin Watts.

Baranskaya, Natalya. 1989. *A Week Like Any Other: Novellas and Other Stories.* Translated by Pieta Monks. Seattle: Seal Press.

Bernatskaia, Marina. 1992. *Serafina, angel moi. Znamia* 2: 38–62.

Brownmiller, Susan. 1984. *Femininity.* New York: Fawcett Columbine.

Friedan, Betty. 1993. *The Fountain of Age.* New York: Simon and Schuster.

Goscilo, Helena. 1993. "New Members and Organs: The Politics of Porn." *Carl Beck Papers*, no. 1007. Pittsburgh: U of Pittsburgh, CREES.

Greer, Germaine. 1992. *The Change: Women, Aging, and the Menopause.* New York: Alfred A. Knopf.

Hughes, Lindsey. 1992. "Russian Beauty: A Novel." *Times Literary Supplement* 4662: 17.

Köchel, Jürgen. 1992. "Leben mit einem Idioten: Der Text und sein Autor, Der Komponist und seine Oper," Alfred Schnittke, *Life with an Idiot* (libretto by Viktor Erofeev). Sony CD S2K 52495: 19–26.

Kunin, Vladimir. 1991. *Intergirl: A Hard Currency Hooker.* Translated by Antonina W. Bouis. New York: Bergh.

Lakhova, E. 1994. "Politicheskaia deklaratsiia s seksual'nym uklonom," interview with E. Lakhova. *Gazeta dlia zhenshchin* 8: 7.

Lauder, Estée. 1985. *Estée: A Success Story.* New York: Random House.

Maiakovskii, V. V. 1987. *Sochineniia v dvukh tomakh.* Vol. 1. Moscow: "Pravda."

McLaughlin, Terence. 1972. *The Gilded Lily.* London: Cassell.

Orlova, L. F. 1994. *Kosmetika.* Moscow: "Studiia-Press."

Perutz, Kathrin. 1970. *Beyond the Looking Glass: America's Beauty Culture.* New York: William Morrow.

Proffer, Carl. 1987. *The Widows of Russia and Other Writings.* Ann Arbor: Ardis.

Rubinov, Anatolii. 1991. *Intimnaia zhizn' Moskvy.* Moscow: Ekonomika.

Rybakov, Anatoly. 1988. *Children of the Arbat.* Boston: Little, Brown.

Sandomirskaia, I., and B. Kuzminskii. 1993. "Pauza i slovo, ili est' li imia u boli [beseda v redaktsii]." *Inostrannaia literatura* 3: 236–45.

Vinikas, Vincent. 1992. *Soft Soap, Hard Sell: American Hygiene in an Age of Advertisement.* Ames: Iowa State UP.

Wolf, Naomi. 1991. *The Beauty Myth: How Images of Beauty Are Used against Women.* New York: William Morrow.

Zekulin, Nicholas. 1993. "Soviet Russian Women's Literature in the Early 1980s." In *Fruits of Her Plume,* ed. Helena Goscilo, 33–58. Armonk: M. E. Sharpe.

Domovoi 1–7 (1994).

Inostrannaia literatura 3 (1993): 236–45.

Iz ruk v ruki (1994).
Kommersant deili (January–June 1994).
Krest'ianka (1960–1984).
Mir zhenshchiny (January–June 1994).
Miss Iks 1–9 (1994).
Newsweek (March 28, 1994).
Ona 1 (1994).
Rabotnitsa (1962–1994).
Sudarushka (January–June 1994).
U.S. News & World Report (March 28, 1994).
Vsia Moskva (1994).
Zhenskie dela 1–6 (1994).

PART II

DOMESTICA-

TIONS

5

DOMESTIC PORKBARRELING

IN NINETEENTH-CENTURY RUSSIA,

OR WHO HOLDS THE KEYS

TO THE LARDER?

Darra Goldstein

Managing a household is not the same as braiding sandals.
(*Dom vesti, ne lapti plesti*)
—Russian proverb

Home is the girl's prison and the woman's workhouse.
—George Bernard Shaw, *Woman in the Home*

THE PREFACE TO THE twenty-second edition of Elena Molokhovets's famous cookbook, *A Gift to Young Housewives*, originally published in 1861, begins with an admonition. This caution, even from the pen of a woman whose stated aim is to ameliorate the position of young wives, reads like yet another attempt to limit woman's role in the world by confining her to the home and entrapping her in domestic duties:

> Cookery is, in its own way, an art; one which, without guidance and the exclusive devotion of some time, can be learned . . . only after decades of experience. A decade of inexperience sometimes proves highly expensive, especially to young spouses; not infrequently one hears of a sad state of disorder, and various unpleasantnesses in family life are thus ascribed largely to the fact that the housewife was inexperienced and did not want to learn all about household management. (Molokhovets i)

Molokhovets explicitly equates an efficient household with a good family life; no doubt she would agree with Tolstoi that all happy families are alike—provided each is well cared for by an experienced homemaker. For Molokhovets, providing for a family means more than just cooking well. In her descriptions of ideal designs for the house or apartment, she affirms the importance of a common room for prayer (Molokhovets

216). Significantly, the family communion was to take place around the table; in this way physical and spiritual sustenance are integrally linked.

Molokhovets takes as her task the guidance of young housewives through what she sees as the pitfalls of domestic life, and her sympathetic understanding of the daily dilemmas of kitchen management endears her to the reader (and likely accounts for the enormous popularity of her book).[1] Writing from a position of both practical and moral authority,[2] Molokhovets aims to reassure the novice by allaying anxiety over food preparation and familial relations. Yet the reader who finally makes her way through the thousand-odd pages of prescriptions for keeping the home fires burning soon realizes that nothing short of heroic labors is required to provide properly for family and friends.

Nineteenth-century writers of Russian fiction (almost all male) would have us believe that these labors were always performed cheerfully, even passionately. We need only recall Pulkheriia Ivanovna of Nikolai Gogol''s "Old World Landowners," the prototype of the great nineteenth-century housekeeper, to see how a woman's self-worth and very identity are depicted as deriving largely from the domestic activities associated with keeping the pantry, and hence her husband's belly, full.

> For Pulkheriia Ivanovna, housekeeping meant continually locking and unlocking the larder, salting, drying, and preserving an endless number of fruits and vegetables. Her home was like a chemical laboratory. A fire was constantly tended under the apple tree; and the kettle or copper vat—filled with jam, jelly, or confections made with honey, sugar, and I can hardly remember what else—was almost never removed from its iron tripod. Under another tree, in a copper cauldron, the coachman was forever distilling vodka from peach leaves, bird-cherry blossoms, from centaury or cherry pits. (Gogol' 214)

Like Molokhovets's ideal housewife, Pulkheriia Ivanovna "always liked to prepare more than was needed, to have some on hand," and the rhythm of her life is determined by the meals she serves. A typical day of eating includes an early breakfast with coffee; a mid-morning snack of lard biscuits, poppy-seed pies, and salted mushrooms; a late-morning snack of vodka, more mushrooms, and dried fish; a dinner at noon of various porridges and stews, their juices tightly sealed in earthenware pots; an early afternoon snack of watermelon and pears; a mid-afternoon snack of fruit dumplings with berries; a late-afternoon snack of yet other delicacies from the larder; supper at half past nine; and finally, a midnight snack of clabbered milk and stewed dried pears, calculated to relieve the stomachache brought on by the excesses of the day.[3] This predictable cadence characterizes an idyllic life, in which temporal boundaries are blurred in relation to gastronomic cycles (Bakhtin 225). Given Gogol''s own food obsessions and culinary skills, it is notable that he never chooses to describe the real labors of food preparation. Instead, we find Pulkheriia Ivanovna overseeing the work of a coachman *cum* alchemist, who magically produces homeopathic brews as he incants over them. The appearance of food on Afanasii Ivanovich's plate as if by magic serves to reinforce the idyllic element of the story, and in its depiction of contentment and ease "Old World Landowners" may be seen as a sort of Slavic Eden before the Fall (Karlinsky 63).

We love Gogol' for these images of alchemy and plenty, which are appealing in their ability to evoke the child's wish for magic that lingers deep within us: secretly we still long for the enchanted tablecloth that lays itself (*skatert'-samobranka*), piling the table high with luscious delicacies. Even Agafiia Matveevna, who ministers to the needs of the lethargic Oblomov (in the novel of the same name) and whose labors the author, Ivan Goncharov, describes in detail, appears connected to the realm of the fantastic: "she doesn't walk, but seems to float from the cupboard to the kitchen, from the kitchen to the larder" (Goncharov 448). Such examples serve to make the preparation of food seem endowed with magical powers; this activity is romanticized.

But what is the position of the real woman, who on a daily basis must strive to prepare or oversee the production of excellent meals for her family in an effort to nurture and sustain it? Even for those with servants to carry out the most odious tasks, there is no question that much of the work required to keep a larder is drudgery.[4] Molokhovets provides a corrective to the rosy picture of women's work proposed by nineteenth-century fiction, without quite intending to. Her recipe for that most Russian of soups, cabbage soup (*shchi*), as prepared in the winter when no fresh cabbage is available, seems simple enough (Molokhovets 123–24):

> Make a white bouillon from two or three pounds of fatty beef chuck, rump, or brisket, or from 2 pounds of beef and 1 pound of ham, along with dried mushrooms and spices; strain it. Squeeze the liquid out of 3 cups of sauerkraut, pour boiling water over it, and drain in a colander; chop the sauerkraut and sauté until soft with 1 spoon of butter, or better yet lard, 1 finely chopped onion, 2 spoons of flour, and ground pepper; then pour on the bouillon and boil until soft. When the meat and cabbage are completely ready, you can add about 1/2 cup of sour cream or heavy cream and bring it to a boil once. Serve with the sliced boiled ham or beef. Many like chopped, rather than shredded, cabbage.

1 lb. beef, 1 lb. ham	3 glasses sauerkraut (1–1/2 lb.)
3–4 dried mushrooms	1–1/2 spoons butter
2 onions	1 spoon flour
5–10 allspice berries	(5 peppercorns)
1–2 bay leaves	1/2 or 1–1/2 cups sour cream

Yet just as Gogol'’s depiction of Pulkheriia Ivanova’s work hides the reality of the labor involved, so Molokhovets’s instructions mask the extensive preparatory work that must be carried out before even the most basic recipes can be prepared; they completely understate the rigors involved in maintaining an aura of plenty in the household. Thus, for the preparation of *shchi*, Molokhovets presumes that the sauerkraut has already been fermented, the beef or pork butchered, the mushrooms dried, and the cream soured. The wood stove has necessarily been stoked, and the accompaniments of fried sausages, fried buckwheat groats, meat pies, or pancake pies (*blinchatye pirozhki*) readied. It is only by perusing the more than eight hundred recipes elsewhere in the book detailing the proper methods for preserving, distilling, brewing, drying, marinating, macerating, and smoking all sorts of products that the true scope of the housewife’s labors is revealed. Molokhovets’s recipes might make cooking seem straightforward, but her book proves that, in fact, quite the opposite is true.

The management of a prosperous nineteenth-century Russian household was onerous enough to ensure that the housewife would remain tied to the home. And far too often her skill in managing the home was simply taken for granted. Even progressive nineteenth-century male thinkers reveal a certain condescension toward women who get their meals to the table, particularly if we take as evidence the writings of Aleksandr Nikolaevich Engel’gardt. A chemist, Engel’gardt was exiled from Saint Petersburg to the Russian countryside in 1871; his letters, commissioned by Mikhail Saltykov-Shchedrin for the journal *Notes of the Fatherland*, provide an interesting perspective on domestic work when he writes of his housekeeper, Avdot’ia. Engel’gardt’s concern with chemistry offers insight into the considerable expertise the successful housekeeper or wife must command:

> Avdotia, who possesses unusual culinary skills and diligence, and also the knowledge every baba has of baking bread, making cabbage soup and meat pies, began to cook for me splendidly, as well as making various supplies for the winter: pickles, marinated mushrooms, fish and crayfish conserves, preserves, creamy cheeses. I explained to her that in making syrup

> from berries, the most important thing is to boil them to the point that, because of the acidity, the crystallized sugar becomes winelike and the syrup thickens so much that no fermentation can take place; I explained that there will be no spoilage in preserves, no mold in pickles, and so forth, as Pasteur showed, if no bacteria or lower organisms fall out of the air into them; I explained the influence of high temperature on bacteria, albumen, and so forth. Avdotia understands all of this splendidly. (Engelgardt 25)

What the chemist knows only theoretically, by way of science, Avdot'ia knows empirically. He may think that she "understands splendidly" all of his explanations, but her true understanding lies in knowing how to go about her work without her master's interference. Though an accurate observer, Engel'gardt proves oblivious to the real nitty-gritty of cooking. Here is how he describes preparations for the Easter table:

> I went to the station and bought wheat flour, sandalwood, raisins, and al-monds. The cooking began. The confectioner cut decorations for the Easter cake and leg of lamb out of different colors of paper; I, with a fellow chemist friend who had come for a visit from Petersburg for the holiday, made a rose out of rose-colored tea paper, perfumed with excel-lent perfume, and put it in the Easter cake. Everything came out wonder-fully. (Engelgardt 28)

The finishing touch of placing the rose on the Easter bread (*kulich*) serves as a perfect metaphor for the way in which food preparation is romanticized; the beauty and aroma of the flower belie the bloody busi-ness of butchering the lamb and the infernal heat of the bake ovens. The master need only make a grand final gesture for everything to turn out perfectly.

Still, it must be conceded that Engel'gardt is generally aware of the ef-forts Avdot'ia expends to keep him happy. He states quite unequivocally that "Avdotia's entire life is consumed by the household she runs." Given its gastronomic implications, Engel'gardt's word choice is of interest here. Is Avdot'ia truly *consumed* by her labors—does she in effect disap-pear, lost behind the work of art that is the perfect meal?[5] Or is it pos-sible that, paradoxically, her activity constitutes a kind of incandescence, a source of heat, light, or even power?

We must be careful not to regard domestic tasks as entirely negative: in servitude there exists power, and drudgery serves as the barrier that both protects and conceals the manner in which this power is exercised.

Walls are confining, but as we have noted, the larder is a place apart, a fantastic realm from which bounty emanates. The wise housewife is aware of the magical powers of the storeroom and will use them to her advantage. This advantage may be construed in several ways. On the most basic level, a well-stocked larder symbolizes domestic prowess; thus it is a source of pride, an emblem of efficiency. In its embodiment of plenty, the larder offers not only a promise of hospitality (as Molokhovets affirms), but also the more crucial appeasement of hunger through motherly or wifely love. If the practical reason for establishing a household unit is to provide freedom from want, then the larder represents the fecundity of the home. Therefore, whoever holds the keys takes control of the site of prolifigacy, and by extension control of her own life, which in many other ways is constrained.[6]

This control takes two forms. On the one hand, it means control over others: The housewife must manage the domestic help, a task which demands constant vigilance, authority, and supple control. Not surprisingly, Molokhovets offers advice in this area, suggesting that the apartment or house be arranged so as to make the role of overseer most convenient. To this end she advises situating the larder (*kladovaia*) adjacent to the maids' room or the pantry (*bufet*); from the larder a hatchway (*liuk*) should lead down to the cold-storage cellar. Such an arrangement proves exceptionally handy for the housewife who because of weak health is unable to visit the unheated larder during cold weather; instead, she can sit at the table in the warm maids' room or pantry and from there manage the distribution of provisions, making sure that nothing extra is smuggled past her out of the larder (Molokhovets 217). In this manner she fulfills the role of the expert housekeeper (*khoziaika*)—household manager, banker, and customs official all in one. (See fig. 5.1.)

This commanding role is not limited solely to the lady of the house but extends as well to the servants in charge of running various parts of the estate. Engel'gardt refers to the old woman who oversees the dining hall as "the commander—I can't call her anything else" (32). That he chooses precisely this metaphor is interesting, deriving as it does from the military, a male province. Engel'gardt's word choice suggests a patronizing kind of deference in place of a genuine effort on his part to "understand splendidly" the complicated patterns of power and subjugation involved in the repetitive tasks of her "command." He goes on to observe that when women are working "*not for the household, but for themselves . . .* all of them know how to work splendidly and in fact do work splendidly" (Engelgardt 164, his italics). Here he recognizes the second, and more crucial, aspect of control associated with household management, for it has to do with a woman's own life.

FIG 5.1. Aleksei Venetsianov, *Morning Report on a Country Estate* (1823). In this early-nineteenth-century genre scene, we see the mistress of the larder going over the inventory with her maidservants. The prosperity of the household is emphasized by the cloth bursting with produce in the foreground.

Much attention has been given the image of the strong woman in Russian literature, particularly in regard to the weak heroes surrounding her. Yet the kind of maneuvering for position that occurs within the domestic circle is less a question of the "transfiguration of humiliation into strength" (Dunham 468) than it is of a conscious desire to wield power. For years, American feminists held a wary (if not contemptuous) attitude toward any celebration of the home, because the woman's position within it seems so obviously bound up with male domination. Yet just as Western critical scholarship has come to reexamine issues of domestic politics,[7] so too must the standard view of the prosperous nineteenth-century Russian woman as victim and martyr be revised. Many women actually enjoyed their domestic role, as we learn from a letter to Molokhovets included in the jubilee edition of *A Gift to Young Housewives*, written by members of the Smolensk Society. They state: "Among those who have signed this address you will not find anyone who is emancipated from domestic work. For us, the rational thriftiness of bees is more appealing" (Toomre 13). Whether in literature or in life, the keeper of the keys need not suffer from a poor self-image or perceive herself as a victim, as long as she can maintain control, the essence of which lies in her awareness of the power to withhold or bestow at will. (See fig. 5.2.) Freedom, after all, is a complicated business. Furthermore, the knowledge that the male observer perceives certain tasks as menial enough to be unworthy of his attention (lest they prove unmanning) enables the woman to carry on as she sees fit. Thus, the activity of many nineteenth-century housewives and housekeepers may retrospectively be seen, in the current lingo, as a sort of "power feminism" (Wolf).[8]

Given this possibility for power, we might speculate that the unhappy lives of the female characters in Karolina Pavlova's 1848 novel, *A Double Life,* could have turned out differently had the women maneuvered in the kitchen instead of in the drawing room. Although Pavlova's story is set almost entirely within interior, domestic spaces, her characters do not stake out the turf where their struggles for power would prove effective. Their battles are waged only socially, with words; they never manipulate with the greater weapon of food. In fact, throughout the novel nothing more substantial than tea ever appears. Pavlova's characters, like their Victorian counterparts, are like decorative pieces in their perfect drawing rooms, exhibiting scant control over the physical space they inhabit; thus it is not surprising that they should have so little control over their lives. Despite the author's obviously negative commentary on women's confinement[9] (the only place Cecily ever feels free is outdoors, riding horseback), she never allows her characters to claim fully autonomous space.

In contrast, an ordinary passage from *Oblomov* illustrates the ways in which women can wield domestic power; it also reveals the complicated combination of subjection and power that is largely concealed from casual view. The housekeeper, Agafiia Matveevna (whose surname, incidentally, is Pshenitsyna, from the word for "wheat," implying both sustenance and fecundity), is busy making pudding in the kitchen when Oblomov enters:

> "Eternally busy!" he said, going in to the housekeeper. "What is this?"
>
> "I'm pounding cinnamon," she answered, looking into the mortar as if into an abyss, and beating mercilessly with the pestle.
>
> "What if I were to disturb you?" he asked, taking her by the elbow and not letting her work.
>
> "Let me go! I still have to pound the sugar and pour off some wine for the pudding. . . ."
>
> "Tell me, what if I were to . . . fall in love with you?"
>
> She smiled.

FIG 5.2. Boris Kustodiev, *Merchant's Wife Drinking Tea* (1923). This prosperous and well-fed woman exudes self-satisfaction and control. The rounded shapes of the teapot, samovar, and creamer mirror her plumpness even as the ripe watermelon and rolls heighten the sense of her fecundity.

"Would you love me?" he asked again.

"Why not? God commanded us to love everyone."

"And if I were to kiss you?" he whispered, bending over so that his breath felt hot on her cheek.

"It's not Holy Week," she said with a smile. (Goncharov 367)

This passage may be read in two opposite ways. The first confirms that Agafiia Matveena's life is one of endless domestic duties. How else should the abyss in the mortar be interpreted if not as a metaphor for the drudgery of her days? In this reading, Agafiia Matveevna is viewed sympathetically as a martyr not only to the domestic cause, but also to the advances of her master. However, the reader knows that Agafiia has already fallen in love with the lethargic Oblomov, even if she can't quite admit it to herself, and this knowledge allows for a second interpretation, in which Agafiia Matveevna, through her labors, transforms not only the ingredients for the pudding but Oblomov as well. Looking into the mortar, she sees an abyss—the erstwhile monotony of her life—but she uses her skill with the mortar to revitalize Oblomov, win his love, and rescue herself from the abyss of dispiriting activity. This ability to transform represents real power.

Goncharov's choice of the word "abyss," in its association with the dark powers, is significant for both readings. In the first interpretation, the seemingly bottomless mortar constitutes an extension of the pagan, and hence unclean, realm traditionally ascribed to women in Russian peasant culture. In the peasant cottage, the corner where the stove is located was also known as the "woman's corner" (*babii ugol*), and it represented profane space. In both physical and metaphorical opposition to the *babii ugol* stood the "beautiful corner" (*krasnyi ugol*), where the icon hung, and which was associated with the sacred domain of the male (Tempest 2, 4). Even in the second, more positive reading of this passage, Agafiia Mataveevna appears as a kitchen wizard who wields an instrument of transformation. Because most men cannot (or choose not to) understand the skill and science underlying menial domestic tasks, they ascribe magical powers to those who carry them out.

Another, quite different, example of the use of food as control comes from Sergei Aksakov's autobiographical saga of life on a Russian estate, *The Childhood Years of Bagrov's Grandson*. In this narrative of his childhood, Aksakov associates his aunt Tat'iana with the larder, which she uses to ensure her own security. The storeroom is off limits to the young Sergei and therefore is a source of great curiosity. One day he sneaks inside and finds a wonderland of goods, including "a large new tub covered with white sackcloth; out of curiosity I lifted the cloth and was astonished to find that the tub was nearly full of bits of sugar" (Aksakov 450). Bursting with his discovery, the boy blurts out his secret to one of the servants, causing her to exclaim: "For twenty years she's been stealing and hoarding this sugar! I bet she has bags of tea and coffee hanging in there, too!" (451). It turns out that Aunt Tat'iana has been squirreling away costly sugar for her dowry; as keeper of the keys, she invests the larder with all of her hopes for the future. The larder represents the sole source of her power—with enough sugar, coffee, and tea, she might be able to bargain for a good marriage. Both Agafiia Matveevna and Aunt Tat'iana, in different ways, use traditional female agency to get what they want; behind their mask of selflessness lies assertive behavior, whether conscious or not. An important distinction between their activities must be noted, however. Unlike Agafiia Matveevna, Tat'iana abuses her position for personal enrichment. Her siphoning off of sugar may seem trivial, but in the long run it threatens the household economy. Twentieth-century Russia offers ample evidence of the ways in which an economy is damaged by the furtive draining of resources from the intended consumers.

At times the distinction between the female keykeeper and the larder she controls becomes hazy in literature, where the larder itself seems to take on female characteristics, and not only because the noun *kladovaia* carries a feminine ending. We have already noted the fecundity that is associated with the larder. We can also perceive a rather prurient interest in the room on the part of certain male characters, who seem more than ordinarily aroused by the secret aspect of the place, by the implicit promise of a "treasure" (*klad*) that they can win by entry. The larder titillates as much as a woman herself does; in this way the secrets of the larder come to be equated with the secrets of the womb. It is hardly surprising, then, that the image of a Peeping Tom should appear, a character type that is not limited solely to the curious young boy, as in Aksakov's tale. We also find a salacious male in Gogol''s story, where Pulkheriia Ivanovna's husband, Afansaii Ivanovich, sits down to observe the activity surrounding the larder. Having just sated his belly with ripe fruits,

> he would sit down under an awning facing the yard and watch how the larder continually revealed and hid its interior and how the girls, pushing one another, would carry in and out piles of all sorts of rubbish in wooden boxes, sieves, and other containers for keeping fruits. A bit later he would send for Pulkheriia Ivanovna or go find her himself and say:
>
> "What might there be for me to eat, Pulkheriia Ivanovna?" (Gogol' 217)

Here the sexual connotations are obvious, strengthened in the original Russian by the juxtaposition of "interior" (*vnutrennost'*)[10] and "girls" (*devki*). Afanasii Ivanovich is fully aware of the larder as the dark recesses of the home, essential to its functioning, and he takes great pleasure in teasing Pulkheriia Ivanovna about this most sensitive area. From time to time, when sleepless at night, Afanasii Ivanovich asks her what would happen if the house suddenly caught on fire. When she doesn't rise to his bait, he continues: "What if our house burned right down, where would we go then?" When Pulkheriia Ivanovna answers that they'd retreat to the outdoor kitchen, he asks, "What if the kitchen burned down?" "Then we'd go to the larder and stay there until a new house was built." Unable to restrain himself, Afanasii Ivanovich triumphantly delivers his final punch: "And if the larder burns?" Pulkheriia Ivanovna can bear no more; the teasing ends with her admonition: "It's a sin to say that, and God punishes talk like that" (Gogol' 218). Significantly, Pulkeriia Ivanovna invokes the highest authority to protect what she perceives as the most sacred part of her home. She genuinely believes in the sanctity of the larder.

The idea of the larder as the innermost core of the home is not without precedent, nor is the belief that power resides within the domestic sphere: The classical world offers evidence enough of this. In Homer's *Odyssey*, for instance, Penelope is the one who holds the keys to the storeroom, symbols of her worthy status. In ancient Rome, the storerooms themselves were protected by domestic gods called penates, whose name is derived from *penus*, the archaic word for larder or cupboard. The *penus* is virtually a sacred place in classical mythology, as the inner sanctum of the temple of Vesta, keeper of the hearth for the entire city of Rome, was known by this name. The Romans immediately understood the meaningful connection between home fires and domestic provisioning. For the Russian peasantry, even up to this century, a house spirit or *domovoi* protected the hearth, and hence the home: It was believed that one could transfer the spirit to a new dwelling by scraping up some of the coals from the old hearth (Ivanits 56).

We can gain additional insight into Russian domestic life by examining the Latin word *domus*, "house," from which *domovoi* derives. Many cultural meanings that result from the root of this word are inscribed with male attributes, such as domination (*dominirovanie*), domineering (*dominiruiushchii*), and domain (*domen*). Through such words, "the house speaks to us precisely as the symbol of rulership, ownership, mastery, power" (Danto 9). Yet, in the Russian language the idea of domesticity is not only related to the masculine sphere of the *domus*; while the adjective *domashnii* can be directly translated as "domestic," another set of words carries the additional connotations of "family- and home-loving" (*semeinyi* and *semeistvennyi*). The etymological and psychological connections between "family" (*sem'ia*) and "semen" or "seed" (*semia*) in Russian should also be noted. Reproduced by seed (semen), the family is a generative entity rooted in place. In Gogol's tale, Pulkeriia Ivanovna's room is bursting with "a multitude of bundles and bags with seeds for flowers, vegetables, watermelons" (Gogol' 213), thereby ensuring the continuity not only of plant life through propagation, but also of the family through nourishment.

As Molokhovets teaches, if you love your family, you must necessarily love your home, and this precept would seem to be as much the Russian ideal as it was in the classical world: "To be a member of a household ... is to be enmeshed in a *philia*, to belong to and to recognize this community as one's own and to have a place in the *oikos* hierarchy" (Booth 20). This idea of communal good is most explicitly represented by the larder, with its promise of sustenance for months and years to come. However, the larder represents more than just plenty; it also demands a special conception of space and time, which requires the keeper to think about ordering and rotating the provisions on shelves as well as regulating their distribution so that the goods will last until the next harvest or, at the very least, sustain the family through the long Russian winter. As anthropologist Mary Douglas writes, "The spacing of provisions provides another aide-memoire for the totality of life within the home" (Douglas 270). If the family is to thrive, there is no place for opportunism or individual self-regard (the Russian proverb states, "A worm spoils the tree; a bad woman ruins the home" [*Cherv' derevo tlit, a zlaia zhena dom izvodit*]). Those who carry the keys to the larder thus wield tremendous power in their ready access to this most important part of the house, which tempts by its very abundance, offering them the chance to dip in or hoard, to think above all of themselves, if they so choose. When necessary, even the most obedient housekeepers will invoke their powers to keep the larder full, as does Engel'gardt's devoted Avdotia, whose sole purpose would appear to be the desire to do everything properly. At the height of the harvest season—coinciding with the height of her powers—she bluntly talks back to her master and actually ends up taking over his house: "During the garden harvest, Avdotia displaced me completely, as though I were not even the master," complains Engel'gardt (Engelgardt 54). This displacement represents a reversal similar to the one that takes place at carnival time, only now, during the harvest, it is women who gain the upper hand, filling the larder with bounty to ensure at least some degree of dominion during the coming year. In this way, from their initial role as mere mistresses of the larder, women are able to move into true *mastery* over the household, becoming both regulators and manipulators of the household, with actual as opposed to titular authority. (See fig. 5.3.)

In ordinary cases, we can assume that this position was not abused. But, like unhappy families, injurious circumstances often prove the most illuminating. Some readers may feel uncomfortable with the treatment of literary text as social document, but nineteenth-century Russian realistic prose actively comments on the daily life that informs it. Reading between the lines, we can learn as much about Russian culture from, say, Tolstoi's description in *Anna Karenina* of what Oblonskii and Levin choose to order in a restaurant[11] as we can from Molokhovets's

Fig 5.3. David Shterenberg, *Breakfast* (1916). A latter-day Eve tempts her mate with an apple. Her direct gaze and gesture contrast sharply with his downcast mien and hidden hand. The cherries are playful, but the knife pointing right at the man threatens. There is no question who controls the foodstuffs at this table.

factual exposition of the recipes for the dishes they eat. The transmission of knowledge works both ways. For many of us, Molokhovets's recipe for *shchi* conjures up all sorts of deeply Russian associations; reading it, we can savor in our minds not only the taste of the soup but a certain atmosphere, a memory of past experience. This associative function explains why Molokhovets's book remains an icon of Russian culture (as the French critic Philippe Gillet has written: "La recette c'est la vie" [Gillet 263]). Literary descriptions can provoke memory and taste in analogous fashion, as Aleksandr Solzhenitsyn poignantly demonstrates in *The Gulag Archipelago*. Even though Solzhenitsyn was starved for reading matter in his prison cell (quite apart from the physical starvation he endured), he could hardly bear to read some nineteenth-century writers: "It was bad, too, to be betrayed by the author of the book you were reading—if he began to drool over food in the greatest detail. Get away from me, Gogol! Get away from me, Chekhov, too! They both had too much food in their books" (Solzhenitsyn 214). Fiction often elucidates the culture from which its characters arise; by scrutinizing what the characters eat and their behavior toward food, we can learn a great deal about societal attitudes.

In this regard, it is instructive to turn to Mikhail Saltykov-Shchedrin's novel *The Golovlevs*, where the autocratic matriarch, Arina Petrovna, wields her power over the larder so perversely that she ultimately destroys her family. In *The Golovlevs*, three generations live out the myth of one big happy family. In the midst of scheming and debauchery, they convince themselves that their most self-centered actions are family-oriented, that their primary concerns are family concerns. Arina Petrovna is in many outward ways a model of nineteenth-century domesticity. Thrifty and pious, she puts up with a drunkard husband and difficult children; what's more, she seems to take the idea of hospitality (*khleb-sol'*) quite seriously (Saltykov-Shchedrin 107). Although Arina Petrovna's privileged life has spared her from ever learning to cook or even lay the table (133), she successfully manages the extensive larders and cellars, and the family estate is filled to overflowing with the fruits of abundant harvests. Most important (and this we learn at the very beginning of the novel), the word "family" is always on Arina Petrovna's lips (104).

By keeping this word on the tip of her tongue, Arina Petrovna plays her part in mythologizing the family. Her children do the same. As Roland Barthes has pointed out, perpetuating myth keeps the reality of one's life at bay and makes the world seem a safe and natural place. This dictum certainly holds true for the Golovlevs. The children, now adults, insist on returning home, hoping for handouts, even though Arina Petrovna kept them half starved in their youth (106). They cannot resist the myth of home as a haven where both physical and emotional sustenance are automatically and unconditionally provided. This conception of home proves entirely false, as does the idea of a nurturing mother always welcoming her children, even the prodigal ones, never ceasing to cater to them.[12]

Instead, the myth of a happy family is revealed for what it all too often is: a struggle for power. Saltykov-Shchedrin accomplishes this debunking by playing in particular on one important aspect of the family myth, that of nourishment. Nourishment becomes the book's prevailing metaphor, a gastronomic conceit that chronicles the family's dyspepsia and eventual demise. Food and eating are used both symbolically and structurally to dramatize the gluttonous appetite for power that the family members share.

In the novel, food indicates familial standing. Arina Petrovna's favorite child is her second son, Porfirii, usually referred to by his nickname, "Little Judas." It is he who always receives the choicest morsels of food from the family table (Saltykov-Shchedrin 108). In Arina Petrovna's code of familial behavior, these "tidbits" (*kusok*, pl. *kuski*) are central; in fact, throughout the novel the *kusok* reappears like so many leftovers day after day. By these tidbits Arina Petrovna wields her power, rewarding or withholding from those around her as she sees fit. The *kusok* is her best manipulative weapon, linked not only to her stinginess (it is, after all, merely a piece, not a whole) but also to her generosity. For Arina Petrovna considers it her maternal duty to give each of her wayward children one last chance after they've gone astray—by tossing them a "bone" or *kusok*. We learn that her deceased daughter, Anna, received the Pogorelka estate as her piece of the pie; and when the eldest son, Stepan, squanders his money, he gets a townhouse in Moscow as his rightful *kusok*. Yet even though Arina Petrovna has many of these *kuski* (112), she feels resentful at the loss of income each tossed "bone" represents. The Russian idiom "It sticks in the throat" (*kusok v glotku ne idet*) would seem to apply here.

Perhaps Arina Petrovna's resentment is well-founded. It turns out that she has been serving up these *kuski* to all of the Golovlev ne'er-do-wells who return to the family hearth, or more aptly, to the larder. As Stepan travels back to Golovlevo after having squandered his *kusok*—consumed his last morsel—he thinks of the others who have returned there before him: his Uncle Misha, whose *kusok* was Arina Petrovna's permission to live on the estate, which he gratefully accepted even though he had to live with the serfs and eat out of the dog's bowl (116); and his Aunt Vera, who eventually died of "moderation" (*umerennost'*, read "malnutrition") because Arina Petrovna reproached her for every bite she took (ibid.). Understandably, such thoughts cause Stepen some anxiety. Already thin and undernourished, he expects he'll get nothing more than dry bread at his mother's (111), but even so the myth of nourishment—emotional if not physical—lures him on.

As Stepan's journey progresses, his anxiety grows, until he begins to doubt that his mother will feed him at all. He calms himself with thoughts of the leftovers and tea she can't possibly refuse him and is heartened by a friend's comment that his own mother could hardly deny him a piece of pie on the holidays—if God in his mercy should intercede on his behalf, that is (114). Stepan's gastronomic musings inflame his appetite, and throughout his journey he assuages his hunger by mooching from others. But even as he appeases his belly, his thoughts (or perhaps the overly salty sausage) lead him toward despair. Suddenly a clear image of his mother appears before him, and he chants four times, "She will devour me" (*zaest ona menia*) (115). As if this consuming image[13] weren't enough, Stepan is greeted upon his arrival home by a cold stare from his mother and a terrifying outburst from his infirm father. Catching sight of Stepan, the old man crows like a rooster, laughs wildly, and cries out three times, "She'll eat you up!" (*S"est! s"est! s"est!*) (116). This word *s"est* continues to reverberate deep in Stepan's consciousness, until he becomes entirely obsessed with eating in his effort not to be eaten himself.

Stepan's mental state is not as odd as it may at first appear. As the critic Norman Brown suggests, to live is to eat or to be eaten (Brown 169). Even though Stepan is powerless, his choice for survival is clear, and he consumes with voracity the spoiled food and leftovers doled out to him. Tellingly, though, his dreams of food and eating are tied up with the idea of family reconciliation, a dream of unconditional love, when everyone will come together "to feast upon the fatted calf" (Saltykov-Shchedrin 118). Arina Petrovna's abuse of her maternal, nurturing, *household* power lies at the root of the family's manifold dysfunctions, and in this respect *The Golovlevs* appears as a cautionary tale not unlike *A Gift to Young Housewives* in its subtext.

Stepan's interest in the household economy is lively, if furtive, and very soon he learns that there truly is something rotten in Golovlevo. The storerooms are filled to bursting, and new produce is continually being toted in, but Arina Petrovna refuses to allow any of the fresh goods to be eaten until the spoiled ones have been used up. This system troubles Stepan, even though he knows that if no rotten meat were on hand for supper, he might not eat at all (125). Stepan eventually comes to realize that nothing more than a myth sustains him and at last relinquishes even this evanescent hope for maternal sustenance. He never again asks his mother for anything; in fact, Stepan never says another word, and shortly thereafter he dies.

Chapter one of *The Golovlevs* ends with Stepan's death; as chapter two begins, his brother Pavel is dying. In the interim the serfs have been

emancipated, and Judas has taken control of Golovlevo as his share of
the divided estate. Arina Petrovna has retained control only of the capital, which soon dwindles to an insubstantial amount. These events pre-
cipitate crises for Arina Petrovna, either real or imagined. She pictures
the liberated serfs eating her out of house and home:

> At other times she pictured herself walking through her deserted house
> while the servants sat in their quarters feeding their faces. Then she visu-
> alized them surfeited, tossing leftovers under the table. Or she imagined
> going down to the larder and finding her maids there gorging themselves,
> wanting to reprimand them but restraining herself as if something were
> stuck in her throat. (132)

Arina Petrovna's worst fears about losing her home come true, though
not because of her former serfs. Rather, the cause is Judas. Unlike other
masters, when Judas inherits Golovlevo he assumes the role of actual, not
just titular, head of household and becomes involved in the minutiae of
estate management. Having learned well from his mother's example, he
calculates the exact amount of food his mother consumes at Golovlevo
and holds her accountable for it. And because he has only recently eaten
at his benefactor's table, Judas's betrayal, like that of his biblical namesake,
appears all the more heinous.

The new balance of power is unbearable for Arina Petrovna, so she
moves to Dubrovino to take up residence with Pavel. For the first time,
she feels how her authority has eroded. This realization causes her to exclaim, "I'm not gnawed remains!" (*Ia ne ogryzok!*) (133). Now that she no
longer holds the keys to the larder, Arina Petrovna is fearful of becoming
precisely that which she fed to her son and her serfs: discards.

After Pavel dies, all of the provisions at Dubrovino as well as
Golovlevo belong to Judas, and Arina Petrovna's fear of being "the
eaten" instead of the eater initially causes her to lose all interest in food.
Because she has been reduced to just another "extra mouth" (*lishnii rot*)
(152) in a household where every *kusok* counts, she no longer feels like
eating. She is calmed only by the thought that she can move to
Pogorelka, the *kusok* she once tossed her daughter Anna; however, this
move places her in the uncomfortable position of eating the metaphorical leftovers. Interestingly, as soon as Arina Petrovna is reduced to beg-
ging food from Judas, we begin to feel sympathy for her and the bad diet
she is forced to endure. Like Stepan before her, she begins to experience
gastronomic daydreams in which she no longer has to tolerate Judas for
the sake of a tidbit (*radi sladkogo kuska*) (157); instead, she dreams "of the

Golovlev stores, of the carp in the Dubrovino ponds, of the chickens being fattened in the poultry yards that had been hers" (156).

The Golovlevs is filled to overflowing with instances of food imagery used to characterize familial relations; enumerating all of them is not within the scope of this essay. But several additional points may be made. First, it is interesting to note that the secrets of domestic power are unveiled in the novel not by Arina Petrovna, as one might expect, but by Judas, the overpampered son, slightly feminized by his favored relationship with his mother. In this tale of extreme abuse, Judas reveals (or rather, true to his name, betrays) the means by which women's power is traditionally exercised. Saltykov-Shchedrin thus offers insight into domestic power from the perspective of a feminized male, who serves as a sort of bridge between the sexes for those unable to make the greater leap to a differently gendered point of view.

A second consideration is that the more obsessed Arina Petrovna and Judas become with food, the more they run off at the mouth; here food as a manipulative device is connected with that other source of oral gratification, talking. Michel Jeanneret has written that "oral pleasure is also a matter of speech, the mouth is also the laboratory where one creates discourse: eating and speaking maintain a relationship of solidarity, of similarity" (Jeanneret 119).[14] The blathering of mother and son becomes a kind of verbal intoxication (*zapoi prazdnomysliia*) (Saltykov-Shchedrin 222), and they can never get their fill. Like other abusive substances, their idle talk is toxic, lacking in any real nourishment, and ultimately harmful to others. Judas in particular manipulates those around him by forcing them both to eat and to endure his prattle before he will agree to any genuine discourse. And it is not surprising that his empty words often center on reminiscences of past meals and abundance. Judas knows that his mother and other keepers of the larder exercise control and indulge their whims in order to test the existence of their informal power, which is not explicitly acknowledged but always felt. By prattling on and holding others in their web, they prove their own power over a captive audience, held frozen at the dinner table by the implicit threat of the carrot being removed.

Judas's power plays are often subtly orchestrated, as when he tries to convince Anninka to stay at Golovlevo, but in the case of his mistress Evpraksiia, he makes no bones about offering her tasty morsels in exchange for her favors. Not incidentally, Evpraksiia has a marvelous back, repeatedly and admiringly compared to a stove (*plita*). And Judas finds the temptation to kindle a fire in this "stove" all too great, succumbing to the sin of fornication. To his horror Evpraksiia becomes pregnant; and his embarrassment becomes unbearable when Arina Petrovna gleefully calculates that the intercourse must have taken place on a fast day.

The idea of fornicating on a fast day begs a comparison between oral and sexual forms of graitification, particularly when we see Judas as an indulger in both types of intercourse (although one might question whether prattling, the egocentric and self-indulgent form of monologue, is indeed intercourse or merely masturbation). The real issue is Judas's craving for pleasure and satiation, which for him, as for the rest of his family, is tied up with the thirst for power. The Golovlevs have found a most convenient way to attain and wield power; they do it by means of food, recognizing that at the heart of authority lies the ability to eat. Capriciously, even maliciously, they desire to control the behavior of others, sometimes to the point of risking their survival. Even though the Golovlev tables are lavishly set and their larders full, no real nourishment takes place; eating is merely an empty extension of power. Thus it becomes inevitable that one Golovlev after another should die as the myth of the family as a nurturing body is proved invalid.

Although the Golovlevs represent an extreme case, the novel provides insight into the intricacies of familial relationships and the uses of power within domestic circles. If the mandate of the family is to provide plenty, then Arina Petrovna and Judas abuse their positions as managers of the larder by manipulating the plenty at Golovlevo to control others, in effect transgressing against familial norms. Unlike Pulkheriia Ivanovna, who invokes God's name to protect the larder and is unable to sin even in thought, Arina Petrovna behaves selfishly and hypocritically, and a whole pattern of moral decay ensues. As Molokhovets suggests and the Golovlevs evince, it is not enough for a family simply to eat together; physical sustenance must go hand in hand with the spiritual in order for true nurturing to take place.

Throughout the first decade of this century, domestic life remained fairly stable for those housewives who chose to engage themselves fully in household management. But with the 1917 Revolution, drastic changes occurred as the new society worked energetically to "liberate" women by encouraging them to leave the home. Much of the Soviet propaganda focused on the kitchen, which was viewed as a hindrance to women's full development. The new rhetoric proclaimed women's liberation from domestic chores, but in fact women were not so much liberated from the home as the home was forcibly taken from them. They were urged to think beyond the needs of the immediate family (one hortatory pamphlet from 1923 was entitled "Down with the Private Kitchen!" [Doloi chastnuiu kukhniu! Rothstein and Rothstein 31]) as communal eating was touted over separate family meals. Because women were now expected to nurture not only the family but also the nation, it is hardly surprising that their work should increase.

At home, women no longer commanded extensive larders, which simply did not exist.[15] They did not even have pantries, let alone real cupboard space. Most urban houses had been converted to multi-family dwellings, with a single communal kitchen for each apartment. Thus the site of women's power was severely diminished, and in many cases entirely lost. The cramped, difficult housing conditions of the Soviet era are frequently cited as the root cause of the family's demise, but I would suggest that the problem goes beyond the lack of adequate living space in urban apartments. To paraphrase Molokhovets, many of the various unpleasantnesses in family life can be ascribed to the fact that the housewife is now unable to practice household management: She has lost her larder and hence her control.

Until the period of perestroika, at least some families were able to find comfort in thoughts of the abundance of the communal larder, which replaced their own, personal stores, and government propaganda played on this vulnerability for all it was worth. The 1953 edition of *A Book of Tasty and Healthy Food* (a sort of Soviet *Gift to Young Housewives*) begins with an introduction entitled "Toward Abundance!" (K izobiliiu!). Its eleven pages confirm the old saw that a picture says more than a thousand words: each page contains text within a cream-colored block, surrounded on all sides by sepia-tone photographs of the Soviet Union's bounty. The first page offers a literal representation of the text's enthusiastic title—a field of ripe wheat with a threshing machine looming on the horizon. On the second page, bolstering words of praise for the Communist Party's decrees, the photograph depicts a store with satisfied shoppers looking over an array of baked goods; in heaps and piles are stacked a vast assortment of traditional breads, cookies, and cakes (*vatrushki, sushki, keksy, rulety, karavai, bulki, korzhiki, batony, pechen'ia*). (See fig. 5.4.) The next page shows the same sort of variety, only here we find sausages and meats, from slender hotdogs to massive joints. And so the nation's abundance is celebrated page after page: fish from the sea; preserves; chicken and ducks; all sorts of cheeses; dairy products and coffee; melons and peaches; cauliflower, carrots, cabbages, tomatoes, and potatoes; and finally grapes, apples, and pears. These images bring us to the end of the text and the inevitable "creation in life of mankind's

Fig 5.4. Il'ia Mashkov, *Soviet Breads* (1936). The connection between political power and sustenance is made explicit in this Stalin-era painting depicting the Soviet Union as a literal cornucopia of breads. Mashkov has ingeniously arranged the breadstuffs to represent the union of peasant and worker: The batons in the background appear as sheaves of wheat, while the various round rolls in the center resemble cogs in the industrial wheel.

age-old dream of the building of a communist society, of an abundant, happy, and joyous life" (Sivolap 17).

Despite attempts to eradicate the family kitchen and create a truly communal society,[16] the kitchen did not lose its hold on either the public or the private imagination. We need only recall the site of one of the great ideological spats of this century to realize that the kitchen remains a place of power. In 1959 Richard Nixon and Nikita Khrushchev met in Moscow's Sokol'niki Park, where an American exhibition had recently opened as part of the first cultural exchange following the long Stalin years. The theme of the exhibition was "The American Home," and the historic debate took place in its kitchen, complete with a gleaming stove, an efficient dishwasher, and ample cupboard space. Almost as much as the famous Checkers speech, this modern, all-electric American kitchen helped to further Nixon's career. How could Khrushchev be a major player in the world if he could not even provide his country's women with their own kitchens? Khrushchev did not hold the keys to the world's larder; and with the lure of such shiny cabinets in the background, there could be no real contest between Russia and America.

Had men, then, coopted women's traditional province, turning the kitchen into a place for power plays on a worldly rather than domestic scale? Or had women's space simply become so curtailed and unpleasant that the house (*dom*) is now no more than a *domovina*, the Russian diminutive for "house" that in folk parlance refers to the grave? Sadly, on the eve of the twenty-first century, the latter seems more likely. Here Russian women now reside, captive to the drudgery of their domestic tasks, yet lacking the empowerment that their nineteenth-century forebears could enjoy.

Notes

1. Twenty-nine editions of *A Gift to Young Housewives* were published through 1917, the year of the Russian Revolution (for a complete list, see Toomre 633). With the advent of perestroika, Molokhovets's recipes reappeared in Russia, and her book was reprinted in 1991 (Molokhovets). Before *A Gift to Young Housewives*, the only popular cookbooks were those written by Katerina Avdeeva, who published four between 1842 and 1848 (see Toomre 9).

2. Molokhovets stresses that the responsibilities of a good family woman (*sem'ianinka*) are moral (*nravstvennyi*) as well as domestic (*khoziaistvennyi*) (Molokhovets 216). In this regard her work may be compared to that of the American writer Catherine Beecher, who in her popular *Treatise on Domestic Economy* (1841) takes pains to connect good Christian behavior and women's familial duties. For a discussion of Beecher's work and American domestic politics, see Gillian Brown 13–38.

3. Ironically, Afanasii Ivanovich's stomach pains presage his creator's demise, although Gogol''s extreme discomfort was brought about by a refusal to eat rather than by overindulgence. For further information, Gogol' 1967, 18–19 and Karlinsky 278, who also mentions the perverse detail that in his death agonies Gogol' was surrounded by loaves of freshly baked bread in an apparent attempt to assuage some of the pain.

4. The distinction between housewife and housekeeper is of less concern here than the similiarity of their roles, since the housewife is, in effect, the head servant.

5. In Western society, the "denial of self and the feeding of others" are attributes of the ideal woman (Bordo 1993, 118). Such paragons are vividly portrayed in the English Victorian novel, where many female characters effectively disappear as they waste away from selfless hunger. See Michie 12–29 and Bordo 1989.

6. It must be reiterated that we are speaking of the autarkic household, one that is materially self-sufficient, with a wife or matriarch or housekeeper in charge of a well-stocked larder. The difficult conditions that obtained for peasant women in nineteenth-century Russia obviously do not apply here.

7. For an excellent overview of more than a century's discussion of the place of women in American society, see Kerber.

8. Power feminism above all involves a positive self-image instead of a conception of oneself as victim. The power feminist is a confident woman who embraces a "psychology of plenty" (Wolf 107) that enables her to recognize subleties of thought and to stop seeing the world in terms of antagonistic polarities (female/male, feminist/sexist) that only perpetuate a sense of oppression.

9. Pavlova's highly intellectual concerns aroused the scorn of her contemporaries, who were offended by her lack of domestic interests. The poet Nikolai Nekrasov, commonly praised as the champion of Russia's oppressed women, did not feel as charitable toward Pavlova. His poem "My Disappointment" (Moe razocharovanie, 1851), a parody of Pavlova's poem "Quadrille," relates how the poet meets the woman of his dreams, who is more interested in discussing Hegel and reading Tacitus than in making pickles and preserves. To the poet's horror, he one day finds his love in the kitchen: "Having torn Lamartine to shreds, / My fiancée was placing pies on the paper / And putting them in the oven!! / I watched with horror / As she mixed the dough by hand, / And then tasted the pie" (*Rasterzav na kloch'ia Lamartina, / Na bumagu klala pirozhki / I sazhala v pech' moia nevesta!! / Ia smotret' bez uzhasa ne mog, / Kak ona rukoi mesila testo, / Kak potom otvedala pirog*) (Nekrasov 208–209).

10. Cf. the meaning of "entrails" or "intestines" for the plural form of *vnutrennost'*.

11. To emphasize his refinement, Oblonskii orders an entirely French meal consisting of *soupe printanière, turbot, sauce Beaumarchais, poularde à l'estragon,* and *macédoine de fruits*. In contrast, Levin chooses the archetypically Russian cabbage soup (*shchi*) and buckwheat groats (*grechnevaia kasha*). The dichotomy between the two men, and between the two opposing camps in Russia of Westernizers and Slavophiles, is dramatized throughout the passage by the food they order.

12. In this context it is interesting to compare Robert Frost's gender-differentiated definitions of home, as expressed in his poem "The Death of the Hired Hand": [Husband]: "Home is the place where, when you have to go

there, / They have to take you in." [Wife]: "I should have called it / Something you somehow haven't to deserve." In an interview, Frost remarked that this latter ideal is "the feminine way of it, the mother way," juxtaposing it to the father's way. Arina Petrovna would appear to reverse Frost's conception. See Richard Poirier, *Robert Frost: The Work of Knowing* (New York: Oxford UP, 1977), 255.

13. The image of the devouring woman is present in many cultures. See Bordo 1993, 117.

14. See also Louis Marin's discussion of orality and its relation to the word in Marin, *Food for Thought* (Baltimore: Johns Hopkins UP, 1989), esp. 35–38. Ronald LeBlanc treats orality in Gogol' in his excellent article "Satisfying Khlestakov's Appetite: The Semiotics of Eating in *The Inspector General*," *Slavic Review* (Fall 1988): 483–98.

15. In *House and Family*, a recent encyclopedia of domestic concerns, there is no separate entry for "larder" (*kladovaia*); the word is mentioned only under the entry for "rural house" (*sel'skii dom*). Interestingly, however, the Introduction makes claims similar to those made by Molokhovets a century earlier, namely, that the family is the nucleus of society that provides not only physical but also spiritual strength. See A. I. Timush et al., *Dom i sem'ia. Kratkaia entsiklopediia* (Kishinev: Glavnaia redaktsiia Moldavskoi Sovetskoi Entsiklopedii, 1987).

16. In *The Trial of a Housewife*, an early Soviet *agitsud* or agitational trial in the form of a play, the prosecutor states that "the anti-community feeling of the housewife is an enemy of the socialist state, it hinders the construction of a new way of life" (R. D. 21).

Works Cited

Aksakov, S. T. 1958. *Detskie gody Bagrova-vnuka*. Moscow: Gos. izd-vo khudozhestvennoi literatury.

Bakhtin, M. M. 1981. "Forms of Time and of the Chronotope in the Novel." In *The Dialogic Imagination*, ed. Michael Holquist, 84–258. Austin: U of Texas P.

Barthes, Roland. 1957. *Mythologies*. Paris: Éditions du Seuil.

Booth, William James. 1993. *Households: On the Moral Architecture of the Economy*. Ithaca: Cornell UP.

Bordo, Susan R. 1989. "The Body and the Reproduction of Femininity: A Feminist Appropriation of Foucault." In *Gender/Body/Knowledge: Feminist Reconstructions of Being and Knowing*, ed. Alison M. Jaggar and Susan R. Bordo, 13–33. New Brunswick: Rutgers UP.

———. 1993. *Unbearable Weight: Feminism, Western Culture, and the Body*. Berkeley: U of California P.

Brown, Gillian. 1990. *Domestic Individualism: Imagining Self in Nineteenth-Century America*. Berkeley: U of California P.

Brown, Norman. 1966. "Food." In *Love's Body*, 162–65. New York: Vintage.

Danto, Arthur C. 1990. "Abide/Abode." In *Housing: Symbol, Structure, Site*, ed. Lisa Taylor, 8–9. New York: Cooper-Hewitt Museum and Rizzoli.

Douglas, Mary. 1993. "A Kind of Space." In *Home: A Place in the World*, ed. Arien Mack, 261–81. New York: New York UP.

Dunham, Vera Sandomirsky. 1960. "The Strong-Woman Motif." In *The Transformation of Russian Society: Aspects of Social Change since 1861*, ed. Cyril E. Black, 459–83. Cambridge: Harvard UP.

Engelgardt, Aleksandr Nikolaevich. 1993. *Letters from the Country, 1872–1887*. Translated and edited by Cathy A. Frierson. New York: Oxford UP.

Gillet, Philippe. 1987. *Le Goût et les Mots: Littérature et gastronomie (14e–20e siècles)*. Paris: Payot.

Gogol', Nikolai. 1967. *Letters of Nikolai Gogol*. Edited by Carl R. Proffer. Ann Arbor: U of Michigan P.

———. 1975. "Starosvetskie pomeshchiki." In *Sochineniia v dvukh tomakh*, vol. 1, 209–30. Moscow: Khudozhestvennaia literatura.

Goncharov, I. A. 1984. *Oblomov*. Perm': Permskoe knizhnoe izd-vo.

Ivanits, Linda J. 1989. *Russian Folk Belief*. Armonk, N.Y.: M. E. Sharpe.

Jeanneret, Michel. 1985. "Littérature et gastronomie." In *Papers on French Seventeenth Century Literature*, ed. Ronald W. Tobin, Papers on French Seventeenth Century Literature, Biblio 17. Paris.

Karlinsky, Simon. 1976. *The Sexual Labyrinth of Nikolai Gogol*. Cambridge: Harvard UP.

Kerber, Linda K. 1988. "Separate Spheres, Female Worlds, Woman's Place: The Rhetoric of Women's History." *Journal of American History* 75, no. 1 (June): 9–39.

Michie, Helena. 1987. *The Flesh Made Word: Female Figures and Women's Bodies*. New York: Oxford UP.

Molokhovets, Elena. 1991. *Podarok molodym khoziaikam ili sredstvo k umen'sheniiu raskhodov v domashnem khoziaistve*. Moscow: Polikom. (Reprint of 4th Moscow printing of 22nd edition, Saint Petersburg: Tipografiia N. N. Klobukova, 1901.)

Nekrasov, N. A. 1948. *Stikhotvoreniia 1838–1856*. Vol. 1. Moscow: OGIZ.

Pavlova, Karolina. 1978. *A Double Life*. Translated by Barbara Heldt. Ann Arbor: Ardis Publishers.

R. D. 1927. *Sud nad domashnei khoziaikoi*. Moscow-Leningrad: Gos. izd-vo.

Rothstein, Halina, and Robert A. Rothstein. 1993. "The Beginnings of Soviet Culinary Arts." Paper presented at the conference "Food in Russian History and Culture," Russian Research Center, Harvard University, October 1.

Saltykov-Shchedrin, M. E. 1946. *Gospoda Golovlevy*. In *Izbrannye sochineniia*. Moscow-Leningrad: OGIZ.

Sivolap, I. K., et al. 1953. *Kniga o vkusnoi i zdovoroi pishche*. Moscow: Pishchepromizdat.

Solzhenitsyn, Aleksandr I. 1973. *The Gulag Archipelago, 1918–1956*. Vol. 1. Trans. Thomas P. Whitney. New York: Harper and Row.

Tempest, Snejana. 1993. "Stovelore in Russian Folklife." Paper presented at the conference "Food in Russian History and Culture," Russian Research Center, Harvard University, October 1.

Toomre, Joyce. 1992. *Classic Russian Cooking: Elena Molokhovets' A Gift to Young Housewives*. Bloomington: Indiana UP.

Wolf, Naomi. 1993. *Fire with Fire: The New Female Power and How It Will Change the Twenty-first Century*. New York: Random House.

6

THE RITUAL FABRICS OF

RUSSIAN VILLAGE WOMEN

Mary B. Kelly

The Spiritual Power of Cloth in Village Ritual Life

REMNANTS OF ANCIENT GODDESS beliefs were part of nineteenth-century
Russian folk culture, and rituals to honor the goddess were supervised
by women; it was also her image that they embroidered on their ritual
clothing and textiles. This goddess figure, which duplicates images of the
female deity found on Russian Neolithic ceramics, can be understood as
the protectress of home and families as well as the bringer of harvests
and fertility to people and animals.

The nineteenth-century embroideries discussed in this essay are embellished with strange and archaic-looking goddess figures. Produced,
stitch by stitch, by Russian village women, whose lives were limited by a
lack of formal education and a strictly controlled, stratified society, they
are found throughout Russia, from the far north, down along the Volga,
to the southern borders. The images extend, in slightly altered form, into
Ukraine, Belarus, and parts of Central and Eastern Europe. Found primarily in museum collections, they were collected in areas secluded by
mountains or forests and dominated by agricultural life. Women played
an active role in this life with its seasonal rhythms, taking part in planting
and harvest rites; initiating and controlling rites of birth, marriage, and
death; worshipping female as well as male deities that had come down to
them in folk memory from pre-Christian times; and creating images of
these goddesses on their embroidery and weavings.

Aside from their historical and aesthetic value, these textiles carried a vital spiritual function. This was their most important contribution, for unlike practitioners of other arts, the textile artists had an additional motive: they made the cloths so that the fabric would have spiritual power. Russian ethnography has linked the Great Goddess, whose image appears on so many cloths made for folk rituals, with pre-Christian religious beliefs. Moreover, Russian archeologists point out that this figure, with its upraised hands and accompanying powerful fertility symbols, is similar in style and usage to Russian Neolithic goddess figures. Certainly the goddess symbol was embroidered again and again by Russian women because they believed that her image protected them, fertilized their crops, and sanctified those who enfolded themselves in her fabrics. By reproducing the goddess on cloth, they produced a sacred object that had meaning for them and that they passed down to their daughters and granddaughters in dowries.

Given the recent interest in women's religious history and women's ways of communicating, it is time to reevaluate the role of Russian women in the creation and maintenance of religious folk traditions. Also, as information becomes more available, textiles that were secluded and inaccessible in museum collections can now be appraised and assessed. This essay documents the circumstances under which these textiles were produced, embroidery was taught, and symbols were preserved by a female tradition straddling multiple generations. I shall describe and explain the images of the female deities and their accompanying clusters of symbols, as well as analyze the specific power and significance of the symbols to their makers and users. Russian village women contributed to Russian culture by preserving ancient religious symbols into the twentieth century, enabling us to partially decode their meaning and understand portions of early religious ideas and beliefs.

The Goddess on the Cloth

Who was the goddess, and why does her image appear on Russian cloths and clothing? When first glancing at the figures on the nineteenth-century Russian embroideries displayed in ethnographic museums or published in embroidery texts, many observers assume, as did the earliest collectors and researchers, that they are "dolls" or "dancing girls." However, the perceptive Mme Shabel'skaia, who worked with the village women on her estate in the mid-nineteenth century and eventually assembled a huge embroidery collection, referred to the figures as "idols." She noted their religious nature, commenting that the embroideries served "to decorate the temples of idols, they [the embroideries] hung in the guise of sacrifices on the sacred trees" (Sidamon-Eristoff 2). At approximately the same time (1872), V. V. Stasov, a noted art historian, published the first collection of Russian folk embroideries. The bulk of the plates in this essay show embroideries on which the female deities are central.

A contemporary scholar, Viktor M. Vasilenko, maintains that when Stasov published the designs from the folk textiles, he was the first to identify the antiquity of the folk motifs. He looked at carvings on wooden boards used to mold gingerbread and said, "This is not an art of rough bakers, but an art in which there is much of the past." Vasilenko considered Stasov "very brave" to make this assertion because in the first half of the nineteenth century everybody *knew about* folk art, but nobody *understood* it. Stasov collected it, published examples along with his comments, and then, according to Vasilenko, everybody *saw* its antiquity.[1] Stasov's encouragement of Shabel'skaia and her collection of folk textiles was crucial to the development and preservation of her extensive collection, much of which is now housed in the Ethnographic Museum in St. Petersburg.

In the early twentieth century, the eminent Russian scholar V. A. Gorodtsov identified the figures on the folk textiles as goddesses, remnants of the Great Goddess religion. About the figures on embroideries he said, "Goddess, Queen of heaven and earth, she is the beginning of life and mother of all. To her belongs the air, earth and water. She is Queen of everything" (18). He noted that the figures on the cloth bore many similarities to those from prehistory—specifically their upraised arms, their association with water and grain, their accompaniment by birds. These similarities led Russian ethnographers to take a second look at the textiles as survivals of earlier religious beliefs.

On Russian soil, female deities have been identified in small sculptures postdating the Paleolithic era. Large-breasted and big-bellied goddesses from the Tambov region contrast to slim-figured figurines from the Lake Baikal area. With the change from hunting cultures to agriculture in the Neolithic era, the female deity became "mother of the moist earth" (Rybakov 1981, 474). On Russian ceramic figures from Trypole, the goddess, bringer of fertility to crops, even has grains of wheat impressed into her body (Gimbutas 205). Gimbutas notes that although aspects of the deity change, she is essentially the same goddess. As the bringer of water for good harvests, she has inscribed on her pregnant stomach the "fertile field" symbol, later seen on much nineteenth-century embroidery. "The idea of grain and seed as the beginning of

new life permeates all the plastic art of the middle and late Tripillian periods," remarks Academician Rybakov (1965, 19), whose studies of
Neolithic figurines explicitly link them with symbols found on peasant
embroidery (1981, 471–527).

A Bronze Age bracelet (700 B.C.) from a proto-Slavonic Baltic site
records additional iconography. The goddess, crowned by the sun, with
her hands raised, rides in a double-headed sun chariot. A later version
(600 B.C.) documents the goddess in a sun chariot drawn by birds
(*Russian Embroidery* 16). These features are retained on Russian jewelry,
particularly on women's fibulae from the fifth through seventh centuries
of our own era. Vasilenko documents numerous instances of goddesses
whose upraised arms hold birds or who have sun discs incised on their
bodies that decorate metal fibulae (1977, figs. 30, 31). By 600 A.D.
sources indicate the goddess's name—Berehinia. The sixth-century
Byzantine historian Procopius gives an account of the Slavs who worshipped trees and "bereginy": female spirits of the lake and riverbanks.
Taboo for Christians, "Bereginia" was castigated by clerics who were
afraid of her worship during the annual "Russalye" or Midsummer festivities.

A virgin water deity and bringer of dews and mists for the fields,
Berehinia exemplified one aspect of the goddess's fertile power. A second
name, Mokosh, meaning "bread," "fruitfulness," or "harvest," also comes
down to us as a kind of earth goddess similar to the Greek Demeter.
Human fertility is designated by the name Rozhanitsa, the Mother
Goddess who gives birth to children. Each of these aspects and names
reflects specific needs of the community, and the deities were invoked at
different times and situations. However, over time the attributes became
so muddied and intermingled that it is often impossible to accurately
identify a goddess on an embroidery. In this situation, other researchers
stress the essential power of the female deity as single, yet having multiple attributes or aspects. I agree that this simplifies the discussion, and I
have adopted that premise here.[2]

Textiles recording goddess images date from the late fifteenth century.
In *Russkoe narodnoe iskusstvo*, we can trace the evolution of goddess
images on folk textiles from the fifteenth through the twentieth centuries. I. A. Boguslavskaia includes a photograph of a white fifteenth-
century embroidered cloth on which a goddess, a tree of life, and a deer
are clearly shown (161, 162). Beside it, on the facing page, we see a late-
seventeenth-century Sirin goddess with upraised hands, the figure of a
female deity with the wings and tail of a bird. On an eighteenth-century
pearl headdress the goddess is accompanied by birds and a tree of life

(163), while on nineteenth- and twentieth-century towels we again see the goddess figure with birds and suns (177, 178). Thus in the space of a few pages, the goddess image is shown as it was first seen in the fifteenth century, in its seventeenth- and eighteenth-century versions, and as it appears on nineteenth- and twentieth-century cloth.

Ethnographic data about nineteenth-century folklife, gathered in the 1930s by Vasilenko and others, provide details about who the goddess was and what her worship meant to the agricultural population. Preserved in tales, rites, and festivals, myths of female deities recur in Russia and the whole region extending southward into the Balkans. Bereginia was the subject of many tales and superstitions connected with water. Village women warned Vasilenko not to swim in waters where the Bereginia lived.[3] As a water goddess, she was depicted on embroidery in double-headed boats, while on folk woodcarving she had the form of a fish-tailed mermaid. A springtime goddess, Bereginia was generally portrayed surrounded by plants, sprouting vines, and birds. Given her role as the bringer of springtime sunshine, women showed her holding solar disks or riding in a sun chariot. In fig. 6.1, her head is surrounded by an aureole of solar rays. Two rayed sun disks are shown beside her as she rides on the double-headed solar boat, which is embroidered with small sprouting branches.

Since Bereginia was also the patroness of spinning, women brought their distaffs and spindles to the banks of rivers and brooks on her feast days so that she could spin. This practice, as described by Vasilenko in the interview cited above, involved placing the *prialki* or spinning distaffs up in the branches of the trees along watercourses, particularly on Fridays. On these days, Bereginia's feast, no woman would spin or "the goddess's eyes would be polluted."

Midsummer Night, the goddess's great feast, was celebrated almost everywhere in Russia with fire and water. Huge bonfires were lit; people jumped over them for purification, and later went swimming in brooks and rivers for the same reason. Girls dedicated wreaths to her and sent these or small effigies of the goddess downstream. Wild dancing was characteristic of these celebrations, and, to judge from the sermons against this dancing, women played a powerful role in the festivities. Priests in medieval Russia who saw their congregations led astray assailed women from the pulpit: "For a woman dancing is called Satan's bride and the Devil's lover, spouse of the demon" (Rybakov 1968, 39). A clerical description of the Russalye points out that "at night men, women, and girls come together for excitement and for immoral talk and demonic songs and for dancing and for jumping and for deeds against God" (40).

FIG 6.1. The Goddess, with arms lowered, rides a double-headed sun chariot, sprouting small branches. Her head is rayed, sun-like, and she is flanked by sun disks.

While dancing, women wore decorated bracelets that clicked as they moved, and some of the bracelets that survive today are decorated with images of the wildly dancing women. The ritual cloths made for the festivities also portray the fires and the goddess (Rybakov 1968, 42).

During autumn harvests, the goddess Mokosh was celebrated, and her image on cloth was accompanied by sheaves of wheat. By wintertime, as the agricultural year ended, the Mother Goddess, or Rozhanitsa, was honored by special days extending through the Christmas holidays. We see her birth-giving powers celebrated on cloths made for the holiday on which her figure, with legs outspread, was the dominant image. Facing her, at each side, stand huge reindeer, or large reindeer horns sprout directly from her head. Small children emerge from her body or are shown in her arms or her skirt.

We may never know just who the Russian goddess, in all her aspects, really was, nor what her rites meant to those who participated in them. What is remarkable, however, is how frequently and persistently her image was imprinted on Russian textiles. Museums have collected hundreds upon hundreds of such goddess textiles, and many pieces can be seen in Russia and in the United States, specifically in collections at the Brooklyn Museum, the Cleveland Museum of Art, and the Boston Museum of Fine Arts. Was this goddess the same Great Goddess from prehistory? Again, no conclusive answers suggest themselves, but at least one scholar has remarked on the ethnographic similarities between the archaic material and the nineteenth-century textiles:

> In drawing the connection between the prehistoric and the contemporary, we should add that not only are the actual figures similar, but they are placed in similar settings of plant, animal and human motifs. Furthermore, what we find in extensive ethnographic work that was done in the Slavic and East European areas starting in the late nineteenth century is exactly what we would expect as remnants of a former system of belief in a Great Goddess. In the arts we find sacred cloths such as the one here. In ritual, we find agrarian festivals such as the Russalye, a festival in which a female being is supposed to bring crop fertility to the fields. As might be expected if this were a remnant of a former religious practice, Russalye is both taken seriously by the peasants and looked down upon by the church. (Kononenko 17)

And in *Language of the Goddess,* Maria Gimbutas notes that "the old European sacred images and symbols were never totally uprooted . . . they could have disappeared only with the total extermination of the female population" (318).

Identification and Classification: A Visual First Step

How do we recognize the goddess on these pieces? Russian examples, fortunately, are among the easiest to identify. The goddess figures are large, centrally placed, and clearly delineated. They face forward, are crowned or horned, and have ample skirts. The arms are either raised (in the so-called "maiden position," which indicated springtime embroideries) or lowered (the "mother position," for later solstice embroideries) (*Russian Embroidery* 30). Often the goddess holds aloft in each hand a large flower, a large bird, or a sun disk. In her hands we occasionally see the reins of two facing animals. She may hold horses on which her daughters ride or even the reins of lions. One embroidery (fig. 6.2) shows the spring goddess with hands upraised, while just above her hands two slanting lines, representing the reins, descend to the lion's head.

These figures are highly reminiscent of ancient Greek sculptures showing goddesses having power over animals, specifically lions. We can see this in an example displayed in the collection of the Archeology

Fig 6.2. The Goddess figure, with raised arms, is faced by rampant lions whose reins are shown attached to the upper border.

Museum in Rhodes, Greece, a column representing the triple goddess Hecate. The three goddesses stand back to back, each holding a lion by its leash and by its tail.

When the goddess is depicted on Russian embroidery in the center of the composition, birds, deer, trees of life, or daughters face her at each side. Riders on horseback with hands raised in salute may also face her. Sometimes she rides a double-headed bird or a double-headed boat, as evident in figure 6.1, and rays may emanate from her head as she rides in this "sun chariot."

Some Russian compositions are so formulaic that they have been grouped by researchers according to usage. For example, the "Spring Welcome" complex of images shows a large club-headed goddess, hands upraised, holding the reins of two horses. She stands in the center of a rectangular field, often bordered by birds. Sprouting seeds are shown at her side, or sometimes "fertile field" motifs—the ancient Neolithic figure of a quartered square with a dot in each quadrant—accompany her. Male or female riders salute the goddess with upraised hands. This type of composition is bordered with floral and vegetative decoration and often outlined in red. A characteristic work (fig. 6.3) shows the spring goddess with upraised hands in the center of a square field, flanked by solar images. Sprouting seeds not only are above and below her, but are also in adjacent fields. The whole composition is bordered by floral or vegetative ornament. Thus, all the images signal the use of such cloths in spring planting rituals.

Another composition, the "Solstice" embroidery, occurs in many variations of the same format. In this grouping, made specifically for the celebration of the summer solstice, the goddess is placed at the center of the composition, but her hands are lowered. Often, solar disks are embroidered at each side of her body (fig. 6.4), and sometimes she holds the reins of two horses which face her, ridden by her small daughters, who in turn hold the reins of a foal. More typically, mother and daughter wear elaborate solar headdresses, sprout branches from their bodies, or are horned.

In one instance, the whole grouping is shown inside a shrine (*Russian Embroidery* 82, 85). Ethnographer and textile specialist L. Kalmykova's collection includes a nineteenth-century village towel on which a peaked-roofed shrine, altars, and a large birth goddess are depicted together (19). Ethnographic research also documents such shrines. In the countryside during the early twentieth century, shrines of this type were constructed to celebrate summer festivals. Rybakov describes them as "decorated with garlands of flowers and fragrant greenery," smaller than Christian churches and usually of wood.

> They were hidden in the woods or sometimes placed on a hill overlooking a lake. The residents of the area would gather around that hut, having brought with them choice food and drink. In a round dance formation they would sing and dance around the hut, which represented a kind of pagan temple. (1968, 43)

It is easy to recognize this temple, with the goddess image within it, on many of the summer embroideries.

Another group composition, designed to protect its wearers or occupants from harm, shows long rows or borders of goddesses, their large hands upraised. This type of composition appears on the shirt edgings of pregnant women, on bed hangings, and round borders of ritual towels.[4]

Thus, depending on the time of year or the specific ritual occasion, embroidered figures, varied by their arm positions and their attendant motifs, symbolized the changing aspects of the Great Goddess.

Production of Textiles and Maintenance of Tradition

One of the most noteworthy accomplishments of talented Russian women was the way in which they maintained textile traditions and later transmitted them to their female descendants. The process was accomplished solely by individualized instruction, without any centralized control. There were no schools, no formal teachers, no "experts." Every woman was expected to learn the necessary skills, and each daughter learned the textile traditions from her mother or another female family member. Maslova elaborates:

> Home embroidery was entirely the province of women.... For their own use, the most traditional subject matter and techniques were retained, especially in isolated areas. From the age of eight to nine, peasant girls mastered embroidery, taking in what had been gathered by previous generations. In response to questions about where their patterns came from, the answers were "neighbors," passed down from "generation to generation," "other women," "an earlier towel," "each other," "my girlfriends." In other words, through collective sharing and passing on of tradition. (33)

Let us consider more specifically what this tradition involved. First, theoretical expertise was required. Complex design ideas needed to be mastered, their meaning had to be understood, and the history of each motif and its relation to every other motif had to be learned. "The idiom of Russian embroidery may be compared to an alphabet where every ornamented motif is an independent symbol; in combination, these symbols make up an artistic and semantic entity" (*Russian Embroidery* 30). Learning to identify the motifs may be compared to acquiring a language; learning to combine motifs correctly may be likened to the difficulty of producing or writing a computer program.

Unlike computer use, however, where typing on a keyboard is fairly simple to learn, producing stitches is a highly skilled manual technique. It is as if you had first to build your own computer from plastic, then to master its use, and finally to produce meaningful texts on it. A Russian girl had first to learn the techniques of planting and harvesting flax, preparing the stalks, spinning the thread, threading the loom according to a pre-programmed design, producing the linen cloth, ornamenting it with counted stitches so fine that one could hardly see the background linen, and finally embellishing it with golden thread and pearls. In addition, every motif she embroidered had to convey a precise meaning and had to be created with the right technique so that it would have the necessary power. This early work was carefully overseen by her mother or other female relatives.

Fig 6.3. Embroidery for spring planting rituals showing "Spring Welcome" motifs. The Goddess figure is at the center with solar disks. Sprouting seeds are shown above and below. The Neolithic "fertile field" symbol is also shown in several fields. The whole piece is bordered by vegetation motifs.

An object thus produced would be valuable in our eyes today, if only because of the time and effort necessary to finish it. More important for the women undertaking this labor was the protection vouchsafed them and their families by these beautiful and meaningful textiles. They needed specifically ornamented textiles for the rituals to have the desired effect. We have only to read a simple description in a museum catalogue of a woman's ritual haymaking shirt to understand her special genius. The shirt she made for bringing in the harvest would not be covered by any other clothing because it would be too hot to wear her apron or sarafan. Thus all the lovely "counted thread work in red and blue linen, colored silks and wools, the insertion of bobbin lace and gold lace trimming" could be seen. This simple work shirt is covered with

Fig 6.4. A "Solstice" embroidery. The Mother Goddess is shown between two birds. Daughter Goddesses ride the birds. All goddesses wear floral crowns.

tree of life and bird motifs. The sleeve is worked in an all-over pattern of geometrical plant forms. The front hem is occupied by a three-part composition of a "bird-boat" with a stylized Tree of Life, flanked by birds. Three highly conventionalized Trees of Life, flanked by minor opposed birds, add to the ornamentation at the back hem. (*Russian Embroidery* 229)

Note here that in order to gather the harvest, female haymakers wore ritual clothing stressing plant motifs. Stylized trees of life are arranged around the haymaker's skirt, and the goddess motif protects the neck. The design, a one-of-a-kind piece of work, was stitched in beautiful silk and gold threads so that the harvest would go smoothly and the hay would be safely brought into the barns. The dress made and worn by the woman ensured this.

Such dresses are common in Moscow museum collections, and many are reproduced in Russian publications such as the work cited above. The function of the dresses is clearly specified by the label "Ritual Haymaking Shirt," and the text makes clear that the motifs described above "symbolize the cyclic extinction and regeneration of the sun, they are prayers for rich harvests and symbols of that harvest" (317).

Textile production continued throughout women's lives, and the large carved trunk found in every village home would contain many home-produced textiles. This precious casket held all the textiles used for the special occasions in a woman's life. Here were the long linen shirts she made to wear on the first day of haying season, heavily embroidered with plant motifs. Other shifts, also displaying fertility designs around the hems, wrists, and neck opening, were set aside for her wedding day. Ritual towels, many six feet long and embroidered on either end with red solar and goddess designs, were carefully folded in anticipation of the day when they would be used to bind the couple ritually in marriage, to wrap the sacred trees in the spring and the graves on Memorial Day. They would also be hung from the beams overhead for the woman in labor to pull on, and later would swaddle her baby. Wedding shirts and ritual clothes were also made for her future husband to wear. These ritual fabrics accompanied the woman who made them for the duration of her life. In fact, she might already have made her embroidered shroud for her burial.

A woman not only created her own ritual textiles but also inherited those made by her mother and grandmother. The old pieces displayed the same time-honored motifs that she herself learned to embroider and that she passed on to her daughters. For her traditional wooden chest contained a woman's dowry, all the wealth she would ever own. It constituted both a library and a treasury in her life.

As noted earlier, pieces were handed down from one generation of women to the next. Kalmykova, who documented this process in twentieth-century villages, notes the "steadfastness of local tradition in embroidery" in the area around Tver', north of Moscow. This continuity is due in part to the seclusion of the villages and the "old-fashioned mode of life, with its age-old customs, rites, and beliefs surviving from the paganism of the Early Slavs" (196). The aesthetic education of the child began very early at home, contends Kalmykova.[5] It was grounded in home life and the natural world. Girls were taught stylized forms of embroidery designs and were encouraged to add forms from nature. Textile traditions were controlled and taught entirely by women. Each woman, according to Kalmykova, had access to her mother's and grandmother's textiles, as well as to other family pieces, such as those belonging to her mother-in-law.

The child artist drew on all these textiles for ideas. The result was embroidery on which styles combined in varying formats. Images repeated themselves again and again as the child's skill and body of work grew. The girl did not draw the design on the cloth, according to Kalmykova, but let the design grow in the process of the embroidery without pre-planning. In addition to embroidery, the child was also taught various techniques such as lacemaking, appliqué, and tape weaving, all processes that combined in a single costume. Purchased ribbons and patterned fabric were also used, but all the diverse elements were interpreted in a pleasing textural arrangement that yielded a harmonious image.

Several pieces in the Zagorsk Folk Art Museum collection overseen by Kalmykova were obviously produced by young embroiderers: the stitches were crude, somewhat inept. But one could easily recognize in these early works the same motifs as the adult embroiderers used; suns, goddesses, and trees of life were all carefully repeated.

The most important motif, however, remained that of the Mother Goddess. Since her image and accompanying fertility symbols were necessary to the growth and well-being of fields, crops, and family, they were also woven on the long cloths that overhung the icon. Her image was similarly outlined in rows along the bed curtains, her uplifted hands protecting the occupants from evil as they slept. The long cloths show the rites of the season: the goddess holding birds and sun disks, and riding a solar chariot in the spring; the goddess overseeing the Midsummer Night fires and bringing in the summer solstice; the harvest goddess with sheaves of wheat; and the Mother Goddess giving birth to children at the winter solstice.

Sacred Embroidery: The Power of Cloth in Ritual Usage

The young girl needed to learn from her mother more than technique and identification of motifs. The "library" she inherited was not there simply for her to copy. The embroidery motifs constituted a symbolic language that she first had to learn to read. Then, in a new, creative way, she had to combine the sacred images on her own cloth so that it would produce the same powerful effects as the embroideries of her predecessors. The spiritual power of the ritual cloth demanded that the symbols be used correctly, their meaning made specific to their purpose.

Although the young girl may not have known it, the meanings of the images stretch back into the distant past. L. Efimova notes that Russian embroidered ornamentation dates from the twelfth century. From antiquity, towels were used as religious accessories at solemn ceremonies and family festivals (Efimova and Belogorskaia 255). The image of the Mother Goddess with her upraised hands, accompanied by fabulous creatures and symbolic animals, may stem from a kind of "Russian pagan paradise before the appearance of Christianity" (ibid.). In the earliest representations of the female deity, she is crowned by a solar disk, surrounded by suns, and seated on a solar chariot. Clearly, these early representations found their way onto ritual cloth, the images apparently having a sacred character. And as James Mellaart and others demonstrated in a study of contemporary village kelim carpets in Anatolia, textiles retain meaning longer than almost any other medium. Religious motifs from Neolithic wall paintings are still being woven by village women there, and these researchers note:

> It seems that the repertoire of religious symbols became firmly established in Anatolia during the Neolithic period. There are three reasons why certain of these symbolic motifs should have survived on kelims. Firstly, the religious significance of the motifs survived for millennia; secondly, the nature of the kelim technique allowed designs to be taught easily by an experienced weaver to a learner; and thirdly, the rural weavers faithfully adhered to their traditional designs. (Vol. 4, 11)

As in Anatolia, the Russian sacred textile motifs were carefully handed down and faithfully reproduced by daughters following their mothers' tuition.

If we examine the ritual cloths and clothing on which women recorded these motifs over hundreds of years, we can isolate some of the more obvious themes that help us to understand their motives for selecting specific items for representation. From the many symbolic textile motifs available to the young girl, I have chosen to analyze four general areas of usage: motifs associated with protection; motifs embroidered so as to indicate identity or identification with the goddess; motifs intended to ensure fertility of humans and crops; and finally, motifs that expressed ritual good wishes or ratified contracts between groups.

The first group of symbolic motifs express a desire for protection from the elements, from sickness and from barrenness, which was clearly vital for the women and their families. Embroidering a powerful goddess on a cloth would, they hoped, protect the newborn child wrapped in it from sickness. In a society at the mercy of natural forces, protection from the elements or from "evil" was paramount. Therefore cloth outlined with protective goddesses covered the windows and doors. It covered the icons, the beds, and the bread.

Kalmykova provides a useful catalogue of specific motifs used in Russian villages for protection against evil forces: the goddess figure, double-headed birds, the color red, and circular forms. Why did Russian women wear circular beads, headdresses, belts—even hems and wristbands circled with red? Kalmykova maintains, "It is because the woman is the mother. She protects the family and the circle protects *her* from the dark forces" (interview, May 1988). Tat'iana M. Rasina, researcher at the Moscow Institute of Folk Art Production, also confirms that the goddess was "a guardian and a protectress." So when a Russian woman was "appropriately" dressed and guarded by the correct symbolic goddess motifs, she was protected.

She was also identified. In a sense, the ancient Slavic white linen shirt worn by men, women, and children alike was a kind of skin, an alter ego that delineated them against nothingness. Ornamented as it was at the neck, wrists, and hems—in short, at all the openings where evil could attack the body—the shirt became both a protective skin and an identifier of the person. People in all Slavic countries believed that they needed to be buried in their shirts, particularly their marriage shirts, so that they would be known by family and kin, so "that they would be recognised as a human being in the next world" (Mihailova 36). Placing a white shirt "protected" by red thread on a newborn also identified it as human; only after it was clothed could a child be addressed by its name.[6]

Over this identifying "skin" of the shirt Russian women wore either a wraparound skirt called the *poneva* (southern Russia) or a sleeveless jumper called the *sarafan* (northern Russia). In contrast to the shirt, both were highly decorated with brocade, pearls, gold embroidery, or, for the poorer woman, braid, bugles, and river pearls. Decoration indicated a woman's social status, her village, her age, and her marital and maternal status. Like the calling card of a Victorian lady, the Russian village woman's dress proclaimed her identity.

Crowning this costume for married women was a gorgeous headdress called a *kokoshnik* or *soroka*. These were the most expensive and expressive part of her dress. For from ancient times, women's hair was bound up with superstitions regarding its strength and power. Women were said to cover their hair for the protection of their home and kinfolk. According to ancient Russian beliefs, hair could do various harm (Maslova 41). People collected their hair so that it could be buried with them and thus not harm anyone, or alternatively, their burial shirt would be embroidered with human hair as a protection for life beyond the grave. But the headdress a woman made to cover her crowning glory became more beautiful than her hair. Made of velvet, gold embroidery, pearls, or feathers, these gorgeous creations still astonish us with their intricacy and opulent splendor. We can hardly conceive that women proudly wore their kokoshniks every day. Each was decorated with special shapes and colors, and some had long red horns. Sorokas with glittering beads, feathers, hanging pompoms, and pearls were made in the south. Each woman made her own headdress, one appropriate to her village and station in life. More than anything else she wore, the headdress transformed a woman into a goddess.

Indeed, important similarities exist between the headdresses worn by the women and those depicted as worn by the goddess on goddess embroideries. The goddess, as mentioned earlier, is sun-headed, with rays emanating from her face. In some cases her face was embroidered in shining gold silk thread to heighten this effect (see fig. 6.5). In like fashion, the soroka, made of glittering beads, spangles, and feathers, made the woman's head brilliant and sunlike. Just as the goddess is often seen with red horns, so were the ladies from Riazan' Province, whose huge red-horned headdress was accented by gold lace and hanging beadwork (*Russian Folk Clothing*, Photograph #21). The goddess's floral crown depicted on some embroideries is echoed in most sorokas, which resemble a crown densely covered with artificial beaded flowers and ribbons.

Similarly, in the images picked out in pearls and gold thread on the kokoshniks we discern the image of the Mother Goddess, flanked by birds facing her. The entire iconography of goddess religion—the deer, the sun chariot, and the chain of daughters—is depicted on the headdresses. The Russian woman wearing the kokoshnik was both protected by the goddess and displayed *as* a goddess to her viewer. Her clothing, which she herself made, communicated her identity, her pride in her abilities and creativity, and her oneness with the deity she revered.

Besides protecting her and her family and serving as an identifier, the embroidered cloth made a plea for another important power—that of fertility. As mentioned earlier, fertile harvests were perhaps the most desirable bounty in peasant life. The embroideries were worked to ensure that both fields and flocks would continue to produce generously. Hence the goddess bringing down the sun, the rains, and the dews and guarding the newly sprouted seeds is repeatedly shown on ritual cloths.

The cloths also symbolically entreated human fertility. Brides' shirts were covered with fertile field motifs, while the shifts of pregnant women were embroidered with pregnant birth goddesses to encourage the safe birth of the new child. Maslova remarks that little was done to discourage women from embroidering fertility motifs because both the church and family members may have believed that it was better not to meddle in anything as important as fertility (171). The repetition of the birth goddess image on cloths and clothing throughout the Russian territories testifies to the primacy of this motif.

Ritual cloths were also used as sanctifiers, binders of contracts, and granters of good wishes. For example, in Russian wedding ceremonies, the engagement contract was ratified by the exchange of an embroidered towel. The couple were "bound" in marriage by an actual cloth bound around their hands. Cloth sanctified the place where they made their vows. Together they stepped upon a *shirinka*, a holy cloth, as they solemnized their marriage vows (Maslova 24). At the wedding supper, the bride's brother led her to the table by a ritual cloth tied around her wrist. He gave the ritual cloth to the groom, who led (and thus wound) the bride three times around himself before seating her beside him at the table.

Just as ritual cloths designated a holy place during weddings, so the "beautiful corner" of the peasant home was sanctified by the icon draped with a ritual cloth. This eastern corner usually had a shelf on which valued family mementos, as well as flowers and a lamp, were kept. Like the hearth, the corner typified the home, and it was from this corner that the bride left to go to her new home.

Cloth was also used for ritual presents. Honored guests would receive a specially embroidered ritual cloth or, at the wedding, the bride would give guests cloths she had made. Sometimes as many as one hundred ritual cloths were made for presentation by the bride and her family. On special occasions such as births, name days, and memorials for the dead, special cloths were embroidered and distributed as a kind of greeting card or were spread on the grave for the ritual meal held forty days after a death (Maslova 18).

FIG 6.5. The Goddess rides a double-headed horse.

A Belief System Recorded in Symbolic Language

So ritual cloth and clothing, covered with symbolic designs, were used for specific occasions and effects. In addition, among themselves, women used the symbols as a kind of language, a symbolic belief system that reinforced their solidarity and religious faith. As we know, most of the women who produced these textiles were illiterate, and they used the patterned cloth as a symbolic language, communicating ideas in coded visual terms. In the nineteenth century, these cloths conveyed ideas through symbols that could be read by others who had learned to decode them.[7] Could it be that this embroidery was also meant to communicate with us, cross-generationally? Could these symbols represent meaningful communication from women who could not communicate in writing?

In the society from which they came, embroideries really had no need of verbal "titles" any more than we really need titles on paintings today. At the time, the artistic work spoke for itself. For centuries women had learned how to communicate through cloth and how to teach their daughters to do the same. The fabric they produced contained the very essence of their culture, their heritage of ritual beliefs, their remembrance of things long past, and their hope for future blessing, protection, and fruitfulness. It encoded an ancient belief system with its myths and traditions, much as a library does for us today.

It may be that the ultimate accomplishment of Russian folk women was their ability to preserve the symbols of their ancient culture, passing them down to our era with some of the meanings still intact, so that, with diligence, we also may learn to decode them and understand something of their religious history and ritual ideas. If contemporary women are ever to find remnants of their own religious and ritual history, it will be because their Russian predecessors took the trouble to record what they knew on their fabrics, and because contemporary women will take the trouble to try to understand the messages they recorded in thread.

From the above-described record of Russian textiles we can suggest a tentative reading of some of these messages. First of all, the embroidered communications were undoubtedly religious or ritual in character. They ranked what was important and what was not by what they chose to reproduce and what they omitted. In a sense, the embroideries resemble poetry, emphasizing ideas by repetition, duplication, and mirroring of images; they evoke music in that there are refrains, motifs, and variations. They are a religious litany of sorts, in that the cloth helps us visualize their prayers or wishes for those elements most important for their world, such as protection from evil, storms, and sickness; holiness; fertility and good health of crops, cattle, and families.

The importance of birth, whether of humans or plant or animal life, is primary in the religious messages recorded for us. For Russian villagers all life was holy; all were born of the Great Mother, hence the continued emphasis on life and its preciousness in many of the images on Russian textiles. Protection of all life on the planet is a prime tenet. The beauty of life and of the earth is the source of the aesthetic beauty of the embroideries. Again and again, like a litany, we see images surrounded by small "life" signs, spirals or tendrils that cover much of the surface of ritual embroidery, repeating the message of life's primacy.

Another message relates to power and its source. Although the goddess images are visually tremendously powerful, they do not derive their power from violence, weapons, or warfare. They carry no arms, kill no animals, and wield no power over slaves or captives, as depicted in Mesopotamian or Egyptian art. There is no hierarchy in the realm of deities, except that of mother to daughters or large animals to smaller ones. The nature of this hierarchy indicates the chain of life, inasmuch as one gives birth to the other. Power in these embroideries comes from the ability to give and sustain life.

Women most often depicted daughters as companions to the central goddess. Although they clearly were able to represent both males and females, they embroidered the chain of female descent, the mother-daughter bond, much more frequently than they did sons. Male figures rarely appear on these textiles, and what few male riders are depicted on the cloth face the goddess and salute her with one hand upraised.[8] Most frequently (fig. 6.6) the central mother goddess holds the reins of horses on which her daughters ride. She has given birth to the small females— and the horses are also accompanied by small versions of themselves, showing the animal chain of life.

Other symbols, those which stress polarized forces, are commonly portrayed: the sun is balanced by water motifs, for instance, or a bird; a sky symbol is balanced by a snake, an earth symbol. In these cases, what holds center stage is the unity of the symbols, the balance of opposites. Partially this is accomplished by the symmetry of composition. With the goddess in the center, a bird perches on either side of her, and a snake guarding her womb is shown twice, also at each side. Thus all variations are balanced by the Great Goddess. Indeed, life, death, and the renewal of life are the focus of the rituals on the ritual cloths.

Conclusion

Russian village women contributed substantially to their culture by preserving archaic traditions from their distant Slavic past. Not only were they able to teach new generations of women to produce beautiful cloth and stitchery, but through tireless tutelage they preserved sacred pre-Christian motifs on their resplendent ritual cloths and clothing into the nineteenth and twentieth centuries. They recorded their beliefs on cloths that were invested with both meaning and power. The visual symbols they used enable us to decode their messages and to understand something of their religious priorities and beliefs. For all women whose heritage has been so fragmented, the preservation of these visual remnants of the ancient goddess religion represents a brilliant feat of salvaging and articulation.[9]

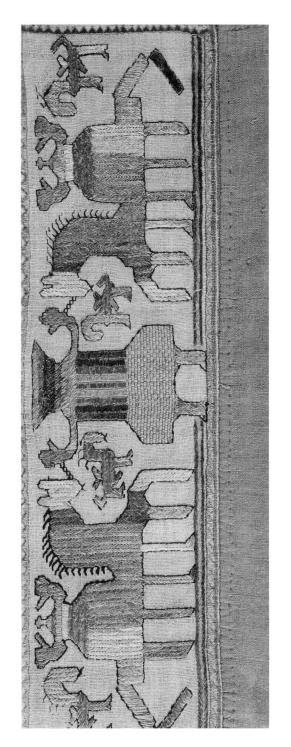

Fig 6.6. "Chain of Life" motif linking female generations. The central Mother Goddess holds the reins of stylized horses which her daughters ride. The smaller horses are indicators of the Mother's role as Mistress of Animals.

The meaning of ritual cloth symbols, which once had far-reaching power and a meaning that was clear to all, gradually faded. The urgent necessity in the nineteenth century to invigorate the fields by evoking the goddess was replaced in the twentieth century by the surer mechanisms of the fertilizer truck and the tractor. Similarly, reproductive fertility, once considered the prime glory of women, became a nuisance as crowded housing made large families burdensome. Birth control negated the powers the birth goddess once held. No longer were the fires lit on Midsummer Night to purify and kindle love between men and women. Life could go on without the goddess's intervention.

In the late twentieth century, however, interest in women's religious history and ways of communicating has revived. For centuries, women recorded on their embroideries beliefs that were important to them, and now, with all the skill we can muster, we try to understand what it was that they wanted to say to us. Whether we believe in a female deity or not, we can only admire the tenacity of Russian village women, who, in the face of incredibly difficult and complex lives, expended precious time and effort to transmit and preserve the ritual traditions they themselves had inherited.

Notes

The illustrations in this chapter are all from the Shabel'skaia textile collection, assembled in Russia in about 1870. All are ritual towel ends worked in cotton, linen, and silk thread on white linen cloth. Currently they are housed in the Cleveland Museum of Art. I thank that institution for its permission to reproduce them here.

1. Interview with Viktor M. Vasilenko, Professor of Folk Art, Moscow State University, June 1988.

2. Gimbutas argues for this view (5), and Natalie Kononenko adopts this approach as well in the article cited below (17).

3. Consultation with Vasilenko in Moscow, March 9, 1982.

4. In passing we should mention that not all female motifs are goddess motifs. On late-nineteenth-century embroideries, especially bed valances, we see compositions that refer to everyday life: women flirting with soldiers or waving fans. On other clothes, illustrations of fairy tales are shown with women characters. But these embroideries are of a different genre and obviously do not have the same ritual character as the pieces treated in this essay.

5. Interview with L. Kalmykova, textile curator of the Zagorsk Museum of Folk Arts, in Zagorsk, April 19, 1982.

6. In Bulgaria, when a baby (for example, a prematurely born infant) was in danger of dying, a magic ritual that echoes Russian practice was enacted. A shirt

was made by three women who, in the darkness of night, stripped off their clothes and let their hair loose. Standing on the roof of the house, they had to weave a piece of cloth there and sew it into a baby's shirt before the first rooster crowed. This magic shirt was then put immediately on the baby to keep it alive. As noted above, this first shirt was ornamented with protective red embroidery around the neck, and from the moment it was placed on the child, it was interpreted as a human sign, or, more specifically, as human skin, and from that point onward the child was addressed by name (Mihailova 37). Ukrainian tradition preserves a similar housetop ritual.

7. Actual embroidered words were rarely used on textiles, and when they appeared, as Maslova notes, they were occasionally misspelled or individual letters were stitched backward (28). In all probability this was because women were copying from written sources without understanding the letters they were reproducing.

8. The position recalls male riders who salute the Great Goddess with one hand raised on the huge felted hanging found in the Siberian Paszyryk burial mound (600 B.C.).

9. This achievement has been variously appreciated and understood throughout the twentieth century. In the 1930s, Vasilenko discovered in Russian villages that there was still an older woman called the "Verduna" (from the Russian word *izvedovat'*, "to foretell, to advise"). She was the person who knew about the rituals and what symbols needed to be embroidered on the cloths. Vasilenko was one of the first to ask in the villages about the meanings of motifs, and he interviewed many of the verduny in the 1920s and 1930s. By that time, the chain of mother-daughter tuition had been interrupted by wars and political upheaval. Sometimes only *she* remembered the ancient motifs and reminded the women of the meaning and value of their embroidery.

This information was elicited in a conference with Vasilenko, in Moscow, March 16, 1990. At the time, he was eighty-four years old, and this was my last meeting with him before his death in 1991. During this consultation, Vasilenko described his interviews with many village "Wise Women" in the twenties and thirties. The name *verduna* is also variously used as *ved'ma* from *videt'*, "to see." Like "wise woman" in the West, this word has been variously used and translated as "witch." Unfortunately, Vasilenko's notes on these interviews were never published, and during the Stalinist period, when Vasilenko was a victim of the purges, his materials were burned by the militia, who taunted him that "not even one spot or speck" of his work would survive.

Works Cited

Efimova, L. V., and R. M. Belogorskaia. 1982. *Russian Embroidery and Lace*. Moscow: Izobrazitel'noe Iskusstvo.

Folk Art of the Russian Federation. 1981. Leningrad: Khudozhnik RSFSR.

Gimbutas, Marija. 1981. *Goddesses and Gods of Old Europe.* Berkeley: U of California P.

———. 1989. *Language of the Goddess.* San Francisco: Harper and Row.

Gorodtsov, V. A. 1926. *Trud istoricheskogo muzeia.* Moscow: Museum Press.

Kalmykova, L. 1981. *Folk Embroidery of the Tver Region.* Leningrad: Khudozhnik RSFSR.

Kononenko, Natalie. 1986. "The Goddess: Prehistoric and Modern." In *Goddesses and Their Offspring*, exhibition catalog. Binghamton, N.Y.: Roberson Center for the Arts and Sciences.

Manushina, T. N. 1983. *Early Russian Embroidery.* Moscow: Sovetskaia Rossia.

Maslova, G. S. 1984. *Ornament russkoi narodnoi vyshivki.* Moscow: Nauka.

Mellaart, James; Udo Hirsch; and Belkis Balpinar. 1989. *The Goddess from Anatolia.* Milan: Eskanazi.

Mihailova, Ganka. 1992. "The Traditional Bulgarian Costume as a Reflection of Folk Notions about the World, Nature and Man." In *British and Bulgarian Ethnography* (Papers from a Symposium). Liverpool: Liverpool Museum.

Russian Embroidery: Traditional Motifs. 1990. Moscow: Sovetskaia Rossiia.

Russian Folk Clothing. 1984. Leningrad: Khudozhnik RSFSR.

Russkoe narodnoe iskusstvo. 1984. Leningrad: Khudozhnik RSFSR.

Rybakov, B. A. 1965. "The Cosmogony and Mythology of the Agriculturalists of the Eneolithic." *Soviet Anthropology and Archeology* 4, no. 2: 16–36.

———. 1968. "The Rusalii and the God Simargl-Pereplut." *Soviet Anthropology and Archeology* 6, no. 4: 43–59.

———. 1981. *Iazychestvo drevnikh slavian.* Moscow: Nauka.

Sidamon-Eristoff, V., and N. P. Shabelsky. 1910. *Antiquités russes.* Moscow: n.p.

Stasov, V. V. 1872. *Russkii narodnyi ornament.* Vol. 1. St. Petersburg: Tipografiia Tovarishchestva Obshchestvennaia Pol'za.

Vasilenko, V. M. 1974. *Narodnoe iskusstvo.* Moscow: Sovetskii khudozhnik.

———. 1977. *Russkoe prekladnoe iskusstvo.* Moscow: Iskusstvo.

7

DIRTY WOMEN: CULTURAL CONNOTATIONS OF CLEANLINESS IN SOVIET RUSSIA

Nadya L. Peterson

To Natalie

The Naked Community

GOING TO THE RUSSIAN BATHS with my mother is a vivid memory from my childhood in the sixties. Although physical cleanliness was an inevitable by-product of our weekly trip, it was not its primary objective, since a modern bathroom with a tub was available at home. Rather, the aim was purification and restoration of spiritual balance, accomplished through sharing and camaraderie. We went to the bathhouse in order to experience, with other naked women and children, a different kind of cleanliness.

Women's strategies for maintaining cleanliness, and the cultural significance of these strategies in Soviet Russia, are the focus of this essay. I define cleanliness as the absence of identifiable traces of all other activities on objects (that which is deemed extraneous is "unclean"), and as the culturally determined arrangement of objects in correct relation to one another (that which is out of place is "disordered") (Frykman and Lofgren 157–74). The dichotomy of clean/unclean (ordered/disordered), in turn, is directly related to the social organization of space (Douglas 1966, 35). Personal cleanliness aims at a distinct separation of categories, and in its enactment of the "rule of distance from physical origin" is particularly attentive to the boundaries between what is "me" and what is "not me" (Douglas 1973, 12). These boundaries become more prominent with the awareness of those differences between the physical and the social self, the private and public realms, that accompany the transition from primitive to civilized cultures (Frykman and Lofgren 170–72).

Furthermore, in modern societies, cleanliness/purity is a symbolically charged value characterized by the interplay among the categories of the moral, the political, and the physical; it is, therefore, eagerly appropriated by the dominant culture in specific historical contexts for specific purposes. In Stalin's time, for example, the "unclean" could signify (separately or collectively) the crossing of the normative boundaries of the sexual (dirty as "loose"), political ("dirty enemy of the people"), and physical ("nonhygienic"). The rituals of cleansing aimed at purification of the "unclean" in Stalinist society exemplify the excessive interpretation of the notions about purity shared by the larger culture.

The perceived violation of purity standards (and in the case of women, sexual and political "impurity" was often seen as one and the same) resulted in cleansing (*chistka*) of entire segments of society, the process propelled by the idea of expiating one's imagined sins before the state in the purgatory or hell of the prison camp. Yet "To Freedom with a Clean Conscience" (*na svobodu s chistoi sovest'iu*), the slogan current at the time, had a different meaning for the punishing authority and the political prisoner (Achil'diev 56). In official parlance, a "clean conscience" signified a "blank conscience," i.e., the eradication of individuality and total receptivity to the political mythologies of the moment, the mechanism operative in the post-Stalin era as well. For those now considered "impure" and punished for it, the dichotomy of clean/unclean becomes destabilized and in need of revaluation.

Cleaning practices related to the body and the environment, overseen by women as the traditional enactors of the domestic order, reflect processes occurring in the larger culture, linking interactive behaviors in a complex and changing network. Here Alfred Rieber's notion of "sedimentary society" for late Imperial Russia is helpful in understanding the dynamics of women's participation in and appropriation of Soviet culture as well. According to Rieber, "throughout Russian history a successive series of social forms accumulated, each constituting a layer that covered all or most of society without altering the older forms lying under the surface" (Rieber 353). As in late Imperial Russia, so in Soviet society there was considerable interaction between elite and popular culture. Peasant culture penetrated all levels of society, forming a changing network of shared social values or cultures.[1] Thus, in a curious blending of attitudes, Soviet women's culture exists as a mix of entrenched and modified behaviors: traditional peasant beliefs confront notions of gender quality and middle-class *kul'turnost'* (socially correct behavior in everyday life and demonstrative, socially motivated appreciation of high culture); anti-male bias appears together with patriarchal deference to men; and in such locales as the bathhouse, middle-class notions of propriety are exchanged for a different set of cultural norms.[2]

In the sedimentary society, the bathhouse and the modern bathroom offer venues for two different kinds of cleansing. The modern bathroom at home is a space where the actualization of domestic order occurs, i.e., the practical application of the domestic code as it relates to strategies for maintaining personal hygiene. This area is shared by all members of the family, but it is the woman who is in charge of maintaining current social norms of order, in effect appearing as the "technician of behavior, engineer of conduct and orthopedist of individuality," the terms Foucault uses to describe jailers (Foucault 235). If in her supervision of family hygiene in the home the woman reinforces the Law of the Norm, in the bathhouse she submits to more archaic forms of interaction. The "segregated" bathhouse is a place where men and women act as distinct groups performing the ritual of cleansing; here tradition, much more than "civilization," is the organizing principle of their behavior.[3] (See essay by Condee above.) In Soviet Russia, in the absence of religious culture, communal cleansing in the bathhouse has served as a spiritual outlet of sorts, linking modern urban dwellers with their ancestral traditions. Under the conditions of incarceration, the domestic code of cleanliness is modified, and communal cleansing plays an important part in forming familial prison groups, essential for spiritual and physical survival.

My primary sources for this essay are prison memoirs of several women writers: Evgeniia Ginzburg's *Journey into the Whirlwind* (Krutoi marshrut), Ol'ga Adamova-Sliozberg's *The Path* (Put'), Nadezhda Grankina's *Notes of Your Contemporary* (Zapiski vashei sovremennitsy), Vera Shul'ts's *Taganka in Central Asia* (Taganka v Srednei Azii), Zoia Marchenko's *This Was the Way it Was . . .* (Tak bylo . . .), Maria Ioffe's *One Night: The Story of Truth* (Odna noch: Povest' o pravde), and Irina Ratushinskaia's *Grey Is the Color of Hope* (Seryi tsvet nadezhdy). These writers' notions of what is clean and what is not and, related to that opposition, their perception of spaces, objects, boundaries, and bodies (conditioned by their social position, personal history, and family background) are brought into the reality of imprisonment. This is the environment where males are outsiders, and where successful interaction between women inmates is the chief condition for staying alive. Cultural notions about cleanliness, articulated in descriptions of these daily interactions, point to the way women experienced and appropriated Soviet culture from its beginnings in the 1930s through the post–Stalin period.

Spiritual aspects of communal bathing persist in the continuum of Russian culture. Evgeniia Ginzburg's memoir of prison life in the 1930s conveys the sense of communality (of erasure of class and personal differences) and of purification in the bathhouse that pervades my own childhood memories. Ginzburg's account represents communal bathing as a true communion with her kin:[4]

> Such moments are rare in life. True brotherly [*bratskaia*] love reigned between us in this bathhouse. Our hearts had not yet been touched by the caustic, beastly law of the camps, which, in subsequent years, corrupted many human souls. But now, purified by suffering, happy about meeting people after two years of solitude, we were sisters [*sestry*] in the loftiest sense of the word. Each one of us tried to serve the other, to share everything we had. (Ginzburg 1990, 172)[5]

The seemingly paradoxical move from brothers to sisters incorporates the androgynous equality and the ascetic ideal of a universal fraternity into the specifics of a woman's experience. "Brotherly love" in Russian has the broader symbolic meaning of a selfless, platonic, almost pious affection among all people, while "sisters" evokes a community ruled by distinctive norms of gendered kinship.[6] This naked community is bound by the visible manifestations of its phallic "lack," employing, in rituals of cleansing, the time-tested forms of familial cooperation, support, and exchange. Later in the same scene Ginzburg underscores the idea of kinship by referring to the sharing of a "family-size" bar of soap. In Ginzburg's description of communal bathing in the disinfection center at Sverdlovsk, the overall emphasis, too, is on being female and on being spiritually and physically different, the contrast made even starker by the presence of male guards who show awareness of the inmates' nudity:

> The commander, with enviable nonchalance, was walking up and down among the hundreds of naked women. No sooner had we gasped at this than we noticed that two soldiers in full uniform, rifle in hand, were posted at each of the doors leading into the shower room.
>
> "Saints above," wailed Polya Shvyrkova, like a peasant woman, "they must think we're not human, making us walk past the men with nothing on like this. Are they out of their minds or something?"
>
> "Didn't your interrogators teach you in '37 that there are no differences of sex where spies, saboteurs, terrorists, and traitors are concerned?

That being so, we needn't think of them as men either." And Nina Gviniashvili stepped boldly through the door between two soldiers.

"Yes," whispered Tanya Krupenik, "but these soldiers do see us as women and human beings. Just look at their faces."

She was right. Every single one of the sentries was staring at a spot between his feet, as though counting the pairs of heels that went past him. None of them raised their eyes to look. It was a different matter with the Brigand. (Ginzburg 1967, 316–17)

By denying the women their gender, the Brigand and the interrogators strip them of their "humanity"—the ultimate "cleansing" of a person. The inmates' refusal to see the guards as males is an act aimed against this spiritual castration. The women use nudity as a weapon of resistance, forcing the males to avert their gaze, acknowledge the difference, and grant the women their humanity. Adamova-Sliozberg's and Ioffe's descriptions of communal bathing are similar to Ginzburg's in their emphasis on gender difference as an expression of resistance to the coercive authority. (Adamova-Sliozberg 54, 58; Ioffe 42).[7]

Strength comes from the realization that women inmates can survive by forming a familial group in prison. Segregated according to sex and placed behind bars, this community is twice removed from the social structure that institutionalizes inequality, and in prison is free to explore relationships other than those of a nuclear family or of the "great family of the Soviet people." Irina Ratushinskaia, a dissident Soviet poet who served her prison term in the early 1980s, experiences bathing as the primary act in joining a family of women:

It's better to be back home in the Zone than to stay any longer in the icy, filthy hospital. The others heat up two buckets of water for me, and I wash off the hospital's coal dust. I throw my jacket and underwear into the snow outside to kill off any germs they may have picked up in the hospital compound. I'll wash and clean them tomorrow. Washed and dressed in clean clothes, I settle down by our "fireplace." Pani Lida brews tea. I already feel much better within these walls, but even better than the walls of this our home is our friendship. (196)

The paradoxical opposition of a "filthy" hospital and a pure, warm barrack is the opposition between the polluted spaces of the "official" prison and the spiritually unsullied interior of Ratushinskaia's prison family. Coming home is marked by the ritual of purification.

The prison barrack and the bathhouse are places where cleanliness is achieved in the sight of others, where the private realm expands to include the naked bodies of other women, and cleansing the body often acquires a spiritual dimension. Investigation of the dynamics of interaction in these spaces—an interaction that occurs in the absence of and in opposition to the immediate authority of the patriarch (be he the father of the family or the Father of the State)—opens a path into women's culture.

Invisible and Silent: Searching for Women's Culture

Contemporary Russian culture as a whole offers innumerable possibilities for variation in the interaction between the traditional and the "civilized." Reformers from Peter the Great to Mikhail Gorbachev subjected this culture to a daunting series of graftings, and all the participants brought a multitude of personal and national characteristics and perspectives with them into its continually evolving organism. To investigate the elusive notion of "women's culture" in the context of postrevolutionary Russian society is to sift through layers upon layers of accumulated cultural patterns.

Furthermore, a specifically women's culture is not a stable entity but a variety of different behaviors produced within larger cultures at particular historical moments. The multiplicity of these behaviors and their intimate relationship to their own time—involving resistance, adaptation, and transformation (the strategy related to women's perceived minority status)—is but one aspect of the overall complexity of "women's culture." Another is the absence of easily identifiable traces of this culture for anyone attempting to disentangle its strands and locate it within larger cultures (Moore 53).

In traditional Russian peasant society, where the private and public realms were not easily separated (and therefore were not situated from the outset in hierarchical terms of social validity), duties performed in the home have been seen by scholars as a valuable part of the culture. Peasant culture is nonwritten by definition, and the approaches to its history have relied on anthropological (ethnographic) descriptive research. Yet, characteristically, when the focus of analysis shifts from the overarching peasant culture to the narrower confines of women's peasant culture, it shifts from descriptions of a stable order toward expressions of deviations from the established patriarchal norms. Traces of women's daily behavior often become visible only in the recorded acts of negation of these norms—in court records, psychiatric evaluations, hospital files, and petitions.[8] Or, as Bryan S. Turner notes, "all social structures which institutionalize inequality and dependency are fought out at the level of a micro-politics of deviance and disease" (114).

In industrialized societies, on the other hand, domestic activities hide behind the facade of the private sphere, inaccessible to the voyeuristic impulse of the outsider. Moreover, the domestic realm, i.e., women's realm, has often been associated with physiological needs, deemed "natural" and, consequently, not worthy of theoretical attention. As in peasant societies, women's culture in the urban home is invisible because its language (understood broadly as any communication system employing signs that are ordered in a particular manner) is nonwritten and often nonverbal, not lending itself to translation into the dominant (written) discourses. Another notable feature of women's culture in general is its resistance to change; its prolongation is a necessary means of pursuing household survival strategies, even under transformed social conditions (Moore 145). But this complex of behaviors becomes visible only in the shifts between the traditional and the "civilized," between the norm and the deviation—displacements that occur in specific environments and in a specific language.

Two sources of information about norms of conduct and actual behavioral patterns are personal accounts and literary representations of life by participants in culture. In these texts the symbolic structure points to ethical hierarchies shaping the narrator's perception of events; the propriety or impropriety of specific actions is referred to in direct descriptive statements or is signaled by deliberate omissions. Normative narratives provide another source about actual behaviors. Even though aimed at different audiences, and written in different genres and historical periods, these narratives share in the way they represent proper behaviors in opposition to the departures from the ideal norm.[9] Nineteenth-century etiquette books and household management books, for example, are structured around what should not be done in polite society, illuminating in the process people's actual behavior.[10] In Soviet Russia written prescriptions for proper behavior (etiquette books, women's journals, fashion magazines, encyclopedias of domestic life) also stress prohibition, or focus on the results of slip-ups in the performance of the domestic code. In terms of personal hygiene and the cleanliness of the immediate environment, these narratives, implicitly aimed at women as controllers of the domestic sphere, tend to deal mostly with prevention and correction.[11]

Both normative and literary discourses rely on established models of conduct as well as of representation. Glimpses of the "truth" of culture are found in departures from the canon specific to each of these discourses, in the selection of the appropriate models for use, and in the symbolic hierarchies established in the narratives.[12] Prison memoirs, like all biographical literature, "filter the randomness [*sluchainost'*] of real events through the cultural codes of the time. . . . In this process, cultural codes not only select relevant facts out of the mass of life actions, but also become a program for future behavior, actively bringing it closer to the ideal norm" (Lotman 1992, 371). The solipsism of most memoir literature results in a particular narrative structure where the author is the central consciousness, forcefully establishing her right to a biography.[13] All other participants and their actions in the writer's story are there to illuminate her choices.

Ginzburg's portraits of female prisoners are based on narratives rendered familiar by the whole range of cultural images current at the time: the leather-jacketed tough Communists of the 1920s may be found in Boris Pil'niak's novels; the housewives of the elite in journalistic accounts and in the writings of Mikhail Zoshchenko and Il'ia Il'f and Evgenii Petrov; the spoiled, empty-headed daughters of distinguished professors in contemporary movies; and the uncompromising Socialist Revolutionaries in propaganda articles of the revolutionary years. Ioffe's memoir likewise abounds in easily recognized literary allusions; her confrontation with the investigator Kashketin, for instance, draws on Raskol'nikov's duel with Porfirii in Dostoevskii's *Crime and Punishment.* Adamova-Sliozberg's descriptions of hysterical inmates who allow themselves to remember their children, of guards looking for forbidden books after an inmate recites poetry by heart, and of her first encounter with a mirror in a prison bathhouse (in which she sees her mother's face) uncannily resemble Ginzburg's renditions of similar events (Adamova-Sliozberg 31, 57–58). Ratushinskaia's portraits, too, are painted according to patterns conventionalized by prison literature: saintly peasant women (also familiar from "village prose"), uncompromising dissidents, and naive guards. These secondary characters are represented stereotypically, fixed in assigned roles, unfree in their inexorable adherence to a set of behavioral norms imposed by the author. As memoirists, these writers by definition are Others, establishing their sense of self in opposition to the roles that men and women characters are made to play in these narratives. The writer, always at a distance from the events and characters described, draws some subjects into the orbit of her own difference. A reconstituted family, formed by these women in prison as a means of spiritual escape and physical survival, is a select group of women who share the author's background and perception of events, or those who could connect her with the common people (*narod*). All authors discussed here use the dynamics of social exclusion to their advantage by underscoring the value of being different from the rest of society—as a woman, a writer, and a political prisoner.

The New Soviet Woman in Her Prison Home

Prisons, like hospital wards, are microcosms of the social relations outside them, and incarceration—Foucault's "making bodies docile" (and cleansing them of impurities)—is central to the understanding of Stalinist culture and the Soviet culture it spawned. Prisons are "total institutions," their total character symbolized by the barrier to social intercourse with the outside, the breakdown of the barriers separating "sleep, play, and work" in modern societies, and the concerted assault on the selfhood of the inmate (Goffman 4–7). In addition, women and men here are isolated according to gender. In women's prisons, the male is the quintessential outsider. He is the jailer or interrogator, the enforcer of social punishment and the ultimate figure of authority. Women guards, representing coercive authority, practice gestures of oppression as well.

Moreover, life in a women's prison camp replicates in exaggerated form the dynamics of the Soviet urban household. There, too, the male is an outsider, and crucial decisions and actions pertaining to the daily running of the household are made by women. As in a camp, they cannot really escape; they are barred from freedom by the punishing authority of law and by the age-old Russian custom that stresses and enforces the values of family life.[14] Yet women manage to achieve a certain measure of control over their daily lives, practicing hidden resistance to authority as they simultaneously reinforce preexisting power relations within the family.

The prison barrack is a shared living space, a substitute for "home." The scarcity of certain items (the inevitable *defitsit* of Soviet reality), exacerbated by conditions of confinement, serves to illuminate the symbolic and relational importance of specific objects of daily life. Here, just as outside, spaces and objects become mobile, used in private and public contexts, and recycled for various uses. Here also, important differences between individual and communal practices of hygiene are emphasized.

To understand the complex of norms underlying the notions of cleanliness found in these memoirs, one must be aware of the cultural ingredients that collectively created the new Soviet woman of the thirties—a role assumed by Ginzburg, Ioffe, Adamova-Sliozberg, Shul'ts, and Marchenko as members of the new class of Soviet administrators and professionals. This cultural construct, a modification of the revolutionary heroine, appears in Stalin's time as a result of the syncretism between Bolshevik ideology and traditional Russian values (Clements, Engel, and Worobec 20). If the revolutionary heroine of the 1920s was "ascetic, dedicated, hard-working, intelligent, scornful of sexual game-playing, and demanding of equal treatment from men," then in the thirties she acquired new features, instrumental in "strengthening a Bolshevik-ordained social order" (ibid. 21). On the level of public articulation she remained an equal citizen and a loyal worker, but she also became a chaste wife and mother, in the process losing most of her autonomy. Her submissiveness and her responsibilities to husband, children, and society recall populist ideas about Russian peasants, now with a particular emphasis on the woman's domestic virtues (ibid. 20).

As Vera Dunham has shown, in addition to consumerism and *kul'turnost'*, domesticity was a major Stalinist value. The cultural values learned by the new elite were "transplants from Russia's prerevolutionary educated classes, now members of the new Soviet intelligentsia" (Fitzpatrick 35). Ginzburg, the daughter of a Kazan pharmacist, did not have to go outside her own home for middle-class cultural values. Vasilii Aksenov's introduction to the Possev edition of her memoirs paints a picture of a typical bourgeois family, where "the pharmacist Ginzburg, a refined [*kholenyi*] gentleman with a big fluffy mustache," invests in music and French lessons as a way to prepare his girls for eventual studies in Geneva (Aksenov 3). Ginzburg admits discomfiture about her roots, recalling an adolescent desire to have been a worker's child (Ginzburg 158). Her adjustment to the ways of the new elite does not come from emulating the ways of the old bourgeoisie (she does not have to learn what she already knows), but rather from conscious steps aimed at social advancement based on the synthesis of her middle-class upbringing with new ideals. As a student at Kazan University she is an active Komsomol member, deeply involved in the campaign for the political enlightenment of Kazan workers. After graduation she joins the party, marries a prominent Kazan politician, and works as a teacher and journalist. She becomes part of the new elite, eagerly participating in the multitude of roles her position requires (including those of good wife and doting mother). Her transformation into a new Soviet heroine is complete.

Ioffe, Adamova-Sliozberg, Shul'ts, and Marchenko came from backgrounds similar to Ginzburg's.[15] Ratushinskaia, born in Odessa in 1954, represents a new generation of political prisoners, which emerged as a result of the intelligentsia's dissatisfaction with the state of affairs in the country and of the greater degree of openness characterizing post-Stalin society. Her father an engineer and her mother a teacher of Russian literature, Ratushinskaia herself has a degree in physics, taught at the Odessa Pedagogical Institute, and is married to an engineer. A modern Soviet woman *intelligent* of the late Brezhnev era, Ratushinskaia in her memoir subscribes to the notions about women's roles current at the

time, notions quite similar to those inculcated in the 1930s and fundamental to the lives of the women victims of the Great Purges. For
Ratushinskaia, "quiet feminine fortitude" (217) and nurturing abilities
are a woman's most cherished qualities (83), the most dreaded consequence of incarceration is sterility (82), and attention to one's appearance is an inseparable part of being a woman (Ratushinskaia 51).

Like her 1930s counterpart, the new Soviet woman of the 1970s was
"characterized above all by a high level of citizenship, selflessness, steadfastness, responsibility, and confidence in the correctness of her actions,
but [was] also suffused with spiritual softness, emotion, and urge to help,
to ease, to take care of others, to support."[16] Woman's maternal function
was construed as the base for sexual difference, and women were perceived to have a natural attraction for the home environment (Attwood
70). As a supportive, nurturant institution, the family was an antidote to
inadequacies in the society, and the woman was primarily responsible for
the successful functioning of this institution (ibid. 72). The stereotypes of
popular images of femininity and masculinity current at the time suggested that a traditional division of labor with regard to childrearing and
homemaking was natural, universal, and unchanging (Buckley 50).

Notwithstanding the similarities in perceptions of female roles, prison
meant different things for the women of Ginzburg's generation and
status, and for a later generation of inmates (someone such as Ratushinskaia). Imprisonment for the Soviet woman of the 1930s was a confrontation with ultimate disorder, incomprehensible to her as a person and a
committed member of the new society. Ginzburg's memoir therefore
records her search for clarity, an attempt to "clean up the mess," and to
categorize her experience in intelligible terms. For Ratushinskaia, on the
other hand, incarceration is an anticipated and ultimate test of endurance, and an opportunity to consciously defy the system, paradoxically,
from within the confines of a correctional institution—by opposing its
practices, writing about her experience, and disseminating her writings
while still in prison.

In these women's descriptions of prison life, of the many bodies that
surround them and act upon them, traditional peasant perceptions of
order and cleanliness appear together with middle-class and intelligentsia
norms. The hierarchical arrangement of values associated with such
practices points to the way these women interpret and use these behaviors either to assist them in their search for clarity or, in Ratushinskaia's
case, to preach the gospel of a Soviet woman dissident. Unlike women
prisoners of Ginzburg's generation, who served their time in the camps
with people from all walks of life (including common criminals), Ratu-

shinskaia and her fellow women dissidents were isolated in a separate zone without much contact with the rest of the prison population. What Ginzburg and Ratushinskaia share, however, is the idea that the status of a political prisoner and a member of the intelligentsia places them apart from the common folk. For both of them traditional peasant notions of order and cleanliness come filtered through the accretions of a "sedimentary society" and in prison are applied to revalue society's standards of purity and to regain their humanity.

Filthy or Pure? Cleanliness in the Village

Some peasant notions about cleanliness can still be discerned in behavioral patterns of modern Russians. The middle-class *kul'turnost'* of Stalinist time, aimed at bringing workers and recent peasants into the fold of "civilization," proved unsuccessful in eradicating all vestiges of traditional peasant behaviors. For example, the strict separation of the public and private realm of middle-class culture, which prohibits activities related to the body in view of others, is not shared by peasant culture and is not always strictly observed in Soviet Russia.[17] (See Vainshtein's essay above.) The blurring of the boundaries between the private and public realms, purity as a moral concept, physical dirt as beneficial and physical cleanliness as a negative sign of separateness, as well as liminal aspects of communal cleansing are all part of traditional peasant lore, and of particular relevance to the survival strategies of women prisoners discussed here.

According to the traditional peasant mentality, cleanliness is a moral concept, related directly to the omnipresence of evil spirits (unclean power, *nechistaia sila*) in the world, the spirits that constantly threaten the peasant, his family, animals, and immediate surroundings (Rybakov 517).[18] Thus, for the Russian peasant, cleanliness is synonymous with purity, a concept that has much more to do with the need for "ritual construction of a sacred space" than with modern prescriptions of hygiene (Eliade 29). Peasants shielded themselves from the unclean by carefully arranging protective symbols both inside and outside the house, by using holy water (normally done by a priest), and by ritual cleansing of the body and environment (largely a woman's responsibility) (Tian-Shanskaia 115; Zelenin 280–81).

Thus it was possible to achieve "purity" in the Russian village, yet very hard to remain clean. Many Russian huts (*izby*) were crowded and lacked a chimney (*dymokhod*), and during cold weather animals were kept inside (Tian-Shanskaia 123). Women swaddled children in dirty rags and washed them infrequently. Infants received solid food immediately after birth in the form of a *soska* (chewed solid food wrapped in a rag), a custom that led to gastrointestinal disease and death (Ransel 117–18).[19] Excrement from animals and children covered the floor, and adults used either a bucket in the *izba* or a hole in the entryway (*seni*) to defecate and urinate, a practice still observed in the village in the 1930s.[20] Animal feces were a valuable fertilizer, and peasants in some areas saw dirt as beneficial, capable, for example, of shielding children from evil spirits (Baiburin and Toporkov 100). Wiping after defecation was done with leaves or whatever else was available at the moment. Women used rags during menstruation to protect their clothing, but thought nothing of using underskirts to dry themselves after urinating.[21] Urine was considered to have medicinal value and was often used to treat skin infections and other maladies.[22] In some regions women combed their hair and then wetted it with brine or *kvas* (a drink made from fermented bread) before braiding it (Zelenin 280).

Clearly, Russian peasants had a high tolerance for pungent smells. They reacted with equal equanimity to bodily excretions other than feces and urine, such as snot, spit, and sweat, for example. Handkerchiefs were not generally used; peasants relied instead on their fingers (Zelenin 281); a sweaty person was not unclean, since perspiration was part and parcel of hard physical work; spit was used to coat small cuts and abrasions.[23]

Peasant women, who had sole responsibility over the domestic domain, also served as enactors and controllers of cleanliness in settings that stressed cooperation and division of household tasks among female family members.[24] For them, cleaning in general was not a hygienic but a practical and ritual act related to transitional states.[25] Washing the body, whether at home in a bucket or in a bathhouse, marked a passage from one activity to another. Peasants washed before meals, in the morning before work, and always after coitus (Zelenin 281).[26] Cleansing the body was of special importance for marriageable young girls, who washed and groomed more often than married women (Tian-Shanskaia 115). Overall, the traditional attitude toward the body was utilitarian. Peasants made sure their bodies could work and reproduce, protecting themselves from harm (spirits rather than microbes) in any way they could. Dirt was an inevitable part of life, and beneficial; physical cleanliness, on the other hand, was a sign of nonbelonging and, therefore, suspect.

The bathhouse, typical for northerners, was a place most intimately connected with pre-Christian concepts of the life cycle. It was the threshold, the border—between life and death, virginity and marriage, a childless state and parenthood, sickness and health—as well as a place where the child came into the world (Pushkareva 110).[27] The bathhouse was "unclean" because of its strong links with pagan rituals; the water used in the bathhouse was "unclean" as well, and bathhouses never housed icons. Peasants were not supposed to attend church on the day they bathed and had to rinse themselves in "clean" water after bathing. In addition, baths were there to be enjoyed, as evident in the proverb *baba da bania—odna zabava*, "a bath and a woman are equally pleasurable." Here the woman's body is equated with a pagan space; both are sources of sensual pleasure, and both are "unclean" according to the asceticism of Russian Orthodoxy.

Yet its association with liminal states made the bathhouse both a place of danger and a refuge from danger.[28] The use of the bathhouse during delivery, for example, "was not related to modern Western ideas of cleanliness, but was a matter of ritual separation during a time of contamination and, even more, a protection from the influence of people with bad intentions" (Ransel 116). Both men and women used the bathhouse; yet women's connections with it—through the practices of healing, delivery, and witchcraft—were clearly more immediate and frequent. Although women oversaw cleanliness, because of their close links to pagan rituals and spaces, they themselves could not escape being "dirty." The protective aspects of communal cleansing, negative connotations of physical cleanliness, acceptance of dirt, and cleanliness as a moral value are the traditional peasant notions used by imprisoned women members of the Soviet intelligentsia to forge for themselves new standards of purity.

Disciplining the Body: Middle-Class Perceptions of Order and Cleanliness

Peasants accepted dirt as an unavoidable and sometimes useful part of their environment. In a middle-class culture, by contrast, lack of physical cleanliness is seen as an obstacle to equality and improvement, even though the physical body is hidden, and emphasis is placed upon a person's spiritual rather than physiological aspects. Spirituality in this culture is related to a particular kind of morality; to be "pure" is to be a chaste wife and an honest person, and suffering is an important part of spiritual purification.

The process of middle-class enculturation, which starts early in life, involves training in self-discipline, disciplining the body. Both the physical body and the person's environment (including the house and to some extent even nature) are supposed to be clean and orderly. Thus the body is placed at the center of a campaign to conceal its physiology—to reduce the part nature plays in human behavior and to elevate culture to dominant status. An etiquette book titled *The Rules of High Society Life and Etiquette: Good Manners* (Pravila svetskoi zhizni i etiketa: Khoroshii ton), published in Russian at the turn of the century, eloquently illustrates the strategy used to hide and discipline the body. The introduction to the volume stresses the importance of proper upbringing, but reassures the student of good taste that the rules of proper behavior may be acquired by anyone at any point in life.[29]

> [E]xperience shows that any adult, even if raised in the village or behind a shop counter, can successfully reeducate [*perevospitat'*] himself and become a proper [*prilichnyi*] person in the full sense of the word, i.e., master all the rules of social proprieties [*svetskikh prilichii*] to the point where in the best salons of high society, amid born aristocrats, he would not in any way betray his plebeian origins, but would conduct himself with the tact and refinement [*iziashchestvo*] of a true gentleman. (Iur'ev and Vladimirskii 2)

The way to achieve admittance into salons of high society is to master the code of proper behavior, which, according to *Khoroshii ton*, is a set of easily acquired norms. Maintenance of cleanliness (*christoplotnost'*), including cleanliness of the body, dress, living space, and air, is one of those norms. Cleanliness is particularly important for women, "whose obligations include care of the household management, food, and family clothes. Our dress, linen, beds, and bedspreads should be clean" (45).[30] Women should also take particular care of their teeth and hands.

What Vigarello calls "local washing" (hands, teeth, feet, etc.) and the attention given to the visible manifestations of cleanliness (dress, home environment) are clear signs of the strict division between private and public realms characteristic of middle-class society (Vigarello 160).[31] A woman's hands should not *show* the physical results of her work at home (she should protect her hands by wearing gloves); yet a clean house is exclusively the woman's practical responsibility (even though she has servants to help her). The parts of her body that are visible, as well as her dress and surroundings, should conform to the ideal of order and cleanliness.[32]

Order in the house equals the absence of dirt, the proper arrangement of objects, and the efficient management of resources. The woman, especially the mother, is in charge of maintaining this order, and its absence leads to an unhappy household:

> disorder in things, disorder in affairs, disorder in studies, in the very way of life! Everything is in chaos, everything is lost, and prosperity [*blagosostoia-nie*], this child of order, quickly disappears. The terror of sloppiness

[*neriashestvo*] reigns in the home; dress, furniture, food—everything bears the mark of sloppiness. (Iur'ev and Vladimirskii 50)

Women as primary organizers of domestic life, order in the house, prosperity, and personal cleanliness—these middle-class notions of propriety were adopted by the new Stalinist elite and bequeathed to post-Stalin generations of Soviet citizens (Fitzpatrick 35–36). A century after the publication of *Khoroshii ton*, etiquette manuals still insist on domestic comfort (*semeinyi uiut*) as a woman's sole responsibility. Peace and the overall welfare of the family (*pokoi i blagopoluchie*), for example, can be achieved only if the woman is equally attentive to the cleanliness of her home and the hygienic needs of her family members (Agaronian 83). If the woman is sloppy (*nebrezhna*), however, all sorts of dire consequences might ensue, including a divorce (ibid.). A woman's "femininity" and her graceful appearance should be nurtured; to protect her hands from the visible traces of hard work, a woman is still advised to rely on the familiar gloves from *Khoroshii ton* (Arova 86).

Trial by Dirt

For the political prisoner such as Ginzburg, then, prison becomes an experience of total and shocking deprivation; she is robbed of her family, occupation, status, her sense of ordered space, cleanliness, and beauty. Her very gender and humanity are threatened as well. The "cleansing" of incarceration demands that she accept the notion of being "dirty"—politically, morally, and physically—subverting in the process her own standards of purity. Ginzburg's sense of honor is sabotaged by interrogators who demand false confessions. Her affection for a fellow prisoner is construed as dissipation. And her middle-class sensibilities are assaulted by the smells of rotting human flesh, excrement, blood, and urine, by the moldy walls of her cell, by rodents and bugs, by the dirty utensils and half-cooked meals. Personal cleanliness cannot exist under these conditions, in which, paradoxically, dirt becomes her passport to spirituality.[33]

To accept physical and moral dirt for these women is to go against deep-seated notions about order and conduct. Ginzburg's generation of women perceive criminals as dirty—inside and out; the impurity of the inner self overtakes the person's exterior, attenuating its humanity:

> It seemed as though there was no room left in the hold for as much as a kitten—but down through the hatchway poured another few hundred human beings, if that is the right name for those appalling creatures, the

dregs of the criminal world: murderers, sadists, and experts at every kind of sexual perversion. I am still convinced that the proper place for people like this is not a prison or a camp, but a psychiatric clinic. When the mongrel horde surged down upon us, with their tattooed, half-naked bodies and grimacing, apelike faces, my first thought was that we had been abandoned to the mercy of a crowd of raving lunatics. (Ginzburg 1967, 353–54)[34]

Ratushinskaia, who is a born-again Christian, views most prisoners, including the criminals she encounters, with compassion; yet even for her the filth of immorality is linked to physical dirt. For Ratushinskaia, lesbian behavior in the camps (which she, like Ginzburg, equates with "madness") stems from a lack of self-control, an absence of real love, and of culture (217). Yet she places even greater blame on the coercive authority of the state that made these "poor creatures" live "in pigsty conditions, set [them] against one another, humiliate[d] and debase[d] [them]" (Ratushinskaia 217).

To combat the label of impurity for themselves, these women employ a set of strategies drawn both from the intelligentsia norms of conduct and from traditional peasant attitudes. All of the writers perceive cleanliness (*chistota*) in moral terms. When Ginzburg talks of a fellow prisoner who did not sign incriminating papers, she is consoled by his clean conscience (*chistaia sovest'*) (Ginzburg 1990, 59). In her description of the bathhouse experience quoted above, the focus is on purification through suffering (*ochishchennye stradaniem*) rather than on personal hygiene. Adamova-Sliozberg's declaration of innocence is "I am pure" (*ia chista*) (13). Honest work is the only "human and clean" occupation possible in the camp (*tol'ko trud byl chelovechen i chist*) (69).

Like other women writers in Stalinist prisons, Ginzburg shows that the state of moral purity is achieved by adhering to a code of honor, a code that recalls the behavior of another famous political prisoner, Vera Figner. Ginzburg refers to Figner's memoir as a narrative that guided her own initiation into prison life (35). The notions about honorable conduct that Ginzburg shares with Figner are part of the "implicit intelligentsia criteria of cultural literacy, altruism, industry, and sexual modesty" (Holmgren 134). Like Figner, Ginzburg and other women members of the new elite do not want to show emotion when dealing with their interrogators, are unwilling to implicate anyone, and are ready to help others through sharing and self-denial. Ratushinskaia's memoir conveys similar sentiments.

The crucial difference between Figner and middle-class women victims of Stalinist purges is the absence of comprehensible reasons for the latter's detention. Ginzburg longs for an explanation, wishing at one point to have acted against the regime that crushed her life and envying a fellow inmate who is imprisoned for disseminating anti-Soviet leaflets (334). Yet resisting would have meant acting against herself, performing an act of self-annihilation.

In prison Stalin becomes an enemy, and, like the evil spirits of the Russian peasants, the evil of Stalinism infuses the inmates' environment. Ginzburg sees her survival as an act of opposition to this omnipresent force and as an acknowledgment of her debt to her children. For the political woman prisoner of Ginzburg's generation and class, the body is there to endure, to suffer, and, through suffering, to achieve spiritual deliverance, to become "clean." For Ratushinskaia, who served her prison term under the much milder conditions of the late Brezhnev era, the "profane" is the establishment, both inside and outside the prison. Her fight against the authority of the state is Ratushinskaia's way of remaining spiritually unsullied.

The intelligentsia code of honor, shared by all women writers here, sees heterosexual love based on affection and common interests or chastity as the only possible alternatives to sexual impurity. Bartering your body for food or better accommodations is unacceptable, and these women are willing to risk their lives rather than compromise their ethical position. Yet "true" love can find its place in the camps as well, and Ginzburg, for example, views prudish intolerance of sexuality as an excessive gesture of oppression. The female head of the Kolyma camp, Zimmerman (compared by Ginzburg to the notorious Nazi Ilse Koch), is a dedicated party member, a widow with two children, and a beautiful woman who takes great care of her personal appearance. She is intolerant of the prisoners' immoral behavior, punishing Ginzburg for her involvement with Dr. Val'ter, an involvement that Zimmerman considers undignified. "Dissipation [*razvrat*] offended the whiteness [*belizna*] of her widow's garb," explains Ginzburg. Traditionally, Russian mourning dress is black, and the word *belizna* is used by Ginzburg here purely symbolically, both to indicate Zimmerman's virginal intolerance of sex and to point out the jailer's physical difference from the inmates.

Overall, however, Ginzburg is reticent about such physiological aspects of women's lives as sexuality, menstruation, and venereal disease, resorting to euphemisms, medical terms, or silence. This prudishness, also characteristic of Figner's memoir, is not necessarily imitative of Figner. As we have seen, middle-class norms of behavior aim at hiding the body, and Stalinist culture was particularly attentive to this proscription. All memoirs discussed here, even Ratushinskaia's, subscribe in various degrees to this code of silence about the female body.

What is fully acknowledged, however, in these memoirs is that the female body in prison is physically dirty. Here only jailers and traitors can be physically clean. Ginzburg establishes the color white (in two versions: *belosnezhnyi*, snow-white, and *belizna*, whiteness) as suspect because of its anomaly in prison. The whiteness (*belizna*) of the floor in a children's section of the camp, a condition maintained at all cost for "hygienic reasons," is completely incongruous with the general squalor of the barrack (273). Ginzburg describes the prison initiation of a fellow inmate, the wife of an important Kazan politician, in terms of the incongruity that stems from the woman's nouveau riche aspirations. In the cell her snow-white blouse is like a seagull on a pile of trash. Torture "wipes away the pretentious [*pokaznoi*] makeup," revealing her class and ethnic origins, those of "a provincial Tatar girl who used to sell cigarettes in a village shop" (79–80).

The clean white robe (*chistyi belyi khalat*) of a doctor's assistant (the position Ginzburg hopes to get) is presented by the writer in positive terms (331), for cleanliness and, by extension, the purity of the robe fit into the hospital environment as symbols of compassion for the sick. As we have seen, for Ginzburg the word "clean" (*chistyi*) signifies a state of moral purity. The comparative degree "cleaner" (*chishche*), on the other hand, implies a different and antagonistic status, referring to greater physical cleanliness at odds with the prison existence. Here, in a telling reversal of middle-class perceptions of clean and unclean, Ginzburg posits this axiom of prison existence in Russia: "the dirtier the prison, the worse its food, the chattier and rougher the guards, the less immediate danger for one's life. The cleaner [*chishche*], fatter, more polite the guards, the closer is mortal danger" (68). Thus "cleaner" is very different from "clean," and dirt is beneficial for one's health. Adamova-Sliozberg expresses a similar dread of clean prisons where "prison culture is brought to perfection" as a "regulated existence designed for longevity" (*uporiadochennyi byt rasschitannyi na gody*) (106). The excess of cleanliness, signaled by the comparative degree, becomes a sign of ritualized oppression, of the regulated cleansing of difference, and of death.

The "perpetual cultural opposition of *byt* (daily grind) and *bytie* (spiritual being)," where *byt* is condemned and *bytie* elevated—an opposition characteristic of the Russian intelligentsia—is resurrected by these women as a psychological strategy (Boym 61). Middle-class norms of conduct are reversed, dirt becomes a sign of belonging, the profane is equated with the oppressive state, and purity is perceived in moral terms. For spirituality is the sole area where these women can maintain a sense of order and exercise control. Yet for the spirit to endure, the body has to survive.

Survival in Families

Survival hinges on close ties with a community of prisoners whom the inmate considers "her own." For a woman *intelligent* of the 1930s, this group includes either former members of the Soviet elite, who share cultural origins, love of poetry, and views on Stalinism, or women cast in the traditional role of a wise Russian peasant. A prison "family" is formed where domestic and political spheres are integrated, in this case because of the absence of males. Ginzburg's family consists of "sisters" and "mothers" united by "blood ties"; it is matriarchal and based on co-operation, sharing, and exchange (65). Similar communities are formed by other women writers in prison, including Ratushinskaia. As Louise Lamphere has noted, women's strategies in such extended families focus on cooperation for everyday activities, which are "economic" in the sense that they center on the exchange of goods and services. Here objects related to the practice of cleanliness, such as soap, combs, buttons, and thread, are sometimes used for other purposes or exchanged for other objects more necessary for survival.

Ginzburg's description of her barrack life in Elgen places the maternal figure of simple Maria at the center; she is in charge of the "household," able to maintain order and create a sense of home. The focus is on the survival of the body, and all activities in the "household" are directed to that effect. As in the bathhouse, privacy is nonexistent, and natural bodily functions are attended to in everybody's sight. Like the traditional peasant bathhouse, the barrack is a site of refuge from the hostile forces outside. Maria protects her "daughters" from the cold by providing them with makeshift chamber pots; she ensures that the barrack is sufficiently heated and that inmates have enough to eat. As in the Russian village, dirt is an inevitable part of this life and is generally ignored; warmth of dwelling and body are essential for survival, however, and are maintained at all cost (259).

In her interactions with "mothers," Ginzburg is reminded of other Russian women bound by tradition, and she admires their wisdom and ability to function under the most adverse circumstances. At times she reverts to earlier traditional forms of cultural expression, experiencing the joy of communal spirit in the bathhouse or lamenting in the language of her nanny the fate of her children. Yet, as with other members of the imprisoned elite, a sense of distance, of irreconcilable differences between her and "simple folk," always remains. She describes the envy she feels when observing village women doing the laundry in the river and undercuts her glowing description of domestic bliss by focusing on the borscht that one of the women and her husband will "slurp from the same bowl" (*khlebat' iz odnoi miski*). Or she talks about the fate of a former specialist in Scandinavian languages (ironically labeled by Ginzburg a lucky woman, *shchastlivistsa*) who, upon her release from prison, marries a truck driver and has to endure his drinking and physical abuse.

The matriarchal family is essential for Ginzburg's survival, but she finds her true happiness in the second family she creates in the camp. Her life with Dr. Val'ter, both during imprisonment when she works as his nurse and after her release, is a return to the dynamics of Soviet middle-class life. In her description of this family, Ginzburg focuses on the accouterments of propriety and comfort—privacy, intimacy, cleanliness of body and environment, entertainment of friends, and participation in high culture.

Ginzburg's shifts of perspective, from the middle-class to the traditional and back, point to the chaos of symbolic structures facing all members of Soviet society aspiring to inclusion in the new elite. In Stalinist Russia, the upwardly mobile members of the lower classes had to learn the mores appropriate to their new social position from the old bourgeoisie, while struggling to disengage themselves from the "common" ways of behavior. In prison, however, many of the "arrivistes" are shown to revert to the old mores, abandoning the surface layer of culture, together with expensive clothes and personal cleanliness. And Ginzburg is keenly aware of her difference, both from the "simple" folk and from the "arrivistes."

Ratushinskaia's prison world is less complicated, divided into "politicals" (political and religious activists) and criminals. Most "politicals" come from the relatively homogeneous class of post-Stalin intelligentsia, the class whose cultural roots Ratushinskaia shares. Like the women prisoners of Ginzburg's generation, however, she yearns for communion with the "people," yet realizes the impossibility of belonging:

> What motivated them—they, who barely knew anything about the "rights" for which we struggled—to support us despite the risk of being caught? And in the light of their action, what price the theories aired by some that our people are unaware of their oppressed situation and feel no need for civil liberties? When I was much younger and thought myself

unique in my wisdom, I, too, was guilty of such an attitude toward those who grew the bread I ate or sewed summer dresses....

... And in the wondrous realization that they were on our side, and not on the side of our tormentors, I shed my youthful pride, and the arrogance which might have destroyed my soul melted away. (Ratushinskaia, 148–49)

The arrogance might have melted away, but the sense of difference remains. Like Ginzburg, however, Ratushinskaia is saved by a prison community that is equally matriarchal, asexual, and rigidly organized around shared tasks and responsibilities.

In prison—in the absence of males—these women rely on strategies that emphasize female kinship. Ratushinskaia, whose female community in the camp is very close to the ideal established in Ginzburg's memoir, speaks of lesbian families with the condescension and disdain characteristic of the female Russian *intelligent* ("you poor creatures, you poor creatures! To what have they reduced you?" [217]). Ratushinskaia is emphatic about the distance that exists between a member of the intelligentsia, a political prisoner, and the "poor uncultured" lesbian, or a heterosexual woman who finds a lover in the camps ("It's the political prisoners who wait for each other, even up to twenty years" [216]). To be pure is to be faithful to your male companion, even if it means celibacy. Another reason for Ratushinskaia's antipathy toward lesbian groups is the essentially patriarchal structure of such associations:

I have heard, of course, about lesbianism in the criminal camps, but I had had no idea of how widespread it is. These women, mainly young, who were torn away from normal life, compensated by seeking substitute love and creating substitute families. Yes, families—with grandmothers and grandfathers (those were old zeks), mothers and fathers of under-age children. The "children" were young girls who had been transferred from juvenile zones upon turning eighteen. [...]

Men's names were assumed by "stallions"—women who play the male role in lesbian sex. Those who took the woman's role were referred to as "pickers." (Ratushinskaia 214–15)

Ratushinskaia blames the coercion of incarceration for the "warped psyche" of lesbian inmates, and in the hierarchies of power within lesbian families notes distinct similarities with the hierarchies in the "official" prison and outside. To be sure, when Ratushinskaia and Ginzburg return into the fold of a nuclear family, middle-class notions about propriety kick in, *kul'turnost'* reigns, and family hierarchy is reestablished. Yet their ideal family in prison resists the imitation of patriarchal structures outside; it is firmly based on *female* kinship.

Women's culture in prison camps is a product of resistance and adaptation. Behavioral norms of the intelligentsia and those of workers and former peasants emerge as dynamic responses to the threat of ultimate cleansing. A new code of purity is forged, and women behind bars find the key to personal and spiritual survival in the joys of sisterhood, at the feet of an adoptive mother in a matriarchal family, in the traditional Russian rituals for grieving, and in the communal bathhouse.

Notes

My profound thanks to my two indefatigable editors, Helena Goscilo and Beth Holmgren, and to Professors Ben Eklof and David Ransel of Indiana University, for their help, support, and invaluable criticisms.

1. The return (on the level of public articulation) to conventional feminine roles for women in Stalin's time, based on the notion of the primacy of the family, was a return to the values of the prerevolutionary Russian middle class, which were supported and propagated in post-Stalin Russia as well (Attwood 71–75). As in the 1930s, the post-Stalin period witnessed the grafting of new public and professional roles for women onto the family and domestic roles (McAndrew 94). Middle-class notions of propriety and order, reintroduced in Stalin's time after the abandonment of early postrevolutionary experiments with communal living and sexual liberation, still reigned in the household decades later—the household where the father's authority went unquestioned and the mother tended the hearth, even if she was employed outside the home.

2. "Women's culture" is understood here as a changing network of interactive behaviors based on common social values and shared perceptions about gender roles.

3. On this see Cross 40–42. On foreigners' misconceptions about the sexual nature of mixed bathing, see Vowles 68–69 and Levin 49.

4. The memoir appears in English under the titles *Journey into the Whirlwind* and *In the Whirlwind*. Here the translation from the Russian is mine.

5. Paul Stevenson's and Max Hayward's translation of this passage omits "brotherly love." See Ginzburg 1967, 264.

6. "Brothers" here may also involve the linguistic use of the masculine for the general case. (I am grateful to Beth Holmgren for this observation.)

7. Adamova-Sliozberg's bathhouse as paradise stands in a curious direct opposition to Shul'ts's Dostoevskian vision of prison bathing as hell. Both women, however, perceive the bathhouse as a particularly important symbolic site.

8. See, for example, the scope of issues and materials used in Costlow, Sandler, and Vowles and Farnsworth and Viola.

9. For example, the *Stoglav* (Book of a Hundred Chapters, 1551), a written set of regulations codifying religious and secular life in Russia, implicitly posits norms of actual behavior by attacking heresies and pagan superstitions. The

Domostroi, a popular sixteenth-century manual for household management, is similarly structured around behaviors found inappropriate by its authors.

10. An example of how actual behaviors become visible in a clash of different cultural norms (describing what a person of breeding would not do) is found in Lotman's discussion of daily life in Pushkin's time and of the nobility's perception of good manners. Lotman recalls Tolstoi's description of the return of a Decembrist wife from Siberia. Tolstoi points out that, in spite of long years spent by this woman under the harshest conditions of voluntary exile, one could not imagine her other than having been surrounded with respect and all the comforts of life. "To be hungry and eat with alacrity, to have dirty underwear, to stumble or forget to blow her nose—that was impossible. It was physically impossible" (Lotman 1983, 80). Clearly, it is the woman's "breeding," her unconscious adherence to the norm, that prevents her from being influenced by behavior quite common at the time among other classes.

11. *Kratkaia entsiklopediia domashnego khoziaistva* (The Concise Encyclopedia of Homemaking), published in its sixth edition in 1979, is a narrative of scarcity, aimed at maintenance, preservation, and recycling of space and objects (i.e., strategies for gluing crystal, washing laundry and floors, organizing space in a one-room apartment, tending plants in the home for medicinal purposes, and knitting and sewing one's own clothes). Instructions for the correction of problems related to poor hygiene, such as bad skin and teeth, body odor, athlete's foot, and dandruff, abound. Significantly, the narrative completely avoids issues related to the physiological functions of the female or male body. This prudishness can be accounted for by the fact that, although the implied addressee for most of the narrative is clearly a woman, certain topics pertain to traditionally male activities (such as repairs, photography, fishing, etc.). Topics related to sexuality, and generally avoided in mixed company, are possibly deleted because of the likelihood of a male readership.

12. The basic difference between literature designated as normative and other types of discourses lies in its primary "orientation" (*ustanovka*); all discourses are normative in some sense, since they establish hierarchies of value in relation to different behaviors.

13. On the solipsism of prison memoirs, see Gelfand 29. On women writing in prison, see also Harlow.

14. On changes in Soviet family laws in the 1930s, see Juviler 253.

15. Adamova-Sliozberg's father was a successful tailor in Samara. She graduated from a *gimnaziia*, continued her education in Moscow (with Lenin's assistance), and at the time of imprisonment was married to a university professor. Ioffe was a graduate of the Bekhterev Institute of Psychoneurology, worked as a journalist, and was active in party circles. She was married to A. A. Ioffe, the chairman of the Brest Peace Delegation. Marchenko, a teacher's daughter, worked as a stenographer in a government office and was married to the German Communist leader Herman Taubenberger. Shul'ts was a prominent actress married to a professor and had a degree from the department of social sciences at Moscow State University.

16. Iankova 125, as quoted in Attwood 63.

17. An American visitor to Russia in 1992 was shocked to discover that Russians do not wash as often as Americans, that they are impervious to strong body odor and often pick their noses in public; that most women use rags during menstruation or even resort to saving used tampons; that women rarely shave legs or underarms, and bad breath is a common occurrence (personal communication, Sh. Kirilenko). I would not hazard to offer a full explanation for the staying power of peasant practices of cleanliness in Soviet society; social conditions, which preclude privacy and are responsible for shortages of items related to hygiene, obviously play a part; so do family backgrounds and entrenched notions about behavior shared by the larger culture.

18. One word for "dirty" in Russian, *poganyi*, is a derivative of "pagan," sullied with pagan blood (vulg. Lat. *paganus*) or associated with evil spirits (Zelenin 280).

19. The practice of giving the *soska* to infants survived until the early 1930s (personal communication, Anna Khizhniakova, Pskov region).

20. Personal communication, Natal'ia Melikhova, Pskov region.

21. Some Russian and Byelorussian women simply wore a black or red underskirt during menstruation. I thank David Ransel for this information.

22. Personal communication, Khizhniakova, Pskov region. The belief in the medicinal powers of urine persists to this day. Many Russians use urine as a potion to cure internal infections and to enhance the skin's elasticity (small amounts of urine are consumed over the course of several days).

23. Personal communication, Elena Borovikova, Moscow region. Soap, however, was "unclean," and Old Believers thought it a sin to use soap while washing. Women never used soap for washing dishes; if laundry was done with soap, it had to be rinsed in flowing water, otherwise it would remain "unclean" (Zelenin 280).

24. The boundaries of gender in the domestic sphere were inviolable: men did not do women's work in the hut and its environs. The duties of peasant women included child care, tending the kitchen garden, maintenance of the hut, caring for the smaller livestock, and preparing and preserving food. Healing, midwifery, matchmaking, and witchcraft were almost exclusively in the women's domain (Glickman 149).

25. Siberian women, for example, washed the walls of the house several times a year. Yet, notably, this last custom (like other practices of cleansing) was observed most rigidly in households with young marriageable daughters (Zelenin 281). The association between house and female body as entities requiring cleansing may be seen in the film version of Valentin Rasputin's *Farewell to Matera*, where old Daria enacts a ritual related to transitional states by preparing her home for immolation—carefully washing its "body" and decorating it with flowers.

26. Full body washing occurred two or three times a week (depending on the region and time of year). In some regions a widower could not wash his body for six weeks after the funeral (Efimenko 136). Normally, the unwashed

peasant was prohibited by custom from certain tasks, such as tending the bees, going on a journey, or participating in some rituals (Zelenin 281).

27. On bathing at the time of marriage and after sex, see Baron 186.

28. I am grateful to David Ransel for pointing out the complexities of communal bathing in Russian peasant tradition.

29. For a detailed and influential discussion of "civilizing the body," see Elias.

30. The morning ritual of cleanliness includes combing and brushing hair, cleaning and trimming nails, and washing the face, neck, and ears with cold water because cold water invigorates and strengthens. Brushing one's teeth and rinsing one's mouth is important for health reasons and also because of "propriety" (*prilichie*).

31. The authors advise against obtrusively attending to body functions in public and urge the student to refrain from these practices *even when alone* (emphasis added), to ensure that good habits become automatic (Iur'ev and Vladimirskii 49). Some natural functions (such as burping and farting, for example) are discreetly hidden behind the "so on," but are clearly implied as unacceptable.

32. Tidiness of person (*opriatnost'*) is of paramount importance, even though, as the book admits, this state of social grace precludes a number of the most natural actions:

> to scratch your head, to put fingers in your hair, nose, or ear; to bite your nails, spit on the floor, in the fire, or out of the window, to extinguish a candle right under the noses of those present—all these actions are considered improper in society, and particularly during a meal. In addition, it is very improper while at a meal to blow your nose, sneeze, clean your teeth, sniff tobacco, wipe your sweaty face, and so on. When you have an urgent need to spit, use a handkerchief (if you are not on the street). (Iur'ev and Vladimirskii 48–49)

The separation of private and public behavior through disciplining the body evident in the above citation is a strategy that acknowledges the presence of two sets of antagonistic cultures, that of the person "raised in the village or behind a shop counter" (and unaware of the distinction) and that of the aspiring bourgeois.

33. The notion of cleanliness as purity acquires a different aspect in the middle class. The idea of changing bodily habits of the poor to instill better morals, of equating physical dirt with immorality, informed European thinking on the subject in the mid-nineteenth century and gained prominence in Russia in the late Imperial era (Vigarello 192–93; Frieden 77–83, 156–58). All-conquering cleanliness is supposed to bring with it order and virtue (Vigarello 193).

34. A similar equation of the impurity of the inner and outer self is conveyed in Ioffe's memoir (8).

Works Cited

Achil'diev, I. 1989. "Idol." *Iunost'* 10: 50–59.

Adamova-Sliozberg, Ol'ga. 1989. "Put'." in *Dodnes' tiagoteet*, ed. Semen Vilenskii, 6–123. Moscow: Sovetskii pisatel'.

Agaronian, A. S. 1979. *Kul'tura povedeniia (sotsial'no-prakticheskie aspekty)*. Tashkent: "Uzbekistan."

Aksenov, Vasilii. 1985. "Kazhdyi mig, svobodnyi ot stradanii." In Evgeniia Ginzburg, *Krutoi marshrut*, 3–5. Possev-Verlag.

Arova, E. V. 1985. *Bud'te zdorovy: molodoi sem'e o kul'ture chuvstv i povedeniia*. 2nd ed. Minsk: "Polymia."

Atkinson, Dorothy; Alexander Dallin; and Gail Warshofsky Lapidus, eds. 1977. *Women in Russia*. Stanford: Stanford UP.

Attwood, Lynne. 1985. "The New Soviet Man and Woman." In *Soviet Sisterhood*, ed. Barbara Holland, 54–77. Bloomington: Indiana UP.

Baiburin, A. K., and A. L. Toporkov. 1990. *U istokov etiketa*. Leningrad: Nauka.

Baron, S. H., ed. 1967. *The Travels of Olearius in Seventeenth-Century Russia*. Stanford: Stanford UP.

Boym, Svetlana. 1993. "The Poetics of Banality." In *Fruits of Her Plume*, ed. Helena Goscilo, 59–83. London: M. E. Sharpe.

Buckley, Mary. 1985. "Soviet Interpretations of the Woman Question." In *Soviet Sisterhood*, ed. Barbara Holland, 24–53. Bloomington: Indiana UP.

Clements, Barbara Evans. 1981. "The Birth of the New Soviet Woman." Washington, D.C.: *Kennan Institute for Advanced Russian Studies, The Wilson Center, Occasional Paper* 140.

Clements, Barbara Evans; Barbara Alpern Engel; and Christine D. Worobec, eds. 1991. *Russia's Women: Accommodation, Resistance, Transformation*. Berkeley: U of California P.

Costlow, Jane T.; Stephanie Sandler; and Judith Vowles, eds. 1993. *Sexuality and the Body in Russian Culture*. Stanford: Stanford UP.

Cross, A. G. 1991. "The Russian *Banya* in the Descriptions of Foreign Travellers and in the Depiction of Foreign and Russian Artists." *Oxford Slavonic Papers* 24, N.S.

Douglas, Mary. 1966. *Purity and Danger: An Analysis of Concepts of Pollution and Taboo*. London: Routledge and Kegan Paul.

———. 1973. *Nature Symbols: Explorations in Cosmology*. 2nd ed. London: Barrie and Jenkins.

Dunham, Vera S. 1976. *In Stalin's Time: Middleclass Values in Soviet Fiction*. Cambridge: Cambridge UP.

Efimenko, S. 1877. *Materialy po etnografii russkogo naseleniia Arkhangel'skoi gubernii*. Moscow.

Eliade, Mircea. 1961. *The Sacred and the Profane: The Nature of Religion*. New York: Harper and Row.

Elias, Norbert. *The Civilizing Process*. 1978. New York: Urizen Books.

Farnsworth, Beatrice, and Lynne Viola, eds. 1992. *Russian Peasant Women.* Oxford: Oxford UP.

Fitzpatrick, Sheila. 1988. "Middle-Class Values and Soviet Life in the 1930s." In *Soviet Society and Culture: Essays in Honor of Vera Dunham,* ed. Terry L. Thompson and Richard Sheldon, 20–38. Boulder: Westview P.

Foucault, Michel. 1984. "The Carceral" (from *Discipline and Punish*). In *Foucault Reader,* ed. Paul Rabinow. New York.

Frieden, Nancy Mandelker. 1981. *Russian Physicians in an Era of Reform and Revolution, 1856–1905.* Princeton: Princeton UP.

Frykman, Jonas, and Orvar Lofgren. 1987. *Culture Builders: A Historical Anthropology of Middle-class Life.* New Brunswick: Rutgers UP.

Gelfand, Elissa D. 1983. *Imagination in Confinement: Women's Writings from French Prisons.* Ithaca: Cornell UP.

Ginzburg, Evgeniia. 1990. *Krutoi marshrut: khronika vremen kul'ta lichnosti.* Moscow: Moskovskii pisatel'.

———. 1967. *Journey into the Whirlwind.* New York: Harcourt Brace Jovanovich.

Glickman, Rose L. 1991. "The Peasant Woman as Healer." In Clements, Engel, and Worobec *Russia's Women,* 148–62.

Goffman, Erving. 1961. *Asylums: Essays on the Social Situation of Mental Patients and Other Inmates.* New York: Anchor Books.

Grankina, Nadezhda. 1989. "Zapiski vashei sovremennitsy." In *Dodnes' tiagoteet,* ed. Semen Vilenskii, 149–74. Moscow: Sovetskii pisatel'.

Harlow, Barbara. 1992. *Barred: Women, Writing and Political Detention.* Middletown, Conn.: Wesleyan UP.

Holmgren, Beth. 1994. "For the Good of the Cause: Russian Women's Autobiography in the Twentieth Century." In *Women in Russian Literature,* ed. Diana Greene and Toby Clyman, 127–48. Westport, Conn.: Greenwood Press.

Iankova, Z. A. 1978. *Sovetskaia zhenschina.* Moscow.

Ioffe, Maria. 1978. *Odna noch': Povest' o pravde.* New York: Khronika.

Iur'ev and Vladimirskii, eds. 1889. *Pravila svetskoi zhizni i etiketa: Khoroshii ton.* St. Petersburg. Rpt., Moscow: Ripol, 1991.

Juviler, Peter H. 1977. "Women and Sex in Soviet Law." In Atkinson, Dallin, and Lapidus, *Women in Russia,* 243–66.

Lamphere, Louise. 1975. "Women and Domestic Power: Economic Strategies in Domestic Groups." In *Being Female: Reproduction, Power, Change,* ed. Dana Raphael. The Hague: Mouton.

Levin, Eve. 1993. "Sexual Vocabulary in Medieval Russia." In Costlow, Sandler, and Vowles, *Sexuality and the Body in Russian Culture,* 41–52. Stanford: Stanford UP.

Lotman, Iurii. 1983. *Roman A. S. Pushkina "Evgenii Onegin": Kommentarii.* Leningrad: Prosveshchenie.

———. 1992. *Izbrannye stat'i v trekh tomakh.* Vol. 1. Tallin: Aleksandra.

Marchenko, Zoia. 1989. "Tak bylo. . . . " In *Dodnes' tiagoteet,* ed. Semen Vilenskii. 309–25. Moscow: Sovetskii pisatel'.

McAndrew, Maggie. 1985. "Women's Magazines in the Soviet Union." In *Soviet Sisterhood*, ed. Barbara Holland, 78–115. Bloomington: Indiana UP.

Moore, Henrietta. 1988. *Feminism and Anthropology*. Minneapolis: U of Minnesota P.

Pushkareva, N. L. 1992. "The Woman in the Ancient Russian Family." In *Russian Traditional Culture: Religion, Gender and Customary Law*, ed. Marjorie M. Balzer, 105–21. London: M. E. Sharpe.

Ransel, David. 1991. "Infant-care Cultures in the Russian Empire." In Clements, Engel, and Worobec, *Russia's Women*, 113–32.

Ratushinskaia, Irina. 1988. *Grey Is the Color of Hope*. New York: Knopf.

Rieber, Alfred. 1992. "The Sedimentary Society." In *Between Tsar and People: Educated Society and the Quest for Public Identity in Late Imperial Russia*, ed. Edith W. Clowes, Samuel D. Kassow, and James L. West. Princeton: Princeton UP.

Rybakov, Boris A. 1987. *Iazychestvo drevnei Rusi*. Moscow: Nauka.

Shul'ts, Vera. 1989. "Taganka v Srednei Azii." In *Dodnes' tiagoteet*, ed. Semen Vilenskii, 185–221. Moscow: Sovetskii pisatel'.

Tian-Shanskaia, Olga. 1993. *Village Life in Late Tsarist Russia*. Edited by David L. Ransel. Bloomington: Indiana UP.

Turner, Bryan S. 1984. *The Body and Society: Explorations in Social Theory*. London: Basil Blackwell.

Vigarello, Georges. 1988. *Concepts of Cleanliness: Changing Attitudes in France since the Middle Ages*. Cambridge: Cambridge UP.

Vowels, Judith. 1993. "Marriage à la russe." In Costlow, Sandler, and Vowles, *Sexuality and the Body in Russian Culture*, 53–72.

Wright, Lawrence. 1980. *Clean and Decent: The History of the Bath and Loo*. London: Routledge and Kegan Paul.

Zelenin. D. K. 1991. *Vostochnoslavianskaia etnografiia*. Moscow: Nauka.

PART III

PERFORMING

ARTS

8

WOMEN ON THE VERGE OF A NEW LANGUAGE: RUSSIAN SALON HOSTESSES IN THE FIRST HALF OF THE NINETEENTH CENTURY

Lina Bernstein

AT THE TURN OF THE nineteenth century, the Russian literary salon served as an important forum for the development of a Russian literary language, and its female members played a key role in this process.[1] Although few became published writers, women participated actively in Russian cultural life of this period. In particular, hostesses of literary salons were acutely aware of the social and cultural importance of their private gatherings, for these facilitated the fusion of the social and the literary at a time when Russian letters were rapidly developing. As M. Aronson maintains in his evaluation of salon culture: "At the beginning of the nineteenth century educated society was saturated with literature through and through. So there is no need for us to distinguish salons of that time as literary or non-literary . . . any salon could be a place where literature was being cultivated and disseminated" (Aronson and Reisner 24).

The salon was inextricably tied to the social presence of women, and to social and intellectual interaction between men and women. It provided a place where women could make use of their education and intellect. Recognition as a salon hostess meant a woman could enjoy public affirmation of her abilities and talents and could acquire a visible and significant social position. Women's presence in the salon became a reality in Russia in the eighteenth century, after Peter the Great (1672–1725) mandated women's integration into Russian high society: he ordered the wives and daughters of the nobility to participate in public functions, to attend his "assemblies," and to be present at theater performances and receptions for foreign ambassadors and diplomats. This

"feminization" of society, along with its secularization and greater openness to Western mores, facilitated the creation of Russian salons, which
took as their cultural model the French salon of the seventeenth and
eighteenth centuries.[2] Their development into a literary establishment
was furthered by eighteenth-century reforms in women's education.[3]

Moreover, educated Russian women contributed very specifically to
the linguistic and literary developments of the time. Nikolai Karamzin's
linguistic reform was directed toward a woman reader and a woman
interlocutor, whose "tender style" was to serve as a measure of the perfection of language.[4] Karamzin and his followers were not alone in their
perception of women as the ultimate linguistic arbiters. Even Admiral
Shishkov, the most powerful opponent of Karamzin's reform, affirmed
this evaluation of women's role in literary life: "Industrious minds
invent, write, compose expressions, and define words; women, reading
them, learn purity and correctness of language: but this language, passing
through their lips, becomes clearer, smoother, more pleasant, and sweeter."[5]

Although Shishkov draws a sharp distinction between the roles of
men and women in the creation and development of the Russian language, he does not define women's role as exclusively passive. Rather,
educated women were the chief imitators and consumers of the
changing language: they tested and improved it, and the salon, hosted
and attended by women, was one of the places where the refinement of
language occurred. Women's receptivity to the developing Russian
idiom can be explained by the fact that women had not been overly exposed to the written Russian language. They were neither versed in the
sciences nor engaged in business correspondence. The heavy language
and style of these discourses were alien to them, and their language was
less likely to have been contaminated by rude and folk expressions.

Women exerted overt power as salon hostesses, for they determined
the salon's lifespan, atmosphere, and cultural success.[6] They cultivated the
salon as a meeting place for writers as well as a vital link between writers
and their audience, on whom creative experiments and ideas were tested.
The literary taste of the salon's female "legislator" or *zakonodatel'nitsa*[7] was
an indicator of the response of the writer's audience. The drawing room
of such a "legislator" defined the values of both literature and public life
in general, especially in an era when these two spheres were almost indistinguishable. By virtue of their erudition, personal talents, social grace,
and animated interest in the life of the mind, such remarkable salon hostesses as V. A. Iushkova, E. A. Karamzina, Z. A. Volkonskaia, A. P. Elagina, S.
D. Ponomareva, E. P. Rostopchina, A. O. Smirnova-Rosset, and E. A.
Sverbeeva, to name just a few, attracted not only professional writers, but
also a highly educated and artistically inclined public.[8]

The gatherings hosted by Varvara Afanas'evna Iushkova (née Bunina), a remarkably well-educated woman and an outstanding musician, represent one of the first documented Russian literary salons. Significantly, this salon flourished not in the capitals but in Tula, a provincial town two hundred kilometers south of Moscow and a seat of the old Russian nobility, who spent their summers on their estates in the Tula and Orel regions and their winters in town. Although well-versed in French and German, Iushkova was also at home in Russian language and literature. She organized literary evenings at which "the latest creations of the school of Karamzin and Dmitriev became, immediately upon publication, the subjects of reading and critical discussions" (Brodskii 18). Russian was the language of conversation in her home, and Russian literature was at the core of her circle's intellectual life. Iushkova was also instrumental in creating the Tula Russian theater, which flourishes to this day.

For at least ten years preceding Iushkova's death in 1797, her Tula house served as a forum for Russian language and literature, its representatives, and its audience.[9] Iushkova's provincial literary salon predated similar developments in the capital by at least twenty years. The Russian language was first heard in the drawing rooms of St. Petersburg high society only after 1812, and even then only in certain drawing rooms. Sof'ia Dmitrievna Ponomareva's Petersburg salon serves as a representative case. Although all of Ponomareva's guests were concerned with Russian poetic language, discussions there were often conducted in French. That dualism is exemplified by one of Ponomareva's admirers, Prince A.I. Orest Somov, who wrote poems dedicated to her in Russian, yet left a collection of lengthy love letters to her written in French.

In a recent book, literary scholar Vadim Vatsuro demonstrates the cultural and literary significance of this salon in particular, and of the institution of the salon in general. He shows that the crowd of fawning admirers gathered around Ponomareva did not merely pretend to engage in the love games orchestrated by their playful hostess. (Her album contained a picture of a basket full of hearts with the inscription "Toys of Sof'ia Dmitrievna" [Vatsuro 186].) The real love and admiration inspired by the charming, witty Ponomareva also prompted literary "exercises" by both dilettantes and professionals, who submitted their creations for their muse's judgment. Ponomareva herself commissioned these exercises, and they provoked serious literary discussions in her circle. The hostess, moreover, was supremely equipped to conduct such discussions. One of her guests noted that "her education was most brilliant: she easily conversed in all four European languages [*sic*] and had a perfect command of Russian, which was a rarity at that time; she knew well light foreign literature and our own domestic product" (Vatsuro 16). In addition,

Ponomareva was a talented pianist. On her tomb the poet A.E. Izmailov attested: "She was as charming as a Grace, / As educated as a Muse." Elsewhere he itemizes her talents: "And mind, and beauty, Amiability, talent, Exacting taste, wit, Pleasant and rare knowledge" (Brodskii 93).

Ponomareva was quite in tune with the spirit of the 1810s. Vatsuro portrays her as a highly gifted young woman engaged in the artistic creation of her own life. The image she chose to project was a product of the Romantic age in which she lived: a charming child who convinces those around her that she is even younger than she really is and who inspires and outsmarts her "grown-up" guests.[10] Her salon provided a literary environment that gave birth to and nourished a new light poetry. Baratynskii and Del'vig, among others, left cycles of poems inspired by and dedicated to Ponomareva. Vatsuro quotes one of the guests of her salon, P. L. Iakovlev, who testifies to women's salutary influence on the Russian written language:

> Albums disseminated among us a taste for reading and writing—gave us a taste for literature. . . . It has long been said that only women are able to teach us to speak and write pleasantly, it has long been maintained that only their genuine, fine taste can compel us to give up the strange and base language in which the heroes of Russian novels find expression. . . . Thanks be to women! They introduced the custom of albums. . . . I am even convinced that since the introduction of albums we have begun to write better, more pleasantly, to express ourselves freely, more appropriately, and more closely to the language of public discourse. . . . (45)

Thus a contemporary perceived Ponomareva's salon as a site for both development of the Russian language under female influence and the socialization of men and women.[11]

Another remarkable and representative hostess was Aleksandra Osipovna Smirnova-Rosset, who made her debut in St. Petersburg society in the second half of the 1820s and whose beauty and intellect attracted the best of the literati. Born in Odessa, Smirnova spent her childhood in southern provincial towns. Her first memory is of herself at the age of three conversing with her father in French. French, evidently, was the common language of her parents, a Swiss-Italian father, Joseph Rosseti, and a half-German, half-Georgian mother, Nadezhda Lorer. Amal'ia Ivanovna, a devoted German governess, taught the girl German. "No one taught us Russian," Smirnova recalls with bitterness in her memoirs (Smirnova-Rosset 97). Yet Russian speech surrounded the girl: her grandmother, aunts, and guests spoke a curious mixture of Russian and Ukrainian that Smirnova later captures when reporting their conversations in her memoirs. Many of her contemporaries remarked on her wonderful faculty as a conversationalist and storyteller. P. A. Viazemskii paid her this tribute: "Even silent you would have gained renown for your cleverness. The gift of the word, wit—all this is a luxury in you" ("To A. O. Rosseti," in Smirnova-Rosset 492).

Many urged her to write, but she realized that "to tell and to write are two very different things; thought or word does not come from the pen as easily" (613). Although her diaries, letters, and memoirs contain valuable information about a critical time in the cultural history of Russia, and portraits of the remarkable people she met and those she knew well, the language of her writings is a hybrid of Russian and French. Praise for her style came from those who knew her personally and could vividly imagine her conversation, which combined Russian with French, and sometimes German, English, or even Italian. Although her memoirs represent an invaluable source for literary history, they have little importance as a monument of the Russian language.

Smirnova obtained a real education only at the age of eleven in the Ekaterininskii Institute, whose educational program corresponded to contemporary programs in boys' schools. In his published memoirs Viazemskii somewhat anachronistically recalls Smirnova's thirst for knowledge:

> With some she could pass for an academician in a bonnet. Her knowledge was multifaceted, her reading was instructive and serious, although not to the exclusion of novels and journals. Even theological questions and reading enticed her. A professor from the theological academy would not be superfluous in her woman's study, nor would a diplomat, nor Pushkin or Gogol'. . . . Sometimes she would appear in her reception room . . . after a lesson in the Greek language, by means of which she wanted to study Eastern theology. (234–35)[12]

Yet, like Ponomareva, Smirnova was described as childlike by such contemporaries as Aleksandr Pushkin: ". . . And like a child she was kind, / Laughed at the foolish crowd, / —Judged sensibly and clearly . . ." (Smirnova-Rosset 485).

The childlike qualities emphasized in descriptions of both Ponomareva and Smirnova reflected the Romantic perception of childhood as a harmonious time of life, when judgment is unbiased ("Judged sensibly and clearly") and free of the prejudices of "the foolish crowd." At the same time, the poem quoted above shows what was expected of the hostess by her male visitors: she was the poet's audience and informal critic, accepting or rejecting his work. The same sentiments are expressed in Sobolevskii's epigram: "Not for your luxurious shoulders, / Not for your black eyes, / But for your intelligent speech / Do I adore you. / By

your eyes you are revealed a mischievous imp, / By your soul a child"
(Aronson and Reisner 1984).

In constructing both Ponomareva and Smirnova as unbiased children
who speak freely and sometimes even extremely critically, their male
contemporaries correlated the women's personal behavior with fashionable Romantic images. The social roles these women chose for themselves were influenced by the literature they read; the poems they
inspired reflected those elements of their characters that fit general formulas. Both were playful, as children should be, Ponomareva constantly
mystifying her visitors, Smirnova at seventeen playing the sophisticated
hostess to the dignitaries of her time.

Their salons fostered similar environments, with somewhat different
clientele. Ponomareva's salon provided a meeting place for the older and
younger generations of poets, who, on account of the extreme differences in their literary views, would otherwise not have come together—
an important characteristic of many salons. These meetings resulted in
open and fierce literary debate (Vatsuro 1989). Apart from the literati, the
audience at Ponomareva's consisted of military officers and government
servants. Many of Ponomareva's guests at one time or another were in
love with her, and flirtation was a necessary element of her soirées.

Compared to Ponomareva's salon, the circle of guests in Smirnova's
drawing room was more wide-ranging and distinguished. Smirnova provided a venue for meetings between the principal literary figures of the
day and the highest society, including the tsar himself. Although at different times Smirnova was, as Prince Viazemskii puts it, "in a relationship"
(*v otnosheniiakh* [234]) with some of her visitors, this was not the focus of
her gatherings. What Ponomareva and Smirnova had in common and
what appears to have been central to their success, apart from an excellent education, talent, and a lively intellect, was a certain playfulness and
lightness of character and a youthful charm or beauty that inspired
poetry.

Both Ponomareva and Smirnova were engaged in creating a vital
social milieu, one of the main elements of which was literature, although
this literature was conceived almost exclusively as poetry.[13] N. Aleksandrov characterizes the format of and participants in Smirnova's
gatherings: "Here . . . sometimes literary evenings are organized where
poets read their works, and the hostess criticizes or praises them" (311).
The guests he mentions are predominantly poets: Pushkin, Zhukovskii,
Viazemskii. Smirnova's own diary entry confirms this: "The empress
asked me whether my poets would be coming to my house this evening" (Aronson and Reisner 185). This common conception of literature
as poetry was based on a poetic vision of life. Life's practical, "prosaic"

side interfered with Romantic aspirations and the sublime realm of poetry. Prosaic thinking, which presupposes the importance of everyday detail and serves as the basis for the development of prose, must have been alien to Ponomareva and to the young Smirnova. Their interest was primarily in Russian poetry, and neither of them was much concerned with conversational literary Russian.

Whereas most Petersburg salons retained French as their principal language, many of their Moscow counterparts adopted Russian instead. As the examples of Ponomareva and Smirnova demonstrate, the language of discourse in large part indicated the nature of the salon and the role of the hostess. Salons that favored Russian and created an atmosphere that nourished Russian literary language were mostly family affairs. A.P. Elagina, a daughter of the aforementioned Iushkova, hosted one of the most prominent Moscow literary salons.[14] Russian was the preferred language of this salon, where the theories of the Slavophiles first took shape. As one of Elagina's biographers remarks:

> Avdot'ia Petrovna Elagina's salon in Moscow was the focal point and meeting place of the entire Russian intelligentsia, of all that was the most enlightened, literary, and knowledgeably educated. . . . Avdot'ia Petrovna was not a writer, but took part in the movement and development of Russian thought more than many writers and professional intellectuals. (Kavelin 1899, 1115, 1125)

Elagina was born in 1789 near Tula, on her father's estate. Her father, Petr Nikolaevich Iushkov, held a prominent administrative position in the Tula district during the reign of Catherine II, and belonged to a well-known noble family (ibid. 1116). Elagina's mother, Varvara Afanas'-evna Iushkova, who, as mentioned earlier, was hostess of a literary salon in Tula, paid particular attention to the education of her four daughters. In addition to subjects such as French, German, and music, studied by most children of their class, the Iushkov girls received instruction in the Russian language. Their Russian instructor was Feofilakt Gavrilovich Pokrovskii, a poet and historian of the Tula region who wrote for the *Political Journal* and other publications. Her mother's ideals and aspirations had a profound effect on Elagina. As Bartenev summarizes in the *Russian Archive* (*Russkii Arkhiv*): "From an early age [Elagina] acquired the habit of replacing feminine needlework . . . with reading, note-taking, and in general working at her desk: all her long life she was either copying something . . . or translating from foreign languages, or drawing. . . . To translate and to write were for her a necessity" (487).

Women of strong character predominated in Elagina's immediate surroundings. Both her grandmother, Mariia Grigor'evna Bunina ("famous for her independent character," as Bartenev puts it), in whose house Elagina lived after her mother's death, and her aunt Ekaterina Afanas'evna Protasova, whose daughters Mariia and Aleksandra became Elagina's closest friends, possessed strong personalities and exerted a great influence on the younger generation around them. Like the older women of her family, Elagina had a strong will and determination. These traits of character affected the relationships in Elagina's own family and left their mark on the lives of her children, and even on her children's friends.

Her husband also affected her development. In 1805, at age sixteen, Elagina married Vasilii Ivanovich Kireevskii (who was around thirty at that time), and his influence on her left a lifelong imprint. Together the couple read works on history and Russian Orthodoxy. A sizable portion of her later translations are of a historical, ethnographic, or moral character.

Most of the people who surrounded Elagina in her youth and who imparted their values to her neither aspired to high public office nor desired to ascend the social ladder. Their primary goals were to improve their education and to enrich their spiritual lives. Kireevskii, for example, knew five foreign languages, was a serious chemist, and maintained a well-equipped chemical laboratory at home. His magnificent library attests to his and his wife's historical and philosophical interests. In his activities Vasilii Ivanovich did not distinguish between private and public. Thus, when in 1812 he found the conditions in the Orel hospital unacceptable, he unhesitatingly took over its administration, bought supplies with his own money, and prescribed medicine to the wounded French and Russian soldiers. Unfortunately, he caught typhoid fever in the process, and his twenty-three-year-old wife was left a widow with three small children: Ivan, Petr, and Mariia.

Yet even before her formative marriage to Kireevskii, Elagina and her sister Anna (the future writer Anna Zontag) were seriously engaged in translation. In 1808 and 1809, when V. A. Zhukovskii assumed the leadership of the journal *Messenger of Europe* (Vestnik Evropy), Elagina became his collaborator. She not only carried out copy work for the journal, but also completed a number of translations for publication. Mikhail Gershenzon remarks that "all her life she [Elagina] was translating from foreign languages. . . . her translations, the greater part of which were not published, could comprise many volumes" (91).[15]

After her husband's death, Elagina spent a number of years on her Dolbino estate, where the famous poet Vasilii Zhukovskii often stayed with her. When Zhukovskii wrote his Dolbino poems (1814), Elagina performed the function of professional editor for him, and the poet accepted her judgments, discarding the poems she did not approve

(Kavelin 1899, 1225). She divided her time between her children and Zhukovskii (between the "prosaic" and the "poetic"). By the time Elagina moved to Moscow in 1821, she had married her second husband, Aleksei Andreevich Elagin, who also shared her interests. Elagina's letters to Zhukovskii indicate that the move was made not because she wanted to leave the countryside, but because she thought it necessary to provide a proper education for her children. Elagina's knowledge of country life, her love and appreciation of folk culture, and her work collecting folktales and songs, carried out together with her sister Anna and undertaken on Zhukovskii's advice, all later defined the spirit of her salon.[16] There was no conflict between Elagina's first-rate European education and her acute feeling of belonging to Russia. These two components of her upbringing complemented each other, producing a stable, conservative worldview.

Elagina gradually acquired a reputation in Moscow society as an engaging conversationalist. Her house soon attracted society's most educated members, and by the end of the 1820s it had become one of the most important Moscow centers for cultural exchange. Elagina's salon spanned almost thirty years and had two apogees, in the late 1820s and the early 1830s and again in the early 1840s, coinciding with the coming of age of Elagina's two sets of children. The Elagin-Kireevskiis were a close family, and the salon was a family affair. At seventeen Elagina was already a mother. Indeed, there was practically no generation gap between her and her older children, Ivan and Petr, and as the younger children came of age they upheld the existing pattern of friendship and closeness. Elagina possessed the rare quality of being simultaneously a teacher and a student. Young people who came to her house as her children's friends quickly became her friends as well. They found an interested and serious interlocutor in this mature woman whose conservatism did not prevent her from being open to new knowledge and ideas.

Perhaps the most important characteristic of Elagina's salon, and one that explains its longevity and vitality, was that Russian was its language of intellectual discourse. Elagina's salon remained an active and important literary establishment late into the 1840s, thus spanning the Golden Age of Russian poetry and continuing well into the age of prose. To be sure, poetry and poets were much welcomed and appreciated in Elagina's house. Zhukovskii, Adam Mickiewicz, and Karolina Pavlova visited her salon at different times. Pushkin appeared there in 1826, immediately upon his return from Mikhailovskoe. Nikolai Iazykov often stayed at her house when visiting Moscow, and Evgenii Baratynskii was a close friend of the family. But the dominant mode of discussion may be called prosaic, and this mode grew stronger with the years. Even poets turned to prosaic issues at Elagina's. Pushkin conversed about the importance of collecting and publishing Russian folklore; the exiled Mickiewicz told of Poland and its sufferings. The remoteness of Petersburg and the government enabled the assembled company to voice with comparative freedom their sympathy for the Decembrists and disapproval of the tsar's cruel treatment of them. The university professors who came to tutor the children became family friends and active participants in the salon.

In comparing Elagina's salon with Zinaida Volkonskaia's gatherings in Moscow, Brodskii attempts to minimize any difference between the two. Yet he unwittingly draws an important distinction between their poetic and prosaic orientations:

> It is impossible to draw a sharp distinction between the salons of Zinaida
> Volkonskaia and A. Elagina: if in the former, first-rate talents captivated
> their listeners by their poetic creations in verse and prose, improvised,
> played, and sang, in the latter, outstanding minds shone before their listen-
> ers with their oratorical gifts, eloquently touching upon all possible ques-
> tions, which, however, did not touch the foundations of the social
> existence of the assembled audience. (II)

He suggests two characteristic modes of discourse: Volkonskaia's salon is "poetic," and Elagina's is "oratorical." In Elagina's case, the "oratorical" extended from the hostess's own example. Although constantly surrounded by poets, immersed in Russian poetry, and knowing hundreds of poems by heart, Elagina rarely wrote poetry herself. All her known translations are works of prose, as is, of course, her masterful correspondence. Her letters, written in an era in which Russian was still "not accustomed to epistolary prose" (*k pochtovoi proze ne privyk* [*Eugene Onegin* 67]), are exemplars of epistolary style—warm, humorous, and stylistically sophisticated. Bartenev emphasized the value of her letters for later generations: "Her letters . . . may be called models. To preserve them for posterity is a duty for the sake of Russian letters and for the history of our society" (488).[17]

Elagina's salon provided a forum for the art of conversation in Russian, and with it the art of thinking in Russian, both necessary foundations for the development of Russian prose. It is no coincidence that Elagina's son Ivan Kireevskii, in a review of Russian literature (1829), predicted that the future of this literature lay in prose. The spirit of his mother's salon prompted this insight:

> But if prejudice against women writers has not yet been entirely elimi-
> nated, it seems that another prejudice, against the Russian language, is al-

ready beginning to pass. Not to speak in French is still impossible: thus is our society still formed; thus is our language not yet formed. But at least those who are now beginning to write are of course beginning to write in Russian, and, indeed, that famous example of Russian talent [Zinaida Volkonskaia] is no longer possible; that talent was taken from Russia by French literature, and the more we might expect from it for Russian letters, the more regret it awakens within us. It is not necessary to go on saying that I have in mind here the woman writer who lends to French literature the poetic side of the life of our ancient Slavs. (1984, 103)

Thus, because "prosaics" was a way of life for Elagina, she became a socially important and well-known figure only in the second half of the 1820s.[18] Elagina was described as clever, esteemed, respectable, caring, possessed of high moral qualities and a sharp sense of humor (Kavelin 1899; Bartenev; Koshelev), but never dazzling or childlike. Although she could claim a clear mind and a first-rate education, Elagina could not boast of being a poet's muse or attracting a crowd of admirers seeking her favors. Unlike Ponomareva and Smirnova, whose husbands provided them with material wealth and social position but were otherwise estranged from them, Elagina had true friends and partners in both her husbands. Seductiveness was not her style. There are at least two known portraits of Elagina, one of her as a young woman and one from her later years. The face which looks at us from both portraits has pleasant, clear-cut features and a firm gaze; her image is not posed as that of beauty or child. In fact, by the time Elagina's drawing room opened its doors to Moscow society, she was no longer in her first youth. The life of her salon was intimately connected with the life of her family, with her growing children, and with the necessity to educate them—that is, with the "prosaic." Thus, Eros is absent from her salon, the atmosphere of which is colored by motherly guidance and nurture. Bartenev, implicitly contrasting Elagina with another hypothetical female "type," asserts: "She had not that saccharine nature or sentimentality which can appeal for a minute and then become repellent: she was spared this by constant work and the strict fulfillment of her family obligations" (488).

At times, the gatherings at Elagina's salon resembled university seminars on literary, philosophical, and moral issues. The upbringing she received in her formative years, the values instilled in her by her education and surroundings, her own gifts, her absolute mastery of Russian, and all of her aspirations and principles coalesced to enable her success as a literary salon hostess during the prose-dominated 1830s and 1840s.

Sometimes the success of a woman of a past era is measured by her performance in a male-marked role. Yet in Elagina's day there were other roles that society viewed as no less important and worthy of respect than those of a successful writer or statesman. In an educated Russian family of the first half of the nineteenth century, a woman was responsible for the religious, moral, and aesthetic upbringing of her children. In the case of Elagina this obligation expanded to include the extended "family" of her literary salon, and especially the younger generation that constituted its core.

Indeed, according to the nineteenth-century Russian historian and philosopher, K. D. Kavelin, the role of Elagina and women like her was absolutely essential to the moral and aesthetic formation of his generation of the Russian intelligentsia.[19] Salon hostesses opened their homes for culturally and socially important discussions, assumed a public role, and gained social visibility, participating in the development of Russian language and literature, and making their voices heard. In the capitals and in the provinces, the drawing rooms of salon hostesses attracted a well-educated and intellectually vital part of society, providing a place for the exchange of ideas, social and political news, and new literary works. Salon hostesses constituted the primary audience for both emerging and established writers, who sought out and valued these women's judgments. Salons exhibited a high tolerance for a variety of aesthetic and political allegiances, and hostesses took it upon themselves to protect freedom of expression and fairness toward diverse points of view. Thus, for example, both Slavophiles and Westernizers met at Elagina's, and two aesthetically opposed camps crossed swords at Ponomareva's. The role of a salon hostess was multifaceted: she was inspiration, model, critic, and umpire, and sometimes a patron and a close friend.

Salons were based on ties of family and friendship, with friendship constituting an invaluable counterweight to official social restrictions. As the correspondence of the period shows, salon hostesses provided such friendships as well as an environment in which they could be forged. The importance of personal relationships in the creation and transmission of culture—relationships central to the institution of the salon—remained important in Russia well into the twentieth century. (See below, Holmgren, "Stepping Out/Going Under.")

Notes

1. Literary language here is understood broadly to include the language of educated conversation and epistolary prose as well. See Levin. The Russian linguistic scene at the beginning of the nineteenth century was extremely complex, with Old Church Slavonic, Russian, a mixture of those two called "Slavonic-Russian," and French all present in both written and oral exchanges. In 1800

there was no standard and commonly accepted literary Russian, and in the absence thereof the principal language of the educated Russian elite was French. The widespread dominance of French among the upper classes and their neglect of Russian greatly diminished interest in Russian literature, thereby retarding the development of a Russian literary language, especially of Russian prose. A mature prose requires a broad conversational basis and is built upon the habit of thinking in the language of conversation. See Levin; Lotman and Uspenskii.

2. Although Russian salons imitated their French predecessors, unlike French salons they were almost solely the domain of educated women. A number of Russian salons were hosted by influential men such as A. Olenin, V. Odoevskii, M. Viel'gorskii, and V. Sollogub. However, all of these men were employed at court or in the civil service, and salons were their avocations.

3. Women's secular education in Russia before the eighteenth century was virtually nonexistent, but under Peter I several private schools that accepted both girls and boys opened in Moscow and Petersburg. The first half of the eighteenth century also witnessed the first attempt to create the salon as a public forum for the development and refinement of the Russian language by poet and philologist Vasilii K. Trediakovskii (1703–1769), who was inspired by the salon culture of seventeenth-century France, where salons, hosted by women, cultivated and enriched literary French. But the literary salon established itself in Russia only after the decisive advance in women's education accomplished under Catherine II, who in 1764 issued a decree under which two new women's schools were founded—the Society for the Education of Young Women of the Nobility (Vospitatel'noe obshchestvo blagorodnykh devits) and its affiliated school for girls of the petty bourgeoisie (meshchanskie devitsy). These schools became a model for public schools that opened their doors to students of both sexes. However, the upper class considered it indecent to send their daughters to public schools, and many young women continued to be educated at home. But where earlier the home tutors had been recruited haphazardly and often were without particular qualifications, now they were the same teachers and professors who taught at the schools: professionals had replaced amateurs.

4. See N. M. Karamzin's "Why Are There So Few Authorial Talents in Russia?" (1802); Hammarberg. Hammarberg states that "the budding author was faced with a dilemma: . . . he ought to write as 'dear women' spoke, [at the same time] he needed to provide them with Russian models of how to speak elegantly and sensitively" (96). Women were testing out Karamzin's reform in social settings, further developing and enriching it. The turn of the nineteenth century witnessed a proliferation of publications directed toward women (e.g., *Aglaia, Zhurnal dlia milykh*). One energetic advocate of women's participation in the public forum was a follower of Karamzin, the journalist Petr Makarov. For more on Makarov see Levin; Lotman and Uspenskii; Mordovchenko.

5. A. S. Shishkov, *Rech' pri otkrytii Besedy, Chtenie v Besede liubitelei russokogo slova,* 1 (1811), 42–43, quoted in Todd 1986, 24.

6. The importance for a salon hostess to be in tune with her age is illustrated by the telling example of the poet E. P. Rostopchina. Her Moscow salon at the end of the 1840s, which she opened upon returning from her stay abroad, contrasts sadly with her very successful Petersburg salon of the 1830s. Khodasevich notes that her "rather luxurious salon" "is at odds with contemporary currents" (35), a fact acknowledged in Rostopchina's own poem, which starts with the words: "I have parted ways with the new generation . . ."

7. The term *zakonodatel'nitsa* was coined by Pushkin in *Evgenii Onegin*.

8. According to Aronson and Reisner there were four hundred Russian salons in the first half of the nineteenth century. It is not clear whether this number includes the provinces as well.

9. Iushkova played a decisive role in V. A. Zhukovskii's education, signing him up in the Nobility Pension of the Moscow University. Zhukovskii, Iushkova's half-brother and godson, who lived in her household during her adolescence, credited her with the awakening of his talent. Her name appears in his correspondence throughout his life.

10. Ponomareva certainly succeeded in this: the *Encyclopedia* of Brockhaus and Efron gives 1800 as the year of her birth, whereas she was born in 1794.

11. It is revealing to compare Iakovlev's words about women's beneficial influence upon the Russian language with Charles Townsend's assessment of the language of Princess Natal'ia Dolgorukaia in his introduction to her memoirs. Townsend considers Dolgorukaia's language "neither the ornate and turgid prose, weighted down with Church Slavonicisms, which was so typical of eighteenth century Russian belles-lettres, nor is it the language of the government and the court, with its overlay of Western European and Ukrainian elements which sifted in during Petrine and pre-Petrine periods. At the same time, it is not vulgar or regional speech; the Princess's background precluded this. When Prince Mirskii comments on the 'beautiful undefiled Russian' used by the Princess, he is reacting as would almost any reader to the natural and unadulterated Russian, which is remarkably similar to the modern standard tongue; much closer to it, in fact, than most of the well-known works of eighteenth century literature" (1). These comments echo Herzen's words about his wife's style: "The difference between Natalie's and my styles is very great. . . . In my letters, side by side with sincere feeling there are broken phrases, refined efficacious words, the clear influence of Hugo and new French novelists. Nothing of the kind in her letters, her language is simple, poetic, true" (part 3, 293).

12. Here Viazemskii has put together impressions of Smirnova that he had accumulated over the years. Smirnova became interested in theology and Greek only in the mid-1840s.

13. See Todd's treatment of Pushkin's Tat'iana in her role of salon hostess in his "Eugene Onegin: 'Life's Novel'" (1978, 226–27). Todd's assessment of Tat'iana's role as a creator of social life parallels Vatsuro's assessment of Ponomareva's achievements.

14. On Elagina's salon and literary interests and activities, see archives of Avdot'ia P. Elagina, Rossiiskii Gosudarstvennyi Arkhiv Literatury i Iskusstva

(RGALI), f. 198, op. 1, ed. khr. 107, f.236, op. 1, ed. khr. 67, and Rossiiskaia Gosudarstvennaia Biblioteka (RGB), f. 99, k.1, ed. khr. 8, 9, 16.

15. Elagina's prose translations received high praise from her contemporaries. Indeed, Bartenev concludes that "her translations were not distinguished by strict accuracy, but the thought of the author was always captured and found for itself a superb Russian expression" (488). The story "The Monk" (Chernets), translated into Russian by Elagina from Veit-Weber's *Sagen der Vorzeit* and published in the first issue of *The European* in January 1831 (53–84), earned accolades from the exacting Prince V. F. Odoevskii: "Who translated the German tale? I've never seen a better manner of telling a story! I jumped for joy:—this is exactly the manner which I am looking for in my stories but cannot achieve" (V. F. Odoevskii, TsGALI, f. 236, op. 1, 1.3. Quoted in Vatsuro and Gillel'son 119).

16. For more about this, see Blagoi et al. 15.

17. Not long before her death, Elagina, in official acknowledgment of her contribution to the development of Russian literature, was made an honorary member of the Society of Lovers of Literature (Obshchestvo liubitelei slovesnosti) at Moscow University.

18. The longevity of Elagina's salon may be compared with that of E. A. Karamzina's salon in Petersburg (one of only two significant salons in that city where Russian was the language of discourse), which remained active and vital until Karamzina's death in 1851. Karamzina (née Kolyvanova) was P. A. Viazemskii's stepsister. The gratitude and encomium expressed by Rostopchina in her poem in honor of Karamzina and her salon contrasts sharply with Tolstoi's portrayal of Anna Sherer's salon, where the guests think and speak in French. Describing Karamzina's salon, Rostopchina characterizes it in terms equally applicable to Elagina and her salon: "There they speak and think in Russian, / There their hearts are filled with feeling for the motherland" (quoted in Aronson and Reisner 164). See Koshelev, writing in his *Zapiski* about Karamzina's salon. "They were the only gatherings in Petersburg where they did not play cards and where they spoke Russian" (164).

19. The editors of a recent collection of works by K. D. Kavelin (1989) included, along with his essays on Belinskii, Granovskii, and Dostoevskii, a biographical sketch of Elagina.

Works Cited

Aleksandrov, N. 1924. "A. O. Smirnova." In *Istoriko-literaturnyi sbornik, posv. V. Sreznevskomu*. Leningrad.

Aronson, M., and S. Reisner. 1929. *Literaturnye kruzhki i salony*. Leningrad: Priboi.

Bartenev, Petr. 1877. *Russkii Arkhiv*. Moscow.

Blagoi, D., et al., eds. 1968. *Literaturnoe nasledstvo. Pesni, sobrannye pisateliami. Novye materialy iz arkhiva P. V. Kireevskogo, v. 68*. Moscow: Nauka.

Brodskii, N. L., ed. 1930. *Literaturnye salony i kruzhki*. Moscow-Leningrad: ACADEMIA.

Elagina, A. P. Letters. Rossiiskaia Gosudarstvennaia Biblioteka (RGB, formerly Lenin Library), f. 99, k. 1, ed. khr. 8, 9, 16.

———. Rossiiskii Gosudarstvennyi Arkhiv Literatury i Iskusstva (RGALI), f. 198, op. 1, ed. khr. 107, f. 236, op. 1, ed. khr. 67.

Gershenzon, Mikhail. *Obrazy proshlogo.* Moscow: Okoto, 1912.

Hammarberg, Gitta. *From the Idyll to the Novel: Karamzin's Sentimental Prose.* Cambridge: Cambridge University Press, 1991.

Herzen, Aleksandr. *Byloe i dumy.* Moscow: Khudozhestvennaia literatura, 1967.

Kavelin, K. D. *Sobranie sochinenii.* Vol. 3. St. Petersburg, 1899.

Khodasevich, V. *Stat'i o russkoi poezii.* Petrograd: Epokha, 1922.

Kireevskii, I. V. "O russkikh pisatel'nitsakh." In *Izbrannye stat'i.* Moscow: Sovremennik, 1984.

Kireevskii, I. V., ed. *Evropeets.* Moscow, 1832, #1.

Koshelev, A. I. *Zapiski,* reprint of Berlin, 1884 edition. Newton, Mass.: Oriental Research Partners, 1976.

Levin, V. D. *Ocherk stilistiki russkogo literaturnogo iazka kontsa XVIII–nachala XIX v.* Moscow, 1964.

Lotman, Iu. M. "'Ezda v ostrov liubvi' Trediakovskogo: funktsii perevodnoi literatury v russkoi kul'ture pervoi poloviny XVIII v." In *Problemy izucheniia kul'turnogo naslediia,* 222–30. Moscow, 1985.

Lotman, Iu. M., and B. A. Uspenskii. "Spory o iazyke v nachale XIX veka kak fakt russkoi kul'tury." *Uchenye zapiski Tartuskogo universiteta* 358 (1975): 168–323.

Mordovchenko, N. I. 1959. *Russkaia kritika pervoi poloviny XIX v.* Moscow–Leningrad.

Pushkin, A. S. 1949. *Eugene Onegin.* In *Polnoe sobranie sochinenii, v 10-ti tomakh,* Vol. 5. Moscow-Leningrad: Akademiia nauk, 1949.

Smirnova-Rosset, A. O. 1989. *Dnevnik. Vospominaniia.* Moscow: Nauka.

Todd, William M. 1978. *Literature and Society in Imperial Russia, 1800–1914.* Stanford: Stanford University Press.

———. 1986. *Fiction and Society in the Age of Pushkin.* Cambridge: Harvard University Press.

Tolstoi, L. N. 1951. *Voina i mir.* In *Sobranie sochinenii v 14-ti tomakh,* vol. 4. Moscow: Khudozhestvennaia literatura.

Townsend, Charles. 1977. *The Memoirs of Princess Natal'ia Borisovna Dolgorukaia.* Columbus: Slavica Publishers.

Viazemskii, P. A. 1876–96. *Sochineniia.* Vol. 8. Petersburg: Izdatel'stvo Sheremeteva.

Vatsuro, V. E. 1989. *S. D. P. Iz istorii literaturnogo byta Pushkinskoi pory.* Moscow: Kniga.

Vatsuro, V. E., and M. I. Gillel'son. 1986. *Skvoz' umstvennye plotiny.* Moscow: Kniga.

STEPPING OUT/GOING UNDER:
WOMEN IN RUSSIA'S TWENTIETH-
CENTURY SALONS

Beth Holmgren

When Is a Salon . . . ?

OUR READIEST IMAGES OF THE salon and salonière (the hostess who makes it happen) often surface in period dress and arrayed decorously in upper-class quarters, whether these be the tasteful seventeenth-century Parisian drawing rooms of the Marquise de Rambouillet or, closer to our Russian purview, the palatial St. Petersburg residence of Zinaida Volkonskaia. Certainly these extravagant early models, centered on the bountiful, beautiful, convivial hostess and constellated with the talented and powerful, have excited many succeeding generations to envy and partial imitation. But, as Lina Bernstein has already demonstrated on nineteenth-century Russian examples, the look and character of salons vary considerably from region to region and age to age.[1] Even Western European salons of the late eighteenth and early nineteenth centuries flaunted their differences: the social whirl of Parisian gatherings contrasted with the intellectual weightiness of London's "bluestocking" salons, and the Jewish salons of Old Regime Berlin deviated from both in their daring mix of Jewish and Gentile participants.[2] As we survey twentieth-century culture, these variations become the more pronounced with fundamental changes in the salon's basic building blocks of domestic space and class distinction. In Europe, these changes are perhaps nowhere more drastic, and salon variations more contrastive, than in twentieth-century Russian and Soviet society. As this society careened through a chaotic cultural renaissance, political revolution and class warfare, and varying

degrees of totalitarian repression, its salons coped with very different accommodations and clienteles and produced a fascinating diversity of
salonières.

It is this progression of different salonières that intrigues me, because
they not only epitomize the larger changes in Russian salon culture, but
also confirm, through their very differences, the centrality of women's
images and roles in the development of most salons. Yet in order to make
sense of their differences, it is imperative first to establish some basic connections, to posit a framework that is not so dependent on familiar pre-
twentieth-century models. As the rooms grow smaller and the costuming
less elaborate, we will need more structural clues for comparison. By way
of answering the question of when a salon is a salon (and the consequent
question of what a salonière might be), I offer here a rather improvised
blueprint of the salon's conditions, features, and players.

Generalizing from many specific instances and other historically
grounded studies, we can tentatively conclude that a salon depends on
(1) an environment of relative political stability, (2) a concentrated populace (in either major cities or provincial centers), and (3) an economic
prosperity that fosters luxury spending and at least the sense of a leisured
society among the upper and middle classes (Hertz 15; Quennell 11).[3]
Whereas a salon is almost always situated in a private home, it projects in
various ways a liminal space between private and public—by including
public figures, mixing different social groups, eliciting small-scale public
dialogue. Just as the salon is at once private and public in orientation, it
very often performs the double function of "social and intellectual
event," serving as a venue for debating ideas and showcasing new works
as well as for conversation, entertainment, and more than a little matchmaking.[4] Its participants mirror this hybridity in their reasons for attending and modes of self-presenting. Yet whatever their composition in
terms of class, professional status, and vocation, they constitute a self-
selecting, self-distinguishing group set apart from extant professional associations and occupied with other than mainstream forms of entertainment.

Gender mixing is also a staple feature of the salon, although, historically speaking, this is rarely manifest as an equal distribution of men and
women. Women do not host all salons, and in most cases men predomi-
nate numerically as participants; the fact of women's presence in no way
guarantees the emergence of a specifically "female literary network or
subculture" (Hertz 114). But, given its locus and functions, the salon
regularly enlists women's participation and control because it happens in
their traditional domain and relies on those hostessing and socializing
skills women are conventionally assumed to possess. Moreover, a salon

generally owes its very existence to an attractive, facilitating personality (or personalities), a role women have earned more often on the strength of their gendered image: In contrast to men's more intellectualized public personae, women's charisma could obtain in the admissible combination of spirit and flesh, inner and outer beauty, intellect and virtue, wit and social graces.[5] And women's traditional advantages as salon hostess have been the more enhanced because the salon so often declares its cultivation of a "female sensibility"—a variable package that might claim emotional sensitivity, intimate atmosphere, physical charm, social adeptness, or a dilettantish freedom and verve as exclusively female features.

As spare and generally applicable as this salon blueprint may seem, it still begs some important questions about the always peculiar Russian case. Did the salons of twentieth-century Russia and the Soviet Union retain the private/public orientation and social function that made them so accessible to women? If not, what roles did women play in these gatherings? How did the figure of the salon hostess metamorphose with the liquidation of the aristocracy and the fledgling bourgeoisie? Indeed, was a salon possible in a totalitarian society? What constituted a "female sensibility" in Russia over these years? My analysis of twentieth-century Russian salon culture basically follows its roller-coaster chronology, but specifically juxtaposes the two most distinctive points of the ride: the prerevolutionary years of the so-called Silver Age in Russian culture (1890s–1917) and the post-Stalin decades of the Soviet period (roughly the 1950s through the 1980s).

Stepping Out in the Silver Age

Although it no longer rested comfortably on a nineteenth-century class system, fin-de-siècle Russian society certainly afforded the conditions necessary for salon development. Class boundaries had grown more fluid, and a new class—merchants become industrialists—had superseded the aristocracy as economic leaders and patrons of the arts.[6] The economic prosperity of this period was not evenly distributed, as frequent worker strikes and uprisings attest, yet the combined influences of class mobility, urbanization, improved networks of communication and transportation, advances in education, and the involvement of informed and enthusiastic cultural patrons fomented an extraordinary boom in all kinds of cultural activity.[7] More Russians than ever before were equipped to indulge in leisure pursuits; an unprecedented number of groups formed to explore an unprecedented variety of artistic movements and enterprises.

Many of these groups, which ranged from artists' colonies and workshops to weekly social gatherings, differed from nineteenth-century salons in their educational and professional aspirations, a trend encouraged by a vibrant and diversified cultural market. For example, the famed artists' colony at Abramtsevo, actively sponsored by the industrialist couple Savva and Elizaveta Mamontov, quickly marshaled its residents to *apply* their art—to stage theatrical productions, build a church, found a museum, and even stock a handicrafts gallery for public consumption.[8] The World of Art group, born of a Saint Petersburg schoolboy society dubbed the Nevsky Pickwickians, improvised a pattern of professionalization much copied by its successors: Their informal meetings developed into concentrated exercises in cultural self-education and eventually spawned a highly influential journal and a series of national and international art exhibits.[9] Yet, especially in their founding stages, these groups evinced the public/private and social/intellectual dichotomies characteristic of so many salons. In large part, they had come into being in reaction to the limitations of official organizations. Artists and intellectuals dissatisfied with the bias of government-sponsored academies found greater freedom and meaning in their own informal gatherings, which were sponsored (when project needs arose) by independent patrons. While their meetings privileged intellectual discussion and artistic output, social interaction and social skills remained important. The World of Art, built on schoolboy ties and first convened in the parental homes of Alexander Benois and Dmitrii Filosofov, overtly pursued a "cult of dilettantism" throughout its existence.[10] The Abramtsevo colony, which included various families and sets of friends, was responsible for at least one successful match (the marriage of Vasilii Polenov and Mariia Iakunchikova).

Different features of the salon recurred in many other groups of this period—the Religious-Philosophical Society organized by the poet couple Zinaida Gippius and Dmitrii Merezhkovskii, the "Tower" gatherings at the residence of Viacheslav Ivanov and Lidiia Zinov'eva-Annibal, the Guild of Poets led by poet Nikolai Gumilev and graced by his then wife, the poet Anna Akhmatova. The ever-expanding audience and market for culture encouraged these groups' professionalization and public outreach, but the participants still conceived of themselves as a hybrid social/intellectual network meeting on private grounds and distinguished from official organizations and mainstream cultural production. For the most part, therefore, the old invitation to women was still extended, and, as the above examples indicate, women continued to figure importantly in the new salon variations. Almost none of these groups revolved around a solo hostess, yet most were significantly shaped, maintained, and exemplified by their prominent female participants. As art historian Camilla Gray surmises, even the all-male World of Art could partly trace its "extreme sophistication" to the salon of Filosofov's mother, Anna, "a fashionable hostess whose drawing-room was the centre of the intelligent minor aristocracy" and "a very cultivated person in her own right who had been a founder of the first 'Women's University Courses' in Russia" (39).

Their participation, however, had become more "plotted." These influential salon women echoed general fin-de-siècle tendencies toward cultural synthesis and eclectic revival by mixing and matching certain nineteenth-century hostess paradigms. In such figures as Elizaveta Mamontova, Varvara Morozova (the daughter of a textile magnate who hosted a political salon), and Princess Tenisheva (patron of the Talashkino artists' colony) we can recognize the attributes of the Lady Bountiful (Volkonskaia) and the involved maternal mentor (Elagina). The poets Zinaida Gippius and Anna Akhmatova and the writer Lidiia Zinov'eva-Annibal reprised, in their own idiosyncratic ways, the role of attracting beauty (Volkonskaia, Ponomareva, Smirnova). And it is remarkable that virtually all of these women chose to present themselves as companionate intellectuals and artists, as women who were equal to, yet carefully partnered with, their men. To some extent, this stance recalled the partnerships of such prominent nineteenth-century radicals as Nikolai Nekrasov and his co-editor and common-law wife, Avdot'ia Panaeva.[11] Yet the fin-de-siècle couples deviated from late-nineteenth-century models on two rather contradictory counts: On the one hand, the two partners were more often seen as distinctly and equally important (at least the woman's artistic accomplishments were not subsumed by the man, as in Panaeva's case), and on the other, the very fact of their coupledom was purported to be of vital philosophical, if not metaphysical, importance. In lieu of solo hostesses (with absentee husbands) or solo hosts (with facilitating, self-effacing wives), Silver Age salons featured male/female couples (or in some instances *a ménage à trois*) who held court together in an emblematic demonstration of some higher complex unity—perhaps the "new church" proposed by Gippius and Merezhkovskii or the Dionysian ecstasy supposedly embodied and projected by Ivanov and Zinov'eva-Annibal.[12]

We might speculate, then, that the salonières of the Silver Age had relinquished some of the solo luster of early-nineteenth-century hostesses in a bid for intellectual and artistic equality: They stepped down from their pedestal for a place in the action. Or, viewing them in conjunction with later models, we could argue that these women successfully stepped out from the shadowed roles of quiet facilitator and intellectual helpmate prevalent in the late nineteenth century. Whatever our tally of their wins and losses, we should note that fin-de-siècle Russian society was generally reworking, revaluating, and even reassigning long-established gender

Лидия Димитриевна, Вера, Вячеслав Иванов (ок. 1905).

FIG 9.1. Portrait of Lidiia Zinov'eva–Annibal'. Courtesy of Atheneum Press and Lidiia Ivanova.

images and roles and that this grand experiment had a profound impact on women's function and value in the salon.

As individual cases demonstrate, this experiment kicked open stubborn old doors for women. In past salons, Russian women penned verse (for which they were charmingly praised), translated treatises, or anonymously co-authored entire novels, but it was only at the turn of the century that the largely male critical establishment pronounced them (at least a highly visible few) to be first-rate writers. For example, critics acclaimed the poetry of both Gippius and Akhmatova to the extent of ranking it above their husbands' work; Zinov'eva-Annibal's creative output went less remarked, but her novel depicting a lesbian affair, *Thirty-three Abominations*, was something of a *succès de scandale* (Zlobin 5; Haight 20). Several developments paved the way for this recognition: improvements in women's higher education, the critical and practical inroads made by previous generations of women writers, and, perhaps above all, the increasing visibility of women in the professional sphere.

By the end of the nineteenth century, women had gained ever greater access to various public roles and professions, especially those in the arts that enabled them "to engage in public self-display and self-assertion" (Engelstein 400). Although their work ranged widely over the cultural spectrum, and the phenomenal success of popular female artists did not win highbrow approval, many women earned power and prestige in the public eye.[13] Female artists and performers were overcoming their traditional entrapment as creatures, creations, or, at best, creative auxiliaries, to attain the vaunted position of creator and the respected status of professional. Women could approximate the artistic stature and creative depth of their male peers; by extension, as the fin-de-siècle salon became more professionalized, its female members could participate fully and openly in this process.

Yet if this new blending of gender roles opened old doors for salon women, it also led them into new mazes and occasional dead ends. For while their professional opportunities multiplied and improved, their social currency became more contested in this deliberately aestheticized age. I have underscored the self-conscious synthesis of salon women's roles in the Silver Age (a synthesis of both style and personal association); their varied role-playing also reflects that era's fascination with the visual and performance arts. Fin-de-siècle Russian culture favored all kinds of performance and display—in theater, dance, painting, and most provocatively, daily life. Art Nouveau, the dominant European artistic movement in the early years of the century, aimed to transform the everyday world through art; the World of Art eagerly took up this cause on Russian soil, advocating and practicing an art "which embraces the whole of life" (Chernevich 39; Gray 37). At roughly the same time, writers (particularly poets) practiced a similar conflation of life and art by cultivating singular verbal, visual, and performative self-images.[14] As one astute contemporary remarked, these artists equally prized "the gift of living" and "the gift of writing" (Khodasevich 8). They not only wrote their persona, but also dressed and emoted the part, sometimes to regrettable extremes.[15]

The salon, with its public/private ambiguity, afforded a natural stage for such "in life" dramatics. In its rarefied but not altogether theatricalized atmosphere, an artist could easily tease the boundary between natural and scripted emotions and actions, and could play his or her donned image as "real." Of course, some sort of image-making had always been a prerogative of salon members, whether for the beauties who "made" the salons or for the attendant dandies bent on romantic conquest. But the Silver Age ethos differed in that such posing had become more generally prescribed, generally desirable, and cosmically meaningful. The old gender assignments no longer applied. Women could not lay exclusive claim to the power of the body; more and more men in the salons evinced the same concern for and attached the same significance to their physical image.[16] In this regard, it is intriguing that both women and men in the salon showed keen interest in the numerous portraits made of them, as if they were seeking a suitable imprint of their own "life art."[17]

This is not to say that Silver Age women were actually eclipsed or even equaled by men in their image-making, only that the potential for competition had been theoretically approved and, in some cases, realized. Women still dominated visually in the salons, especially in the "couple" configurations I have noted above. Of these, Gippius was perhaps the most assiduous player, a woman who "devoted a great deal of time to her appearance" and affected such *outré* costumes and cosmetics (elaborate shawls and furs, brick-red rouge) that she earned "the reputation of being a Messalina or, at least, of being extremely affected" (Zlobin 59, 180). Whereas her partner-husband "did not even take notice of other people," Gippius put in calculated performances as salon hostess, always dressed (or undressed) to elicit comment, "reclining on a couch in Mme de Récamier fashion," and engaging her guests with her trenchant and often abusive wit (Berdyaev 145; Matich 1991, 60).[18]

Zinov'eva-Annibal, the hostess of the "Tower" Wednesdays that superseded the Gippius-Merezhkovskii salon, eschewed playing centerpiece for the role of set designer.[19] One eyewitness characterizes her as the "soul and psyche" of these gatherings: "She did not say much and she offered no ideological judgments, but she created an atmosphere of gifted femininity that permeated all our talk and interaction."[20] The notion of "gifted femininity" goes unexplained, but it appears that this atmosphere was tangibly composed of the candlelight that illuminated the salon—with candles stuck in every available holder—and the hostess's fanciful study, painted orange and strewn with brightly colored mattresses and variegated pillows (Deschartes 92). Zinov'eva-Annibal, who reportedly looked Greek and often dressed in a Duncanesque Greek costume, charged the bohemian atmosphere with her bohemian antics: If a speaker proved to be too boring or esoteric, she and a few fellow bohemians would form an impromptu peanut gallery and pelt the bore with apples and oranges (Engelstein 392; Deschartes 18,92).

Clearly, both Gippius and Zinov'eva-Annibal functioned (albeit in different guises) as the visual attractions, even the physical incarnations, of their respective salons. The poet Anna Akhmatova, in turn, fulfilled something of the same role for the entire poetic movement of Acmeism, a group forged in the Guild of Poets. Although her husband, Gumilev, conducted the Guild as more lecture than salon, Akhmatova's striking physi-

cal image—matched by her poetic personae—evoked a salon-like cult of
her person and a lifelong series of portraits and other artistic tributes.[21] Yet
these women's iconic power, so characteristic for salonières in the past,
had become more problematic in their current context of gender blending and revaluation. It seems that the experiment had not gone far
enough; an old double standard lingered in a reductive perception of
woman as body alone. In the Silver Age men were able, if not always interested or equipped, to cultivate their physical image without forfeiting
intellectual control or artistic scope. Such male poets as Valerii Bruisov
and Aleksandr Blok could cut a dashing figure in life and verse and still be
received as serious cultural critics. But successful female image-makers
such as Akhmatova and Gippius chafed at gender-specific boundaries;
both perceived and resisted a marginalization inherent in their female
iconography. Even as Akhmatova developed personae based largely on
women's images and experience, she balked at her "diminished" reputation as "a poet for women" or "poetess." Gippius waged a more dramatic
(and treacherous) battle for respect by appropriating the masculine in her
work and life, adopting a male pseudonym for her critical writing, using
masculine endings in her poetry, and recasting her various femme fatale
poses as androgynous (a curious blend of female beauty and dandyish
Don Juan).[22] Her strategies may have stemmed from her actual biology (as
at least one critic contends), but they also point to a tension between the
"male aesthete" and the "new woman" that has yet to be explored in the
Russian case.[23] By her actions Gippius endorsed widespread claims that
the male-identified androgyne was intellectually and aesthetically superior to the flesh-bound, fetishized female.[24]

Like the salons they co-created, the salonières of the Silver Age
seemed caught in a moment of profound transition. Their diverse roles
and images reflected their summarizing, synthesizing position in Russian
history, for they combined attractive past models and styles from both
Russian and European cultures and projected a new sort of male/female
partnership. As their society grew more urban, worldly, and market-
driven, their status, like the character of their salons, gradually shifted
from that of dilettante to that of professional artist; indeed, even their
supposedly private actions and relationships were increasingly designed
and played as works of art. In terms of professional recognition and
social function (now redefined as social *performance*), these women appeared to be gaining (and perhaps also losing) their way to parity with
their male counterparts. At the same time, however, their experimentation with gender roles had not yet resulted in full equality and a fundamental revaluation of masculine and feminine. Despite all its symbolic
and aesthetic attractions in this era, the female form and the female artist

who manipulated it were still diminished by restrictions, grounded in the flesh.

Going Under in the Post-Stalin Era

Instead of completing this transition, the postrevolutionary years swept Russian society in a very different and much more narrowly defined direction. With the 1917 October revolution and the consolidation and eventual Stalinization of the Soviet Union, the conditions for some facsimile of salon culture drastically eroded and finally collapsed. The new government's chaotic and then ruthless programs of political and economic mobilization destroyed any sense of social stability and private leisure activity. Government-directed class warfare not only reshuffled the class hierarchy, but also ensured that the new privileged classes (workers, party bureaucrats) were absolutely dependent on official favor and bound to official policies. The professionalizing groups already apparent in the Silver Age gave way to official institutions; salons such as the "Tower" and the Religious-Philosophical Society were displaced by such writers' organizations as Proletcult, Pereval, RAPP, etc., all of which necessarily defined themselves as supportive of the new government. By the early 1930s, government agencies had preempted any private associations and were at once patronizing and policing all social, cultural, and intellectual production. Under Stalin, the very notion of a private society was criminalized, suspected as a subversive departures from the state's wise and total control. If a salon was to survive in such conditions, it had to go underground; it operated conspiratorially, not as a public/private space.

After Stalin's death in 1953, these regimenting agencies remained in place and continued to block the emergence of any wholly independent group aboveground. But they no longer exerted absolute control. As the mobilization of the prewar and war years relaxed and de-Stalinization spurred a de facto liberalization in politics and culture, Soviet society responded with a new variant of salon culture.[25] Aside from the prohibition of an independent public culture, all the basic ingredients were present: greater economic and political stability, dominant urban centers, the presence of a privileged class (largely educated white-collar workers) with the time and money to invest in leisure pursuits and, just as important, a well-developed antipathy to many of the official associations and entertainments available to them. This privileged class spontaneously devised a new sort of gathering, variously called *kompaniia* or *kruzhok* (a nineteenth-century Russian term for "intellectual circle"); these proved to be even more wide-ranging in their social and intellectual functions

than past salons.[26] In a sense, the *kruzhok* or *kompaniia* evolved to dis-
place all the official venues its members had come to distrust.[27] In the
words of one participant, such gatherings constituted an alternative society, a freewheeling composite of "publishing houses, speaker bureaus,
salons, billboards, confession booths, concert halls, libraries, museums,
counseling groups, sewing circles, knitting clubs, chambers of commerce,
bars, clubs, restaurants, coffeehouses, dating bureaus, and seminars in literature, history, philosophy, linguistics, economics, genetics, physics,
music, and art" (Alexeyeva and Goldberg 83).

I have argued elsewhere that the development of such unofficial
salons reflected growing trends toward privatization and dissident action
in post-Stalin society and that both these trends particularly involved
women.[28] Whatever their professional obligations, women throughout
Soviet history were tacitly responsible for the domestic sphere, which,
under Stalinist conditions, served as the one possible locus for the private, the unofficial, and, potentially, the dissident. Just as the antagonism
between public and domestic spheres forced a new variant of the salon,
so the specific functions and images of salon hostesses were more determined by present context than by past models. Even in the relatively
relaxed atmosphere of the 1960s, the intervening decades of political terror and material hardship rendered past preoccupations with style and
performance burdensome and somewhat superfluous. The affluence of
post-Stalin society was a very relative thing and material provision an all-
consuming quest; salon hosts were hard-pressed to stock their parties
with appropriate food and drink and the latest in (usually Western)
entertainment. As the designated shoppers for, and keepers of, the home,
women were the hardest-pressed of all. Therefore, one of their chief
functions in the *kompaniia* (or its subsequent incarnations) was that of
actual provider and caretaker. Given the cramped living quarters and
material deficits characteristic of Soviet society, the post-Stalin salon
overlapped literally and figuratively with the kitchen, and the salon hostess was de-glamorized from Lady Bountiful into hands-on shopper,
cook, and cleaning woman. Her baldly pragmatic role was valued rather
than disdained; expectations of a hostess were attuned to the exigencies
of Soviet life, and a woman who played (and dressed) the part of a
Volkonskaia or even a Gippius would have seemed frivolously or suspiciously out of place.

Yet this does not mean that the women in the post-Stalin salons were
simply effaced, stripped of all finery, and reduced to a pair of dish-pan
hands. Rather, as I have indicated above, past images of belles, bohemians, and androgynes were simply inappropriate for a society barely
surfacing from a devastating world war and totalitarian repression. Such

roles recalled an era of decadent self-absorption that irresponsibly allowed for revolution and terror. If the women (and men) in the post-Stalin salons adopted any sort of costume, it was that of Western clothing, the imported or imitative goods that signaled their mild dis-satisfaction with Soviet products and Soviet priorities. (See essay by Vainshtein above.) As the Cold War waxed and waned, a vague pro-Westernism (and especially pro-Americanism) circulated in the clothing, entertainment, and talk of these more or less private parties.[29]

Moreover, the post-Stalin salon sanctioned one new context-specific image for women—that of the aged, surviving witness. After the devas-tation and disruption wrought by Stalin's purges, when millions were executed or incarcerated and most of the country's political and cultural talents were repressed, the so-called "Thaw generation" began to unearth and court the survivors. These included the few artists who escaped extinction—great poets such as Akhmatova and Boris Pasternak—and those who were related or somehow connected to the famous wronged dead. On account of their lesser political persecution and longer life expectancy, women more often assumed this central role, whether they were themselves established artists or artists' companions and witnesses (what the late scholar Carl Proffer has termed "literary widows"). Indeed, in both cases the woman figured as a kind of symbolic caretaker, the embodiment and articulation of a martyred past; the image handily evoked her traditional roles of mother and mourner. Whether these female survivors hosted their own salons or were featured guests of honor in other households, groups of admirers flocked to them in hopes of connecting with that past and earning moral or artistic recognition from their life-suffered authority.[30]

In the post-Stalin salon, then, women once again projected an image based on certain traditionally gendered features, but, in comparison with the gamut of synthetic Silver Age roles, this image proved to be at once more empowering and binding. Its influence became particularly appar-ent in the relationship between image and authorship, a relationship that now scrupulously shunned the extravagant theatricality of fin-de-siècle Russian culture. Whereas Silver Age roles showcased physical beauty, sexual allure, and playful synthesis (mixed styles, gender blending), the post-Stalin image hallowed the solitary, victimized, and aged female body, a woman who bore the authentic stigmata of her or her loved ones' persecution and her place in Stalinist history. The shift enacted something like a religious conversion: Unofficial Soviet society re-nounced an eclectic aestheticization of the body as well as the interim Stalinist images of committed worker and supportive wife for the holy verities of living relic and oracle.[31] We can see this shift conveniently incarnated in Akhmatova, perhaps the star Silver Age survivor in the post-Stalin era. In prerevolutionary years, her hooded eyes, striking profile, world-weary expression, and slim pliant figure case her as the Garbo of the Russian cultural scene.[32] Long decades of bereavement, persecution, and illness then purified and amplified her (quite literally) into a living monument of her suffering nation.[33] The gray-haired, heavyset Akhmatova of the post-Stalin years truly embodied the image she had predicted for herself in *Requiem*, her narrative poem focused on the harshest purge years: the monument of a poet who physically allies herself with all the tyrant's victims. Once her image as artist was fundamentally transformed from companionate beauty into lone relic, a whole new generation of nascent poets revered and served her as a touchstone for enduring poetic and spiritual values.[34]

We can identify similar attitudes in the circles attending Nadezhda Mandel'shtam (the widow of the great poet Osip Mandel'shtam) and, more recently, the poet Marina Tsvetaeva's surviving sister, Anatasiia, although the pitch of sanctimony wavered according to the personality of the worshipped.[35] It is intriguing, however, that almost all of these women, regardless of their literary qualifications, were heeded and read as vital witnesses. In this regard, reverence was automatic and absolute. The embodiment of the caretaker apparently required her articulation; flesh and word were bound together in sacred consonance. Just as the post-Stalin context sanctioned the particular image of the survivor-witness, so it seemed to dictate a correspondent style of testimonial that told a repressed past and commemorated the dead. As long as the author had earned the moral and physical credentials to bear witness—had shared the sufferings of other Stalinist victims and had retained her purity or renounced her blindness—then her work was esteemed and her authority entrenched. Especially in the immediate post-Stalin context, truth-telling, or at least the illusion of it, outholied all other values (ideological correctness, stylistic finesse) in the unofficial judgment of literature.

On the one hand, these new standards enabled many more women to achieve the respected status of author. Unlike the Silver Age artists, these writers did not have to jump through professional hoops, for the truths they told were printable only in the unofficial media of *samizdat* (clandestine self-publishing) or *tamizdat* (publishing abroad), media concerned more with exposing taboo topics than with shaping an official canon. This contemporary emphasis on truth-telling also tended to minimize highbrow distinctions between writer and witness, poet and chronicler. A "literary widow" such as Nadezhda Mandel'shtam, who had dared to preserve her husband's works or to relate his martyrdom, commanded as much regard in her circle as a "true poet" such as Akhmatova. Mandel'shtam, for example, had not worked professionally as a writer (her training was in painting and set design) and began to write only decades after her husband's death in a labor camp, but her first set of memoirs (Englished as *Hope against Hope*) was received as a major literary event and helped establish her modest two-room Moscow apartment as a meeting place for "the best minds, the most talented artists, writers, theologians, priests and philosophers" (Proffer 19). Mandel'shtam's paradigm demonstrates how a "mere companion to the artist" could aspire to the double authority of the caretaker's image and speaking part.

Her subsequent experience, on the other hand, reveals the strictures of this authority. In her second volume of memoirs, Mandel'shtam resumes her analysis of her husband's life and work and the Stalinist context they endured together, but she repeatedly and vehemently oversteps the modest role of testifying widow, critiquing even those presumed to be "pure" and conducting her own idiosyncratic "Day of Judgment" on all the personalities and trends of that era.[36] Her departure from the sanctioned model provoked a telling storm of protest not only from those who felt that they or their associates had been defamed, but also from a community outraged by their icon's betrayal. Their monument had grossly misbehaved. The written responses to Mandel'shtam's second volume angrily demoted her from "witness" to "slanderer" and, in a very interesting act of "defleshing" the relic, from "widow" to "shadow" (Gershtein 89; Kaverin).[37] In ironclad sequence, many of her former admirers condemned her person along with her persona and boycotted her salon: "in a fairly short time, she went from being a literary lioness to being almost an outcast in literary Moscow" (Proffer 31).

The sustained outburst of Mandel'shtam's second volume recalls the frustration with conventional female scripts that we saw in the earlier responses of Akhmatova and Gippius. Yet it is significant that very few women followed her provocative lead. Most of the vaunted "caretakers" in post-Stalin society dutifully kept to the straight and narrow in their behavior and writing and so retained their place by the altar. It is only in the *glasnost'* period, when even dissident society came under close scrutiny, that we encounter Liudmila Petrushevskaia's fictional critique, the story "Our Crowd," in which a late-Soviet female variant of Dostoevsky's Underground Man cynically dissects her motley salon with its "priestess of love," sexual games, unfulfilled "intellectuals," and petty political exploits.[38] Given this general hesitation, it seems, then, that the "caretaker" script, despite its restrictions, may have afforded women more authority, respect, and latitude than the various female icons of the Silver Age, perhaps because the post-Stalin context itself was more circumscribed. In a society still physically traumatized by cataclysmic events

Fig 9.2. Portrait of Nadezhda Mandel'stham in her later years. Courtesy of Ardis Press.

and politically battered into absolute polarization, the combined roles of material provider and moral exemplar placed women at the material and spiritual center of unofficial Soviet life. Certainly this later script better satisfied a demanding artist such as Akhmatova, who consistently strived for a "universal" reputation.

The Ties That Bind

The contrast is almost misleading: the candlelit semicircular room of the "Tower" decorated and dynamized by the togaed Zinov'eva-Annibal; the tiny Soviet kitchen of Nadezhda Mandel'shtam with the wizened, chain-smoking hostess holding forth on her ancient couch. We move between two vastly different salon worlds generated by vastly different contexts. Proliferating in a period of capitalist growth and cultural renaissance, the Silver Age salons relied on comfortable settings and exotic props, and burgeoned into part professional association, part philosophical experiment, and part private theatrical. They invited a grand engagement with the contemporary cultural scene. The salons of the post-Stalin era emerged more circumspectly as a release from and an alternative to a politicized, regimented public life. Coping with an external world of diminished material comfort and narrowed cultural horizons, these salons improvised a homey, unofficial society that was more recuperative than experimental in nature, restoring connections with a forbidden past (the first decades of the century) and a forbidden present (the West).

Yet, as I have labored to show (with worn blueprint in hand), these very different-looking salons share certain enabling features, one of the most important of which is women's role in their shaping and expression. The sharp contrast between the bohemian Zinov'eva-Annibal and the down-to-earth Mandel'shtam really underscores their similar function. The Silver Age salonières flamboyantly realized the traits of their salons; they took the show home. They explored and, in many cases, emblematized a new philosophy or artistic movement; they excelled in staging, costuming, and enacting the "in life dramatics" of the age; they most pointedly illustrated the shift from dilettante to professional with their own successful professionalization. In keeping with a general retreat from public conformity to private pursuits, the women in the post-Stalin salons exchanged Silver Age theatricality for domestic and spiritual commitment; they *replaced* the show (now a ponderous public spectacle) with a new version of home. These women facilitated the very existence of the salon in their capacity as domestic caretaker (shopper, cook, housekeeper, hostess), and those who qualified as surviving witnesses directed, embodied, and articulated the cultural and moral recovery their salons undertook.

In fact, compared with their nineteenth-century predecessors, both sets of twentieth-century salon women exerted a wider range of authority over their respective groups, in large part because of the greater array of professional and social options open to them. Perhaps most impressive was the fact of their recognized authorship: The salon women of the twentieth century were not only rapturously beheld, but also seriously read. But, even with the bonus of authorship, one characteristic remains constant and ambivalent for nineteenth-and twentieth-century salonières alike: Their significance and influence (including their textual influence) seem ineluctably tied to the body, to their physical images, actions, and capacities. Men participate in and are associated with the salon, but its tangible character—its physical space and atmosphere—tends to bear the imprint of and imprint itself on the person of the hostess. As my comparison of the Silver Age and post-Stalin era demonstrates, the valence of this bond between space and flesh can depend on the value society attaches to the female body or one particular type of female body; that body can be fetishized or sanctified. Yet, as many salon women have discovered, this bond is always at once creative and constraining, for while it surely enables a salon to *be*, it may well penalize a salonière for *becoming* beyond its set images and scripts.

Notes

My thanks to Lina Bernstein, Helena Goscilo, and Nicole Tonkovich for their comments and suggestions, and to Mark Sidell for photographing the illustrations.

1. See Bernstein's chapter in this volume on women in nineteenth-century Russian salons.

2.   For an excellent study of this last phenomenon and a useful overview of the features of the salon, see Deborah Hertz's book *Jewish High Society in Old Regime Berlin*.

3.   Quennell's anthology, *Genius in the Drawing-Room: The Literary Salon in the Nineteenth and Twentieth Centuries* (curiously enough, issued under the separate title *Affairs of the Mind: The Salon in Europe and America from the Eighteenth to the Twentieth Centuries* by New Republic Books in the same year), surveys a wide array of salons, including such twentieth-century examples as Mabel Doge's gatherings in Greenwich Village and Lady Emerald Cunard's salon in 1930s and 1940s Britain.

4.   "Whereas some salons provided a workaday atmosphere in which rough drafts were read aloud for criticism and new plays and books evaluated, others were known mainly for sparkling conversation, elegant dinners, and musical performances" (Hertz 17–18).

5.   See, for example, chapter 2 of Carolyn C. Lougee's *Le Paradis des Femmes: Women, Salons, and Social Stratification in Seventeenth-Century France*, in which she discusses seventeenth-century arguments for "feminine authority" based on women's imagination, sentiment, physical sensitivity and weakness, and capacity for love.

6.   For a succinct overview of these changes, see Fitzlyon 21–38.

7.   Fitzlyon argues the importance of the new industrialists' personal interest in the arts: "It was a constructive and discriminating encouragement, relying on the patron's own taste, ability and flair and not, as so often happened in the West at the same time, on experts' and middlemen's advice" (37).

8.   Camilla Gray outlines these activities in her pioneering survey *The Russian Experiment in Art, 1863–1922*. In strictly chronological terms, the founding of the Abramtsevo colony predates the fin-de-siècle period by about ten years, but this colony served as an extremely influential model for later developments.

9.   On the formation and evolution of the World of Art, see Janet Kennedy's *The "Mir iskusstva" Group* and John E. Bowlt's *The Silver Age*; also Bowlt's essay "The World of Art" in the 1975 anthology entitled *The Silver Age of Russian Culture*.

10. "Although it was precisely for its 'dilettantism' that the World of Art was attacked, its amateur enthusiasm, haphazard methods and youthful extremism were characteristic of it from the first meetings of the Pickwickians' Club to the last entanglements of Diaghilev's *Ballets Russes*" (Bowlt 1975, 402).

11. In her excellent article on Gippius, "Dialectics of Cultural Return: Zinaida Gippius' Personal Myth," Olga Matich identifies the poet's important lifestyle connections with the Russian radicals of the 1860s—specifically the characters of Nikolai Chernyshevskii's novel *What Is to Be Done?*

12. See Matich's discussion of the various philosophized relationships prevailing in fin-de-siècle Russian modernist circles, "The Symbolist Meaning of Love: Theory and Practice." Matich posits the different categories of "homoerotic love," "celibate marriage," and "triangular love." Such metaphysical unions did not always result in an equal partnership, as we can see in the relationship between the Symbolist poet Aleksandr Blok and his mystically veiled and humanly misunderstood wife, Liubov' Mendeleeva-Blok. For a discussion of the Gippius-Merezhkovskii "church," see chapter 4 of Temira Pachmuss's *Zinaida Hippius: An Intellectual Profile.* Olga Deschartes provides an extensive account of Ivanov and Zinov'eva-Annibal's relationship in her introduction to Viacheslav Ivanov's *Sobranie sochinenii, I.*

13. Charlotte Rosenthal explains the special popularity of women writers in this period in her essay "Achievement and Obscurity: Women's Prose in the Silver Age."

14. For a wide-ranging analysis of the phenomenon of *zhiznetvorchestvo* (life creation), see the 1994 anthology *Creating Life: The Aesthetic Utopia of Russian Modernism*, ed. Irina Paperno and Joan Delaney Grossman (Stanford: Stanford UP, 1994).

15. Khodasevich investigates *zhiznetvorchestvo* with an eye to its disastrous consequences. One of his essays in *Nekropol'* chronicles the unhappy "plotted" romance between Symbolist poet Valerii Briusov and the "life artist" Nina Petrovskaia.

16. Briusov serves as a most interesting example of this new type. Khodasevich comments on the poet's self-importance and penchant for theatrical and mysterious gestures (33–37).

17. In his diaries Briusov relates at least two instances in which Gippius is eager to show him her portrait. Elsewhere he makes ample note of his own portrait by the famous Silver Age painter Mikhail Vrubel' (96, 115, 134).

18. Zlobin recalls the black dress Gippius had made for the first meeting of the Religious-Philosophical Society, a session attended by church dignitaries: "It was designed in such a way that, with the slightest movement, the pleats would part and a pale pink lining would show through. The impression was that she was naked underneath" (46).

19. The "Tower" refers to the Ivanov–Zinov'eva-Annibal' apartment, which was situated on the top floor of a large Saint Petersburg apartment building and featured a semicircular towerlike room used for their salon. John Malmstad claims that "[b]y 1906, the 'Tower' had become not only the leading intellectual

center of the capital, but a special world with a powerful attraction for the widest possible groups of people" (119).

20. Quoted from N. Berdiaev's "Ivanovskie sredy," in *Russkaia literatura XX veka*, kn. 8, 97–100, by Deschartes 93.

21. A half-century later, Nadezhda Mandel'shtam categorized Akhmatova, along with her close companion Ol'ga Glebova-Sudeikina, as "belles" of early twentieth-century Petersburg society (*Hope Abandoned* 437, 456). In her biography of Akhmatova, Haight proffers a brief description of the meetings of the Guild (17–19). For a more extensive discussion of Akhmatova's iconography, see Holmgren 70–72.

22. Note Gippius' portrait in male dress by Leon Bakst: "Dressed in the exquisite costume of a fop, Gippius is portrayed in a chair, exuding contempt, blasé indifference, and affectation. The portrait definitely contributed to Gippius' dandy-like androgynous image, which provided a striking contrast to her poetry and metaphysical concerns" (Matich 1991, 58).

23. In his introduction to Zlobin's memoir on Gippius, Simon Karlinsky decides that the poet was probably a biological androgyne: "Primarily, though apparently not totally female physically, she felt herself to be a male intellectually and spiritually" (10).

24. Discussing the uneasy relations between "decadents" (often a euphemism for male homosexuals) and "new women" in fin-de-siècle England, Elaine Showalter cites the representative stance of Oscar Wilde, whose "model of homosexuality is implicitly one of gender differentiation, the most perfected form of male aestheticism, a 'romance of art' rather than a romance of the flesh," and whose subtext conveys an "escalating contempt for women, whose bodies seem to stand in the way of philosophical beauty" (176).

25. Ludmila Alexeyeva describes this shift: "Under Stalin, when informing had become the norm, unofficial contacts between people had been reduced to a bare minimum. As a rule, two of three families would associate only among themselves, and there were very few homes where many people gathered. After the fear of mass arrests had passed, people threw themselves at each other, deriving satisfaction from merely being together. A normal Moscow circle numbered forty to fifty 'close friends'" (269).

26. In their joint memoir, *We Lived in Moscow* (My zhili v Moskve, 1956–1980), Soviet dissidents Raisa Orlova and Lev Kopelev describe the transformation of the post-Stalin era *kruzhok* into a new sort of salon (27–29).

27. "No matter which *kompaniia* I was invited to, no matter which corridor I walked down and which door I opened, I sensed that those people were like me. They grew up reading Pushkin and Akhmatova, disliking Pavlik Morozov, tuning out party activists, and considering themselves outsiders. They grew up thinking that they were pitiful beings who did not fit into the 'healthy collective'" (Alexeyeva and Goldberg 84).

28. See Holmgren, chapter 8.

29. In his memoir, *In Search of Melancholy Baby*, Vasilii Aksyonov remarks on the importance of American pop culture products—films, jazz albums, clothes,

cigarettes—in shaping the post-Stalin party scene and its vaguely dissident mentality (12–19). He describes a sort of preview of the *kompaniia*—a 1952 private party in the home of a Moscow diplomat: "I scrutinized the mysterious young beauties gliding across the darkened room—the shiny hair so neatly parted, the suave, white-toothed smiles, the Camels and Pall Malls, the sophisticated English vocabulary ('darling,' 'baby,' 'let's drink')—and their partners, so elegantly attired in jackets with huge padded shoulders, tight black trousers, and thick-soled shoes. Our gang in Kazan did everything it could to ape American fashion; our girls knit us sweaters with deer on them and embroidered our ties with cowboys and cactuses. But it was only imitation, do-it-yourself. This was the genuine article, made in the USA" (13).

30. This category of witness might also be extended to the women and men who belatedly took up the struggle against Stalinist injustice and became dissident activists and central figures in unofficial gatherings. The case of children's writer Frida Vigdorova, as related by Raisa Orlova, serves as one such example (262–84).

31. See Clements and Fitzpatrick for discussion of these two interim images.

32. I am indebted to Claudia Roth Pierpont for this wonderfully apt characterization of Akhmatova.

33. For a more detailed account of how Akhmatova's iconography evolves, see Holmgren 72–76.

34. Haight describes these visits in her biography of Akhmatova: "Now in these easier times other young poets made pilgrimages to recite their works to her and she recited hers to them. Others came for advice or to ask questions about those who had been alive in the early part of the century or who had died in the purges or the war, people with whom Akhmatova was a living link" (176). For a more personalized account of the older Akhmatova's relationship with her admirers, see Naiman.

35. Mandel'shtam, for example, scorned the sort of deference her friend Akhmatova clearly relished in her followers. She cultivated an informal and sometimes deliberately irreverent atmosphere in her makeshift salon. For descriptions of Mandel'shtam's gatherings, see Polivanov and the first chapter of Proffer.

36. The poet Joseph Brodsky specifically names this "Day of Judgment" in his review of Mandel'shtam's second volume of memoirs (13).

37. Kaverin decries Mandel'shtam as a "shadow" of her husband to emphasize her utter inability to sit in judgment. He chose to circulate his countercritique in an open letter to the community.

38. I note here that while Petrushevskaia wrote "Our Crowd" in 1979, it was printed only in 1988, and even then, "[a]ccording to Petrushevskaya's own comments and the letters that bombarded *Novyi mir*, 'Our Crowd' offended many and earned her enemies among the very intelligentsia which purportedly is the strongest supporter of glasnost" (Goscilo xxxiv).

Works Cited

Aksyonov, Vassily. 1989. *In Search of Melancholy Baby*. Translated by Michael Henry Heim and Antonina W. Bouis. New York: Vintage Books.

Alexeyeva, Ludmila. 1985. *Soviet Dissent: Contemporary Movements for National, Religious, and Human Rights*. Translated by Carol Pearce and John Glad. Middletown, Conn.: Wesleyan UP.

Alexeyeva, Ludmila, and Paul Goldberg. 1990. *The Thaw Generation: Coming of Age in the Post-Stalin Era*. Boston: Little, Brown.

Berdyaev, Nicolas. 1951. *Dream and Reality: An Essay in Autobiography*. New York: Macmillan Co.

Bowlt, John E. 1975. "The World of Art." In *The Silver Age of Russian Culture: An Anthology*, 397–432. Ann Arbor: Ardis.

———.1982: *The Silver Age: Russian Art of the Early Twentieth Century and the "World of Art."* Newtonville, Mass.: Oriental Research Partners.

Briusov, Valerii. 1927. *Dnevniki* (1891–1910). Prepared by I. M. Briusova, with introduction by N. S. Ashukin. Moscow: Izd. M.; S. Sabashnikovy.

Brodsky, Joseph. 1974. Review of *Hope Abandoned*. *New York Review of Books*, 7 February, 13–16.

Chernevich, Elena. 1990. *Russian Graphic Design*. London: Studio Vista.

Clements, Barbara Evans. 1991. "Later Developments: Trends in Soviet Women's History 1930 to the Present." In *Russia's Women: Accommodation, Resistance, Transformation*. ed. Barbara Evans Clements, Barbara Alpern Engel, and Christine D. Worobec, 262–78. Berkeley: U of California P.

Deschartes, Olga. 1971. "Vvedenie" to Viacheslav Ivanov's *Sobranie sochinenii, I*, ed. D.V. Ivanov and O. Deschartes, 5–227. Brussels: Foyer Oriental Chretien.

Engelstein, Laura. 1992. *The Keys to Happiness: Sex and the Search for Modernity in Fin de Siècle Russia*. Ithaca, N.Y.: Cornell UP.

Fitzlyon, Kyril. 1977. "Russian Society in the Reign of Nicholas II." In *Before the Revolution: A View of Russia under the Last Tsar*, ed. Kyril Fitzlyon and Tatiana Browning, 15–70. London: Allen Lane.

Fitzpatrick, Sheila. 1988. "'Middle Class Values' and Soviet Life in the 1930s." In *Soviet Society and Culture: Essays in Honor of Vera S. Dunham*, ed. Terry L. Thompson and Richard Sheldon, 20–30. Boulder: Westview P.

Gershtein, Emma. 1988. "Mandel'shtam v Voronezhe." *Pod"em* 7: 84–105.

Goscilo, Helena. 1990. "Introduction: A Nation in Search of Its Authors." In Glasnost: An Anthology of Russian Literature under Gorbachev, ed. Helena Goscilo and Byron Lindsey. Ann Arbor: Ardis.

Gray, Camilla. 1962. *The Russian Experiment in Art*, 1863–1922. Revised and enlarged edition. London: Thames and Hudson.

Haight, Amanda. 1976. *Anna Akhmatova: A Poetic Pilgrimage*. New York: Oxford UP.

Hertz, Deborah. 1988. *Jewish High Society in Old Regime Berlin*. New Haven: Yale UP.

Holmgren, Beth. 1993. *Women's Works in Stalin's Time: On Lidiia Chukovskaia and Nadezhda Mandelstam.* Bloomington: Indiana UP.

Kaverin, Veniamin. Letter to Nadezhda Mandel'shtam. Fond 2788, op. 1, ed. khr. 625, in TsGALI, Moscow.

Kennedy, Janet. 1977. *The "Mir iskusstva" Group and Russian Art, 1898–1912.* New York: Garland Publishing.

Khodasevich, V. F. 1976. *Nekropol'.* Paris: YMCA.

Lougee, Carolyn C. 1976. *Le Paradis des Femmes: Women, Salons, and Social Stratification in Seventeenth-Century France.* Princeton. N.J.: Princeton UP.

Malmstad, John. 1977. "Mixail Kuzmin: A Chronicle of His Life and Times." In M. A. Kuzmin, *Sobranie stikhov III,* 7–319. Munich: Wilhelm Fink Verlag.

Mandelstam, Nadezhda. 1974. *Hope Abandoned.* Trans. Max Hayward. New York: Atheneum.

Matich, Olga. 1991. "Dialectics of Cultural Return: Zinaida Gippius' Personal Myth." In *Cultural Mythologies of Russian Modernism: From the Golden Age to the Silver Age,* ed. Boris Gasparov, Robert P. Huges, and Irina Paperno, 52–72. Berkeley: U of California P.

———. 1994. "The Symbolist Meaning of Love: Theory and Practice." In *Creating Life: The Aesthetic Utopia of Russian Modernism,* ed. Irina Paperno and Joan Delaney Grossman, 24–50. Stanford: Stanford UP.

Naiman, Anatoly. 1991. *Remembering Akhmatova.* Translated by Wendy Rosslyn. London: Halban.

Orlova, Raisa. 1983 *Memoirs.* Trans. Samuel Cioran. New York: Random House.

Orlova, Raisa, and Lev Kopelev. 1988. *My zhili v Moskve, 1956–1980.* Ann Arbor: Ardis.

Pachmuss, Temira. 1971. *Zinaida Hippius: An Intellectual Profile.* Carbondale: Southern Illinois UP.

Paperno, Irina, and Joan Delaney Grossman, eds. 1994. *Creating Life: The Aesthetic Utopia of Russian Modernism.* Stanford: Stanford UP.

Pierpont, Claudia Roth. 1994. "The Rage of Aphrodite." *The New Yorker,* 7 February, 90–98.

Polivanov, Mikhail. 1988. Introduction to Nadezhda Mandel'shtam's *Vospominaniia. Iunost'* 8: 34–35.

Proffer, Carl R. 1987. *The Widows of Russia and Other Writings.* Ann Arbor: Ardis.

Quennell, Peter, ed. 1980. *Genius in the Drawing-Room: The Literary Salon in the Nineteenth and Twentieth Centuries.* London: Weidenfeld and Nicolson.

Rosenthal, Charlotte. 1994. "Achievement and Obscurity: Women's Prose in the Silver Age." In *Women Writers in Russian Literatuare,* ed. Toby W. Clyman and Diana Greene, 149–70. Westport, Conn.: Greenwood P.

Showalter, Elaine. 1990. *Sexual Anarchy: Gender and Culture at the Fin De Siecle.* London: Penguin Books.

Zlobin, Vladimir. 1980. *A Difficult Soul: Zinaida Gippius.* Edited by Simon Karlinsky. Berkeley: U of California P.

10

PLEASURE, DANGER, AND THE
DANCE: NINETEENTH-CENTURY
RUSSIAN VARIATIONS

Stephanie Sandler

WHEN THE HEROINES AND HEROES of a story dance, great changes in emotional expression and the rules regarding sexual play may take place. Narrative progression stops for an aesthetic of motion, and though the limits of the literary text require that dance be evoked through verbal means, words about dance can work new wonders. Lorrie Moore works this magic in her story "Dance in America" (1993), a tale of broken-down lives and a child's serious illness that loses all fear and pain in a final scene of raucous family dancing.[1] In nineteenth-century Russia, dance scenes were more usually associated with aristocratic romantic liaisons. Nowhere more easily than in the ballroom could lovers arrange secret meetings, flirt with daring, or try to discover the true nature of each other's feelings. Particularly in an age of codified sexual mores and fairly rigid gender expectations, as was true for the upper classes in varying degrees throughout the nineteenth century in Russia, dance offered an occasion to violate these norms—or, if not to reject them so completely as to permit any real violation, then to test, to stretch, to push at the limits of behavior in ways that were themselves thrilling and often quite satisfying. Punishment came swiftly and inevitably: there are no dance scenes from nineteenth-century Russian literature where experiments and errors go entirely unpunished, though the severity varies greatly.

In this essay I chart several variations on this theme, variations that differently attend to moments of pleasure, discipline, and punishment.

The variations almost map onto discrete time spans in the nineteenth century (the age of Pushkin, post-Pushkinian romantic writing, and the very end of the century), but my argument is not entirely historical. In part, this is because no compelling, unified historical narrative really emerges from this material. Attitudes toward dance, or toward sexual liaisons, did not change in an easily identifiable progression, though the forms of punishment grew more violent at the turn of the century. Tales of repression were penned alongside some of the most remarkable celebrations of the dancing body, sometimes in the same story. My analysis will depend rather on the interactions between genre conventions and particular anxieties about gender and sexual expression as they change across the decades. I also note shifts in the relationship between danced theatrical entertainment (chiefly ballet) and social dancing. Specific dances prove meaningful: even tales that elide precise dance steps rely on readers' knowledge of cultural practices and social symbolism. The rules of the waltz, the mazurka, and the cotillion turn out to play an inordinate role in determining who gets to enjoy the pleasures of the ballroom, and at what price.

Pleasures of the Dance in the Age of Pushkin

The fullest imaginable sense of liberation in dance enlivens the opening chapter of Aleksandr Pushkin's novel in verse *Eugene Onegin* (Evgenii Onegin, 1823–31). No one can forget the sensual freedoms and recollected pleasures of Istomina dancing, or the heady joys of the foot digression (the focus on feet, legs, and movement also link the foot digression to the ballet scene). More than one Pushkin scholar has found the Istomina stanza so riveting as to study the sounds and rhythms very closely (Briggs 16–21). The discipline of dance remarkably parallels the exigencies of form facing a poet (Todd 19). Visual pleasures and sensual stimulation enter *Onegin* whenever the narrative pauses for dance, and these pleasures are made possible by what William Mills Todd III calls a "grammar of dance." The tension between freedom and control, a familiar theme in this novel, also characterizes its first scene of dance. Unlike the dance scenes we will examine in a moment, dance is not shown as a break in social decorum that leads to punishment and a restoration of social norms; rather, dance itself is governed by rules that have symbolic as well as real value.

The romantic plot of *Eugene Onegin* also relies on a dance scene, the name-day party (chapter 5) at which Onegin dances with Olga. These stanzas contain beautifully poetic and culturally precise descriptions of two dances that had special status at balls of that period, the waltz and the mazurka. Here is Charles Johnston's translation:

> And now, monotonously dashing
> like mindless youth, the waltz goes by
> with spinning noise and senseless flashing
> as pair by pair the dancers fly.
> Revenge's hour is near, and after
> Evgeny, full of inward laughter,
> has gone to Olga, swept the girl
> past all the assembly in a whirl,
> he takes her to a chair, beginning
> to talk of this and that, but then
> after two minutes, off again,
> they're on the dance-floor, waltzing, spinning.
> All are dumbfounded. Lensky shies
> away from trusting his own eyes.
>
> Now the mazurka sounds. Its thunder
> used in times past to ring a peal
> that huge ballrooms vibrated under,
> while floors would split from crash of heel,
> and frames would shudder, now we resemble
> ladies who glide on waxed parquet.
> Yet the mazurka keeps today
> in country towns and suchlike places
> its pristine charm: heeltaps, and leaps,
> and whiskers—all of this it keeps
> as fresh as ever, for its graces
> are here untouched by fashion's reign,
> our modern Russia's plague and bane. (Pushkin, 1977, 152–53)

As Iurii Lotman has observed, Pushkin's account of the mazurka stresses the intervals of solo performance by the male partner (Lotman 86–88); this opportunity of watching as well as dancing characterized other dances of the period that were performed with intervals of dancing and resting, such as the quadrille. Such displays of skill made social dancing quite like the theatrical performances of ballet (Gasnault 11–12; Boulenger 5–18; Lillian Moore 36); ballet masters of the theater were often engaged to coach gentry youth and adults; and certainly a continuum can be said to exist in *Eugene Onegin*'s presentation of dance in both the theater and the ballroom (Todd).[2]

Nowhere was the mazurka enjoyed more than in Russia and Eastern Europe: French and English dance books complained of its complexity to justify their nations' preference for other dances.[3] It became the culmination of Russian balls (as it is in the *Onegin* scene) because the mazurka offered dramatic opportunities for skill in performance. With its possibilities for improvisation and individual expression, the mazurka would have been very much in the spirit of *Eugene Onegin*.[4] Pushkin's narrator laments the more subdued versions of the dance as it was increasingly practiced in Russian cities (though in a canceled stanza he savagely parodies the aggressive male performances in country versions and has the men whipping women into action like stable boys working wild horses [Lotman 184–85]).[5] In the final version, the narrator merely notes the quieting of once thunderous steps, but he retains the impression of gendered tension: the men now glide along like women. This diminished masculinity is played out more generally in *Eugene Onegin*, a novel in which the roles of men and women are highly differentiated but rendered equal in terms of agency when Tatiana's refusal of Onegin forms the symmetrical response to his earlier refusal of her. More relevant to our discussion is the implicit performance by the male partner, the moment for masculine display: this is something seen in a few other literary examples (including Count Rostov's performance of Daniel Cooper in *War and Peace* [Voina i mir, 1863–69], and the praise in that same novel of Denisov's excellent performance of the mazurka). Such examples balance the typically greater stress on women's performances, though they do not diminish the stronger association of women's dance with sexual availability: to return to *War and Peace*, for example, we may recall that Hélène Bezukhova praises the dancing of Duport at the opera, but the body that stays in our memory of the opera scene is her own, hardened by the varnish of the thousands of glances that have scanned her person.

Pushkin does not take the occasion to comment on men's and women's roles when he describes the waltz in the first quoted stanza, perhaps because he is more concerned to show Onegin's desire for revenge on Lenskii than to give a woman's account of the dizzying sensation of being carried along in this dangerous dance. And dangerous it was, to judge from the ways the waltz was frequently associated with sexual transgression or with the heroine's first inclinations to let down her guard (as in Flaubert's *Madame Bovary*, 1857).[6] In 1820 the waltz was still banned at court in France (Perrot 285; Boulenger 20). Yet it was so popular in the early nineteenth century that dance handbooks found description superfluous (indeed, they would have had little to say in any case about a dance so simply performed); they nonetheless excoriated the waltz for the possible closeness of the partners and the building intensity of a dance consisting entirely of the same steps performed over and over (Lotman 85–86).[7] Perhaps most important, the waltz freed the dancing couple from the organized contact with others required in the mazurka, the quadrille, or the earlier minuet (Boulenger 3): the pair could focus their attention on each other, making the waltz all the more a form of erotic temptation.[8]

While Pushkin characteristically does not moralize about the waltz, Onegin presumably chooses this moment to get even with Lenskii precisely because of the waltz's associations with seduction. The specifics of dance again prove meaningful to Pushkin, even if the dance itself is barely mentioned. Pushkin generally handles questions of error and punishment less aggressively than many of his successors. In part, that has to do with his having portrayed relations between men and women less puritanically and with considerable psychological complexity. The difference is also one of form: The foundation of verse rules and repeating rhythms enables not fixity but graceful and ever-changing poetry. As with the scene of Istomina dancing, control mixes with passionate expression. Women are allowed agency at nearly all levels. In prose and some poetry, other writers seem less able to find counterbalancing language that is beautiful; one poetic tale exudes an ugly spirit of revenge.

A literary genre that more dramatically contrasts flights of romantic fancy with moral sternness is the society tale (svetskaia povest'), which flourished in Russia from about 1820 to about 1850. The society tale frequently takes the ballroom as a key location for romantic plots, as several scholars have noted (Iezuitova; Shepard; Andrew); thus it is attractive for our purposes because it nearly always describes dance. One of Joe Andrew's key points is to read the semiotic coding of the ballroom: When a woman is frequently said to love dancing at balls, for example, we know that she is being represented as superficial, narcissistic, and perhaps sexually transgressive. Memoir accounts of Pushkin's wife, Natal'ia Nikolaevna, make this association;[9] literary examples include Princess Lidiia in Vladimir Odoevskii's tale "Princess Zizi" (Kniazhna Zizi, 1839) and the self-recriminations of Evdokiia Rostopchina's poem "Temptation" (Iskushen'e, 1839)—Rostopchina ironically observes that being a woman renders one helpless before this silly passion for the ball.[10]

Most society tales traffic in a form of romantic fantasy that offers love as an escape from confined daily life; the experience of dancing is associated with an irruption of pleasure and perhaps sexual power. This

association works principally for women, who were among the important producers, consumers, and heroines of society tales; the pleasures
women enjoy in the ballroom are inevitably contained by fairly harsh
invocations of social restrictions. The means for enforcing these norms
varies: in *Onegin* a duel emerges from the improprieties of the waltz, and
dueling frequently punctuates society tales. A less violent form of discipline is enforced by women as well as men: gossip.

Talk in the Ballroom

No European or American writer was closer to Pushkin in spirit than
Jane Austen, and her novels give frequent accounts of the way conversational wit could be used as a means of control (in *Pride and Prejudice*) and
the ways talk itself could be transgressive (in *Emma*). It is in *Pride and
Prejudice* (1813) that Austen gives us her most memorable scenes of
dance. She has a minor (and disagreeable) character, Miss Bingley, try to
create some competition between dancing and talking when Miss
Bingley observes, "It would surely be much more rational if conversation
instead of dancing made the order of the day" (Austen 100). But as
Austen shows, interludes of dance were themselves punctuated by conversation. Elizabeth Bennett provokes a nearly silent Mr. Darcy during
their first dance together with these words: "It is *your* turn to say something now, Mr Darcy.—*I* talked about the dance, and *you* ought to make
some kind of remark on the size of the room, or the number of couples"
(Austen 133–34). Even if Elizabeth's comment appears to reveal the
emptiness of most ballroom chatter, her words suggest wit and her abiding sexual vitality.

In the ballroom scenes of many society tales, talk virtually replaces
dance. Some tales make passing references to particular dances, but the
comments are formulaic and the women rarely have the sassiness of Jane
Austen's heroines. An exception is Karolina Pavlova's *Quadrille* (Kadril',
1843–59), where four women narrate poignant and knowing romantic
histories. *Quadrille* quite literally substitutes words for dance, since the
frame story of these four individual tales shows the women gathering to
attend an evening's ball. They keep delaying their departure to hear each
other's tales, and, given the intelligent and deprecating views they all
hold with regard to how men treat women at these balls, it is thoroughly
obvious that they prefer each other's understanding and like-minded
company. Talk also figures in important ways in the tales they recount
(that is, their adventures thematize the dangers or pleasures of speech).
Ol'ga's story recalls her first ball and her first dance. It is the mazurka,

and the young man is voluble. He clutches her too closely during their dance, but the striking and offensive part of their encounter is his effusive and, as it turns out, fulsome declaration of love. In Countess Polina's story, mazurka chatter is called a kind of verbal swordplay, a competition of clever words, and indeed throughout *Quadrille* Pavlova exposes the aggressiveness and maneuvering that romantic liaisons in the ballroom often involve.

The inclusion of talk is in part an effect of the way the mazurka was danced (and not just the mazurka—this would be true of all forms of round or square dancing where the choreography demanded patterns of couples taking turns with their movements), since regular interludes of seated stillness punctuated one's opportunity to glide across the room (Aldrich; Lotman). The dancers are not the only ones who talk, of course. Observers evaluate the behavior and appearance of dancers and thus discipline their desires. Gossip is the most extreme form of this talk: Whispering denunciations shape the ballroom scenes of *Woe from Wit* (Gore ot uma, 1824) and *Dead Souls* (Mertvye dushi, 1842). In society tales that focus more on romantic fantasies, gossip punishes flights of fancy; indeed, the gossip itself is often a tissue of lies, as in Vladimir Odoevskii's "Princess Mimi" (Kniazhna Mimi, 1834), which ends in early deaths and duels all around.

"Princess Mimi" offers a strong example of what is being disciplined in many dance scenes. Ballrooms expose women at their most sexual. They are elaborately costumed and made beautiful by cosmetics and jewelry. More of their flesh is showing than in any other setting save their own bedrooms. The paucity of descriptions of actual dance in society tales often goes unnoticed, given the extravagantly compensatory accounts of lace, net, and floral trims, intricate hairpieces, brilliant gems, and remarkably eye-catching flesh. What such ballroom scenes are about, and what must be disciplined, is the abundant display of women's erotic capacities, with the suggestion that it is they who might control their sexuality. (See essay by Goscilo above.) In many literary texts, it is women who seem to control the movements in the ballroom with their shrewd observations of who is dancing with whom, their plans for matchmaking and marriage, and their gossip (as in "Princess Mimi"). In what seems a women's domain, the sexual expressions can appear uncontrolled—which some of the stories I will now examine clearly translate into a lack of control by men. Not all fictions accept this view— Pavlova's *Quadrille* is again a vivid exception, particularly in the passages in Ol'ga's story that meditate on the powerlessness of a young woman new to balls. Still, most tales, even without showing the illicit joys of the dance, suggest that something very dangerous happens in the ballroom, and more generally whenever defenseless men are exposed to the sexual wiles of women.

Evgenii Baratynskii's remarkable narrative poem "The Ball" (Bal, 1828) images the dangers of women quite memorably.[11] The heroine Nina, a passionate woman who seems to elicit jealousy and gossip on all sides, was modeled on the great beauty Agrafena Zakrevskaia,[12] who figures in Pushkin's poetry as the "lawless comet" (*bezzakonnaia kometa*) and in Baratynskii's verse as a woman who could weep like Mary Magdalene but also laugh exultantly like a mermaid.[13] Commentaries characterize Zakrevskaia as fiery in temperament and free in behavior. No wonder Baratynskii describes the heroine of "The Ball" as having lips beyond reproach, black eyes bright with luster, moist with passion (*neporochnye usta* and *iarkii glianets chernykh glaz, / Oblitykh vlagoi sladostrastnoi*; Baratynskii 190). More important, this is a woman whose passionate anger, especially when infused with jealousy, gives vent to terrible words, and at such moments she is to be feared—a "dangerous charmer" (*prelestnitsa opasnaia*; Baratynskii 191). Her aura of danger interests us, and Baratynskii figures it very aggressively:

> Beware this dangerous charmer,
> Do not approach: She is surrounded
> By an enchanted boundary;
> The air encircling her is filled
> With a passionate disease! Pity on him
> Who enters into its sweet intoxication:
> A whirlpool draws the fisherman's boat
> To death in this way!
> Fly from her, she has no heart!
> Fear the besotting lure
> Of her insinuating speeches;
> Do not catch her infatuated glances:
> The fire in her comes from a drunken Bacchante,
> It is the fire of fever, not the fire of love. (Baratynskii 191)

You would never know from this description that it is not her lover who is at risk (he will desert her rather quickly for a former love). Nina herself is in danger in this poem. She is at once the source and the target of harm; thus her suicide offers the only possible violent outcome in this plot. The poem ends with a recapitulation of the first ballroom scene, which Nina flees precipitously. Something—we are never told what—causes her to flee, and she is next seen at home, suspiciously unmoving in her bedroom armchair. The poem takes great care to show how Nina adorned herself for the ball (dress and jewelry are constant markers of the woman destined for dance; see Aleksandrov; Pavlova); but in the end the enumerated details of pearls, diamonds, and rouge serve as grotesque decorations on a dead woman. Lest we miss the point that this death is the price for a moral failure, Nina's mother comes into her bedroom. Unaware that she stands over a dead daughter, the mother delivers a speech about Nina's lapses from the righteous paths of religious devotion and family duty. Baratynskii, having begun with a vivid representation of the dangers posed by women, ends with a funeral. The ballroom's music has been replaced by a surge of gossip about Nina, gossip that is said even to find its way onto the pages of the *Ladies Journal* (Damskii zhurnal). Commentators note that this closing is Baratynskii's joking swipe against a journal that had criticized his poetry,[14] but the journal's name also suggests that *women* have spread the malicious gossip about Nina after her death (just as moralizing is imputed to women by having Nina's mother pronounce such a vicious speech over her daughter's dead body). Again, men are exonerated from any responsibility for this woman's terrible fate, which is to say that the tales produce an illusion of women's agency and control even when women are shown as victims.

In the society tale and in the romantic long poem, erotic urges nearly always meet powerful obstacles and transgression meets punishment; social harmony is thereby restored. The ballroom in a society tale often sets a scene for young romance, where it might be a girl's first ball (as it is for Ol'ga in "The Quadrille") or a further opportunity for encountering a beloved man whom her parents oppose (as in Rostopchina's prose tale "Rank and Money" [Chiny i den'gi, 1838]). Variations on this pattern appear in Karolina Pavlova's *A Double Life* (Dvoinaia zhizn', 1848), a prose and poetry text that juxtaposes adult machinations with young female innocence; and in a number of society tales about adulterous liaisons, such as "Princess Mimi," Elena Gan's "Ideal" (1837), and Mariia Zhukova's "Baron Reikhman" (1837). In all these examples, gossip is actually the gentlest form of discipline. Duels are frequent, as are premature deaths for the women. That is to say that verbal censure frequently gives way to more violent forms of control; coercion is not foreign to these polite societies, though it is usually cloaked in social niceties. As some of these examples have suggested, the demand that women's sexual behavior be controlled is fully sufficient grounds for this violence. But tales written somewhat further from the norms of the society tale or the long poem, and more closely attuned to the utilitarian social criticism urged in intellectual circles beginning as early as the 1830s, show us a different side of this violence. This is a world where the continuum between dance and talk is ruptured: Here, actions speak louder than words, and no act seems able to restore the social harmony so valued in the society tales examined thus far.

Dance and War

For the narrator in Prince Vladimir Odoevskii's short sketch "The Ball" (Bal, 1833), the ballroom changes from a scene of dancing pleasure to a reminder of mass death on the battlefield. "The Ball" is part of Odoevskii's *Russian Nights* (Russkie nochi, first collected in 1844). The tale substitutes for the narrative of romance a decidedly masculine meditation on war, wounds, and death. Joyful exclamations of a military victory frame "The Ball," but the prize has been taken with considerable toll. There are 10,000 dead and 30,000 disabled soldiers. The booty includes banners splattered with the brains of the enemy and marked with bloody handprints. Odoevskii describes one celebration ball briefly but intensely:

> The ball burned hotter with each passing hour; thin fumes passed in waves over countless dim candles; brocade curtains, marble vases, golden tassels, bas-reliefs, columns, and pictures flickered in the haze; heated air rose from the bared breasts of beautiful women, and often, when the dancing pairs, seemingly torn from the arms of an enchanter, passed before one's eyes in swift turns, it was as if one were in the dry steppes of Arabia and suddenly overcome by a burning, smothering wind; with each hour the fragrant curls came undone; wrinkles of smoke whirled freely above flaming shoulders; the pulse beat faster; hands met more frequently; red-hot faces drew closer; glances grew more languid, laughter and whispering more audible; old men rose up from their places, straightening out their weak limbs, and in half-closed, dazed eyes bitter envy mixed with bitter memories of the past. And everything was turning, jumping, as if possessed by sensual insanity. (Odoevskii 45)

Among the many remarkable qualities of this description is its appearance of emanating from no particular point of view. Odoevskii introduces within a paragraph a first-person narrator who describes with horror his impression that howls of pain and death mix with the music. Every sound tears at his nerves and makes him shudder. As the music hangs oppressively over the dancers, our narrator observes equally horrifying changes in the dancing itself. Every beat of the music urges forth images of a face turned pale from torture, of eyes laughing insanely, of the quivering knees of a murderer, of caked dry lips on a dead man. Drops of blood and tears seem to spill onto the parquet floor, and the velvet dance slippers of beautiful women start to slip. And, in a paragraph Odoevskii later deleted (presumably because the *danse macabre* allusions were more than adequate),[15] the narrator comes to see the dancing people as spectral reminders of death. In quick movements, first clothing, then hair, then flesh itself drop from the dancers' bodies, leaving only skeletons that bump into one another as the dance whirls on in its devilish frenzy.

Odoevskii's brief story ends when the narrator runs out into a church, where he seeks but does not find purification. For all his romantic clichés and purple prose, he gives us a fairly straightforward substitution of the violence of the dance for the destructiveness and death of war. While one might take this young male narrator as a victim of the war, his psychic wounds so disabling that he cannot look at the innocence of a ballroom dance without seeing instead the movements of the dead, it could also be argued that he merely sees the dance for what it is. This is surely why Odoevskii gives us the first description of heat, smoke, insane sensuality, and frenzied movement as if from a neutral perspective. Many other texts contain the metaphor of battle, usually as the battle between the sexes. Elsewhere, Odoevskii himself refers to the struggles of women with men, or simply the ways in which women are routinely trivialized and diminished. He includes bitter commentary about gendered inequality in "Princess Mimi," his shrewd exposé of an unmarried older woman who takes revenge on a culture that systematically devalues her. He conveys even stronger sentiments about the trivialization of women in his fable "A Tale of Why It Is Dangerous for Young Girls to Go Walking in a Group along Nevskii Prospect" (Skazka o tom, kak opasno devushkam khodit' tolpoiu po Nevskomu, 1834), where a girl is turned into a doll by a magical shopkeeper in a story quite reminiscent of the tales of E. T. A. Hoffmann. Her upbringing has long ago turned her into something mechanical, Odoevskii suggests, laying the blame at the feet of mothers, writers, and commercial culture. In "The Ball," however, Odoevskii sharply turns away from an analysis of the ballroom as a scene for gendered battle, preferring to use this site of cultural celebration (and one-time cultural harmony, as Lotman and Todd have noted) as a trope for violence and social discord.

A somewhat different diatribe informs a story by N. F. Pavlov, "The Auction" (Auktsion, 1835), but the difference disguises a similar spirit of social criticism. The Pavlov story also reminds us of the suggestion made by Todd that performed and ballroom dance in *Eugene Onegin* work on a continuum; for all the differences between *Onegin* and "The Auction," a similar continuum appears in the latter. Pavlov begins his story this way:

The Bolshoi Theater was presenting one of those innumerable plays that no one pays any attention to; but the production was embellished by a ballet, and ballet attracts viewers because many Muscovites have preserved whole the habits of the eighteenth century. Many of them speak enthusiastically of Noverre, Vestris, and Duport as great men unfairly forgotten by their descendants; they ecstatically enthuse about the elegant patterns arranged by Didelot, as if these were works deserving the rays of immortality!

How did ballet come to Russia, a country where bashfulness was carried out to the point of perfection, where beautiful women were born, flourished, and faded in the isolation of the sublime *terem*; where not all the beards were shaved off; where you could go nine months without hearing about a Zephyr? And what *is* ballet? What is in it for us, for an age of history, politics, and economics? Ballets can possibly warm the blood of a chilled seventy-year-old, but that is all! What do they contain for the thoughts and soul of 1834? (Pavlov 447)

The narrator's objections to this popular spectacle are first that it is not essentially Russian—in fact, it was difficult to imagine how normally chaste, prudish Russians overcame their modesty to look on this explicitly sexual and foreign spectacle; second, ballet is not serious, its outmoded pleasures hardly merit attention from an age defined as historical, political, and economic.[16] Pavlov finds dance trivial,[17] a view that is itself informed by an ideology of gender, we note, since Pavlov's narrator prefers the image of beautiful women secluded in the *terem* to the more available (hence tainted) beauties of the stage. The story tries to create an illusion of meaninglessness around this scene of ballet, since this particular description would seem to have absolutely nothing to do with the tale that follows.

The ballet scene is not, of course, so inscrutable, nor is the continuum between ballet and social dancing so irreparably broken. Two subsequent ballroom dancing scenes occur in "The Auction," the first offering an occasion for a jealous young man (named T.) to squeeze a woman's hand to the point of pain. What he really wants is to do her real physical harm, however. And thus T. rages against the fact that she is a woman since, he believes, it is ever more difficult to take out one's vengeance on women:

"Oh why isn't she a man? . . . It would be easy for me to throw off this weight of offense! If only I could find a fresh wound in her heart and stick my fingers into it, so that she would groan with pain, lose her senses with the insult! . . Yes, yes! . ." His eyes shone brighter than a fireplace. "There is an offense comprehensible and felt by only one sex, not both, an offense created for woman." (Pavlov 450)

The imagery here is explicitly sexual, but it is also passionately aggressive. The hero wants to wound a formerly loved woman as if she were a man (compare the bizarre story "Erotida" by A. F. Vel'tman [1835], where the man kills his disguised and cross-dressed young love in a duel.) In "The Auction," the woman's offense is that she has turned up married to another man. T. feels betrayed by her. He appears in her rooms and declares his undying love, only to rise in apology once he has her attention, and remind her with a cruel smile of her holy obligations in marriage. She is "different" to him now, he tells her, and, satisfied that he has left her motionless and unable to respond, he laughs and leaves. He has chosen a form of emotional, figurative wounding rather than physical injury, but his intention and his effect have been to neutralize her sexually.

As we have noticed, the sexual power of women, which seems to be more frightening in the physicality and sensuality of dance scenes, produces a reaction of violence in some men who stand in a romantic relation to them; when imaged as a battlefield, the ballroom also attributes violence to the scene of dance. It is no accident that the usual opposition to the realm of the ballroom is the quintessentially masculine world of the military. Any number of society tales assume the attractiveness of the man in uniform, and some make the military background quite explicit. A vivid example of the sharply distinguished worlds of women and men where the male military context is repulsive, rather than sexually attractive, is Elena Gan's story "Ideal." Even when the men with whom women dance and flirt are not themselves in the military, men hold for themselves the privilege of resolving conflicts about romance through the duel. Thus a normally stable set of gender oppositions (masculine/feminine, serious/trivial, strong/weak, physically violent/emotionally distressed) appears in many of these tales, but in the two stories to which I now turn, these oppositions are called into question.

Two Variations on Violence

In the two stories with which this essay concludes, the violence that counterbalances scenes of dance is extreme. In part that has to do with the era in which the stories were written: the first decade of the twentieth century. The more extreme anxieties about gender and sexuality in turn-of-the-century Europe have been well documented (Showalter), and Slavists have noted greater tensions in literary and cultural explorations of sexual experience in Russia (Engelstein; Karlinsky). Many Russian fictions from this period explore the sexual anxieties of men, not women, as in Count Leo Tolstoi's "After the Ball" (Posle bala, 1903), where a nobleman looks back on an incident from his youth in the 1840s. He recounts an ethereal ball where he danced nearly the whole night with a young woman named Varen'ka; after the ball, he walks through the streets and sees a Tartar recruit being forced to run the gauntlet, his bloodied body nearly unrecognizeable as human. This violent ending to the story cannot but be shocking, and a sustained reading of "After the Ball" has devoted considerable attention to details of folklore origins, religious and ritual setting, and imagistic and lexical repetitions that join the two seemingly disparate parts of the story (Zholkovskii).

The story splits into two halves not only because of its radically different choreographed scenes of bodily performance, but also in terms of how the narrating hero describes himself. He was an excellent dancer and not bad-looking (his precise formulation is coy: *tantseval ia khorosho i byl ne bezobrazen*; Tolstoi 10: 383); his listeners prod him to admit that he was a real beauty in his youth, which he brushes aside. But this is a false modesty. He proudly describes his clever and graceful moves on the dance floor, moves that place him next to Varen'ka in group dances. His pride marks him, in fact: When Varen'ka must guess a character trait in order to choose him as her partner in one dance, the guess that he remembers her hazarding is pride.[18]

The narrator's pride dissolves when he comes across the scene of the Tartar being beaten. He feels excruciating shame: "I was so extremely ashamed that, not knowing where to cast my eyes, as if I had been discovered in the most shameful act, I lowered my eyes and hurried home" (Tolstoi 10: 390). What produced this reaction is not just the sight of the Tartar's bloodied body ("something so motley, wet, red, and unnatural that I could not believe that it was the body of a person" [389]), nor the spectacle of cruelty when the presiding officer strikes a young soldier who has not beaten the Tartar with sufficient brutality. The shocking detail is that the narrator recognizes the officer as Varen'ka's father, as the man whose graceful dancing he had lingeringly admired at the ball that evening. The tune that haunts the narrator is that very mazurka the father had danced, and the dancing body that he had described with impeccable details was the father's (not Varen'ka's—the narrator recalls her as disembodied).

The father turns away from the narrator in this punishment scene, pretending not to recognize him, and it is from this gesture that the shame emerges. Why shame, one asks; indeed, why should the narrator feel ashamed (rather than, for example, outraged) at what he sees? Shame, as some psychoanalysts have argued, is constitutive of identity (Sedgwick 1993a); that is to say, the sensation of having done something shameful sits at the core of identity for many people. It is the conflict on which their neurotic anxieties pile up. For our narrator, this scene indeed becomes foundational. He describes it as the source of his not having joined the military or any public service. But the shame is also linked to a kind of ignorance, a sense of not understanding something that others implicitly know. He thinks to himself, seeing the father before him, "'Obviously, he knows something that I don't know [. . .] if I knew what he knows, I'd understand what I've seen, and it wouldn't torment me. [. . .] If this was done with such confidence and acknowledged by everyone as necessary, then it follows that they knew something that I don't know,' I thought, and tried to find it out. But no matter how I tried, even afterwards I couldn't find it out" (Tolstoi 10: 390). Shame comes from ignorance about some set of rules, some sort of knowledge that others possess.[19]

The move from pride to shame delineates the two parts of this story, showing that the narrator has internalized the punishment as if it were inflicted on him (he is also ashamed at what he has seen, in a way that suggests that performing and viewing are once again interchangeably intertwined). The task of the story has changed, too: He began his story as a kind of first-love tale, as if the loss of Varen'ka could explain why he never married; but he concludes with the more disturbing scene of punishment, which purports to explain why he never entered public life. He has been disabled by a kind of ignorance that, until that moment, he did not know he possessed. What he does not know makes him not fit in, makes him "queer" in a sense one can recognize from childhood moments of terror at not understanding what others are talking about.[20]

Yet the two parts of the story do interrelate quite precisely, in that the punishment and the shame are connected through dance. We recall that the ballroom was often a venue for sexual transgressions in society tales, and that Tolstoi, writing at a later date, is describing scenes from the 1840s, when society tales were still quite popular. In society tales, as we have seen, moral failures would typically be punished by gossip or early deaths, but Tolstoi chooses a much more graphic scene of punishment and sets the violence outside the ballroom. As in *Anna Karenina* (1873–77), the body is subjected to physical torment.

Tolstoi's great substitution is not merely the scene of punishment but its object, for in contrast to *Anna Karenina* or "The Kreutzer Sonata," it is not the woman who here falls victim. One explanation for that switch is that in this story women play no role important enough to merit punishment. Varen'ka initially seems an important memory, but only in a trivialized, debased form of the cycle of error and reproof. The dance most frequently mentioned in the story is the mazurka (though often enough in contexts where the narrator says he is not dancing the mazurka, or not dancing with Varen'ka—another example of his being disabled): We recall from *Eugene Onegin* that this dance features the male partner's display of skill; thus, when the narrator recalls the father's dance with Varen'ka, she fades into the background, and the narrator focuses his attention on the movements of the father. But the final dance of this evening is the quadrille, which itself becomes the context for Varen'ka's mock acts of "punishment."

The quadrille, as it was called earlier in the century, or later the cotillion, was a dance filled with games. Tolstoi shows us a figure of the cotillion where a woman chooses between two men by guessing some character trait that one of them has assigned himself. If she guesses right, she gets to dance with the man.[21] In other games of the dance, a man might be handed her fan or umbrella to hold while she dances with another; he would have to hold the umbrella over the dancing couple, or fan them—not being chosen thus had an aspect of mock humiliation (Raffé 128; Aldrich 181–86). Our narrator in "After the Ball" plays these games with some skill, but the key word in this game, "pride," is his downfall. The overwhelming sense of shame that ends the story suggests that he has chosen his trait in error.

The punishments to be administered, however, cannot occur in the silly games of the cotillion. The discipline of men comes at the hands of other men, and it is unsurprising that Varen'ka fades so quickly from memory. Her femininity is itself rather dubious: Zholkovskii sees her as an Amazon, and as masculine,[22] the narrator, we recall, is shocked when his listeners challenge his idea of her as disembodied, but for him she really doesn't have a body, or, more precisely, it is not her body that matters.

That framing scene of narration, of men sitting in conversation about their past lives, reinforces the sense that the emotions and errors of this story exist in a world of men. (It stands in vivid contrast to the sharing of stories by women in Pavlova's *Quadrille*, where loss and pain are acknowledged as unavoidable, indeed normal.) Tolstoi's ballroom dance story is recollected by men who find stories of first love nostalgically amusing but impossibly disrupted by a violent scene of punishment. It is a Tartar, an "other" who is also a man, who offers up the spectacle of harm; the supervising presence of the father, whom the narrator has admiringly watched dancing with his daughter, closes the circle of this story about men and for men. The homoerotic overtones are not subtle, but they are unspeakably taboo. Ultimately, "After the Ball" is mostly about how men disable each other sexually and how they keep each other in line by inflicting violence on the body of another.

The violence of Tat'iana Shchepkina-Kupernik's "The First Ball" (Pervyi bal, 1905) is as extreme as in Tolstoi's story, though it is configured quite differently in terms of gender and politics. In its juxtaposition of dancing pleasure with violence, it reconceives the punishment fetishized by Tolstoi, and it does so by introducing an analysis of class.

The heroine is Ol'ga, a young woman whose mother is mystified by her indifference to fine clothes and handsome young men. Ol'ga spends her time with questionable friends in unknown places, and she has a strange relationship of equality with her servant. So it is a delightful surprise to Ol'ga's mother when she expresses a desire to attend a ball. Readers of the story rather quickly come to suspect that the desire is not what it appears to be, but before the story has its abruptly tragic denouement, Shchepkina-Kupernik gives us six pages of description that convey the ball's atmosphere; she shows the ball's seductive lure even for a young woman as resistant as Ol'ga to its superficial charms. At first, the description is predictable, as if this ball were a typical social gathering where all that happens is a function of repetition.[23] Shchepkina-Kupernik appears to invoke the conventionality of society-tale ballroom scenes,[24] but only to overturn convention when her heroine discovers special pleasures in this ball.

Ol'ga recalls her friend Sonia Gregorovius as a way to ward off the dizzying attractiveness of the scene before her. Sonia had been forbidden to dance because of her weak constitution, and she told Ol'ga how she would steel herself not to envy those who could dance. She used to say to her: "'I just pressed my ears closed very, very tightly in order not to hear the music. And suddenly I didn't feel envy—I found it funny. Everyone was jumping around, making various strange movements; they were all red and crumpled like crazy people" (329). Unlike the young man in Odoevskii's story, who feels involuntary repulsion at the sight of dancing bodies, Ol'ga takes courage from her friend's account of willed estrangement (*ostranenie*). The dancing seems momentarily ugly, as in Pavlov's view of the ballet in "The Auction." Ol'ga's attention is caught by young Prince Gordynskii and his remarkable and powerful dancing. She is drawn to the beauty of what she sees, despite the ugly things she knows about this man. We know from a comment earlier in the story that he has led a military campaign to suppress peasant rebellions, and surely it is this association that causes Ol'ga to feel uneasy at the sight of him.

So Ol'ga squints her eyes shut and calls to mind a different scene in which a woman sees her husband shot by intruding soldiers in a case of mistaken identity. Ol'ga spares herself no details, recalling the woman's sobs and the blood-stained wall she had seen with her own eyes:

> And is this woman a solitary example? Dozens, hundreds of women stretched forth before Ol'ga. The same kind of long line that right now was winding its way around the ballroom to the sounds of music . . . Beaten down, exhausted women . . . disheveled, sallow faces . . . Girls, young girls, practically children, shamed, dishonored by bands of "guards" . . . A crazed old woman whose only son was shot before her eyes for not going to work . . . A woman still breast-feeding her child, whose milk stopped coming on the day her husband was killed before her eyes because they found a revolver on him . . . A mother whose eleven-year-old little boy was shot dead because he did not move off the road as ordered . . . All of them impoverished, abandoned, hungry, with children dying of hunger . . . Oh what a terrifying *sarabande*! . . They lurch forward, groaning, tearing their hair, tearing at their breasts . . . Their eyes are full of bloody tears, their gums swollen and white with hunger . . . How many of them there are, how many. (331–32; all suspension points in the original)

If this story were written with the ideological clarity that marked the stories by Odoevskii and Pavlov cited earlier, to say nothing of nine-teenth-century utilitarian writings and later Soviet fictions, Ol'ga would now open her eyes wide and see the dancing before her as a grotesque falsity, but Shchepkina-Kupernik has something else in mind: Ol'ga is invited to waltz, not by Gordynskii but by an appealing young baron.

> Having known about dance only from the required *gymnasium* lessons, which her friends had regarded as the equivalent of prison servitude, Ol'ga had no idea of what it would be like to dance with a good dancer. And the baron danced splendidly. He held his lady easily, somehow both tenderly and firmly, at times seeming to lift her off the floor. The floor seemed to swim beneath her. For a time she was seized by complete for-getfulness and by a feeling of utter physical bliss, known from childhood when she would ride in her swing. (332)

She is dizzy, she has to stop, her partner offers her icy champagne as refreshment, but he refuses to let her stop dancing, calling it a form of military skill (*voennaia khitrost'* [333]). So the dancing goes on, now even more intoxicating because of the champagne. She feels the blood hot beneath her skin, and she does not want the waltz to end. The waltz again plays its role as choreographed seduction. Ol'ga sees in the eyes of her partner and all the men there that she has made an impression, that the typical tributes to beautiful women can be hers this evening, and she is profoundly tempted. The music stops, reality returns, and once she has sent her dancing partner off for ice cream, Ol'ga locks glances with the fateful Prince Gordynskii. Shchepkina-Kupernik is right to emphasize the force of this mutual gaze, not only because it lets Ol'ga see through to the cruelty beneath the prince's smiling beauty, but also because it is a moment when the prince sees in her eyes something other than infatuated femininity. In the instant that her panicky hatred is transmitted to his face, in the amount of time it takes him to turn pale, Ol'ga removes a gun from her corsage and shoots her man dead.

Shchepkina-Kupernik's story is superbly successful in its psychological portraiture. A young woman who believes herself immune to the trivialized rewards of femininity is drawn in almost beyond her capacities to resist. The ballroom is the locus of that femininity, but also the site of feminine revenge. This is not the male fantasy that women, when permitted to be sexual, are dangerous to men, but a feminine nightmare where the things you believe you have trained yourself not to feel nearly wreck your determination to accomplish a difficult and martyring political deed. Perhaps Ol'ga takes vengeance on a man who has elicited unbidden erotic feelings in her, but, more important, she allies herself with the impoverished women whose families are destroyed by Russia's autocracy, and in this story we see more clearly than in any other that the barriers of class and wealth delineate the pleasures of the ballroom. We see, too, the effects of the continuum between men decked out in uniforms of battle and women dressed for dancing, between officers parading their might and dancers choreographed in expressions of apparent beauty. Beneath beauty, this story suggests, is ugliness, or, to put it differently, there are no forms of aesthetic beauty, either performed before an audience or experienced by a dancer as loss of self, that are so complete as to vanquish the violence of daily life.

This depressing conclusion seems far from the pleasures of Pushkin's *Eugene Onegin*, farther still from the relief found in Lorrie Moore's contemporary American story "Dance in America," mentioned earlier.[25] Russia may have developed a more puritanical tradition in presenting dance in narration; that is, its authors may have more uniformly and

more intensely felt that the pleasures of erotic expression must be disciplined if they are to be shown at all. Specific dance forms were drawn
into these acts of discipline, either as counterpoints to more aggressive
physical punishments or as pretexts for gossip. Women and men interchangeably play nearly all possible roles in the stories we have considered: audience, dancer, flirt, dreamer, victim, assassin, spreader of gossip,
witness of shame. Scenes of dance do not so much neutralize gender difference, however, as offer occasions for individual men and women to
challenge gender norms. Particularly at the end of the nineteenth century, when sexual experimentation was both more common and more
disturbing, the challenges to femininity and masculinity became more
violent. The tales authored by women, particularly Pavlova's *Quadrille*
and Shchepkina-Kupernik's "First Ball," give voice to women's frustra-
tions with these arrangements. Neither they nor the stories and poems
written by Pushkin, Baratynskii, Odoevskii, Pavlov, and Tolstoi can wish
away the cultural norms that consigned women to fewer choices and
more predictable punishments for sexual transgressions—but some of
these tales successfully reveal that the ballroom's pleasures were not all
false and trivial, and that there are some dances that are worth the punishment that soon follows.

Notes

I am grateful to several friends and colleagues whose comments and suggestions have helped me in writing this essay: Jehanne Gheith, Helena Goscilo,
and Beth Holmgren; faculty and graduate students in the University of
Southern California Slavic Department, who responded generously to an
earlier version; and Michael Kasper, whose bibliographical wizardry was indispensable.
    1. This kind of transformation is not unique to the introduction of dance
into a story: As scholars have long noted (though with particular fascination
most recently), the conventions of ekphrasis similarly interrupt and facilitate
changes in mood, tone, and aesthetic norm (Krieger).
    2. One difference between ballet and social dancing ought to be noted,
particularly for post-Pushkinian writing: Ballet dancers, like actresses, were culturally marked as sexually available, whereas women engaging in social dancing
might well be the sorts of innocent young girls to be protected from male sexual incursion (or they might be quite sexually experienced—we shall see both
types in the society tales that follow).
    3. Boulenger 51–52; Richardson 96 also notes that an observer from the
1840s called the mazurka the "Russian Cotillon" when it was introduced into
England by a recent visitor to Russia.

4. As one observer of European dances in 1847 noted: "The real dancer of the mazurka not only varies his steps, but more frequently invents them, creating new ones that belong only to himself, and which others would be wrong in copying with servility" (cited in Richardson 96).

5. Johnston's translation omits the comparison to the stables, but he does give the following lines:

> [. . .] and bounding
> Buyanov's heels have split the wood
> and wrecked the flooring-boards for good:
> there's crashing, rumbling, pounding, trotting.
> The deeper in the wood, the more
> the logs; the wild ones have the floor;
> they're plunging whirling, all but squatting.
> Ah, gently, gently, easy goes—
> your heels will squash the ladies' toes. (Cited in Pushkin 1977, 153)

6. Flaubert writes: "They began slowly, and went faster. They were turning: everything was turning around them, the lamps, the furniture, the panelling, the parquet floor, like a disc on a spindle. Passing near the doors, Emma's dress, at the hem, caught on his trousers; their legs entwined; he looked down at her, she looked up at him; a lethargy came over her, she stopped. They set off again; and, quickening the pace, the Viscount, pulling her along, disappeared with her to the end of the gallery, where, panting for breath, she almost fell, and, for a moment, rested her head upon his chest. And then, still spinning round, but more slowly, he conducted her back to her seat; she slumped against the wall and put her hand over her eyes" (41). The syntax here precisely reproduces the original.

7. The scandals of the waltz did elicit comment, however, in dance hand-books, perhaps nowhere more sternly than in American conduct books. One lady noted in 1833:

> The waltz is a dance of quite too loose a character, and unmarried ladies should refrain from it altogether, both in public and private; very young married ladies, however, may be allowed to waltz in private balls, if it is very seldom, and with persons of their acquaintance. (Aldrich 154)

C. H. Cleveland, Jr. Was still more strict in 1878:

> The author is compelled to say, that he has sometimes seen ladies and gentlemen waltzing to our furious music, in attitudes that more plainly il-lustrated the language of Melnotte in "The Lady of Lyons" than any acting he has ever seen on the stage. (Aldrich 153)

Mr. Cleveland intends his description as a warning, and adds that the "remedy for the evil" is entirely in the hands of women, who should refuse to dance with men whose style is "not respectful."

8. Boulenger also observes that throughout history, moral judgments have been rendered against those dances which were excessively easy to perform; he brings this up to his own day, when the tango was seen as a reprehensible dance (64–65). In terms of the argument I make in this essay, one might argue that the very strictness and complexity of the rules governing many social dances introduced the experience of social discipline into the physical expression and erotic exploration attaching to all dancing. The waltz's dangers, then, would extend to an unarticulated perception that this dance was generally without rules, that it was a moment when anything could happen (and thus often did).

9. I do not cite the examples because I have discussed them at length elsewhere. See Sandler.

10. Rostopchina's poem ends: "And I, I am a woman in all the senses of the word, / I am fully subject to all women's inclinations; / I am only a woman,— and ready to be proud of it, / I love the ball! I want more of them!" (Rostopchina 101).

11. I call the poem remarkable based on my own views, and on those of Pushkin. See his review of the poem, which was first published conjointly with his own scandalous tale "Graf Nulin" (*Polnoe, sobranie sochinenii* 7: 58–61).

12. As acknowledged by Prince Viazemskii in a letter to A. I. Turgenev; cited in Baratynskii 634.

13. See Pushkin, "Portret" (1828), in *Polnoe sobranie sochinenii* 3: 66; and Baratynskii, "Kak mnogo ty v nemnogo dnei" (ca. 1824–1826), in Baratynskii 54.

14. Pushkin judged the closing an inappropriate and poor joke, though he praised "The Ball" enthusiastically in this brief review (*Polnoe Sobranie sochinenii* 7: 61).

15. For a discussion of how Odoevskii changed this story (the long description I cited earlier was also taken out), see Odoevskii 1975, 278.

16. The impression that ballet was outmoded might be taken to mean that the rage for ballets by Didelot, noted by Pushkin in *Eugene Onegin*, was waning; indeed, there was a period in the 1830s when Didelot seemed a glory of the past, and what we now recognize as the fame of Marie Taglioni had not yet been established. See Wiley 81–82.

17. Compare the comments of Belinskii about Rostopchina in Belinskii 3: 458. For an earlier version of these sentiments (which were common), see Lermontov's *Maskarad*, where Arbenin compares life to a ball from which you come home tired, wrinkled, and having forgotten the entire evening (Lermontov 3: 461).

18. The narrator later recalls the second instance: "I saw her before me at the moment when she was choosing between two partners and trying to guess my trait. I heard her sweet voice saying '*Pride*, isn't it?' and she joyously gave me her hand" (Tolstoi 10: 387).

19. This is the opposite of the superior knowledge that marks Pozdnyshev in Tolstoi's most famous tale of sexual hysteria, "The Kreutzer Sonata"

(Kreitserova sonata, 1883): Pozdnyshev knows what others are far from knowing, but the narrator in this story is marked by his embarrassing ignorance.

20. I use the work "queer" as it has been developed in gay and lesbian studies in the last few years. See, for example, Sedgwick, *Tendencies* 5–9.

21. In such moments of choice, the cotillion resembles the mazurka: we recall from Pushkin's *Queen of Spades* (Pikovaia dama, 1834) the scene where Hermann is approached by two women and he must choose one of them by guessing which word (*oubli ou regret*) the woman has taken as her emblem. In Tolstoi's scene, we note, it is the woman who must choose a man.

22. This point is made in the longer, conference version of "Morfologiia i istoricheskie korni rasskaza *Posle bala*," pp. 12–13.

23. This is Joe Andrew's point, drawing on Bakhtin's idea of the chronotope:

> The ball (like the drawing-room or salon) is a place for meetings, intrigues: a place where women (with or without bronze ornaments, though usually with) will parade to be gazed upon. There is an interest here on the (relatively at least) glittering social scene—chandeliers, a thirteen-piece orchestra: every detail immediately alerts us to the fact that we will enter the world of the *svet*, with all the connotations this has at this period in generic literary development. All is typical, a "recurring occurrence"—the flirting, the gossip and arrangement according to taste. It is a world where social and gender roles are seemingly *immutable* (whatever Olga's mother may think), where behavior is ritualized and customs are repeated. In other terms, the power of the sociolect is absolute. All this leads to an emphasis on the narrowness of this (woman's) world, where everything is, moreover, mundane, trivial and banal. (94)

(Andrew's reference to "Olga" is not about the heroine of "The First Ball": he is discussing Elena Gan's story "Ideal.") The chronotope of the salon is remarkably similar. For a good discussion based on a Pushkin fragment, see van Baak.

24. The comparisons of dancing women and ornamented ballroom to floral arrangements are also routine, and the enumeration of colors and swirling forms is familiar to us from a tale such as Odoevskii's "The Ball," for example, as is the growing emphasis on how this scene is being perceived by one very conflicted potential dancer.

25. Moore ends her story with a narrator's bodily pleasure in dance: "I am thinking of the dancing body's magnificent and ostentatious scorn: this is how we offer ourselves, enter Heaven, enter speaking" (85).

Works Cited

Aldrich, Elizabeth. 1991. *From the Ballroom to Hell: Grace and Folly in Nineteenth-Century Dance.* Evanston: Northwestern UP.

Aleksandrov, A. (pseud. N. Durova). 1839. "Dva slova iz zhiteiskogo slovaria: 1. Bal." *Otechestvennye zapiski* 7, no. 8: 38–52.

Andrew, Joe. 1993. *Narrative and Desire in Russian Literature, 1822–49*. Houndsmills: Macmillan.

Austen, Jane. 1972. *Pride and Prejudice*. Edited by Tony Tanner. Harmondsworth: Penguin.

Baratynskii, E. A. 1982. *Stikhotvoreniia. Poemy*. Moscow: Nauka.

Belinskii, V. 1953–59. *Polnoe sobranie sochinenii*. 20 vols. Moscow.

Boulenger, Jacques. 1920. *De la walse au tango: La Danse mondaine du 1-er Empire à nos jours*. Paris: A l'Enseigne du Masque d'Or chez Devambez.

Briggs, A. D. P. 1992. *Alexander Pushkin: Eugene Onegin*. Cambridge: Cambridge UP.

Engelstein, Laura. 1992. *The Keys to Happiness: Sex and the Search for Modernity in Fin-de-Siècle Russia*. Ithaca: Cornell UP.

Flaubert, Gustave. 1992. *Madame Bovary*. Edited by Geoffrey Wall. London: Penguin.

Gan, Elena. 1980. "Ideal." In *Russkaia romanticheskaia povest'*, ed. V. I. Sakharov, 435–82 Moscow: Sovetskaia Rossiia.

Gasnault, François. 1982. "Les salles de bal du Paris romantique: décors et jeux des corps." *Romantisme* 38: 7–18.

Griboedov, A. S. 1969. *Gore ot uma*. Edited by N. K. Piksanov. Moscow: Nauka.

Iezuitova, R. V. 1973. "Svetskaia povest'." In *Russkaia povest' XIX veka. Istoriia i problematika zhanra*, ed. B. S. Meilakh, 169–99. Leningrad: Nauka.

Karlinksy, Simon. 1989. "Russia's Gay Literature and Culture: The Impact of the October Revolution." In *Hidden From History: Reclaiming the Gay and Lesbian Past*, ed. Martin Bauml Duberman et al., 347–64. New York: NAL Books.

Krieger, Murray. 1992. *Ekphrasis: The Illusion of the Natural Sign*. Baltimore: Johns Hopkins UP.

Lermontov, M. Iu. 1976. *Sobranie sochinenii*. 4 vols. Moscow: Khudozhestvennaia literatura.

Lotman, Iu. M. 1980. *Roman A. S. Pushkina 'Evgenii Onegin': Kommentarii*. Leningrad: Prosveshchenie.

Magri, Gennaro. 1988. *Theoretical and Practical Treatise on Dancing*. Translated by Mary Skeaping. London: Dance Books [originally published Naples, 1779].

Martin, John. 1939. *Introduction to the Dance*. New York: W. W. Norton.

Ménil, F. de. [1905] *Historie de la danse à travers les âges*. Paris: A. Picard and Kaan.

Moore, Lillian. 1965. *Images of the Dance: Historical Treasures of the Dance collection, 1581–1861*. New York: New York Public Library.

Moore, Lorrie. 1993. "Dance in America." *New Yorker*, June 28, 82–85.

Odoevskii, V. F. *Russkie nochi*. Edited by V. F. Egorov, E. A. Maimin, and M. I. Medovoi. Leningrad: Nauka.

———. 1981. *Sochineniia*. Edited by V. I. Sakharov. 2 vols. Moscow: Khudozhestvennaia literatura.

Pavlov, N. F. 1950. "Auktsion." In *Russkie povesti XIX veka 20-kh–30-kh godov*, ed. B. S. Meilakh, 2 vols., vol. 1, 447–53. Moscow-Leningrad: Sovetskaia Rossiia.

Pavlova, Karolina. 1964. *Polnoe sobranie sochinenii*. Moscow-Leningrad: Sovetskii Pisatel'.

Perrot, Michelle, ed. 1990. *A History of Private Life: From the Fires of Revolution to the Great War*. Translated by Arthur Goldhammer. Cambridge: Harvard UP.

Pushkin, A. S. 1977. *Eugene Onegin*. Translated by Charles Johnston. London: Penguin.

———. 1977–79. *Polnoe sobranie sochinenii*. 10 vols. Leningrad: Nauka.

Raffé, M. G., ed. 1964. *Dictionary of the Dance*. New York: A. S. Barnes.

Richardson, Philip J. S. 1960. *The Social Dances of the Nineteenth Century in England*. London: Herbert Jenkins.

Rostopchina, Evodkiia. 1986. *Stikhotvoreniia. Proza. Pis'ma*. Edited by Boris Romanov. Moscow: Sovetskaia Rossiia.

Roustang, François. 1988. *The Quadrille of Gender: Casanova's "Memoirs"*. Translated by Anne C. Vila. Stanford: Stanford UP.

Sachs, Curt. 1937. *World History of the Dance*. Translated by Bessie Schönberg. New York: W. W. Norton.

Sandler, Stephanie. 1993. "Pushkin's Last Love: Natal'ya Nikolaevna in Russian Culture." In *Gender Restructuring in Russian Studies*, ed. Marianne Liljeström, Eila Mäntysaari, and Arja Rosenholm, 209–20. Tampere, Finland: Slavica Tamperensia.

Sedgwick, Eve Kosofsky. 1993a. "Queer Performativity: Henry James's *The Art of the Novel*." *GLQ* 1: 1–16.

———. 1993b. *Tendencies*. Durham, N.C.: Duke UP.

Shchepkina-Kupernik, T. L. 1988. "Pervyi bal." In *Tol'ko chas*, ed. V. Uchenova, 317–34. Moscow: Sovremennik.

Shepherd, Elizabeth C. 1981. "The Society Tale and the Innovative Argument in Russian Prose Fiction of the 1830s." *Russian Literature* 10, no. 2: 111–62.

Showalter, Elaine. 1990. *Sexual Anarchy: Gender and Culture at the Fin de Siècle*. New York: Viking.

Todd, William Mills III. 1993. " 'The Russian Terpsichore's Soul-Filled Flight': Dance Themes in *Eugene Onegin*." In *Pushkin Today*, ed. David M. Bethea, 13–30. Bloomington: Indiana UP.

Tolstoi, L. N. 1975. *Sobranie sochinenii*. 12 vols. Moscow: Khudozhestvennaia literatura.

van Baak, J. J. 1990. " 'The Guests Gathered at the Dacha . . .': The Dynamics of a Drawing Room." In *Semantic Analysis of Literary Texts: To Honour Jan van der Eng on the Occasion of His 65th Birthday*, ed. E. de Haard, T. Langerak, and W. G. Weststeijn, 51–66. Amsterdam: Elsevier.

Vel'tman, A. F. 1991. "Erotida." In *Tot divnyi mir*, ed. N. D. Tkachenko, 139–64. Moscow: Sovetskaia Rossiia.

Wiley, John, ed. 1990. *A Century of Russian Ballet: Documents and Accounts, 1810–1910.* Oxford: Oxford UP.

Zholkovskii, A. 1992. "Morfologiia i istoricheskie korni rasskaza Tolstogo 'Posle bala.'" In *Bluzhdaiushchie sny: Iz istorii russkogo modernizma*, ed. A. Zholkovskii, 109–29. Moscow: Sovetskii Pisatel'.

Zhukova, M. S. 1986. *Vechera na Karpovke.* Moscow: Sovetskaia Rossiia. 1986.

11

"THE INCOMPARABLE" ANASTASIIA VIAL'TSEVA AND THE CULTURE OF PERSONALITY

Louise McReynolds

LONG RED HAIR SWEPT UP in the latest fashion, stunning gowns accentuating the figure, brilliant jewelry, and a beautiful face made Anastasiia Dmitrievna Vial'tseva the most popular female concert performer in turn-of-the-century Russia. Her mezzo-soprano voice, though, could not sustain notes as effectively as its owner did attention. Critics lauded the clarity of her pronunciation and her unique timbre, but also tacitly agreed that the performance more than the music made her a star in the age of the truly great Fedor Shaliapin. Consensus held that "this is not a singer . . . but an artist of words, an enchantress with a charming smile, an original creation" (Kizimova 31).[1] Like movie stars, she "personified feminine charm, beauty, and sex appeal" (Nest'ev 50). Prominent newspaper columnist Vlas Doroshevich noted that "the serious critic, of course, writes that Vial'tseva's artistic qualities are limited, but Vial'tseva is a phenomenon [*iavlenie*]. . . . An event!" (Nest'ev 63).

My purpose here is not to belittle Vial'tseva because her voice could not fill the Bol'shoi, but rather to emphasize her celebrity status in order to discuss what the "Vial'tseva phenomenon" can tell us about the changing roles of women in Russian society at the turn of the twentieth century. Many aspects of women's lives were in flux during this era of rapid industrialization, and the growth of consumerism associated with celebrities provided one important cultural context for change. Concert star Vial'tseva, an object of consumption and a consumer her-

self, represented important facets of the new woman in this environment. Her fans called her "The Incomparable One" (*Nesravnennaia*) because of the mixture of allure and style with which she presented herself,
a century before image became everything. The Russian songbird anticipated Madonna's observation that people could become famous simply
for being famous; like Madonna, Vial'tseva owed her popularity to capti-
vating performances and her rapport with the new audiences.[2] As much
as the singers themselves, these audiences embodied a culture reorient-
ing itself away from conservative hierarchies, including that of gender.
The world of culture and consumption, inhabited by stars and audiences
alike, was a significantly new space, positioned between the private
world of the home and the public world of business and politics. Yet this
sphere of leisure also overlapped with parts of the other two, and this
shaded area of overlap allowed both men and women access.

The fame Vial'tseva enjoyed at the height of her career abandoned her
after 1917. The scratchy recordings that survived her may well reveal the
limits of her talent, but they do not explain her nearly complete absence
in histories of the end of Russia's old regime, even those that emphasize
art and culture. With its gaze fixed on party polemics, the historiography
of the era has overlooked the extent to which the personal, too, was becoming political. To turn an old cliché, Vial'tseva was neither fish nor
fowl, in this case neither feminist nor socialist, and therefore she stood
outside the "women's question" as posed from the limited perspective of
female political emancipation. But the "Vial'tseva phenomenon" represented a different sort of liberation: its beneficiaries enjoyed unprecedented opportunities to maneuver through the new urban spaces; they
climbed a social hierarchy undergoing reconstruction; they negotiated a
cultural divide decreasingly polarized into "elite" and "mass." Despite
tsarist Russia's amply studied fixation on class, this peasant girl attained
celebrity status irrespective of her social origins. She marked Van Wyck
Brooks's notion of "middlebrow," embodying the evolving consumerism
in Russian society and the growing preoccupation with personalities
who offered images of success based on individual effort, measured in
salaries, and showcased in luxury. As both article of consumption and
conspicuous consumer, Vial'tseva appeared a caricature of the emerging
middle-class woman.

The idea of a cultural "middle" raises a host of conceptual problems,
and not only for Russia. "Middlebrow," like "middle class," is a nebulous
term because it essentially refers to a socioeconomic situation in flux,
with those in the middle sharing aspects of culture and values in
common with those at both ends of the more easily identifiable high/

low spectrum. But the middle also creates its own culture. Middle classes stand perennially accused of taking the best of high culture and, in the process of pulling it down to their level, disfiguring it by forcing it through a system of values that differs from the one that created it.[3] Both Vial'tseva's detractors and her admirers used "middle" and its synonyms, especially "bourgeois" and its Russian variant, *meshchanstvo*,[4] to characterize her. Vial'tseva personified as well as entertained Russia's middle: the indigent peasant who grew up to live with a noblewoman's elegance because of her own initiative and talent. Yet she downplayed the effort involved in establishing herself. She claimed to be an innocent bystander in her own career, someone who simply satisfied an unspecified public demand. Despite her prominence in the public world of entertainment, she could appear less threatening to the "man's world" of business by denying responsibility for her success. Her posture of nonchalance, though, did not change the fact of her formidable presence.

Vial'tseva's life, so integrated into the transformations of the period, provides insights into the uniqueness of Russia's bourgeoisie, especially its female element. As a performer, a star, a caricature of the emerging modern woman, Vial'tseva is especially appropriate for study. Her life exaggerated both the obstacles and the successes of other women, but they could recognize enough in her of themselves, or at least of their aspirations, to make her their idol. As Philip Rieff has argued, when social structures change, so do the cultures that hold societies together. When this occurs, new "modal types of personality" emerge, "bearers of the new culture" (Rieff 2). As a modal type, Vial'tseva suggested the possibilities of a future with fewer restrictions on mobility. This can be seen in both the actual and the constructed stories of her life, her repertoire, and her multiple audiences.

From childhood, she moved up and out both socially and geographically. One biographer commented on the "melodrama" of her life (Shebuev 12), and it certainly offered considerable action scored to music. Born in 1871 in the village of Altukhovo, Orlov Province, this daughter of a peasant woodcutter and his laundress wife grew up in poverty with her two brothers. Soviet biographer S. Kizimova, more taken with Vial'steva's social origins than were her contemporaries, romanticized the little peasant girl who delighted the neighbors with her songs as she did her chores (Kizimova 9). This image might sustain a publicity hype, but the facts speak of greater hardships and a supremely willed ascension, not an effortless one. The untimely death of their father left their mother alone to raise the children, whom she took to Kiev in hopes of finding better work for all of them. (Perhaps the "peasant stage mother" should be recognized as the first new female character type in this story.) Not even sixteen, the young Vial'tseva began her work life as an apprentice seamstress, but her mother soon found a better position for her as a maid in a hotel frequented by the theatrical crowd. She hoped that someone with connections would recognize her beautiful daughter's talents and help to launch a stage career.

Russia's after-dinner entertainments at that time included increasing numbers of variety theaters and amusement gardens from the 1860s. Modeled on the French café-chantant, or "place where people sing," these houses began to proliferate in the 1890s, multiplying almost exponentially after the turn of the century. Modernization was putting new money into circulation, and those who earned and spent it held different notions of fun from those of their more traditionally minded predecessors. These new "city people," less concerned with social estate, developed a more tolerant view of women in the public spaces formerly occupied by men and the kind of women men did not marry. When in the 1870s Anna Zhiudik delighted the audiences of St. Petersburg's Bouffe Theater with a cancan or her infamous "suggestive . . . cynical . . . ditties" (Kuznetsov 117), she was helping society to free itself from rigid notions of propriety in entertainment. The next step entailed destabilizing class and gender hierarchies; Zhiudik paved Vial'tseva's way.

Vial'tseva integrated the entrepreneurial spirit with the broadly based consumerism upon which it depended. The cliché of rags to riches sooner fit her life than that of the overnight success. At thirteen, impatient to be discovered, she left a life of manual labor for the stage. She approached I. Ia. Setov, director of a Kiev-based operetta company. Initially, she simply wanted to perform, and all Setov could offer was a chorus line.[5] Hardly the first singer to begin a career dancing in a revue, Vial'tseva stepped into the theater world. Dancing in the line for thirty-five rubles a month, she remained with Setov until his company broke up almost two years later. Like many businesses in the unstable entrepreneurial world, this one soon folded, putting her back on the job market. Most commercial theatrical companies did not enjoy a long lifespan because of the stiff competition for the entertainment ruble. New ones sprang up with each failure, and entrepreneurs might change cities as easily as they would the type of entertainment they were promoting; none suffered a dearth of ambitious performers. In this precarious and competitive environment, Vial'tseva spent the next few years in amateur (liubitel'skie) productions around Kiev, moving erratically up the ladder of show business, earning little money but showcasing her voice and expanding her repertoire.

Fig 11.1.
Anastasiia Vial'tseva.

She returned to stable employment when entrepreneur K. N. Nezlobin hired her in his touring company at seventy-five rubles per month.
Similarities in the backgrounds of the entrepreneur and the entertainer
are worth mentioning because they emphasize the degree to which the
theater allowed for so many different forms of social mobility. Nezlobin
had come from a merchant rather than a peasant background, but he
dreamed of more excitement than the family business offered. He
worked as both an actor and a director before finding his niche in
management.[6] Vial'tseva, in the meantime, did a stint in Moscow's most
popular operetta company at the Akvarium Theater. In 1893 she ended
up in St. Petersburg, engaged by one of the leading entrepreneurs in imperial Russia, S. A. Pal'm.[7]

Vial'tseva, however, chafed under the strain of her ambition.[8] Like
Anna Zhiukik or the even more sensational Miss Julia Pastrana, the

"monkey woman" who capitalized on the fascination with Darwinism (Kuznetsov 21), she might have ended up on the fringe of the entertainment world, celebrated but still primarily a star only in the world of male entertainments. The determined chorine, however, took one of the best-tested paths to stardom: She found a wealthy and distinguished admirer interested in helping her career. Legend had her striking up an acquaintance with lawyer N. V. Kholeva, an amateur performer and a sophisticated gentleman-about-town, at the Saturday evening gypsy concerts at the Malyi. Arranged by P. F. Levdik, one of the featured entertainment critics for the "boulevard" newspaper the *Petersburg Gazette* (Peterburgskaia gazeta), these concerts tapped into the "gypsymania" of the age and brought professionals together with amateurs to indulge in a shared passion. Kholeva attended regularly because he enjoyed the music, while Vial'tseva stayed backstage, picking up songs and performance tips. Taking her into his home, Kholeva sponsored voice lessons for her with S. M. Sonki, director of the Petersburg Choral Society and distinguished for his work on vocal cords. Sonki was credited with developing Vial'tseva's unique timbre, her subsequent hallmark. In 1905 she hired pianist, composer, and vocal specialist A. V. Taskin as her permanent accompanist. Thereafter she never appeared without him; the status of having a professional accompanist lent her an air of distinction and undoubtedly helped her performances.

Kholeva oversaw the training not only of her voice, but also of her social persona. He told her what to read and schooled her in the arts of conversation and hostessing. Their relationship continued several years, and although it did not end in marriage, she left the professional stage and performed almost exclusively at soirées in his home and under his surname (Shebuev 9). Henry Higgins to Eliza Doolittle? Whether sugar daddy or Dutch uncle, Kholeva gave the peasant songstress the polish she needed to enter society through other than a stage door (Kizimova 14). Later, she married a colonel in a guards' regiment, V. V. Biskupskii, although he kept his distance from her limelight. The queen of the concert stage could cheerfully admit her humble origins because she was taken for a lady; simply stated, Vial'tseva demonstrated how dress and behavior had the potential to render hereditary social estate increasingly insignificant (ibid. 9).

Vial'tseva had made a calculated move toward respectability, but for her to have achieved it meant that society also must have expanded its notions of the permissible. Although not even the "yellow" press reported scandalous personal details with the enthusiasm it does today, Vial'tseva's peasant background and relationship with Kholeva were hardly state secrets. Of course, the theater offered creative license offstage as well as on, but we should bear in mind that this was also the sphere from which Rieff's modal types were emerging. Parallels with non-Russian female performers illustrate the significance of the situation. Like Sophie Tucker, the diva of American vaudeville who also rose to stardom in the 1910s, Vial'tseva personified the growing acceptance of women in public places. The stage door opened other doors for them that previously would have remained closed to women in general, especially to peasant girls and Jewesses. Yet for her social world to have expanded as it did, the *chansonette* had to have attained a certain respectability.[9] Deference for performers reflected two changed attitudes: Not only did many nightclub singers distance themselves from images of a can-canesque debauchery, but "decent" women themselves appeared more frequently as patrons of these clubs, moving into the previously sexually separated sphere of nightlife.[10] All-female orchestras, for example, became a fashionable novelty in this milieu, where wives and husbands danced alongside mistresses stepping out with their lovers.

After Kholeva's death, Vial'tseva moved back to Pal'm's company and quickly attained celebrity status. Her voice training permitted her to graduate to featured roles, although second to such established names as "the King of Romances," A. D. Davydov. As Katy in the operettic revue "Gypsy Songs in Live Performance," she finally became the overnight sensation that she had worked so long to be. Her rendition of "I Want You, I Love You" stirred the audience to cry for more, and the critics to liken her to Vera Zorina, wildly popular in the 1880s for her torrid gypsy romances. Pal'm quickly moved her up to leads, but Vial'tseva now fielded better offers. In 1897, thirteen years after embarking upon a stage career, Vial'tseva had made it.

Ia. V. Shchukin, entrepreneur at Moscow's prestigious Hermitage Theater, and himself a former footman, offered her a contract at 750 rubles a month, and soon added an extra 133 rubles per performance.[11] A cross between a nightclub and a theater, complete with a mirrored stage in its summer garden in addition to the main hall, the Hermitage mixed genres as easily as it did patrons. Fundamentally commercialized, this was a place where the most revered could earn top salaries for single performances. For example, Shchukin would engage the likes of dramatic actress Vera Komissarzhevskaia to give his theater a patina of sophistication. The talented Komissarzhevskaia's appearances at the Hermitage demonstrated that she was also a celebrity, famous for being famous. The middlebrow audiences who frequented the Hermitage could pay to see (and be seen seeing) the controversial actress

without having to sit through an incomprehensible avant-garde production at her own financially troubled theater. The Hermitage put Vial'-
tseva under the same roof as Komissarzhevskaia, in front of the same
audiences.[12] Even when Vial'tseva left Shchukin in 1909 to work in St.
Petersburg for "the Russian Barnum," P. V. Tumpakov, at his Bouffe
Theater, she returned regularly to perform in the Hermitage. When she
moved to Tumpakov, she linked her name to every major impresario and
variety theater in turn-of-the-century Russia.

Vial'tseva's voice, and perhaps especially its limitations, defined much
of her stage persona. The distinctive timbre enhanced by her various
singing coaches and the deep emotionalism of her style made her a
natural for romances—songs of nostalgia for love gone wrong or about
the capricious heroine toying with her lovers' affections. Although
Vial'tseva is sometimes identified with gypsy songs, they constituted a
minor part in her repertoire. She sang about desire: "I Want, I Want It
All," "Why Love, Why Suffer?," "I Thirst for a Rendezvous," and her
most famous of all, hurrying the coachman along the road to love, "Gai-
da, Troika." She also continued to perform in operettas, the most popular
of which was Jacques Offenbach's perennial crowd-pleaser "The Fair
Hélène."[13] The basis for her attraction, though, lay in her concerts of
Russian songs, consisting largely of undiluted schmaltz: "I fall in and out
of love at will." Her fare reflected the tastes of her bourgeois audience;
bored by the ponderous legitimate stage and opera, this crowd nonetheless sought something more uplifting than "monkey women" and more
refined than dirty ditties.

Just as her career was entwined with the growth of the entertainment
industry in general, so too must Vial'tseva's stardom be read as an indicator of changing attitudes toward celebrities, who were becoming increasingly associated with the values implicit in consumption. The
"Vial'tseva phenomenon" marked a significant shift in Russian culture,
and it was emblematic of the broader "culture of personality" then
taking shape. By christening her "The Incomparable One," her fans suggested that although her charm and talents might lie beyond their reach,
she was, paradoxically, worthy of emulation. Fandom itself was hardly
new to Russia. Pushkin, for example, by the end of the nineteenth century had evolved from a poet influential among the literate elite of his
own generation into a cult figure. But by century's end fandom had
become a commercial commodity, and the poet's status as a celebrity
charted the changes: infamous in court circles for his purported inspiration of the Decembrist revolutionaries and burdened with the tsar as his
personal censor, fifty years after his fatal duel in 1837 he had achieved a

new sort of popularity when his face appeared on chocolate wrappers. The political persona had become a commercialized personality. This was the atmosphere in which Vial'tseva reigned.

In his study of trends in American culture at the turn of the twentieth century, Warren Susman points out the consumer-oriented outlook reflected in the fans' selection of "personalities" over "characters" as role models. Like Leo Lowenthal and other students of the interaction between politics and culture, Susman argues that idealized "characters" embodied the virtues of discipline and restraint, social qualities mandatory for the early stages of industrialization. "Personalities," in contrast, enjoyed the fruits of their labors. They could indulge in the benefits of industry, from the increased leisure time made available by technology to the more readily available fashions, because new salary scales and job opportunities had made them more affordable (Susman 271–85).

Unfortunately, Vial'tseva's personal archive does not yield a cache of fan mail, but it is relatively simple to track her popularity through the growth of publications devoted to entertainment that began to appear especially around the turn of the century. These journals included *The Artist and the Stage* (Artist i stsena), *Theater and Art* (Teatr i iskusstvo), *The Variety Theater* (Teatr variete), *Footlights and Life* (Rampa i zhizn'), and finally the eclectic *News of Theaters, Skating Rinks, and Movie Theaters* (Novosti teatrov, sketing-ringov i kinemateatrov). These more specialized periodicals complemented the "boulevard" press's increasing coverage of leisure-time activities in general. Moreover, fashion magazines and other female-oriented publications testified to both new audiences and their diversified interests. Interviews, photographs, and gossip columns could turn public performers into private individuals, ersatz personal acquaintances.

The publications gave audiences license to cast performers in new roles. As Richard Sennett has argued, "a 'role' is generally defined as behavior appropriate for some situations but not for others." He further notes how the line between stage and street had become fluid in the late-nineteenth-century urban environment, a development that complicated efforts to present the self (Sennett 33). Entertainers who could master fame and fortune yet also evidence the personal touch made ideal role models because they could combine multiple behaviors. For fans, they personified the myth of success in an age when industrialization enabled growing numbers to indulge in conspicuous consumption, even as conventional morals questioned such consumerism as a *modus vivendi*. Under these circumstances, for example, it became imperative for female performers to be able to apply a domestic touch. A photo display in the family journal *The Russian Sun* (Russkoe solntse) brought readers inside the private train car in which Vial'tseva lived when she toured. "Decorated with tsarist elegance, reminiscent of a society matron's salon" (Shebuev 9), the private car was the site of her private life. Three photos spotlighted various aspects of her character, elegant but sincere: One shows her lounging in a peignoir, hair cascading down her back; in another she poses in an evening gown, with an ostrich plume atop her wide-brimmed hat; and the third reflects a staple pose for Russian entertainers intent on proving their seriousness in a society that privileged intellectuals—Vial'tseva sits primly, writing at her desk.[14]

The intimacy presented in the photographs dimmed the distinction between her public and private selves, an overlap indicative of the trends developing in the art-*cum*-business of publicity. Performers still posed in costume, in the personae of their roles, but the public now also hungered to see them "at home." This phenomenon appeared in turn-of-the-century commercial theater journals in all Western countries and later became a mainstay in Hollywood, where studios found themselves taxed to present wholesome images of less-than-virtuous stars; *Mommie Dearest*, the autobiography of Joan Crawford's adopted daughter Christina, exposed the hypocrisy of this publicity, but long after the gullible readers had swallowed the images.[15] Vial'tseva and her husband never had their own family, but several children lived with her off and on in quasi-foster parent arrangements (Kizimova 46–47). Would their stories have presaged Christina's? Reality mattered little here, for image was primary. However stylish this implicit domesticity, made explicit in the promotional shots, it accentuated the need to impart respectability to a profession that aroused suspicion for its excessive freedoms. As modal types, then, the stars could demonstrate basic connections with their bourgeois audience.

At the same time, though, the celebrities had to transcend the banality of bourgeois existence through their conspicuous consumption. Success could be quantified in financial terms, if not always in critical reviews. Vial'tseva's earnings offered stunning possibilities for conspicuous consumption. An article in the *Petersburg Gazette* in 1910 reported with admiration and perhaps a touch of envy the "monstrous salaries" earned by top performers; it placed Vial'tseva in Shaliapin's category of those who earned more than 100,000 rubles a year. Vial'tseva's contract to record ten romances for 10,000 rubles, the impressed reported calculated, would bring her 333 rubles per minute. Noticeably, she was the only Russian female included in this list of millionaires. She fell just shy of actress Sarah Bernhardt and soprano Adelina Patti, two of the dominant female cultural personalities of the nineteenth century (*Pg*, no. 306). Vial'tseva's income "kept other singers awake nights" as they fantasized about taking in 100,000 rubles per tour (*Artist i stsena* 3). Earning up to 20,000 rubles in the two capitals, and 1,400 per operatic performance at the Bouffe, she drew better than foreign stars (Nest'ev 54). And she spent lavishly; in addition to her fancy train car, she boasted a large estate, Kamenka, on the banks of the Dvina River in Vitebsk province, purchased from a count for 150,000 rubles.

The core of her audience can be identified from the theaters in which she performed and the roles she sang: the Bouffe rather than the Bol'shoi, "The Fair Hélène" instead of "The Queen of Spades." No fixed date or concert made her "incomparable," but once the nickname was coined, it made for natural advertisement. Champion wrestler Ivan Poddubnyi paid her an appropriate compliment when he considered her, along with Maksim Gorkii, a star of his magnitude; an earthy balance of pride and profanity, they make a fitting triumvirate of celebrity idols for fin-de-siècle Russia (Kugel' 288–90).

Vial'tseva was essentially an urban songbird. The crowds of new money gathered in the cities, and the bittersweet romances she sang echoed the transitory contacts made in the milieu of modernity (Nest'ev 58–66). Her brother Iurii idealized her as "a street singer; she lived the uncomplicated dramas of the heroines depicted so vividly in her romances. . . . An innocent compassion, and even a touch of vulgarity, touched her very distinctive beauty" (*Novoe vremia*, no. 13258). Also categorized as a "salon singer" because of the ambience she created, Vial'tseva sometimes sang at private gatherings—for example, at the home of actress Mariia Savina, herself a personality as well as a talent (Nest'ev 57). Theater critic A. R. Kugel', who remembered Vial'tseva from Pal'm's chorus line, called her style "conventional" and "petty bourgeois," but he also found in it a "universal atavistic passion" for love.[16] Biographer Kizimova blamed the "uncultured merchants" for demanding romances, as though Vial'tseva would have preferred to sing political anthems (Kizimova 29). True, shortly after her death an embittered Taskin decried the tyranny of the fans, who insisted on the old favorites, shouting down her attempts to introduce anything new. "I am a serious musician, I hated playing [the old songs], but I accompanied her," he said. Yet Taskin's interviewer doubted that Vial'tseva lamented her repertoire. "Maybe she did," he wrote, "but only until she sang the first note. It was the kind of hatred we have for someone with whom we are head-over-heels in love. Once she sang the first note, she would lose herself in the song" (Shebuev 15).

Fig 11.2. Vial'tseva in her most popular role, "The Fair Hélène."

In addition, the behavior of her fans told as much about her celebrity as the packed houses she drew. Vial'tseva sometimes had to pay theater owners a deposit in anticipation of damage wreaked by rambunctious enthusiasts. In fact, the police often patrolled her shows in an effort to keep down disturbances. As her star began its ascent, this rhyme floated about her in St. Petersburg:

> A muffled cry of envy,
> Such a concert singer!
> The whole capital is enraptured
> with Vial'tseva!

Incidents of lovestruck young men leaping from the balconies to declare their devotion were commonplace. One smitten admirer took his date's fan, pinned to it the mortgage to his house, and offered it to Vial'tseva. This conduct differed from that of the stagedoor Johnnies who hoped to escort beautiful young stars to intimate dinners. These "suitors" were more interested in taking part in the performance themselves than in actually seducing Vial'tseva (Kizimova 21–25).

Vial'tseva could not have achieved her extraordinary fame by performing only in the two capitals, and the true foundations of her stardom lay in the provincial cities. She had traveled with various operetta companies from the beginning of her career, and in 1904 entrepreneur L. L. Pal'mskii organized the first concert tour that she headlined. In 1905 she began the biannual provincial tours that continued until her death eight years later. In the age before movies, the tours approximated mass reproduction. They stimulated consumers' appetites for the photos and postcards of her that promoted a sense of intimacy, for the sheet music she plugged, and for the recordings that technology now distributed on a mass scale. In short, they fetishized her. One writer claimed, "In provincial cities her excursions became holidays." Like Savina, she proclaimed, "The train car is my life!" covering a grueling 110,000 miles on tour in her last five years. These tours often landed her in comical situations with local authorities, some of whom simply fleeced her manager to obtain prized tickets or to ensure the inclusion of favorite songs (Shebuev 9–10). Her generosity on stage was legendary; she would sing as many as twenty encores for crowds who had weathered hours in line for tickets. Her need for applause seemed to fuel her psychologically, but the peasant girl craving adoration purchased it at a tremendous personal cost to her health.

Members of the cultural avant-garde also counted themselves among her fans (Kizimova 32); to assume otherwise would be to ascribe an impossibly sharp polarization to Russian culture. If she depended upon middlebrow tastes for the foundation of her fame, by virtue of being a "phenomenon" Vial'tseva could also appeal to those who enjoyed prestige in highbrow circles. After-hours cabarets enjoyed great vogue in artistic circles, where the Stanislavskiis and the Meyerholds could escape to poke fun at the seriousness of the new trends in drama.[17] At one regular Friday presentation, comparable to the present-day "roasts" of entertainers, Vial'tseva was the slated object of burlesque. Isadora Duncan was also appearing in St. Petersburg that night. The cream of culture, Shaliapin, painter Il'ia Repin and his wife, and author Leonid Andreev, gathered in Duncan's dressing room after the show. Duncan declared herself a great fan of Vial'tseva's and, although the tired Repins begged off, the others set out for the cabaret. They created quite a stir when they arrived shortly before the guest of honor. At midnight, Vial'tseva made an entrance with husband and Taskin in tow. Laughing, she "struck the Vial'tseva pose" and then broke into a comical rendition of Mussorgskii's "Fleas." Like headliners in Vegas who take in each other's shows both as a matter of professional courtesy and for a touch of publicity, the famed in the audience did not avoid the spotlight. Giacomino, featured clown at Petersburg's Cirque Moderne, was also in attendance. No single performer could hold center stage all night. Duncan entreated artist A. Ia. Golovin, who chanced to be in the audience, to put together a costume on the spot for her in an impromptu competition of self-parody. The dancer upstaged the singer by winning this contest, but then the crowd settled in and kept Vial'tseva til morning, demanding their favorites (Shau 30–31).

However happily she bathed in the admiration of the cultural elite that evening, Vial'steva was not their professional peer. The impresario who had organized Sarah Bernhardt's most recent foreign tour proposed the European circuit for Vial'tseva, but she declined, insisting that she was a "Russian singer" (*Obozrenie teatrov*, no. 34). "Others go abroad in search of glory; I have already found it in Russia," she asserted (Nest'ev 53). Nationalism was an essential element in her persona, and her repertoire of romances included foreign songs only in translation. This probably bolstered her relationship with her middle-class audience, which characteristically would be prone to prefer a national to a cosmopolitan identity, and be less familiar with foreign languages. Vial'tseva's sparse private archive contains a poem in which she rhapsodized, "I am a Russian, born with a love for my native soil, which is holy for me" (RGALI, f. 950, op. 1, d. 1, 1.1). With much fanfare she traveled to the front during the Russo-Japanese War to nurse her wounded husband.[18] In Manchuria, she also gave concerts for the troops, at the personal expense of the 26,000 rubles she would have earned had she followed her contractual schedule (Nest'ev 53). Her voice would have gone to the front anyway; Commander-in-Chief General Aleksei Kuropatkin took his phonograph and her records with him.[19] She also claimed a stake in national interests when she joined with Shaliapin and tenor Leonid Sobinov to raise funds for a scientific expedition to the North Pole (Kizimova 48).

Her hesitation to tour Europe, however, quite likely derived as much from fear of music critics as from a nativist tradition. Vial'tseva could please the crowds, but not persuade the reviewers that her voice merited critical consideration. A 1903 attempt to cultivate the highbrows with an appearance in the title (male) role of A. G. Rubinshtein's "Demon" prompted the snide reviewer in the *Russian Word* (Russkoe slovo) to include her among the "contemporary elements in opera and drama who remain distant from art." Humiliated, she responded with a letter in a competing newspaper, *Newsday* (Novosti dnia), asking, "How can such a weak woman as I respond to such slander?" (Nest'ev 56). But the fans loved her. Her premiere at the Bol'shoi as Delilah in 1905 once again generated a better response from the audience than from the critics. She did not attempt the legitimate opera again until four years later, when S. I. Zimin, founder of a private opera company in Moscow where Shaliapin, Sobinov, and others of that caliber performed, invited her to sing "Carmen" and "Mignon." She filled the house, bringing in the largest profits at Zimin's box office for 1907. The critics, however, devastated her, and she left the highbrow stage for good.[20]

The ridicule and accusations she suffered from those who preferred a strong voice to a dazzling performance may have hurt her pride, but the delicate beauty was very much an Iron Butterfly. Failure to reach the pinnacle of cultural prestige disappointed Vial'tseva, but did not stop her from attempting to change the terms of acceptance by the public. She offered a new role for women in her own time, many of whom were in search of direction because their social world was in transition at the end of the tsarist era. Her accomplishments, although larger than their lives, were nonetheless human. She helped to make personal independence appear less menacing than earlier in the century, when notions of traditional community had dominated the social organizations of the various estates, including the merchantry. This community was itself increasingly a casualty of urbanization, and if Vial'tseva could triumph from the dislocation, so could others.

This idol worship of certain female entertainers reflected the more extensive transformations of Russia in the throes of modernization. On the one hand, Vial'tseva represented a woman making it in a man's world, an ostensible symbol of equality. On the other hand, it would be misleading to emphasize that aspect of her career because most female entertainers played no active role in the feminist movement. Studying successful female entertainers fills a lacuna in our understanding of Russia's women because it can throw light on how differences between the sexes could be used to the benefit of "the fair sex," as some of these women consciously saw themselves.[21] In Russia the politics of the "woman question" was for the most part subsumed under the larger issue of social justice; in a country where the peasants had so recently been emancipated and no one enjoyed suffrage, many women found feminism a rather narrowly based social issue to pursue (Edmondson). Postrevolutionary historians have also generally adhered to this prioritization.[22] Women such as Vial'tseva, when they are mentioned at all in this sociopolitical paradigm, usually have their subjective charitable actions singled out to illustrate their political consciousness.[23]

This approach, however, establishes very limited criteria for measuring the empowerment of women: it fixates on political power in an undivided public sphere instead of distinguishing between separate, gendered spheres of power and influence. In addition, this perspective ignores the politics implicit in the evolving culture of personality represented by the favorite stars. A 1911 interview in the *Petersburg Gazette* with Vial'tseva on a peculiar labor issue illustrated the orientation she represented: Vial'tseva was among several professionals, including a lawyer and a psychiatrist, whose opinions were solicited about a woman suing her tailor because when she refused to pay him, he showed her fiancé how she had been lying about her proportions. The fiancé then called off the wedding. "The 'Incomparable One' smiled her charming Vial'tseva smile," the story read. Avowing that she always maintained good relations with her tailors, Vial'tseva named them and then boosted national pride with an added observation that "the art of Russian tailors is not a cut below that of the Parisians" (*Pg*, no. 151). In her frivolous response, Vial'tseva ignored the question and simply took advantage of the opportunity to promote her own magnanimous personality and sense of style. Like the romances she sang to large crowds about private love, this interview took her to the public without putting her in the public sphere of political power. In fact, she specifically rejected that possibility by using the occasion to enhance instead the gendered space of feminine wiles in which she found empowerment, as opposed to the public sphere of social policy that the story in fact addressed.

Vial'tseva seemed to deny that the personal was political, despite the extent to which her life said otherwise. By highlighting her role as a fashionable personality, Vial'tseva entered, albeit through the back door, the politicized debate about the rising preoccupation with individualism and the role of the artist in society. Russia's intelligentsia struggled to come to terms with the politics of individualism that accompanied modernization. Some published their confusion in the 1909 collection of essays *Landmarks* (Vekhi), whose tone of retreat from public life to concentrate on private, personal growth upset many others. Historians have misplaced Vial'tseva in this setting, putting her under the rubric of "escapism." Soviet historian I.V. Nest'ev wrote that "the fascination with complex forms of symbolist theater, the new poetry . . . could hardly fail to incite a certain backlash. Many listeners—including people in the highest intellectual circles—gravitated toward the elemental emotional arts" (Nest'ev 13). He cited Vial'tseva's following as a prime example of the flight to fancy. Certainly many paid to see her because they wanted to spend a few hours in a world of charm and beauty, but to evaluate the

"Vial'tseva phenomenon" essentially as a diversion is to miss a fundamental social change that she represented. The intellectuals might have been loath to admit it, but they were, together with Vial'tseva, epiphenomena of the same fundamental changes in the structure of Russian society: the individual coming into his and her own, breaking free from rigid social and economic hierarchies and assuming political burdens in new forms. This emancipation was never fully realized, but the extent to which it was under way by 1917 raises new questions about Russian society on the verge of revolution.

A significant and understudied arena in which the "Vial'tseva phenomenon" speaks to changes in female consciousness is the fashion world. Herself a fashion plate, Vial'tseva made a point of appearing in contemporary gowns rather than in period costumes (ibid. 68). A widening eye for fashion was further reflected in the spate of small, inexpensive pocket books offering guidance on how to dress, how to fix one's hair, how to improve appearance in general. *What Becomes Me?* asked the title of an 1891 handbook on "how to dress with taste." The targeted audience may be pictured from the editors' calculation that readers had an annual household budget of approximately 2,000 rubles, only a small portion of which could go for clothes. Such books gave the sort of generalized advice necessary for women thinking about style for the first time. Significantly, they spoke to women who would spend time both in church and somewhere that bathing costumes would be worn, advice in itself as indicative of changing attitudes toward modesty as of the new money in circulation (*Chto mne k litsu?* 3. 10. 173–79). These statements on style signified an awareness of the self and how to present it in public, one that cut across the boundaries that previously had separated women when the clothes they wore by and large identified their social estate.[24] With a sewing kit, cut-out patterns from a number of inexpensive family journals, and imagination, women could imitate Vial'tseva's wardrobe on their considerably smaller budgets.

Sadly, the hoopla surrounding Vial'tseva's premature death from pleuritis in February 1913 provides perhaps the clearest illustration of how her personality had transcended her mortal self, at least in the temporal sphere. One obituary noted, "The fairy tale of her life ended as extraordinarily as it had begun" (*Rampa i zhizn'*, no. 5), which suggested that the writer, undoubtedly like many of her fans, was unaware of the effort involved in creating Vial'tseva. The singer probably contracted the blood disease in the spring of 1912, but after a summer recuperating at Kamenka she refused to cancel her punishing autumn tour. In November, singing in Kursk, she collapsed on stage. Once she returned to her bed in St. Petersburg, she never left it. By the end of January 1913 her condition had seriously worsened, and the press, led by the *Petersburg Gazette*, began a death watch, providing up-to-the-minute bulletins on her health that "the public read as eagerly as they did political or military news" (*Pg*, no. 37). A German specialist was flown in from Berlin to give her experimental drugs (Kizimova 57).[25] Biskupskii gave his wife so much of his own blood that he was feared to have contracted pleuritis himself; the press quickly noted how his sacrifice repaid hers of following him to Manchuria (ibid. 58–59). Nothing, however, could spare the sick and exhausted songbird. A newspaper columnist used the flowery language of her romances to stress the symbolism of her deadly disease: "Drop by drop, in all corners of Russia, she dissipated her strength, the juice of her nerves, the blood of her heart, and wasted away like a lily torn off at the stalk" (*Rannee utro*, no. 29).

Her funeral was statist in its proportions, the fascination with the style of her life carrying over into that of her death. The body lay in an open coffin in her apartment on the Moika Canal for friends and admirers to pay their last respects, and artist V. I. Demchinskii was commissioned to create a death mask; a small entertainment-oriented magazine published photos of both corpse and mask (*The Modern Accordian* [Sovremennyi baian] no. 2). Thus did her fans canonize this secular saint. Six white horses drew her casket through the streets of St. Petersburg, lined by an estimated 150,000 mourners, and the parade to the cemetery at the Aleksandr Nevskii monastery was filmed for newsreels.[26] Three separate services were held; famed ballerina and former mistress to the tsar Matilda Kseshinskaia reportedly struggled for almost an hour to get through the crowd to attend private ceremonies (*Pg*, no. 37). The devoted Biskupskii, weakened by the blood transfusions, could appear at the cemetery only long enough to lay a wreath (*Pg*, no. 37). Vail'tseva, whose fortune was estimated at 2.5 million rubles, bequeathed her property in St. Petersburg to the city, specifying that it be used for a clinic (RGALI, f. 950, op. 1, d. 3, 1. 5). Taskin and the local press worked together to collect funds for a sculpture and a chapel at her grave, but war and revolution interrupted their undertaking.[27]

Celebrated for her personality, her salary, and her private train car, Vial'tseva embodied the contradictions of the turn of the century. While most histories focus on the developing social and political consciousness of Russians, a biography of Vial'tseva turns attention to concepts of individualism, of personality rather than morality as a motivating force, and of conspicuous consumption over self-sacrifice. Objectively, Vial'tseva was a social upstart who internalized the bourgeois values of hard work and competitive individualism in a business potentially open to all comers. Yet by presenting an image of grace and untroubled poise, she turned these virtues into something resembling happenstance. No Horatio Alger she, but rather a model of feminine talent and leisure. Despite a life of opening back doors, she adapted quickly to walking in through the front when the opportunity arose.

Vial'tseva's greatest significance as a cultural icon derived from her personification of this paradox. Within the broad context of modernization, her acceptance as a modal type evidenced different ways of thinking about the self, of facing the demands of individualism. The space in which leisure was enjoyed, which in Vial'tseva's case consists of the concert halls in which she sang, offered a third and competitive space where influence could be exercised. This third sphere contained something from both the public and the private spheres. Vial'tseva's importance to Russian history expands enormously when she is recognized as an agent of the larger transformation then taking place. If her voice and beauty set her apart, it was the charm and the kind of adulation that feeds upon itself that made her a personality, a female harbinger of changes that ultimately were not realized.

Notes

I would like to thank Dan Kaiser, Joan Neuberger, and the editors of this volume for comments on an earlier draft.

1. Much of the biographical material comes from Kizimova's slim volume, the collection of sources begun in honor of the 100th anniversary of her birthday by staff members of the Briansk regional archive, the region whence Vial'tseva hailed. Vial'tseva seems to be enjoying something of a resurgence in post-Soviet Russia. A 1993 made-for-television movie entitled "The Incomparable One" portrayed a kind and extremely talented peasant girl whose voice and charm enraptured the people, not just the wealthy and powerful. However, the television Vial'tseva appeared far more politically sensitive than the real one, an indication that even in commercialized Russia, "personality" alone does not suffice.

2. In certain respects, Metro-Goldwyn-Mayer's "Iron Butterfly," Jeanette MacDonald, makes a more appropriate parallel than Madonna. Another lovely redhead, MacDonald enjoyed great popularity in film, but her soprano was noticeably weaker than the baritone of her perennial co-star, Nelson Eddy, who also performed in opera companies.

3. See especially the critique of middlebrow culture launched from the Frankfurt School in Max Horkheimer and Theodor Adorno, *The Dialectic of Enlightenment* (New York: Herder and Herder, 1977).

4. *Meshchanstvo* was the Russian estate designation for the urban dweller; by the end of the nineteenth century, it had the same derogatory cultural connotation as "bourgeois."

5. Soviet biographer Kizimova exaggerated greatly when she argued that the singer took this job because she "wanted to serve art" (11).

6. On K. N. Nezlobin, see *Teatral'naia entsiklopediia*, 5 vols. (Moscow: Sovetskaia entsiklopediia, 1965), vol. 4, 11.

7. See S. A. Pal'm's obituary in *Rampa i zhizn'* 37 (1915): 6–8. The son of minor playwright A. I. Pal'm, among his many other accomplishments he was the first to invite Sarah Bernhardt to Russia.

8. Theater critic A. R. Kugel' (Homo Novus) remembered her voice even from when she was primarily a dancer in the line.

9. Lewis Erenberg wrote of Tucker, "The informal world of entertainment in general, and the cabaret in particular, brought her into contact with the successful in urban life and opened up for her a wider world than was previously available for women from her social background." Lewis Erenberg, *Steppin' Out: New York Nightlife and the Transformation of American Culture, 1890–1930* (Chicago: U of Chicago P, 1984), 177.

10. I. I. Miasnitskii (Baryshev), a premier chronicler of the Moscow merchantry from the 1880s, described, for example, a typical evening at the Hermitage with women from the demimonde (*polusvet*) alongside merchants' wives. "V Ermitazhe," in *Prokazniki*, 4th ed. (Moscow: D. P. Efimov, n.d.), 302–25.

11. In 1910, however, the manager at the Hermitage complained to a reporter that her extraordinary salary was costing him more than she was bringing in because he had to fill so many cheap seats. *Petersburgskaia gazeta* 160 (20 June 1910).

12. Coincidentally, Vial'tseva and Komissarzhevskaia both flew as "seagulls" in the popular imagination. The part of Nina in Chekhov's famous play of that title became Komissarzhevskaia's signature role, and it was also the name of Vial'tseva's last popular song.

13. Entrepreneurs felt that their greatest profits were guaranteed if they could sign her for this show. RGALI, f. 853, op. 2, d. 58, 1. 94.

14. The photos are in Shebuev 9–15. In another example, the cover of *Rampa i akter* 15 (1909) showed the dominant actress of the "legitimate" stage, M. G. Savina, also writing at her desk.

15. My mother, for example, and some of her friends vividly recall being impressed by a *Photoplay* spread of Joan Crawford baking in her kitchen.

16. Nest'ev 58–59*fn*3 discusses the indignation of certain intellectuals that Vial'tseva's death caused so much greater a stir than Anton Chekhov's had eight years earlier.

17. The most recent and comprehensive work on the Russian cabaret is L. I. Tikhvinskaia, "Russkie kabare i teatry miniatiur," Dissertatsiia na soiskanie

uchenoi stepeni doktora iskusstvovedeniia (Moscow: Russkii institut iskusstvoz-naniia, 1992).

18. *Teatr i iskusstvo* 22 (1905): 347.

19. Ibid., 54.

20. Information on her March 1907 performance at the Zimin Opera is located in Moscow's Bakhrushin Archive, f. 104, ed. khran.18, 11. 103–105, and ed. khran. 46, which contains annual box office returns.

21. Linda Edmondson recently pointed out that insufficient attention has been paid to the reigning theories of sexual difference in the nineteenth century in studies of emancipation. See Edmondson, "Women's Emancipation and Theories of Sexual Difference in Russia, 1850–1917," in Marianne Liljeström, Eila Mäntysaari, and Arja Rosenholm, eds., *Gender Restructuring in Russian Studies* (Tampere: U of Tampere P, 1993), 39–52.

22. Richard Stites's work makes a case in point. His research puts him at the forefront of both Russian/Soviet women's and cultural histories. Yet successful entertainers do not appear in his *The Women's Liberation Movement in Russia: Feminism, Nihilism, and Bolshevism, 1860–1930* (Princeton: Princeton UP, 1978, 1990). Moreover, Vial'tseva merits but a paragraph, and no citation in the index, in his *Russian Popular Culture: Entertainment and Society since 1900* (Cambridge: Cambridge UP, 1992). I am not criticizing Stites, but pointing out that if he does not mention these women, who else would?

23. Kizimova 50, for example. Kizimova modifies her political hagiography somewhat when she suggests that when Vial'tseva lent her voice to a concert that ultimately helped raise money for the Bolsheviks' *Pravda*, she probably was not making an informed political decision.

24. See especially Mary Ellen Roach and Joanne Bubolz Eicher, *Dress, Adornment, and the Social Order* (New York: John Wiley and Sons, 1965). In his famous 1882 novelization of Moscow's merchantry, Petr Boborykin, the "Russian Zola," used the details of women's clothes to illustrate the relationship between dress and estate. Some of his younger merchant women were using fashion to make a political statement, refusing to dress like their mothers.

25. Kizimova, in an absurdly Soviet aside, blames Vial'tseva's death in part on the Western specialist's ignorance of Russia's more advanced knowledge of treatment for blood diseases.

26. The newsreel can be viewed at Moscow's Tsentral'nyi gosudarstvennyi arkhiv kinodokumentov, film no. 1–12210. Vial'tseva was interred close to Komissarzhevskaia, who, among other things, shared with the songstress a premature death from an illness contracted on tour.

27. The city duma never fulfilled its obligations with respect to her will, which remained in court for years. Surprisingly, given her patriotism, Taskin commissioned a French sculptor for her funerary statue; the First World War and the Bolshevik Revolution prevented its completion. Kizimova 59–60, 71–72.

Works Cited

"A. D.Vial'tseva." 1913. *Teatr i iskusstvo* 6: 132–33.

Artist i stsena 1 (1911): 3.

Chto mne k litsu? Sbornik sovetov dlia dam. Kak odevat'sia s vkusom. 1891. SPB: Knigaizd. German Goppe.

Edmondson, Linda. 1984. *Feminism in Russia, 1900–17.* Stanford: Stanford UP.

Kizimova, S. 1976. *Chaika russkoi estrady.* Briansk: Briansk. oblast. otdel.Vseros. obshchestva okhrany pamiatnikov istorii i kul'tury.

Kugel', A. R. (Homo Novus). 1967. "A. D.Vial'tseva." In *Teatral'nye portrety*, 284–93. Leningrad-Moscow: Iskusstvo.

Kuznetsov, Evgenii. 1958. *Iz proshlogo russkoi estrady: Istoricheskie ocherki.* Moscow: Iskusstvo. A section of this book has been translated as "Shaping the BourgeoisVariety Theater," in Louise McReynolds, ed., "Russian Nightlife, Fin de Siècle," *Russian Studies in History* 31, no. 3 (Winter 1992–93): 11–24.

Nest'ev, I.V. 1970. *Zvezdy russkoi estrady (Panina, Vial'tseva, Plevitskaia): Ocherki o russkikh estradnykh pevitsakh nachala XX veka.* Moscow: Sovetskii kompozitor. The first chapter, " A Bit of History," is translated in Louise McReynolds, ed., "Russian Nightlife, Fin de Siècle," *Russian Studies in History* 31, no. 3 (Winter 1992–93): 25–49.

Novoe vremia (Nv) 13258 (7 February 1913).

Obozrenie teatrov 34 (1907): 1.

Peterburgskaia gazeta (Pg) 306 (7 November 1910), "Chudovishchnye gonorary"; *Pg* 151 (5 June 1911); *Pg* 35 (5 February 1913); *Pg* 36 (6 February 1913); *Pg* 37 (7 February 1913).

Rampa i zhizn'.

Rannee utro 29 (5 February 1913).

RGALI, f. 950, op. 1, d. 1, 1. 1.

RGALI, f. 950, op. 1, d. 3, 1. 5.

Rieff, Phillip. 1966. *The Triumph of the Therapeutic: Uses of Faith after Freud.* New York: Harper and Row.

Sennett, Richard. 1974. *The Fall of Public Man.* Boston: Faber and Faber.

Shau, Roman. 1961. "Kuindzhinskaia piatnitsa." *Teatral'naia zhizn'* 9: 30–31.

Shebuev, N. 1913. "Koroleva tsyganskaia." *Solntse Rossii* 6: 8–15.

"Smert' Vial'tsevy." 1913. *Rampa i zhizn'* 5: 12.

Sovremennyi baian 2 (February 1913): 3, 5.

Susman, Warren. 1984. " 'Personality' and the Making of Twentieth-Century Culture." In *Culture as History: The Transformation of American Society in the Twentieth Century*, 271–85. New York: Pantheon.

PART IV

CREATIVE

LICENSE

12

FLIRTING WITH WORDS:
DOMESTIC ALBUMS, 1770–1840

Gitta Hammarberg

TWO KINDS OF FLIRTING, one courtship-related and the other literary (flirtation with the idea of authorship), characterize the private albums popular in Russia in the late eighteenth and early nineteenth centuries.[1] Apart from their inherent interest, these albums, many of which are preserved in Russian libraries and archives, are invaluable as illustrations of the "feminization" that literature underwent in Russia around the turn of the century.[2] Despite earlier attempts (at least since Trediakovskii) to incorporate women's linguistic usage into literature, it was the Karamzinists who finally succeeded in "feminizing" Russian literature. They not only suggested that writers should imitate women's conversations and that women themselves should participate in the literary enterprise, but they also modeled the "feminine" narratorial pose in their own texts. Women's presumed sensitivities and "tender" language, as well as the light genres and topics perceived as feminine, defined the Sentimentalist movement, which addressed itself to an ideal (and many a real) female reader. Increasingly, women turned to writing, while established male poets (e.g., Kheraskov and Derzhavin) turned from bombastic solemn odes to Anacreontic poetry and light verse. The appearance in 1779 of the first literary journal for women, Nikolai Novikov's *The Fashionable Monthly, or Library for Ladies' Toilette* (Modnoe ezhemesiachnoe izdanie, ili Biblioteka dlia damskogo tualeta) is a manifestation of the emerging "feminization," as are the numerous satires against "learned ladies" and effeminate dandies in various satirical journals.[3]

The stigma attached to women writers, however, was so firmly entrenched in Russian society that apart from a minority of women who published their creations, most wrote only for domestic circles. Domestic gatherings and salons provided an unthreatening and socially acceptable forum for limited oral circulation of women's literary efforts. Albums, occupying the border between public and domestic spheres, were the corresponding written forum. Literary albums also offered men an ideal medium to address women and to display and test forms and styles presumed pleasing to "the fair sex." The albums that survive thus document practices in what Hume called the "conversible society" presided over by women and promoted as the ideal nurturing environment for budding writers.[4]

Writers needed models, and just as lyrical "middle" genres such as idylls, eclogues, elegies, and songs provided patterns for intimacy, so did parlor or boudoir conversations with "the fair sex." If women needed to be entertained and amused, the most admired qualities for wooing by wit were effortless mastery of various forms of light verse (some already established in the Greek Anthology, others of more recent French vintage), together with lighthearted improvisational skills and a spontaneous ability to invent new forms.[5] These forms and their intimate context define the content of private albums. The frequent journal references to women's boudoirs as the setting for literary activity reflect the era's preference for the intimate environment of refined femininity, and for literature as a discourse of flirtation and desire.[6]

The shift in emphasis from public space to the most intimate of domestic spaces, the boudoir, is only part of the major paradigm shift that occurred in Russian literature at this time. Attention also shifted from important personages to beloved women as the main addressees of poems; from solemn odes to minor madrigals as the most common vehicles for flattering them; from a pompous and weighty tone to trivial fun and games; from heroic strength and nationally significant victories to personal weaknesses and minor private events as leading literary themes. "Less" became "more," as miniaturization triumphed. If the gender analogue to this miniaturization was female, the genre analogue was album verse. Iurii Lotman (249–50) even called the new literary quality "albumness" (*al'bomnost'*). The practice of literature became a friendly social event rather than a formal exchange between author and patron or a lonely affair between reader and book. Domestic circles and their hostesses fostered literary play, amateur poetry, and music making; the "poetry of private life" turned into a creative laboratory for some of Russia's greatest poets, such as Karamzin, Zhukovskii, and Viazemskii.

Functioning somewhere on the border between literary and extraliterary fact (a position conducive to literary innovation, according to Tynianov), albums represent a transitional form both as marginal discourse and as pronounced polyphony within a single set of covers. Most albums were kept by women as prime participants in "conversible society."[7] Many hands wrote entries, recording diverse voices; although addressed to the owner of the album, entries were intended simultaneously for display and to be read by the owner's friends (most of whom were also known to the contributor). A peculiar form of double address, with a sideward glance at potential other readers, including fellow contributors, resulted. The possibilities for incorporating various kinds and degrees of *otherness* and *insider codes* were endless. Contributors were thus engaged in an open-ended dialogue that they could enter more than once as *readers* or *writers*. Indeed, albums were a logical continuation of live dialogues and sometimes served as the pretext for pleasant conversations with "the fair sex," as Shalikov's album verse "To a New [Female] Acquaintance" (Novoi znakomke) attests:

> I spoke with you—and my heart repeated
> In my breast, your lovely words!
> I spoke with you—and happiness lit up
> My imagination, thinking, and feelings!
>
> I spoke with you—and my opinion was confirmed,
> that you are gifted with talents, mind;
> I spoke with you—and secretly was delighted
> That I'll *write verse in your priceless Album!*
>
> Ia govoril s toboi—i serdtse povtorialo
> V grudi moei slova liubeznye tvoi!
> Ia govoril s toboi—i schast'e ozarialo
> Voobrazhen'e, mysl' i chuvstviia moi!
>
> Ia govoril s toboi—i v mnen'i utverzhdalsia
> Chto ty odarena talantami, umom;
> Ia govoril s toboi—i taino voskhishchalsia,
> Chto *napishu stikhi v bestsennyi tvoi Al'bom!* (Shalikov 1819, 254)

Albums circulated in domestic settings. Trivial and lighthearted, they were fashionable among young people and aimed at pleasing their owners, who were mostly women. These attributes were criticized by the learned literati, but in these very "weaknesses" lay their strength, as perceptively argued by writer and critic Pavel Iakovlev. Iakovlev contrasted (male) enlightenment, dissertation writing, and nonsensical mysticism to the pleasing female art of albums:

albums spread the taste for reading among us—they gave us the desire for Literature . . . and the reason is obvious! Women, these light, inconstant, flighty, but always dear creatures, women do everything they wish with us, their sincere worshippers. . . . It's been said that only women can teach us to speak and write pleasantly, that only their sure, delicate taste can wean us from the strange lowly language flaunted by every hero of Russian Novels. . . . Thanks to women! They introduced albums and provided young men with a pleasant and useful activity! I'm even convinced that since the appearance of albums, our people began to write better, more pleasantly; to express themselves more freely, more politely, closer to society conversation.

He even defended flattery, perhaps the most salient and most maligned aspect of album writing:

So what? Are coarse words more pleasant than flattery? And you, Messrs moralists! Do you really in all your modesty take *all* the praise *your* fans heap on you to be the truth? Believe me, women *are used to* the sort of pleasantry that often turns your learned heads! Women can distinguish between truth and deceit. Don't think that a girl who has heard a hundred times that she is beautiful, nice, smart, lovely, . . . don't think that she loses her mind over this . . . like our Mystics, Politicians and Ministers! No! She laughs at the flatterers, has fun with the madrigals, and preserves her album . . . as you preserve your Academicians' diplomas! (Izmailova 6–11 ob.)[8]

Characteristically tongue-in-cheek, Iakovlev pinpointed a crucial feature of album appreciation: namely, the female etiquette of reading with a smile rather than taking things too literally.[9] He further stressed visual and recollective pleasures, concluding that an album is to a woman what Aristotle is to a pedant.[10]

There were many kinds of albums.[11] The simplest and oldest was the German-inspired *Stammbuch*, which came into fashion in Russia in the 1770–80s and contained highly formulaic inscriptions vowing eternal remembrance, friendship, and love, or short *sententiae*, favorite aphorisms, songs, and a place, date, and often family heraldry and mottos. Clearly intended to instruct rather than entertain, these early albums tended to stress the traditional "feminine" virtues of modesty, chastity, and honesty. The formulaic entries were soon superseded by more creative entries, varied in form and language—mostly French and Russian, but frequently others as well. Indeed, one of the hallmarks of albums is their linguistic polyphony in its most concrete sense.

With time, albums were embellished with red morocco covers, gold embossings, decorative metal clasps, and pastel-colored pages of better quality. They became daintier, more "feminine" in size. Like other kinds of literature for women (e.g., Karamzin's almanacs), albums were linked to fashion. In fact, women's literature *was* fashion, as indicated by magazine titles such as *The Fashionable Monthly, or Library for Ladies' Toilette*, mentioned above. Album contributors soon began to vie with each other by including decorations, miniature paintings, literary games, or intricate multimedia miniature toys. Miniature painting, drawing, embroidery, and other domestic crafts were common skills in high society, hence the exquisitely embroidered album covers or entries, intricate silhouette cutouts, and compositions made by a technique of hole punching on paper. Charades incorporating different media in montage fashion, as well as various cutouts (for instance, small spiral-shaped cutouts that when lifted become cages hiding "secret" mementos, miniature poems on birch bark, or drawings), also showed the era's tendency to a synaesthetic appeal to several arts and crafts.

Flowers were the most frequent album illustrations and appeared as watercolors of botanically correct flower specimens, or in artistically arranged bouquets, wreaths, or sprigs with or without verbal inscriptions. Sometimes the visual and verbal media were combined into shaped poems, such as the beautifully calligraphed rose-shaped riddle, depicting in red and green ink a rose that spells out a riddle (to which the answer is "rose"), once in the red ink of the petals and a second time in the green ink of the stem and leaves (to make sure the reader gets the point, the riddle is once more spelled out "normally" on the reverse page).[12] The objects themselves (dried flowers and pressed leaves, theater tickets, invitations to balls, etc.) might be affixed to the pages, artistically arranged as part of charade compositions, or simply inserted between the album pages—often, no doubt, with special amorous connotations. Such entries once more emphasize that albums existed on the boundaries between art and life.

Domestic crafts gained artistic prominence during this period of "feminization" in high literature as well. Numerous poems by Derzhavin and Shalikov praised women's talents for playing various instruments, singing, sewing, cutting silhouettes, creating interesting straw decorations and wallpapers, or participating in domestic theatricals.

The dedications of albums were often rich in information about other customs and values of the era. For instance, one of the prime album poets, A. E. Izmailov, presented his wife of twelve years with an elegant album entitled "Concorde dans le mariage" (2–3; see also Kornilova 86), inscribed with a humorous renewal of their marriage vows—a domestication of the more solemn official church vows. Playfully calling himself a good husband and rhymester, he fulfills her "capricious" wish for personal verse and affirms his eternal love, while wondering if she really will read his poetry.

Such "proper" married flirting shows how domestic happiness entered literature and literature entered women's domestic sphere. Exhortations to women to try their hands at writing (often accompanied by regrets about their preference for French over Russian)[13] yielded results in some marriages. Among numerous contributions by women to Izmailov's own album are several original poems by his wife. The spouses' extended literary dialogue via their albums teems with domestic details and descriptions of their personal occasions for poetry. For his name day she presented him with a poem that functioned as an inscription to her gift of their newborn daughter in her arms (28–29 ob.).

Mariia Borisovna Dargomyzhskaia (b. Kozlovskaia) was another accomplished album poet (also published in journals such as *The Flowerbed* [Tsvetnik] and *Northern Flowers* [Severnye tsvety]). Her "miniature autobiography" confirms the importance of trivial forms, especially Karamzin's trendsetting 1797 collection, *My Trifles* (Moi bezdelki), to women's writing:

> I loved Poetry from my very childhood,
> I loved to read songs and fairy tales;
> In them I found consolation,
> When my peers thought only of playing.
> I got bigger, more thoughtful,
> Wanted to turn to something better.
> Shouldn't I start reading authors as soon as possible?
> I took Karamzin's "Trifles," read them;
> In the "Trifles" I found things sensible, practical,
> And the more I got into them
> The stronger grew my taste for Poetry,
>   And what did I dream up?
>   I might as well write myself! . . .

> Ia s samykh detskikh let Poeziiu liubila,
> Liubila pesenki i skazochki chitat';
> V nikh uteshen'e nakhodila,
> Togda kak sverstnitsy lish' dumali igrat'.
> Pobol'she stala ia pomyshlennei stala,
> Poluchshee chem-nibud' zaniat'sia ia zhelala.
> Ne vziat'sia l' avtorov chitat' mne poskorei?
> Vziala Karamzina, "Bezdelki" prochitala;
> V "Bezdelkakh" del'noe, priiatnoe nashla,
> I chem ikh bolee, prilezhnei razbirala
> Sil'nee tem vo vkus Poezii voshla,
>   I chtozh ia vozmechtala?
>   Davai sama pisat'! . . . (*The Loyalist* [Blagonamerennyi] 5
>   [1826]: 288, as cited in Pekelis 54)

The ideal of "feminine" spontaneity and "speech from the heart" bred such genres as the impromptu (*èkspromt*) or *bouts rimés* of various kinds, often accompanied by notes contending that "these lines" were composed on the spot, at the request of a woman. Verses for special occasions and *bouts rimés* were endlessly varied in verse and prose. Stories were composed incorporating set words, sometimes using them in the order given (T. T[olstaia] 71 ob.); set rhyme words were used in special patterns, and verse dialogues were composed with alternate stanzas expressing opposing opinions (I want/I don't want). An agile poet even managed to conclude several stanzas with different set proverbs in Temira Tolstaia's album (82 ob.).

New lyrics to familiar tunes and adaptations of one's own or someone else's poetry to fit specific occasions and persons, or genres, such as the rondo and the triolet, were also popular album entries. The inscription genre generated innumerable album entries. Inscriptions were made for the most varied objects, often presented to a woman as a gift: portraits, sculptures, jewelry, snuff boxes, statues of cupids (and for the different parts of a cupid's body), park benches, or tree trunks (to commemorate amorous promenades or favorite spots)—in fact, just about anything could be accompanied by an inscription. The necessity for women to be creative within strict social constraints is here echoed in several genres where creativity and wit flourish within strict literary constraints.

Domestic word games entered album pages with great frequency. They might be used to express the common theme of love and friendship, which *because* of its very triteness demanded some sort of *pointe* or witty play in order to stand out. Elegant wit came to be particularly treasured—flirting became more refined as the erotic was supported by an aesthetic dimension and the aesthetic by an erotic one. One of the most frequently encountered "Love and Friendship" poems belongs to Karamzin (234):

> Love is useful to us only
> When it is like dear friendship;
> And friendship is lovely only
> when it equals love.
>
> Liubov' togda lish' nam polezna,
> Kak s miloi druzhboiu skhodna;
> A druzhba lish' togda liubezna,
> Kogda s liuboviiu ravna.[14]

In the spirit of playful games and literary conceits, love declarations moved to a metalevel: love was declared by discussing and playing with the word "love," as in a rather typical French poem:

Je ne dirais jamais *j'aime*
Le mot commence à s'user
Ce n'est pas dans le mot *j'aime*
Que consiste l'amitié.
Souvent ceux qui disent *j'aime*
Sont ceux qui n'aiment rien
Pour moi sans dire que *j'aime*
Et sans me flatter de rien
Il est sûr que je vous aime
Et que *je vous aime bien.* (Izmailov 3)

Among the numerous variations on this theme both in Russian and in French is a clever poem with each verse line ending on a variation of "you"—"toujours toi, n'est que toi, c'est par toi, encore toi," etc. (Barataev 17; Dargomyzhskii 86–87; Izmailova 32–32 ob.). Equally popular (Barataev 33; Bakunina 62) was the French tongue twister: "J'aime, qu'on m'aime comme j'aime quand j'aime," or the Russian one: "Milo s milym veselit'sia / Milo s milym slezy lit' / Milo s nim dushoi delit'sia / Milo milu miloi byt'" (Barataev 34 ob.–35 ob. and 41, respectively). A poem entitled "Les plus jolis mots" and its Russian adaptation vary the theme by discussing "J'aime" as the first words uttered by an infant to its mother and the last ones by a lover to his beloved, followed by a word of caution about false lovers who abuse the words and true lovers who use them only sparingly (Kurakina 21 and 68; T. T[olstaia] 72). Such poems presume that women are gullible creatures, easily swayed by form over substance.

Metacommentary on album writing and poetry itself was typical of album verse. New literary genres emerged in albums. In Izmailov's album we find perhaps the most peculiar transformation of the solemn Horatian "Exegi monumentum," into a minor "Joke" (Shutka):

I erected myself an indestructible monument:
Neither thunder nor storms have the power to influence it!
Guided solely by my Genius,
I wrote the first Russian Homonym.
Thus all of me will not die! [. . .]

Ia pamiatnik sebe vozdvig nesokrushimyi:
Ne v silakh grom, ni vikhr podeistvovat' nad nim!
Edinym Geniem moim rukovodimyi,
Ia pervyi napisal Rossiiskii Omonim.
Tak, ves' ia ne umru! [. . .][15]

Logocentrism of this sort was widespread in albums, for language was one of the most popular playthings in an era when adults were particu-

larly fascinated by all sorts of toys and games. Charades in words and pictures, riddles, logogriphs, acrostics, and other verbal guessing games and
even mathematical puzzles became particularly viable forms of album
art.[16] The interactive nature of literary games and the fact that many
poems were collaboratively composed in domestic circles show that the
roles of reader and writer were interchangeable and the identity of the
"real" author mattered little in "feminized" literature.

The album that Mariia Dargomyzhskaia prepared for her newborn
daughter Liudmila reflects the era's gender-specific social and moral attitudes to love. A moving testimony to maternal love and concern for the
education of daughters, the album opens: "I wish that not fashion but
reason might guide you, my friend, and therefore you will not find in this
book anything passionate, anything romantic, anything that might be
pleasant while we are young but pernicious for the rest of our life!" The
rest of the album contains verse in Russian and French of a largely moralizing and instructive bent. Verses alternate with pictures, such as an allegorical drawing of a dozing blindfolded Cupid and the goddess Athena,
leading a child away from him, accompanied by the poem:

> Here is an abyss before you,
> In it is the dwelling of blind love,
> It is more dreadful than the tomb,
> Run, my friend!—run as fast as you can.
> Do not think of stopping
> To frolic with the dear child,
> I don't advise you to enjoy yourself at once,
> He is pretty hard to amuse . . .
>
> Zdes' bezdna pred toboi, Liudmila,
> Liubvi slepoi zhilishche v nei,
> Ona strashnee, chem mogila,
> Begi, moi drug!—begi skorei.
> Ne vzdumai ty ostanovit'sia
> S ditiatei milym poigrat',
> Ne vdrug sovetuiu teshit'sia,
> Ego trudnen'ko zabavliat' . . . (Dargomyzhskaia 6)

Caution against fashion, against flirtation, and especially against erotic
love and passion was extremely common in young girls' albums. Not
only parents but also cousins, uncles, and girlfriends stressed reasonable
behavior, chastity, and innocence. The theme of love was treated contra-
dictorily: although dangerous for women, love was also obligatory. As
Shalikov (1803, 134) noted à propos verses solicited by women: "Love,
naturally, had to be the subject—the poem is for a lady!" The innumer-

able variations on poems and illustrations entitled "Love and Friendship"
debated the merits of each and, more often than not, favored friendship.
The cult of friendship was particularly intense at this time, and the semantic territory of "love" and "friendship" became virtually identical
(Lotman 265–77). Lotman relates this semantic shift to a special gender-
based women's language as understood at the time.[17]

As might be expected, advice to young girls about how to select a
proper husband recurs frequently. "Just say no" is certainly a more
common piece of advice than its opposite, but making the appropriate
choice is deemed paramount:

> Girls, if you don't want
> To suffer love's misfortunes
> Accept with gratitude
> The advice I give
> It is useful for you to decide to do so
> My advice is not difficult at all
> The whole point is not to err
> About when to say *yes*, when to utter *no*.

> Devitsy esli ne khotite
> Podvergnut'sia liubvi bedam
> S priznatel'nost'iu primite
> Sovet kotoryi ia podam
> Polezno vam na to reshit'sia
> Ne truden vovse moi sovet
> Vsia sila chtob ne oshibit'sia
> Gde *da* skazat', gde molvit' *net*. (Temira Tolstaia 73 ob.–74 ob.)

The three following stanzas advise girls to reject flatterers, old men who
declare their passions, important men who try to impress by rank, dandies who sigh a lot, heroes who aim for yet another conquest, or
Croesuses who tempt with gold. "Yes" is to be reserved only for a lovely,
pleasant, and kind young man who displays true and tender passions that
elicit the heart's consent. Marriage is definitely the most desirable solution, as a certain Petr Mikhailovich makes perfectly clear:

> Here's the point of my verses
> I wish that you and your sisters
> And all the girls I know in this town
> Soon find worthy fiancés.

> Vot mysl' moikh stikhov
> Zhelaiu ia tebe, tvoim sestritsam
> I vsem zdes' v gorode znakomym mne devitsam

Nemedlenno naiti dostoinykh zhenikhov.
(T.T[olstaia] 12, see also 146)

Many of the entries that were strong expressions *against* any kind of flirting whatsoever engaged in coquetry of a different kind, with a distinct note of self-congratulation for verbal virtuosity. However, the mere fact that flirting and the expression of erotic feelings were mentioned even obliquely meant that some perceived the new openness between the sexes as a real danger. And, indeed, flirting and love declarations on the pages of albums proliferated.

Sometimes these took the form of commonly known love songs or romances copied into the albums, often personalized (for instance, with names made to fit) and, no doubt, with a private subtext. Codes became important, and strange alphabets were devised. In some cases such messages are irretrievably lost, whereas in others we have the original coded message together with subsequent decipherings penciled in above the lines.[18] Such entries tapped the old emblem tradition (faith, hope, and charity depicted as cross, anchor, and heart), color and flower codes were imported from France or Germany or personally devised, and album fanciers would jot down entire dictionaries of flowers or colors—sometimes in verse. A few examples of the phenomenon will suffice: "Le gris de lin," a poem in French, goes through the symbolism of several colors and states in a refrain a preference for flax gray as the color of eternal love (Bakunina 44 ob.). A short poem written in blue ink lists several colors and concludes that "celestial" blue is "your" color—a case where the message is conveyed both visually and verbally (Varvara Tolstaia 150). A botanical piece entitled "Air de la Leçon de Botanique" lists items linked to various plants (memory - pansy, peace - olive, victory - laurel, and woman - rose; Varvara Tolstaia 136). A simple list of colors and the corresponding human qualities (black - grief, white - innocence, coffee - tenderness, etc.) are included in the album of T.T[olstaia] (112).[19] Of flowers, the rose and the forget-me-not were particularly popular, and it made a difference whether the rose was red or white. All of this was a crucial part of the literary courtship ritual. A couple of rather typical examples of rose flirtation will suffice to convey their general tonality:

> Tell me, Rose, whose image you depict?
> Of course, that of the owner of the album you adorn.
> As tender as a spring rose
> May your beauty blossom
> May pure calm joy
> Live in your soul.

Chei obraz, Roza, ty, skazhi, izobrazhaesh'?
Konechno toi, al'bom chei ukrashaesh'.[20]
Kol' vesenniaia roza nezhna
Pust' tvoia krasa tsvetet
Radost' chista bezmiatezhna
Pust' v dushe tvoei zhivet.[21]

The classic example of extended flower coding is the entry in A. P. Kern's journal that begins: "I have thyme, I dream of mignonette, my mimosa needs much yellow nasturtium to hide the marigold and sweet-briar that torment me" (Petina 1985, 28).

Lack of color (white, the most ordinary of album page colors) could also become artistically significant, as in Derzhavin's 1808 (118–19) poem "Album," written for N. A. Koltovskaia's album. The extreme popularity of flowers and flower metaphors implies an idealization of beautiful, fragrant, and innocent women and a voyeuristic emphasis on external sex appeal. Not only the color of the page, but also the composition of entries on it and its place in the album were meaningful—the first and last pages had special significance, just like an epigraph in a novel or a rhyme word in a poem, and, as we know from *Eugene Onegin*, that fact also became a viable topic for album poets. The best space was presumably reserved for a prospective suitor, indicating that courtship actually influenced album layout. P. P. Iazykova's album contains a poem by a seemingly unsuccessful lover that starts out: "Were my hand / a happy one / I'd start your Album from the first page" (Petina 1985, 27).

A friendly competition for the owner's amorous attentions is often expressed in playful dialogue. In the album of Mariia Strugovshchikova there is an 1808 entry by Gavriil Gerakov: "Friendship is more precious than love, because love is nothing but a morning shadow, which gets smaller with every passing moment; friendship, on the other hand, is like an evening shadow: it grows to the very moment of death." Below it is a slightly ironic repartee dated 1809 and signed G. F. T [Count F. I. Tolstoi]:

> One must be very experienced—like you—to agree with you; but I can't do that yet and say:
>
>> What can be holier than love?
>> Only it gives us bliss,
>> In love our life is a hundred times dearer to us;
>> Love if you want to live!—everything repeats to us.
>>
>> Chto mozhet byt' liubvi sviatee?
>> Ona odna blazhenstvo nam darit,

V liubvi zhizn' nasha nam stokrat milee;
Liubi, kol' khochesh' zhit'!
    —vse nam tverdit. (Strugovshchikova 6)

Two pencil drawings initialed by the same Tolstoi depict two allegorical cupids, one of them accompanied by a quatrain penned by a third contributor, Aleksandr Vasil'evich Argamakov:

> Little god, don't wave your wings,
> Break up your new quiver:
> The power to strike the heart with arrows
> Has been given Strugovshchikova.

> Ne makhai, bozhok, krylami,
> Prelomi kolchan svoi novyi:
> Vlast' razit' serdtsa strelami
> Otdana Strugovshchikovoi. (Strugovshchikova 32)

Entire chain reactions were frequently set off in this way. Besides dialogizing the entries, such interchanges fostered wit and elegance in the form of compliments—perhaps the most prominent album genre.[22]

As participants in domestic literary circles that included professional writers and circulated albums as part of their "literary" behavior, women (and nonprofessional men) tended to make compliments in amazingly roundabout litotetic ways: by coquettishly stressing one's own lack of talent. The rhetorical strategy of self-effacement, lack of talent, modest literary skills, difficulties with words, and an inability to write were perceived as female virtues, readily adopted by men. It was also perfectly proper to flaunt one's lack of talent in order to imply superior talent. K. M., for instance, compares herself unfavorably to the album's owner:

> Next to writers thundering with knowledge
> Can I, with my insignificant gift,
> Write in the album of a highly enlightened Poet?
> Literature I love, but I don't have the knack for verse
>   One thing I can tell Izmailov:
>   I ask that he not forget the one
>   Who respects him so much,
>   Wishes him bliss and happiness;
> In whose hand these ten lines are writ,
> For the sake of remembrance, I pray that this page not be torn out.

> V riadu pisatelei gremiashchikh znan'em,
> Mogu l' s moim nichtozhnym darovan'em,

Pisat' v Al'bom Poeta polnyi prosveshchen'ia?
Slovesnost' ia liubliu, no dlia stikhov ne dostaet umen'ia.
   Odno Izmailovu mogu skazat':
   Proshu o toi ne zabyvat',
   Kotoraia ego tak mnogo uvazhaet
   Blazhenstva, schastiia, vsego emu zhelaet;
Chei zdes' rukoi, napisany sii desiat' strok,
V znak pamiati, moliu ne vyrvat' sei listok. (Izmailov 24 ob.)

This verse points to an important aspect of the open-ended nature of albums: the possibility of erasure. One frequently encounters entries blacked out, scribbled over, or "negated" in some other way. The most radical measure was to tear out pages that were too personal, embarrassing, or outdated, or perhaps were simply needed by an artistically inclined child. In that sense, the album was an unstable, changing genre, possibly reflecting another stereotypically "feminine" quality: inconstancy. Erasures created fragmented entries, akin to the fragment genre that became widespread during the Sentimentalist period. Indeed, the album itself can be considered a fragment, reflecting what some feminist critics have regarded as characteristic aspects of a feminist aesthetic: a de-emphasis on endings and an emphasis on anticipation as an end in itself. (Anticipation is a form of waiting which has been considered the central condition of a woman's life.)[23]

The posture of "feminine inferiority" could be turned coquettishly into an advantage—to evoke compassion or to praise the owner's tolerance, true love, or friendship. Furthermore, the message was not necessarily borne out by the medium—apologies for insufficient talent were often made with a great deal of finesse and were clearly recognizable as conscious artistic conceits.

One of the most common album conceits was flattery by various means of indirection that became as common as direct flattery by, say, comparisons to roses or lilies. Realizing that quotation is the sincerest form of flattery, M. K., apologizing for his own lack of talent, incorporates lines from Izmailov's own poetry into his entry in Izmailov's album (37). Mariia Dargomyzhskaia rejects the requisite compliments and proceeds to flatter by *not* flattering, concluding with an ostensibly selfish wish that her children have an Izmailov heart (Izmailov 57).

Flattery by means of *praeteritio*, whereby one states what one *could* do but won't (and of course thereby does), was richly varied. A frequent contributor to the album of Liza Bornovolokova produces a clever variation which lists and rejects numerous album clichés:

One could find a lot
That is praiseworthy in you.
One could cover a whole ream—
And all of it would be inadequate;
But I am truly afraid
That my truth
Will be considered flattery in society;
There a strange idea has spread
That everything in albums is a lie,
And not an ounce of truth;
Better not go against society,
Better not begin to teach;
And there is no need
To write praise of you.
Shall I call you beautiful?
One look from your eyes,
Your dear gaze, your clear image
Say it a hundred times better.
Shall I write that nature gave you
With equal largesse
Both spiritual beauty
And physical beauty?
But you'll express it more clearly
And prove it more strongly
Surely, with a couple of your own words
Than I in a thousand verses.
It is not for me, an ill-starred
Blockhead, to sing your praises;
Believe me, with the most splendid ode
You'll always be yourself.
No, not so daring is
My weak pen;
Better that I say meekly:
Have a look at her.

Mozhno mnogo otyskat',
Chto v tebe khvaly dostoino.
Mozhno stopu ispisat'—
I vse budet nedovol'no;
No boiusia pravo ia,
Chtoby istina moia
V svete lest'iu ne pochalasia;
V nem chudnaia zavelasia
Mysl', chto vse v al'bomakh lozh',

I net pravdy ni nagrosh';
Ne itti zhe protiv svetu,
Ne uchit' nam stat';
Da i nadobnosti netu
Pokhvalu tebe pisat'.
Nazovu l' tebia prekrasnoi?
Vzgliad edinyi tvoikh glaz,
Vzor tvoi milyi, obraz iasnyi
Skazhut luchshe to v sto raz.
Napishu li, chto prirodoi
S ravnoiu tebe shchedrotoi
I dushevnye krasy,
Kak telesnye dany?
No ty vyrazish' iasnee
I dokazhesh' to sil'nee
Verno paroi svoikh slov,
Chem ia tysiach'iu stikhov.
Ne s moeiu goremyshnoi
Pet' bashkoi khvalu tebe;
Ver', chto odoi samoi pyshnoi
Ty vsegda sama sebe.
Net, ne stol'ko derznovenno
Slaboe pero moe;
Luchshe zh mne skazat' smirenno:
Posmotrite na nee. (Bornovolokova 38–39)

This poem implies that verbal description is inferior to female body language. In feminized literature, the body is often mightier than the pen. Aleksandr Argamakov uses similar devices for indirection, listing what he *wants* to do, then stating that at Strugovshchikova's request he *is ready to do* anything; that he is now writing only to please her, and should not be judged too harshly for his lack of talent; what album verse *should* be like and what he therefore *might do* to flatter her. In the process he lists and rejects virtually all the typical clichés, the most typical genres, the most typical imagery and metaphors for album praise, and finally comes to his own variant of the surprise ending: He would do all this, he says, and finally exclaim, "This is You!" but he is just not good enough and cannot *describe* beauty, can only *marvel* at it (Strugovshchikova 49–50).

Argamakov and the unidentified poet in Bornovolokova's album represent a common awed voyeuristic attitude to the female body. Paradoxically, they express the thought that life is superior to art, while using art to do so. Such paradoxes are quite common in album verse and often turn parodic, particularly as regards entries by competitors.

Another way to avoid direct praise was to complain about the inade-
quacy of the medium:"What language would be rich enough / To express all that feelings say?" (Bornovolokova 6 ob.). Mikhail Kamenev-
Liubovskii tried to resolve this dilemma by invoking the skills of a
painter, sculptor, rhetorician, and poet—none of which, however, could
do Izmailova justice (Izmailova 55). Others appealed to feelings over
verbal or artistic skills, or heart over mind, or vowed to remember the
beloved in their hearts rather than on canvas or in marble (Lizogubova
24). More aggressive flatterers, instead of flattering the owner, advised
potential competitors how to write album verse, or discouraged them
from writing altogether, or bemoaned the poor readers, or in other ways
poked fun at their fellow contributors (Maikov 30). These sorts of entries emphasized the very goal of flirtation: to gain, if not the hand, then
at least the attention of a woman, and to beat out the competition. In a
competition among suitors, the album itself might become the ground
on which the duel of flirtation is fought:

> But, Chloe, never fear! I know that another
> Impatiently waits for the *lovely* Album
> (Which, I think, is rarely at home);
> The other's verse might be nicer than mine! ...

> No, Khloia, ne strashish'! ia znaiu, chto drugoi
> Zhdet s neterpeniem *liubeznogo* Al'boma
> (Kotoroi, dumaiu, byvaet redko doma);
> Drugogo mozhet byt' milee stikh, chem moi! ... (Shalikov 258)

An anonymous contributor describes the album writer's dilemma by
posing a rhetorical question and using the topos of silent admiration as a
solution (and in so doing, of course, breaks the "silence"):

> Praise—and they'll call you a flatterer;
> Don't praise—and you'll come across as a liar;
> What can one do? What can one say?
> Be surprised and be silent.

> Pokhvali—tak skazhut, l'stets;
> Ne khvali—tak vyidesh' lzhets;
> Chtozh tut delat', chto skazat'?
> Udivliat'sia i molchat'. (Bornovolokova 6)

A graphic equivalent to silence was simply to pour out "a flood of
black ink" instead of contributing some hackneyed album genre, while,

as it were, realizing the typical "ink pouring" metaphor for album writing:

> Little Herostrate
> "One writes a madrigal, epistle, triolet;
> Another a fable, acrostic, romance, or sonnet;
> One writes prose, another verse;
> Plays with wit, with words.
> What can I do? For I, alas, sing
> Neither in prose nor in verse!"
> "Let me pour ink on these sheets,"
> He said—ink flowed in streams;
> And this *little,* Temira, *Herostrate*
> Is pleased to pour his homage on your album in the future too.

> Malen'kii Gerostrat
> "Tot pishet madrigal, poslan'e, triolet;
> Tot basniu, akrostikh, romans ili sonet;
> Tot pishet prozoi, tot stikhami;
> Igraet razumom, slovami.
> Chtozh delat' mne? Ved' ia, k neshchast'iu ne poiu
> Ni v proze, ni v stikhakh!"
> "Dai na listy sii chernila ia prol'iu"—
> Skazal—potekli strui chernil rekoiu;
> I etot *malen'koi,* Temira, *Gerostrat,*
> Pochesti, i vpered zalit' al'bom tvoi rad![24]

If silence is a relatively passive form of erasure, this poem represents a more active form of erasure (or more properly, "as-if-erasure") and suggests the dangerous potential of not only destroying one's own entry, but enveloping entire albums in "rivers of ink"—a radical form of album writing against album writing, akin to tearing out pages. Both the "silent" addresses to women and the graphic erasure of literary tributes to them aimed at giving women themselves a voice. They can be seen as poetic analogues to the directly stated suggestions that women should begin to write, referred to above.

While many poets, as we have seen, engaged in expressions of verbal or graphic impotence, others contrived to remove the female addressee. Compliments were made by describing her dog or canary or even her clothing or furniture. Such metonymical accoutrements were regarded as luckier than the hopeful lover who was favored neither by the attention paid the pets, nor by the proximity of the other articles to the beloved. Some admirers indeed imagined themselves as pets, for instance "die treue: R. Moller," used as the signature to a watercolor of a faithful dog reposing on a pillow in Aleksandra Khandvig's album (45). Dogs were given human language to tell the world about the virtues of their mistresses in the popular inscriptions on dog collars. Fidèle, for instance, was ready to bite anyone who did not love its mistress, but since she was so lovable, its teeth had been idle (T. T[olstaia] 39). The metonymic displacement of desire in these kinds of entries echoes the elegies that gained in popularity around the turn of the century. The reference to the *absent* object of love is, however, a way of reinscribing love, reminiscent of such "discourses of desire" as Ovid's *Heroides*.[25]

Animals in albums tended to be gender-specific. The puny pooches in women's laps and their caged canaries provided a good illustration of the closed, sheltered (one might even say caged) lives of women. Men's albums, on the contrary, tended to relate their owners to hunting dogs or favorite riding horses and open spaces.

Far removed from the solemn odic form of flattery prevalent earlier in the eighteenth century, miniature album trifles are possibly the best indication of the "feminization" and eroticization of literature created by flirtatious authors in women's albums. As a product of a "feminine" domestic literary environment, albums urged male writers to appropriate a "feminine" voice while also providing women an appropriate forum for self-expression. They capitalized on "feminine" conversational skills, creating amazing variations within strict formal constraints and entire dialogical chains. They relentlessly flattered ideal women while also prescribing the behavior of the innocent and chaste woman-child. It is perhaps a sad comment on the images of women and the "feminization" they inspired that these album poets (male and female) engaged in so many forms of conceits to efface themselves, to flaunt their weaknesses, to pretend to be incompetent fools, constantly making apologies for their writing or coquettishly congratulating themselves.

With time the literary journals would publish models of album verse appropriate to various situations and meant to be copied by those who did not have the skill to create their own entries. Some authors actually chose to include separate sections of album verse, trivial as it was, in their collected works. Such forms of literary sanction signaled that by then albums had become either too formulaic to be viable as an art form or too professional to retain their original attraction as spontaneous amateur art. This happened in Russia in the 1840s, when the peak of album writing and the reign of the "feminine" domestic arts had come to an end.

Notes

1. This study was supported by the Wallace Foundation, Macalester College, and IREX. I am grateful to the staff at IRLI (Institute of Russian Literature of the Academy of Sciences of the USSR [Pushkin House] in Leningrad), GPB (M. E. Saltykov-Shchedrin State Public Library in Leningrad), and TsGALI (Central State Archive of Literature and Art of the USSR in Moscow) for accommodating my research. I refer to archives by their names at this time of my research, and use the standard Russian-language locational abbreviations as transliterated. Album entries are identified according to the album owner and archival location. I have modernized my texts according to standard practice, and, unless otherwise noted, the emphases are original. All translations are mine.

2. The topic of feminization of literature is addressed in Tynianov 21, 42–47; Vinogradov; Levin; Uspenskii 57–65; Lotman and Uspenskii; Vowles; Hammarberg 1994 and 1991, 95–97.

3. On early women's journals see [Koliupanov]; Shchepkina; on dandies, see Pokrovskii.

4. See Hammarberg 1994.

5. On anthology verse in Russia, see Kibal'nik 1990 and 1993.

6. Makarov's review (176) assesses the *slaveno-rossiiskii* style as inadequate for "the luxurious boudoirs of Aspasia." His editorial (6–7) emphasizes the role of women in "moving the throne of Philosophy into the boudoir." His translation, "Fashionable Furniture" (Modnaia mebel) (177), shows how a married woman of *bon ton* receives "an entire gathering of men, reclining on her bed." The boudoir is also the setting for the salon parody in Chulkov's *The Comely Cook* (Prigozhaia povarikha) (70).

7. There were also men's albums which tended to reflect more typically "male" preoccupations, such as drinking or army life. On the differences between men's and women's albums, see Petina 1988, 11; Petina 1985, 33; Vatsuro 41; Kornilova 80–93.

8. A version was subsequently published in *The Loyalist* (Blagonamerennyi) 11 (1820): 373–78.

9. Not all women took flattery lightly. A. P. Bunina in her album (57–59) responds to A. S. Shishkov in an untypical feminist spirit: "Frivolous women like madrigals. A woman who is used to thinking wishes only to be treated with respect. Don't praise her but don't sacrifice your pride either; she will love you more then than when you take it in your head to lavish inappropriate praise on her or when you belittle her with inappropriate patronizing."

10. "Scholasticism" and "pedantry' are easily recognizable as shorthand for bad "male" literary qualities contrasted to "female" virtues.

11. See Alekseev on the evolution of albums from the 1770s to the 1840s; Vatsuro 61–78; Petina 1970; Kornilova describes their appearance with well-chosen reproductions of album art.

12. [Liza] 42–43. The poem is dated 1812 and signed by D. A. Ostaf'ev, identified by Vatsuro (7–8) as part of a literary circle in Nizhnii Novgorod consisting of local landowners and exiled Muscovites (Karamzin, Neledinskii-Meletskii, Murav'ev-Apostol', and others). This album is especially rich in fancy floral entries.

13. See Iakovlev (Izmailova 6–11 ob.); Uspenskii 30–34, 55–67; Lotman 227–37. On Russia's first women writers, see Zirin; Vowles emphasizes women's own perceptions of language and literature and their responses to feminization.

14. The poem appears unsigned in T. T[olstaia] 20 and also in Kurakina 59, where the author is identified as Karamzin, and in several other albums—it was first published in *My Trifles* (Moi Bezdelki) in 1797. See Karamzin 1966, 234.

15. Izmailov 3–3 ob. A corner of the page is torn, and we may never know the full poem nor its author. Later in the album (79) there is a poem in a different hand labeled "Omonim," signed Sof'ia P. This genre (a homonym fits in the category of riddles) gained prominence in Izmailov's *The Loyalist* (Blagonamerennyi).

16. Kornilova is rich in examples of visual-verbal games. It was common to jot down games and puzzles in special booklets. For one such booklet with 20 riddles together with their answers, see GPB, R.O., f. 1000, op. 4, ed. khr. 32.

17. Makarov adds *obozhat'* (primary meaning: "to worship") and *zhelat'* (primary meaning: "to desire, wish") to the same semantic field; see *Moscow Mercury* (Moskovskii Merkurii) 1, no. 1 (1803): 7.

18. The album of Liza Bornovolokova (44 ob.), for instance, contains a message written in rectangles with small protrusions, deciphered in pencil.

19. Petina 1985, 29 cites popular flower alphabets, printed dictionaries, and code books.

20. Petina 1985, 29; the same verse also appears in the album of an unknown person, IRLI, R. I, op. 42, #4, cited in Kornilova 75.

21. Signed M S; similar to other entries in the same hand signed "ta cousine," or Mariia Shul'gina, in Bakunina 47 ob.

22. Strugovshchikova's album has numerous entries, extended over several years, taking sides in the same dialogue. Vatsuro 6–9 identifies the participants as part of a literary-artistic circle which included S. N. Marin and V. L. Pushkin.

23. According to Modleski, these qualities are typical of a contemporary women's genre, soap operas. Albums anticipated the "television aesthetic" of intimacy and continuity, they were composed with "an indefinitely expandable middle," and they reflected the patterns of female sexuality, being "open-ended, slow paced, multi-climaxed," in Marcia Kinder's sense. They did not follow a specific sequence or progression and were thereby akin to women's work of reproduction and maintenance in their repetitive and routine continuity. See Modleski, especially 87, 88, 98. I am grateful to Beth Holmgren for alerting me to the soap opera connection.

24. T[Tolstaia] 179, signed 25. and written in the same hand as those above.

25. See Kauffman 29–61. On the evolution of the elegy in Russia, see
Gukovskii.

Works Cited

Alekseev. M. P. 1960. "Iz istorii russkikh rukopisnykh sobranii." In *Neizdannye
pis'ma inostrannykh pisatelei XVIII–XIX vekov iz leningradskikh rukopisnykh
sobranii,* 7–122. Moscow-Leningrad: Izd. AN SSSR.

Bakunina,Varvara Aleksandrovna (b. Murav'eva). *Al'bom.* IRLI, f. 16, op. 6, #55.

Barataev, Mikhail Petrovich. *Al'bom.* TsGALI, f. 1336, op. I, ed. khr. #3.

Baskakova,Tat'iana Stepanovna. *Al'bom.* TsGALI, f. 1336, op. I, ed. khr. #7.

Bornovolokova, Liza. *Al'bom.* IRLI, R. I. op. 42, #74.

Bunina, A. P. *Al'bom.* IRLI, f. 88, #16012.

Chulkov, M. D. 1971. *Prigozhaia povarikha, ili pokhozhdenie razvratnoi zhenshchiny.*
In *Russkaia proza XVIII veka,* ed. G. Makogonenko, 39–80. Moscow:
Izdatel'stvo Khudozhestvennaia literatura.

Dargomyzhskaia, Liudmila Sergeevna. *Al'bom.* IRLI, R. l, op. 42, #4.

Dargomyzhskii, S. N. *Al'bom. Vsiakina.* IRLI, f. 296, #4408.

Derzhavin, G. R. 1986. *Anakreonticheskie pesni.* Edited by G. P. Makogonenko,
G. N. Ionin, and E. N. Petrova. Moscow: Nauka.

Gasvitskaia,Aleksandra Nikolaevna (b. Pushchina). *Al'bom.* IRLI, R. I, op. 42, #5.

Gukovskii, G. A. 1927. "Elegiia v XVIII veke." In his *Russkaia poeziia XVIII
veka.* (Voprosy Poetiki 10), 48–102. Leningrad: Academia.

Hammarberg, Gitta. 1991. *From the Idyll to the Novel: Karamzin's Sentimentalist
Prose.* Cambridge: Cambridge UP.

————.1994. "The Feminine Chronotope and Sentimentalist Canon
Formation." In *Literature, Lives and Legality in Catherine's Russia,* ed. G. S.
Smith, 103–20. Nottingham: Astra P.

Izmailov,Aleksandr Efimovich. *Al'bom.* TsGALI, f. 1336, op. I, ed. khr. #23.

Izmailova, Ekaterina Ivanovna. *Al'bom.* IRLI, otd. post. #4929.

Karamzin, N. M. 1966. *Polnoe sobranie stikhotvorenii.* Edited by Iu. M. Lotman.
Moscow: Sovetskii pisatel'.

Kauffman, Linda S. 1986. *Discourses of Desire: Gender, Genre, and Epistolary
Fictions.* Ithaca: Cornell UP.

Khandvig,Aleksandra. *Al'bom.* TsGALI, f.1336, op.I, ed. khr. #63.

Kibal'nik, S. A. 1990. *Russkaia antologicheskaia poeziia pervoi treti XIX veka.*
Leningrad: Nauka.

————. 1993. *Venok russkim kamenam. Antologicheskie stikhotvoreniia russkikh poetov.* St. Petersburg: Nauka.

[Koliupanov, N. P.]. 1889. *Biografiia Aleksandra Ivanovicha Kosheleva.* Vol. 1:
Molodye gody Aleksandra Ivanovicha. Book 1, ed. O. F. Kosheleva. Moscow:
Tipolitografiia I. N. Kushnereva.

Kornilova, A. V. 1990. *Mir al'bomnogo risunka. Russkaia al'bomnaia grafika kontsa
XVIII–pervoi poloviny XIX veka.* Leningrad: Iskusstvo.

Kurakina, Natal'ia Petrovna. *Al'bom.* TsGALI, f. 1336, op. I, ed. khr. #31.

Levin, V. O. 1964. *Ocherk stilistiki russkogo literaturnogo iazyka kontsa XVIII–Nachala XIX v. (Leksika)*. Moscow: Nauka.

[Liza]. *Al'bom*. IRLI, R. I, op. 42, #19.

Lizogubova, Evdokiia. *Al'bom*. IRLI, R. I, op. 42, #36.

Lotman, Iu. M. 1987. *Sotvorenie Karamzina*. Moscow: Kniga.

Lotman, Iu. M., and B. A. Uspenskii. 1975. "Spory o iazyke v nachale XIX veka kak fakt russkoi kul'tury." *Uchenye zapiski tartuskogo universiteta* 358: 168–323.

Maikov, Pavel Mikhailovich. *Al'bom*. TsGALI, f. 1336, op. I, ed. khr. #86.

[Makarov, Petr]. 1803a. "Nekotoryia mysli Izdatelei Merkuriia." *Moskovskii Merkurii* 1, no. 1: 4–18.

———. 1803b. Review of Shishkov, A. S., "Razsuzhdenie o starom i novom sloge Rossiiskago iazyka." *Moskovskii Merkurii* 4, no. 12: 155–98.

[Makarov, Petr, trans.]. 1803. "Modnaia mebel'." *Moskovskii Merkurii* 3, no. 3: 175–78.

Modleski, Tania. 1982. *Loving with a Vengeance: Mass-Produced Fantasies for Women*. Hamden, Conn.: Archon Books.

Pekelis, M. 1966. *Aleksandr Sergeevich Dargomyzhskii i ego okruzhenie*. Vol 1: *1813–1845*. Moscow: Izd. Muzyka.

Petina, L. 1970. "Al'bom pushkinskoi epokhi kak vid literaturnogo teksta." In *Materialy XXV nauchnoi studencheskoi konferentsii. Literaturovedenie. Lingvistika*, 36–38. Tartu: Tartuskii gos. universitet.

Petina, L. I. 1985. "Strukturnye osobennosti al'boma pushkinskoi epokhi." In *Problemy tipologii russkoi literatury. Trudy po russkoi i slavianskoi filologii. Literaturovedenie. Uchenye zapiski tartuskogo gosudarstvennogo universiteta*, 21–36. Tartu: Tartuskii gos. universitet.

———. 1988. "Khudozhestvennaia priroda literaturnogo al'boma pervoi poloviny XIX veka." Avtoreferat dissertatsii na soiskanie uchenoi stepeni kandidata filologicheskikh nauk. Tartu: Tartuskii gosudarstvennyi universitet.

Pokrovskii, V. 1903a. *Shchegoli v satiricheskoi literature XVIII veka*. Moscow: Universitetskaia tipografiia.

———. 1903b. *Shchegolikhi v satiricheskoi literature XVIII veka*. Moscow: Universitetskaia tipografiia.

Shchepkina, E. N. 1910. "Zhenskaia lichnost' v starykh zhurnalakh kontsa XVIII-go i nachala XIX-go vv." *Zapiski Neofilologicheskogo Obshchestva pri Imperatorskom S.-Peterburgskom Universitete* 4: 173–75.

Shalikov, P. I. 1803. *Puteshestvie v Malorossiiu*. Moscow: U Liubii, Gariia i Popova.

Shalikov, Petr. 1819. *Sochineniia Kniazia Shalikova*. Part II: *Stikhi*. Moscow: V Universitetskoi tipografii.

Strogovshchikova, Mariia Aleksandrovna. *Al'bom*. IRLI, R. I, op. 42, #91.

T[olstaia], T. *Al'bom*. TsGALI, f. 1336, op. I, ed. khr. #56.

Tolstaia, Temira. *Al'bom*. TsGALI, f. 1336, op. I, ed. khr. #57.

Tolstaia, Varvara. *Al'bom*. TsGALI, f. 1336, op. I, ed. khr. #55.

Tynianov, Iu. 1929. "Literaturnyi fakt." In *Arkhaisty i novatory*, 5–29. Leningrad; rpt., Munich: Wilhelm Fink Verlag, 1967.

————. "O literaturnoi evoliutsii." In *Arkhaisty i novatory*, 30–47. Leningrad, 1929; rpt., Munich: Wilhelm Fink Verlag, 1967.

Unknown. *Al'bom*. TsGALI, f. 1336, op. I, ed. khr. #84.

Unknown. *Sbornik*. [Collection of riddles] GPB, R.O., f. 1000, op. 4, ed. khr. 32.

Uspenskii, B. A. 1985. *Iz istorii russkogo literaturnogo iazyka XVIII–nachala XIX veka*. Moscow: Izdatel'stvo Moskovskogo universiteta.

Vatsuro, V. E. 1979a. "Iz al'bomnoi liriki i literaturnoi polemiki 1790–1830kh godov." In *Ezhegodnik Rukopisnogo otdela Pushkinskogo Doma na 1977 god*, 61–78. Leningrad: Nauka.

————. 1979b. "Literaturnye al'bomy v sobranii Pushkinskogo Doma (1750–1840e gody)." In *Ezhegodnik Rukopisnogo otdela Pushkinskogo Doma na 1977 god*, 3–56. Leningrad: Nauka.

Vinogradov, V. V. 1935. "Russko-frantsuzskii iazyk dvorianskogo salona i bor'ba Pushkina s literaturnymi normami 'iazyka svetskoi damy.'" In *Iazyk Pushkina*, 195–236. Moscow-Leningrad: Academia.

Vowles, Judith. 1994. "The 'Feminization' of Russian Literature: Woman, Language, and Literature in Eighteenth-Century Russia." In *Women Writers in Russian Literature*, ed. Toby W. Clyman and Diana Greene, 35–60. Westport, Conn.: Greenwood P.

Zirin, M. 1990. "Russian Women Writers: An Overview. Finding Their Voice: From Catherine the Great to 1890." Paper delivered at the IV World Congress for Soviet and East European Studies in Harrogate, England, July 21–26.

13

GENDERING THE ICON:

MARKETING WOMEN WRITERS IN

FIN-DE-SIÈCLE RUSSIA

Beth Holmgren

Browsing the Russian Market

FOR SOME TIME NOW, scholars of Western cultures have gone window-shopping with a rather jaundiced eye, taking stock of the merchandise in the first emporia and department stores of the mid-nineteenth century, sharply scrutinizing the busy pages of illustrated magazines and catalogues, dissecting the textual display of goods assembled by authors ranging from Dickens to Dreiser to Joyce.[1] Themselves very often the products of late capitalist society, these scholars have been eager to map the minefield of the market, with its triggers of visual seduction, traps for impulse or serial buying and luxury spending, and all-entangling exploitation of the consumer (especially the female consumer).[2] Now that we in Russian studies are doing a little window-shopping of our own, we might consider ourselves forewarned about the terrain. In fact, our approach to Russian consumer culture is likely to be more apprehensive, given that culture's relatively late development, short duration, and vociferous rejection by so many Russian highbrow writers and critics. From the Russian side, we have been scolded from the market for most of modern Russian history, first by an intelligentsia-dominated culture missing a middle class, then by a totalitarian cultural police. Therefore, as we go browsing through the fin-de-siècle period in Russian history, when consumer culture seemed a fast-growing transplant, we are predisposed several times over to judge and separate: to cherish, on the one hand, a glorious Silver Age of exquisite poetry, painting, and theater, and to denigrate, on the other, a nether culture of serial fiction and cheesecake thrills.

But in my own perusal of the fin-de-siècle Russian press (the most convenient window to shop in this period), I have found that certain "familiar" patterns of marketing were mutating in strange and intriguing ways—especially with regard to the relations between the intellectual and the material and, by conventional extension, the relations between male and female figures. Despite telltale signs of seduction and commodification (mainly the purveying of female flesh), the cultural dividing lines of the Russian market were not at all clear. I cite in example a sequence of ads in the March 1899 issue of *Vol'f Bookstore News* (Izvestiia Knizhnykh Magazinov Tovarishchestva M. O. Vol'f), a lavish magazine-*cum*-catalogue issued by one of the largest publishers of the day. The first ad proffers a copy of S. A. Kiprenskii's famous portrait of the famous poet Aleksandr Pushkin, a portrait "acknowledged to convey the best likeness" of its subject and issued to commemorate the hundredth anniversary of his birth (fig. 13.1). The second ad, which appears on the following page (and on the coveted back cover of the issue), presents a "sumptuous edition" of illustrations depicting "the women of Russian writers" and recommended as a "marvelous adornment for any drawing room"; the pictured samples display a rather Orientalized version of Tat'iana from Pushkin's *Eugene Onegin* and a radiantly neoclassical Natasha from Tolstoi's *War and Peace*[3] (fig. 13.2). In effect, the two ads draw an equation between Pushkin's "authentic" image and the fictional illustrations of a "gallery of female types." The juxtaposition of the two suggests a blurring of that dichotomy between highbrow emblems and material goods, male icon and female cheesecake that we might presume pervaded Russian culture at this time.

Other examples point to an even more radical conflation: Not only lithographs of "female types," but "authentic" portraits of women writers begin to alternate with portraits of such male classics as Pushkin and Tolstoi in the advertising and feature sections of these magazines and newspapers. The icon of the serious Russian writer extant through much of the nineteenth century—always male and only rarely and reverently painted or photographed—was now taking on ever more material, commodified, and even differently gendered form. In consequence, the recurrence of women's images in the press—as predictable commodities or, perhaps, as differently gendered icons—seemed to reflect more than that irritatingly familiar pattern of women's objectification and exploitation. My window-shopping expeditions suggest that these images signi-

FIG 13.1 Advertisement of Pushkin's portrait.

fied important changes in the very definition and function of Russian literature and, more specifically, facilitated and showcased the splashy entrance of women into the literary sphere as new writers, readers, and role models.

Most obviously, this fleshing and gendering of the icon heralded the extraordinary expansion of Russian literature and its readership at the turn of the century, an expansion that meant a great diversification of writers and readers, but was often packaged as a harmonious whole. Over the past decade, such cultural historians as Jeffrey Brooks, Louise McReynolds, and Laura Engelstein have traced the rise of popular fiction and the mass-circulation press in late-nineteenth-century Russia and the attendant rifts obtaining between highbrow and middlebrow producers (to say nothing of the chasm between highbrow and lowbrow). Yet what I find particularly interesting about the Russian mass-circulation press in this period is its strongly evidenced will to level the playing field and integrate the players. Rather than abiding by any pre-existing caste division between an elite intelligentsia and the new readers they sought to attract, the publishers, editors, and writers for the press operated on the premise of a single blended highbrow/middlebrow

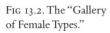

Fig 13.2. The "Gallery of Female Types."

standard.[4] With this premise firmly in place, they effectively revised their relations with a still very powerful highbrow establishment, ignoring its scornful dissociation with a smiling insistence on uniform quality and goals. Although the gap between high and middle was much wider in Russia than in Western cultures, these producers bridged it with the same sturdy strategy of co-option. In a process somewhat like the middlebrow appropriation of the "genteel aesthetic" in American literary history, they invoked the models and traditions of intelligentsia writers to prove the worth of whatever they were trying to pitch.[5] They, too, claimed their product's high moral purpose and value as social critique. And they very shrewdly exercised the familiar intelligentsia role of educator to the masses by cultivating and at the same time cashing in on their new readers' tastes and habits.

Their style of cultivation varied widely. In some cases, they staked out a predictable middle ground with a "family magazine" such as *Niva*, a periodical that reliably reprinted Russian classics and "combined aspects of the informative, instructive, and entertaining elements of other media into a magazine format oriented toward developing a middle-class family audience" (Brooks 113; McReynolds 114). Significantly, *Niva* also "educated" its readers with pictures, inserting full-page illustrations (complete with annotations) of "great works of art" along with decorative kitsch (e.g., depictions of oppressed barge haulers and cute baby animals). Admittedly less "refined" periodicals such as the thin magazine *Ogonek* and the daily *Peterburgskaia gazeta* were less intent on education, but nonetheless anticipated readers' curiosity about the great and the celebrated by including tributes to classic Russian writers and printing informal interviews with artists and public leaders (Brooks 115–16; McReynolds 245–46).[6] More specialized publications such as *Vol'f Bookstore News* conducted aggressive lessons in cultural refinement with articles that counseled readers on whom and how to read and lectured them (with pertinent visual aids) on the acquisition of private libraries, the proper treatment of books, even the creation and maintenance of card catalogues. An article entitled "When and Where to Read Our Poets," for example, specifically prescribes V. Zhukovskii for the early days of courtship, the poetry of T. Shcherbina or M. Lokhvitskaia for the honeymoon, A. Pushkin's "harmonious verses" when one longs for "practical work," and M. Lermontov "in moments of melancholy or helpless anger."[7]

But no matter how deeply they dipped into the intelligentsia's time-honored bag of prestige, all of these publications seemed acutely aware of the exigencies of the new literary market and, above all, the determining market value of the author. The "classic" grew into a very elastic category; the press shied away from exclusive hierarchies of "worthy writers" and instead purveyed an infinitely expandable canon that blended all sorts—foreign and national, highbrow and middlebrow, male and female authors. Just as they guaranteed that any reader (of whatever class background or literary experience) could become a self-made *intelligent* by absorbing their information, so they implied that any writer on their pages was well worth the reader's intellectual and financial investment. Critics for the press self-importantly assumed the intelligentsia role of gatekeeper. When one commentator warned that "we must guard against the vulgar and banal entering our libraries," it was clear that he, rather than any highbrow pundit, would be the one to decide what qualified for inclusion (and very likely his decision would depend on his publisher's book lists).[8]

As the interchangeable visages of Pushkin and Russian "female types" have already demonstrated, this integration was often managed by juxtaposing and equating elements—whether these were visual or verbal. *Vol'f Bookstore News* yields perhaps the best examples of this strategy because it focuses so pointedly on the literary market. The Vol'f publishers developed a special "Literary News" feature that emulated the news miscellanies of other publications and read something like hybrid gossip-reportage. These columns eventually overwhelmed the catalogue, at first filling the back pages and then wrapping around to the inside front cover; they reported on the literary scene without discriminating between purported "classics" and bestsellers. Moreover, they treated "classic" and bestselling author alike as celebrity items, presuming that readers would want to know everything about their works and lives. A typical sequence of entries required the reader to process and connect an incredible variety of "news," ranging in this example from the latest update on Tolstoi's health to official reports on the status of women writers:

> *L. N. Tolstoi went horseback riding recently in Iasnaia Poliana and was thrown to the ground. Fortunately, the count's coachman was driving by and carried him home. The doctor called to the scene confirmed that he had dislocated his left shoulder. The shoulder had to be set. After several days, despite the pain in his shoulder and arm, Tolstoi went out for a walk and covered about five versts on foot. L. N. is as hale and hearty as before, walks a great deal, and continues to work and study.
> *Petersburg women writers have won a new victory: Participants in the so-called "Fiedler" literary luncheons decided to admit women as full-fledged members on the same basis as male writers, i.e., by vote. This right is extended, by the way, to all "women of talent," even if they are not writers. Until now "ladies" were admitted as guests to these dinners only three times a year. (*Izvestiia*, January 1908)

Advertising format followed much the same pattern, and its agenda informed the entire critical apparatus for reporting and reviewing new publications. "Literary News" columns regularly telegraphed a kind of laundry list of new works; classics, avant-garde writers, and bestsellers all received equal billing for their products. In yet another "interim" form of advertisement (one that uncannily anticipates Western advertising methods today), announcements of new publications were accompanied by favorable review blurbs, most of which assured the reader-buyer of the given work's aesthetic, ethical, or educational merits. Hence a 1910 announcement of the second edition of Mariia Bashkirtseva's *Diary* is buttressed by two reviews (from *Novaia Rus* and *Moskovskie Vedomosti*) that proclaim the work's timelessness and general resonance (this perhaps to safeguard against charges of the *Diary's* "too fashionable" topicality).

The Woman in the Window

The expansion of Russian literature, the diffusion of critical authority, the deft jumbling of the canon—all of these trends proved extremely advantageous to women writers (and especially popular women writers), as the cited examples illustrate. With much ado and little defensiveness, the press admitted women into the ranks of "worthy" Russian writers and carefully hiked their "prestige" quotient by association and critical rubber stamp. More surprising, however, is the fact that once women writers were integrated into this august company, their representation powerfully enhanced a new style of representing the company as a whole. Their variant of the icon epitomized a general tendency toward embodying, sexing, materializing, and even theatricalizing the person of the writer.

This tendency was fueled by contextual developments in the arts and sciences and imprinted by the requirements of the press. The Silver Age renaissance in the visual and performance arts, manifest in movements such as the "World of Art" or enterprises such as the Moscow Art Theater, pressed for the aesthetic transformation of the individual and encouraged a conflation of aesthetic and personal style.[9] The mass-circulation press was quick to concretize and capitalize on this aestheticizing imperative by proffering consumers reprints of artwork, illustrated collections of famous people and general "types" (preferably well-dressed or tantalizingly half-dressed), and early versions of coffee-table books on such lifestyle phenomena as costume balls, aristocratic homes, and the rich "material culture" of other peoples. In much the same fashion, the press commodified current scientific and popular interests in human physiology and sexuality, marketing books and models that copiously diagrammed the human anatomy in part and in whole, in sickness and in health.[10] As a result, the body was advertised extensively as artistic object (or at least apt material for artistic makeover) and scientific subject.

For both purposes the press used female figures more often in illustration, relying on certain traditional conceptions of woman as the preferred incarnation of human beauty and the sex more identified with the body.[11] Yet, owing to the combined influences of art, science, and the market, the depiction of these figures—the display and scrutiny of their person, dress, and environs—came to be generalized and applied to virtually all the famous persons of the day, including, of course, the person of the writer. Indeed, "portraits of the artist" had become hot commodities: As the Pushkin commemorative offer indicates, the mass-circulation press printed and peddled scores of their painted and photographed images. If publishers were lucky enough to be featuring a contemporary writer, they could even stage a photographed portrait for special visual and dramatic effect. Focus articles, in turn, were studded with illustrations that posed a writer "at work" (reading, writing, or looking pensive) and toured the grounds of his or her desktop, study, library, house, and local landscape. They also reverently displayed paraphernalia bearing the author's physical imprint—perhaps an inscription, a page of an original manuscript, writing utensils, or something as curiously macabre and physiologically significant as a cast of the writer's hand. And even as the press culled juicy particulars about the writer's life-art connections and material chic, it also dared to scrutinize its subject as scientific specimen. It was in this period, after all, that the press dutifully reported the weight of I. Turgenev's brain (as tangible proof of his genius) and argued that types of literary talent could be detected in the size, shape, and expression of a writer's eyes.[12]

Writers of both sexes were subject to this extensive and invasive coverage, but quite often women writers were shown in especially telling detail. When paraded in a series with male authors, they usually garnered attention as the lone woman; their portaits also seemed more carefully and distinctively composed. For example, a June 1907 photo insert displaying Andrei Belyi, Ivan Bunin, and Zinaida Gippius (a trio dubbed "The Poets of Our Days") clearly highlights Gippius through placement and composition (fig. 13.3). Belyi and Bunin are posed side by side in conventional bust shots; although Belyi looks directly at the viewer, deviating somewhat from Bunin's averted, other-directed gaze (one common in nineteenth-century photo portraits), both men remain stiffly formal and wear sober expressions. Gippius, however, is accorded a solo position below and between the two men and is outfitted with special costume, set, and role. The wide sleeves, drapery folds, and lacy collar of her dress attract the eye; her pose of chin on hands and her three-quarter profile, turned away from the viewer, suggest a girlish dreaminess and vulnerability; she leans her elbows thoughtfully on a betasseled, plushly upholstered chair, playing the scene of a woman espied musing in her parlor (not at her desk). Her portrait of the woman writer invites

FIG 13.3. The photo triangle of Belyi, Bunin, and Gippius.

the viewer to enter her domestic setting and puzzle over her mood, to fathom her more detailed (if rather conventional) character and plot.

Even when women writers were depicted in isolation, their portraits evinced a special knack for dramatic style and aesthetic/emotional engagement. A much-reproduced photo of the bestselling author Anastasiia Verbitskaia revels in a fashionably overblown, somewhat theatricalized display of "the new woman" (fig. 13.4). The subject is literally stacked with emblems of her lavish lifestyle and sexual appeal—the outsized and beflowered hat (its large bloom at once softening and underscoring her determined face); the sensuous upsweep of hair; the accent pieces of beaded jewelry and lace collar; the "fruitful" imagery of flower and her collar's grape-like clusters; the very contrast of textures and materials (lace, jewels, fabrics, hair, skin). At the same time her laden image assumes a fiercely independent pose, her face set in almost stern profile away

FIG 13.4. Anastasiia Verbitskaia as the "new woman."

from the beholder (she definitely does *not* aim to please) and toward some loftier goal implied by the half-empty background of the portrait. Once again, the viewer is required to read the woman writer's portrait as character study, to enter the narrative her image projects—in this case, perhaps, that of a young woman equally bent on material indulgence and personal independence.[13]

Although group portraits by association (artists, writers, inventors, etc.) had acquired a certain cachet in the nineteenth century, it is significant that Russian women writers almost always appeared as solo or anomalous subjects, perhaps in part because they were not yet recognized as a proven collective.[14] Yet, as an overview of contemporary women writers implies, it may be that the increasing differentiation of women's portraiture also discouraged a "group shot." This survey article, published in 1901, exhibits a gallery of seven single portraits that range widely in pose and expression.[15] A photo of an ingenuous Tat'iana Shchepkina-Kupernik begins the series: Face forward and up-tilted, eyes focused on a dreamy middle distance, clad in a soft cloud-like blouse, she rests her arms on a chair back and conveys a younger, more naive, and more accessible version of Gippius's reverie (fig. 13.5). Two other locket-like portraits of the writers Anastasiia Krandievskaia and Mariia Krestovskaia, while less detailed, echo some of Shchepkina-Kipernik's demure dreaminess (figs. 13.6 and 13.7). Yet photos of Gippius, Verbitskaia, and Ol'ga Shapir project quite different scenarios. In contrast to her 1907 portrait, Gippius appears here in mannish costume, with haughty expression and hand in pocket, adopting the androgynous image that became her trademark; Verbitskaia, hatless and with her hair down, almost turns her back on the viewer in a gesture of extreme self-absorption; Shapir adopts the pose of supercilious thinker, affectedly propping chin on hand and elbow on end table, evidently too engrossed in important thoughts to bother with her audience (figs. 13.8–13.10). The most jarring portrait in this gallery, however, is the final photo of Valentina Dmitrieva in pince-nez and schoolmistress uniform (fig. 13.11). Her image recalls the masculinized, stern-expressioned visages of the mid-nineteenth century—a style intellectual and radical women once had to emulate to be viewed seriously—and it falls desperately flat in the engaging company of these girlish dreamers and haughty *artistes*. In the fin-de-siècle market, the writer's attractive (if not provocative) image effectively displaced proofs of her "seriousness."

In itemizing these new visual advantages for women writers, I have implied their role as beneficiaries of a monolithic, omnisciently manipulative press, but that is largely because the details of their agency have been lost. As is often the case with the study of consumer culture (particularly noncontemporary consumer culture), we lack the primary data that would tell us how decisions were made and roles apportioned.[16] It seems probable, however, that Russian women writers did participate in their own portrait-making, choosing the clothes and accessories they were to wear for their photo sessions and working together with the photographer to create a scenario correspondent to their authorial self-conception and (perhaps) the major themes of their works. In this sense, they subscribed to a general tendency in nineteenth-century portraiture

Fig 13.5. Tat'iana
Shchepkina-Kupernik
(1901 article).

to convey identity by a subject's "externals," by what s/he had achieved
or produced (Brilliant 99).[17]

Aspiring to the public arena, these women would also be aware of
how famous female contemporaries had managed the business of image-
making. By the 1890s such internationally renowned actresses and female performers as Sarah Bernhardt and Lillie Langtry had blazed trails
for cultivating female celebrity, improvising the role of living fashion
plate and female bon vivant through publicity photos and product en-
dorsements:

> Sarah Bernhardt cultivated a reputation as an eccentric voluptuary; Lillie
> Langtry portrayed herself as both a lady and an independent woman.
> Both Bernhardt and Langtry were known to favor exercise and reformed
> dress for women. Their immense salaries, their glamorous lives, the adula-
> tion of dramatic critics, and the careful publicity planted by press agents
> brought these actresses enormous public attention. (Banner 180)[18]

Russian entertainers obligingly followed suit and "consented" to
photo spreads of their extravagant dress and lifestyle; they, too, spawned a
subsidiary market of postcard portraits for their fans.[19] In this new era of
social mobility and manufactured celebrity, women writers could ex-

FIG 13.6. Anastasiia
Krandievskaia (1901 article).

periment with some of the techniques of theatrical promotion without
fearing for their reputation or (more important) sales figures.[20] It is
worth noting that authors such as Verbitskaia and Lidiia Charskaia (a
popular writer of children's fiction) enjoyed close connections with
Russian theater culture (Verbitskaia's grandmother was an actress, and
Charskaia herself played character parts).[21] Both women demonstrated a
definite theatrical flair in their promotional photos; Verbitskaia's characteristic shots in profile or with deliberately undone hair suggest affinities
with theater posters, as if the author is playing an actress playing the role
of willful heroine.[22]

Whatever their dramatic or fashionable expertise, women writers
(again, popular women writers especially) were acutely conscious of
their commercial value and specific appeal because they had entered a
capitalist market that insistently addressed women as both consumable
and consumer: "It was above all to women that the new commerce
made its appeal, urging and inviting them to procure its luxurious benefits and purchase sexually attractive images for themselves" (Bowlby 11).
Cheesecake ads directed at a heterosexual male audience still abounded,
but in many cases women were being invited to consume themselves.
The press enjoined female buyers to sample a wide variety of gender-

FIG 13.7. Mariia Krestovskaia
(1901 article).

specific wares—special women's magazines and calendars, shoes, hats, undergarments, cosmetics, lotions, elixirs.[23] The female form recurred in these ads as a commodity marker, still a guarantee of enticement (women would want to look like *that*), but also of identification.[24] Although the evidence remains oblique, it seems that Russian women were signaling their distinctive importance as buyers and readers. As never before in Russian culture, the market accorded them power of representation and satisfaction of their desires.

The Woman in the Text

As other scholars have already surmised, perhaps the most successful satisfiers of women's desires were popular women writers. Brooks identifies Verbitskaia as the virtual creator of the Russian "woman's novel" and attributes her immense popularity to her novels' "success stories and guidebook culture, revolutionary trappings and fleshy individualism, romantic interludes and morbid melodrama" as well as her heroines' "combination of emancipation and submission" (158–59, 160). In a somewhat more positive vein, Engelstein claims that works by writers such as

FIG 13.8. Zinaida
Gippius (1901 article).

Verbitskaia and Evdokiia Nagrodskaia (author of the famous *Wrath of Dionysus*) "provided ordinary women with the stuff of dreams" (400). Focusing on the paradigm of Verbitskaia's six-volume magnum opus, *The Keys to Happiness* (Kliuchi schast'ia), she appreciates the special attractions such female-authored "boulevard fiction" held for women: a vicarious indulgence in adventure and luxury, accessible instruction in world culture and fashion, and, above all, the imagining of their own artistic success and sexual prowess.[25]

Popular women writers had borrowed a page from their publishers' strategy book: They cleverly spiked the traditional intelligentsia writer-

FIG 13.9. Anastasiia
Verbitskaia (1901
article)

reader relationship—the notions of the fictional text as life guide and
valued autobiographical testimony—with visual and commercial allure.
Readers were enticed not only to study and emulate the life plot of the
heroine, but to look and dress and consume in her image. Reading about
the trials and triumphs of the dancer Mania El'tsova (the heroine of
Verbitskaia's *Keys to Happiness*) or the pampered Georgian Princess Nina
(Charskaia's protagonist in her juvenile bestseller *Princess Dzhavakha*)
connected female readers with the tangible satisfactions of the market
and encouraged their own self-regard and cultivation, the more so since
both heroines were highly sensible of the blandishments of fine dress and
decor and well aware of their own attractiveness.[26] Texts such as these
served as both mirrors and catalogues (or department stores, according to
Engelstein and others). By consuming them, women tried on compelling (but returnable) self-images and browsed in a dream world of material possibilities that validated their real-world importance as both
consumers and commodities.

For the most part, readers discovered this visual and commercial
allure in the text itself, yet women writers and their publishers also re-

Fig 13.10. Ol'ga Shapir (1901 article).

sorted to outright illustration. The same photograph that "critically introduced" a writer to her readers on the pages of the press was sometimes recycled as an advertising ploy. In such instances, the visual marker effected a complex sort of identification, stamping the writer's work with her "stage" personality and physical appeal and even implying the body of the writer as her work's embodiment. The dreamy 1901 portrait of Shchepkina-Kupernik later resurfaced as an advertisement for her *Tales of Love* (Skazaniia o liubvi); the composed image of the writer thereby materialized her written product.[27] A photo of Charskaia looking like an adult version of her imperious princesses regularly topped page-long promotions of her work and implied a kind of real-life mentoring: Her proud expression and forthright gaze physically exhorted her young readers to identify with her, to copy her behavior, and to join her remarkable band by purchasing her books (fig. 13.12). Although Russian writers never went to the same marketing extremes as their Western counterparts, generating a line of products based on their works (umbrellas, aprons, shoe polish, etc.), their newly commodi-

FIG 13.11. Valentina
Dmitrieva (1901
article).

fied icon did come to function as combined brand name and personal
guarantee.[28] Their connection of icon and product represented an interesting variation on celebrity product endorsement, for in their case
both icon and product were authored (or largely authored) by the same
person. In place of a Lillie Langtry demonstrating the efficacy of milk
baths or an Elizabeth Taylor hawking her "special line" of perfumes,
Russian consumers were treated to a Charskaia endorsing a possible life
story, her own real-life role model.[29]

To secure reader loyalty, then, it seemed most important that the
writer explicitly vouch for this connection, that she claim both image
and story as "true." Such an endorsement in part would reenact that
comfortingly familiar contract between intelligentsia writers and readers:
The reader could rely on the author's validated authority. Interestingly
enough, it also would answer the expectations of "romance readers," a
good portion of the audience presumably attracted to the Russian
"woman's novel." From what we know of this reading relationship (and
admittedly this is based on studies of late-twentieth-century American
audiences), romance consumers "willingly acknowledge that what they
enjoy most about romance reading is the opportunity to project them-

FIG 13.12. The portrait of Lidiia Charskaia featured in ads for her books.

selves into the story, to become the heroine" (Radway 66); they hope to find the same kind of idealized image incarnated in the person of the author.[30] Perhaps on account of the material bias of the text, romance readers seem to be even more literal than highbrow readers in their demand for physical and material correspondence.

Whatever their reading of their audience, some popular women writers chose to make this endorsement and prove this correspondence through autobiography. Both Verbitskaia's two-volume memoir (*To My Reader* and *My Reminiscences*) and Charskaia's autobiographical tetralogy (*For What?* [1909], *Big John* [1910], *All Life Through* [1911], *Mission Accomplished* [1911]) carefully underscore the similarities between the authors and their heroines.[31] Significantly, both feature family and self-portraits to reinforce visually their readers' sense of identification and emulation. And, to a certain extent, both texts supersede the authors' fictions as an uplifting life guide. Charskaia's autobiography documents a real woman's success and power beyond the age of her famous adolescent heroines. Verbitskaia's texts even redress the ambiguous impressions left by her protagonists, who cannot reconcile professional and personal fulfillment. As Engelstein astutely concludes: "even though the fictional characters failed to achieve fame and femininity at the same time, to be women in public, their authors emphatically did manage to do so. The story of her own life, which Verbitskaia retailed to an eager public, as well as the manifest evidence of her own commercial success, testified to the possibility of enacting that very contradiction" (414).

Compared with the autobiographical narratives of male highbrow writers, these texts sound a more urgent and emotional note, in part because they were written for a sensation-seeking market, but also because they were intent on wooing a female audience with new images and life paradigms. Both writers' double-barreled pitch of autobiography and fiction, icon and product, proved to be right on target; grateful readers quickly elevated Verbitskaia and Charskaia from author to role model. Charskaia, for instance, served as an intimate confidante for the thousands of girls who devoured her books, plied her with gifts, and begged for advice. The ever-ambitious Verbitskaia set up her own publishing house and "specialized in translations of foreign novels about the plight of women" (Brooks 158). She also encouraged her Russian sisters to follow her professional example. The preface of *To My Reader* explicitly addresses her "kindred spirits" (*edinomyshlenniki*):

> And I hope that my simply and sincerely written *Memoirs* will give heart and self-assurance to all my young unknown comrades, who are perhaps even now penning their first literary efforts and are depressed by failure and suffering from spiritual isolation, but—like Bedouins in the night desert—are praying faithfully to the magical star of Art, which leads us mortals into a world of inextinguishable Light and unfading Beauty.

Throughout the nineteenth century, Russian highbrow writers engaged their readers with special prefaces, exhortations, and calls for reform, but they were quite exclusive about sharing any speaking roles. By inviting her readers to follow in her footsteps, to costar in the role of Artist, Verbitskaia articulated a very different perspective on authorship, related more to popular fiction and a kind of feminist activism. She eulogized her writing as spiritual vocation and social mission (she aspired, after all, to intelligentsia status), but she also conveyed it as financial livelihood, self-realization, and an expression of sexual politics. Again, her call to readers intriguingly prefigures the relationship between romance writers and readers in late-twentieth-century America, in which established authors willingly coach readers to "find their own voice" and produce their own money-making novels.[32] Verbitskaia's ad hoc efforts are the more striking, given the dearth of mentoring and networking for Russian women writers in this period.

★   ★   ★

Verbitskaia's invitation spells out an extreme consequence of the gendered icon, whereby the woman writer opts to reproduce other writers in her image and the icon can be cloned *ad infinitum*. Thus, the icon not only represents but *becomes* the flesh. This process might have taken prodigious root in Russia (as it has in other consumer cultures) had the revolution not scattered all these images and opportunities to the winds.[33] Nevertheless, for the lifespan of the market, gendering the icon reflected and effected astonishing changes in the Russian cultural landscape. The new materializing and juxtaposition of male and female images—a Pushkin and a Tat'iana, a Belyi and a Gippius, a Tolstoi and a Verbitskaia—exemplified the expansion, diversification, and manipulated integration of Russian literature; the shifting arbitration of quality and taste; the ever more influential value of the market; even the privileging and generalizing of women's modes of representation and self-representation (however conventionally derived) for all cultural celebrities. As women writers rapidly gained in visibility and popularity, their joining of image with persona, and, eventually, public role model, generated new ways of writing, reading, and being an author that especially involved and enfranchised women.

Just as important, all of these icons placed women on the public stage, and while their poses included the conventionally feminine (we have only to recall those dreamy schoolgirl portraits), none prescribed the rigorously domesticated woman of Western societies. The newly imaged woman of capitalist Russian culture might appear as conspicuous consumer, brilliant performer, tragic lover, or a woman oppressed by husband, family, and inadequate world, but she was never idealized and housebound as happy wife and homemaker. Consumer culture in fin-de-siècle Russia tended to promote spectacle over domestication, individual indulgence over family values. Therefore, despite the undeniable dangers the market posed for Russian women, its repression in the new Soviet Union was ultimately more chastening than liberating in effect. The fin-de-siècle shop windows were stripped of their stylishly dressed models; the new government displays dusted off the old icon of the writer in its puritanical, male-dominated forms. Forbidden sex, style, and material props, women writers could do little but de-gender their image or vacate the stage altogether.

Notes

I thank Helena Goscilo for her comments on earlier versions of this essay, and Mark Sidell for photographing the illustrations.

1. For a representative sampling of this scholarship, see Fox and Lears's anthology, *The Culture of Consumption;* Bowlby's *Just Looking;* Miller's *The Bon Marche;* and Wicke's *Advertising Fictions.*

2. Wicke explicitly criticizes this quickness to judgment, noting scholars' tendency to disdain advertising "as a sinister cultural production with no connection to what seem to be more positive or more transgressive cultural practices—whether evaluated from the left or right end of the spectrum" (11).

3. The other "types" illustrated in this edition are Goncharov's Vera and Turgenev's Liza and Matrena.

4. See Louise McReynolds's article in this volume on the growing importance of the middlebrow in this period.

5. See Rubin's *The Making of Middlebrow Culture* for an interesting discussion of this phenomenon on the American cultural scene.

6. McReynolds notes that *Peterburgskaia gazeta* paid "more attention to personalities than political issues": "Correspondents surveyed public leaders in politics, the arts, and science to bring personal opinions, both trivial and profound, to readers. Topics covered in these questionnaires included 'The Worst Day in My Life,' which gave readers familiarity with the private lives of such celebrities as Miliukov, Gorky, and dancer Isadora Duncan" (245–46).

7. Pl. Krasnov's "Kogda i gde chitat' nashikh poetov" appears in *Izvestiia,* April–May 1901, 81–85.

8. Viktor Rusakov, "Biblioteka v rabochem kabinete intelligentnogo cheloveka," *Izvestiia,* December 1898, 47–52 (48).

9. See Gray, Bowlt, and Slonim for useful coverage of these movements.

10. In *The Commodity Culture of Victorian England,* Thomas Richards demonstrates how the patent medicine industry fattened on a "new, microscopic form of commodity culture: the spectacle of the consumer's body" (169).

11. In her fascinating study of beauty standards in the U.S., Lois Banner notes that in Western cultures women have been defined as more beautiful than men since the Renaissance (10). Analyzing Victorian medical discourse on women, Sally Shuttleworth concludes that "[f]rom the late eighteenth century onward, we find that the traditional, rather undefined associations between woman and the body are strengthened, particularized and codified in medical science" (53).

12. Viktor Rusakov, "Mozg Turgeneva," *Izvestiia,* February 1900, 73–74; L. Mavrov, "Glaza russkikh pisatelei," *Izvestiia,* January 1905, 6–11. McReynolds points out that *Petersburgskaia gazetta* also featured photos of celebrities' handwriting and eyes (247). The periodical *Sinii zhurnal* offers a more playful variant on this theme by depicting the eyes "of our most popular female artists" and bidding readers to guess their names (18 [1914]: 14).

13. A special reading of the portrait may be reinforced by its placement. I have seen this photo reproduced in Verbitskaia's autobiography and also as part of a review of her novel *The Keys to Happiness* in *Izvestiia,* July 1909, 171–74; in

the latter instance, Verbitskaia's image cleverly suggests the proud dreamer-heroine in her work. I am grateful to Nancy Condee for articulating this notion of "narrativizing."

14. In his book on portraiture, Richard Brilliant claims that "[t]his type of voluntary association took on an additional importance in the nineteenth century, when 'to be an artist' carried with it a belief in the assumption of a special vocation with an attendant behavior pattern, which effected at least the partial separation of artists, as a self-defining elite, from the rest of society" (96).

15. "Sovremennye russkie zhenshchiny pisatel'nitsy," *Izvestiia*, August 1901, 111–15.

16. Unfortunately, we in Slavic lack much of the material that informs such studies as Susan Margaret Coultrap-McQuin's *Doing Literary Business: American Women Writers in the Nineteenth Century.*

17. Brilliant also remarks that "any portrait represents some compromise that may be neither understood nor accepted by a third party, a viewer not privy to the intimate psychological exchange between the artist and the person portrayed but whose view often determines the significance of the work, or of the subject" (31).

18. For an informative biography of the great French actress, see Arthur Gold and Robert Fizdale's *The Divine Sarah.* McReynolds describes Bernhardt's triumphal 1881 visit to Russia and discusses the rise of commodity-linked celebrity: "Crowned heads of the new age of consumption, the stars of stage found everything from clothing to confectionery named for them. Dependent upon publicity for fame so widespread that it won them the privileged status of the new age, they developed a symbiotic relationship with the media that introduced them to customers of art, candy, and images" (99).

19. See Banner on postcard portraits in the States. For information on this trend in Russia, cf. McReynolds's essay on the singer Vial'tseva in this volume and Zorkaia 283. Richard Stites remarks on the extension of this practice for film stars: "Russian movie stars were heroes of urban folklore, embodying both the ordinary people who viewed their films and the fantasy they came to see. They earned fabulous sums and were well publicized on placards, photos, screen magazines, postcards, and recordings" (29).

20. Interestingly enough, Richards posits that "[m]uch mid-Victorian advertising was an offshoot of theater advertising" (46).

21. Two other popular women writers deserve mention in this connection: Ol'ga Bebutova, who worked as an actress, and Nadezhda Lappo-Danilevskaia, who had a limited career as an opera singer. For more information about these two, see *Dictionary of Russian Women Writers* 68–69, 363–66.

22. The dramatic hats worn by Verbitskaia and other photo subjects serve as another possible indicator of "theatricality" (Clark 48).

23. S. Ia. Makhonina remarks on the evolution of specialized publications for women and children in the fin-de-siècle Russian press (109). Wicke argues that

in the early twentieth century, all illustrated advertising was presumably ear-marked for women: "Ads became thought of as a sort of minor literature spe-cifically for women, although the fiction persisted that they were easy to entice and that a far 'superior' literature could exist if only men would pay attention" (161).

24. Bowlby offers a slightly different definition: "The model in the window is something both real and other. It offers something more in the form of another altered self, and one potentially obtainable via the payment of a stipu-lated price. But it also, by the same token, constitutes the looker as lacking, as being without 'what it takes'" (34).

25. "This was not only a story that allowed shopgirls to imagine the pleas-ures enjoyed by their social superiors; it was also a tale that allowed women to imagine themselves with the sexual prerogatives of men" (Engelstein 404). For a discussion of the writer Charskaia's attractions for young female readers, see my article "Why Russian Girls Loved Charskaia," in the *Russian Review* 54 (January 1995): 91–106.

26. Princess Nina, for example, loves to wear dashing Caucasian costumes as she gallops through mountain villages. Mania, renowned as a "barefoot" dancer, flits about her husband's estate in a scandalously sheer dress and revels in the body's natural beauty. It is also intriguing that Mania discovers so many of her life dreams and loves in the portraits she sees.

27. We see a similar link of photo and text in the contemporary develop-ment of Russian and Western film. In their fan's eyes, film stars not only acquired a charismatic life story from the roles they enacted, but they also invested each role with the set features of their "star" personality.

28. Wicke identifies Charles Dickens as "the initiator *and* the merchandised product of a new textual confluence between literature and advertising" (53). My list of "umbrellas, aprons, and shoe polish" refers to various products linked with Dickens and imprinted with scenes from his work. In the West, children's fiction especially invited commodification. For a lively, informal discussion of this trend in twentieth-century America, see Bobbie Ann Mason's *The Girl Sleuth*. I should note, however, that enterprising manufacturers and government authorities *did* commodify the images of certain Russian "classic" (and safely dead) authors, producing, for example, bottles in the shape of Pushkin's bust or candy boxes graced with Pushkin's or Gogol's portraits (*Torgovaia reklama i upakovka v Rossii XIX–XX vv.*; Levitt 79). My thanks to Helena Goscilo for the reference to *Torgovaia reklama*.

29. In *Decoding Advertisements*, Judith Williamson provides an excellent analy-sis of the more typical celebrity endorsement (25–28).

30. "This sort of desire to encounter only idealized images is carried over even into meetings with romance authors. Several told of their disappointment at meeting a favorite writer at an autograph session who was neither pretty nor attractively dressed. All agreed, however, that Kathleen Woodiwiss is the ideal

romance author because she is pretty, petite, feminine, and always elegantly turned out" (Radway 98). Janice Radway is the scholar mainly responsible for these studies, and her work is necessarily contemporary, dependent on interviewing a target group of readers.

31. In Russian: Verbitskaia's *Moemu chitateliu* and *Moi vospominaniia* and Charskaia's *Za chto?; Bol' shoi Dzhon; Na vsiu zhizn'*; and *Tsel' dostignuta.* Brooks 156; Holmgren.

32. Radway remarks on the organization of Romance Writers in America in 1981. Trade magazines for romance writers regularly feature how-to articles and workshop advertisements for novices.

33. Indeed, Brooks notes the "unusual" success of such popular women writers as "Bebutova, Verbitskaia, Lappo-Danilevskaia, and, to a lesser degree, Nagrodskaia" by the onset of World War I (160).

Works Cited

Banner, Lois. 1983. *American Beauty*. New York: Alfred A. Knopf.

Bowlby, Rachel. 1985. *Just Looking: Consumer Culture in Dreiser, Gissing & Zola.* London: Methuen.

Bowlt, John. 1982. *The Silver Age: Russian Art of the Early Twentieth Century and the "World of Art."* Newtonville, Mass.: Oriental Research Partners.

Brilliant, Richard. 1991. *Portraiture.* Cambridge, Mass.: Harvard UP.

Brooks, Jeffrey. 1985. *When Russia Learned to Read: Literacy and Popular Literature, 1861–1917.* Princeton, N.J.: Princeton UP.

Charskaia, Lidiia. 1959. *Kniazhna Dzhavakha.* New York: Izdatel'stov Kersha.

Clark, Fiona. 1982. *Hats.* London: B. T. Batsford.

Coultrap-McQuin, Susan Margaret. 1990. *Doing Literary Business: American Women Writers in the Nineteenth Century.* Chapel Hill: U of North Carolina P.

Dictionary of Russian Women Writers. 1994. Edited by Marina Ledkovsky, Charlotte Rosenthal, and Mary Zirin. Westport, Conn.: Greenwood P.

Engelstein, Laura. 1992. *The Keys to Happiness: Sex and the Search for Modernity in Fin de Siècle Russia.* Ithaca, N.Y.: Cornell UP.

Fox, Richard Wightman, and T. J. Jackson Lears, eds. 1983. *The Culture of Consumption: Critical Essays in American History, 1880–1980.* New York: Pantheon.

Gold, Arthur, and Robert Fizdale. 1991. *The Divine Sarah: A Life of Sarah Bernhardt.* New York: Vintage Books.

Gray, Camilla. 1962. *The Russian Experiment in Art, 1863–1922.* Revised and enlarged edition. London: Thames and Hudson.

Holmgren, Beth. 1995. "Why Russian Girls Loved Charskaia." *Russian Review* 54 (January): 91–106.

Levitt, Marcus C. 1989. *Russian Literary Politics and the Pushkin Celebration of 1880.* Ithaca: Cornell UP.

McReynolds, Louise. 1991. *The News under Russia's Old Regime: The Development of a Mass-Circulation Press.* Princeton, N. J.: Princeton UP.

Makhonina, S. Ia. 1991. *Russkaia dorevoliutsionnaia pechat' (1905–1914).* Moscow: Izd. Moskovskogo universiteta.

Mason, Bobbie Ann. 1975. *The Girl Sleuth: A Feminist Guide.* Old Westbury, N.Y.: The Feminist Press.

Miller, Michael Barry. 1981. *The Bon Marche: Bourgeois Culture and the Department Store, 1869–1920.* Princeton, N. J.: Princeton UP.

Radway, Janice A. 1991. *Reading the Romance: Women, Patriarchy and Popular Literature.* Chapel Hill: U of North Carolina P.

Richards, Thomas. 1990. *The Commodity Culture of Victorian England: Advertising and Spectacle, 1851–1914.* Stanford: Stanford UP.

Rubin, Joan Shelley. 1992. *The Making of Middlebrow Culture.* Chapel Hill: U of North Carolina P.

Shuttleworth, Sally. 1990. "Female Circulation: Medical Discourse and Popular Advertising in the Mid-Victorian Era." In *Body/Politics: Women and the Discourses of Science,* ed. Mary Jacobus, Evelyn Fox Keller, and Sally Shuttleworth. New York: Routledge.

Slonim, Marc. 1961. *Russian Theater, from the Empire to the Soviets.* Cleveland: World Publishing Company.

Stites, Richard. 1992. *Russian Popular Culture: Entertainment and Society since 1900.* Cambridge: Cambridge UP.

Torgovaia reklama i upakovka v Rossii XIX–XX vv. 1993. Moscow: Gosudarstvennyi istoricheskii muzei.

Verbitskaia, Anastasiia. 1911. *Moemu chitateliu. Detstvo, gody ucheniia.* Moscow.

———. 1993. *Kliuchi schast'ia: Roman daidzhest.* Vols. I-II. Saint Petersburg: "Severo-zapad."

Wicke, Jennifer. 1988. *Advertising Fictions: Literature, Advertisement and Social Reading.* New York: Columbia UP.

Williamson, Judith. 1978. *Decoding Advertisements: Ideology and Meaning in Advertising.* London: Marion Boyars.

Zorkaia, Neia M. 1976. *Na rubezhe stoletii. U istokov massovogo iskusstva v Rossii 1900–1910 godov.* Moscow: Nauka.

Izvestiia Knizhnykh Magazinov Tovarishchestva M. O. Vol'f.

Sinii zhurnal.

14

DOMESTIC CRAFTS AND CREATIVE

FREEDOM: RUSSIAN WOMEN'S ART

Alison Hilton

"IN THE CLASS OF PAINTING on porcelain, once again women distinguish themselves," wrote Vladimir Stasov in 1889, reviewing an exhibition of work produced by students at St. Petersburg's schools of drawing and applied arts. The eminent critic devoted much of his essay to two important developments: first, the growing attention paid to the applied arts in Russia; and, second, the outstanding success of women in many of the fields represented (Stasov 1889, 42–51). From being marginal figures in the Russian art world, women began to achieve recognition in the last decades of the nineteenth century and enjoyed central roles in early-twentieth-century avant-garde movements. Their change of status owed much to women's activity in the applied arts, work that anticipated a major goal of the revolutionary period: to bring art into daily life.

In nineteenth-century Russia, as in other countries, women were relatively free from the professional rivalries of successful male artists, simply by virtue of not belonging to the upper echelons of the art establishment. Some women artists made up for lack of easy access to prestigious exhibitions and commissions in the favored media of painting and sculpture by exploring opportunities in applied arts. In the 1890s, Mariia Iakunchikova and Elena Polenova developed boldly simplified graphic styles, using elements of Russian folk art as well as European and Far Eastern sources, and two decades later Natal'ia Goncharova made formal innovations based on patterns of textiles and embroidery, media usually associated with women's domestic sphere. The fact that many women artists shared these interests raises questions about the existence of a definable female esthetic in Russian arts (Hilton 1980, 142–45). The notion of a women's art implies practical as well as stylistic concerns. Did some women gravitate toward traditional "women's handwork," embroidery, weaving, and decorative painting, as safe fields, less competitive than painting or sculpture? Alternatively, and more positively, did some artists choose to identify their work with the nonacademic media of applied, folk, and popular arts as a way of maintaining independence?

These questions are not simple. Artists' goals and decisions were influenced by opportunities for professional training, access to certain resources and ideas, and identification with specific cultural values. This essay examines connections between the positive evaluation of applied arts and the involvement of professional women artists with traditional domestic crafts, a distinctive aspect of late-nineteenth-century Russian art that affected the evolution of Russian and international modernism. The first part of the essay focuses on women's artistic education and professional experience in the late nineteenth century, when artistic autonomy was becoming a major issue in the Russian art world. The efforts of women artists in preserving traditional "women's arts," discussed in the second section, were pivotal for the creation of new Russian styles in "high art" at the end of the century. The women artists who managed to achieve the difficult balance between creative integrity and the practical requirements of a career contributed to the more radical (and better-known) Russian avant-garde movements of the early twentieth century—movements characterized by both experimentation in a variety of applied arts media and the prominent role of women artists. In both periods, the artists who searched for new art forms adopted both anti-academic positions and the media and motifs of folk and popular arts. Some may have equated certain forms with specifically female (rather than generally non-establishment or non-elite) cultural experience, although there is little clear evidence because at the time the question was not raised in this way. In the final section of the essay I reconsider these issues from the perspective of some contemporary women artists who deliberately relate exploration of domestic and applied arts to feminist ideas.

Women's Professional Training and Careers

Stasov's review of the applied arts exhibitions offers a starting point for examining not only women's contributions to applied arts but also women's situation within the Russian art world at the turn of the century. Social and institutional as well as artistic factors connected the position of women and the functions of applied arts in Russia. Not only were women artists active in virtually every craft, but many socially concerned upper-class women sponsored training and crafts workshops for peasants, to help them survive economic hardships. Professional artists and codifiers of cultural policies increasingly valued areas of culture often classed as minor.[1] Just as important as the gradual integration of "fine" and "applied arts" was the integration of male and female artists at the most fundamental level, in the studio classroom. This occurred at the very end of the century, as documented by photographs and a large collaborative group portrait by realist painter Il'ia Repin and his pupils (1899, Academy of Arts), showing both men and women working from a nude model (fig. 14.1).

Women first entered studio classrooms in 1842, at the St. Petersburg Drawing School for Auditors (founded in 1840 by the Society for Encouragement of the Arts to help students reach acceptable standards for the academy). The school's separate Women's Section is shown in a painting by a member of its faculty, Ekaterina Khilkova (1855, Russian Museum) (fig. 14.2). Many graduates of the Drawing School, and certainly most women, went on to teach the children of wealthy families such accomplishments as drawing and watercolor painting, or to work in the applied arts, executing designs on porcelain, metal, or other luxury or commercial products. The two major schools of applied arts, the Stroganov School in Moscow and the Stieglitz School in St. Petersburg, also offered training: In the 1840s both opened women's drawing sections to supplement classes in the so-called minor arts—porcelain painting, jewelry making, majolica, lace, furniture, embroidery, and reproductive engraving—and both offered teacher training courses (Moleva and Beliutin 172–75). Khilkova, who studied at the St. Petersburg Drawing School in the 1850s, and later taught drawing, went on to attend classes at the academy. She completed the course in a short four years, and received the title of Artist of the Third Rank—the only rank open to women until the twentieth century. While several women forged successful careers in the "minor arts," it was far more difficult to break into the "high arts": to get proper training, chances to exhibit, or official recognition.

This situation paralleled that in universities and medical schools in the late nineteenth century, although art schools did not have the status of institutions of higher learning. For example, the St. Petersburg Medical-Surgical Academy admitted women student in 1872 and directed them to the midwife training course. Women who wanted to specialize in fields considered more demanding had to study abroad, usually under very difficult conditions. Accounts of women's struggles for education reveal

FIG 14.1. Il'ia Repin and students, *Arranging the Model in Repin's Studio* (1898). St. Petersburg, Academy of Arts.

extraordinary resourcefulness in overcoming obstacles: self-help circles and volunteer teaching to offset most women students' lack of money and often spotty educational backgrounds. Highly motivated female students, perceived as aggressive and radical, inspired both negative and positive characterizations in literature and painting, ranging from the *nigilistki* of Fedor Dostoevskii to the *kursistki* and *progressistki* in paintings by Il'ia Repin, Vladimir Makovskii, and Nikolai Iaroshenko. Iaroshenko's *Kursistka* (1883, Kiev Museum of Russian Art) provoked a volley of attacks in the press about young women who "went against their parents." But it was defended with equal vigor as the embodiment of a new "ideal of self-sufficiency, a new intellectual and spiritual beauty, the prototype of the new woman and the new generation who would bring about far-reaching social changes."[2] In addition to literary descriptions and paintings, some women prominent in the art world helped to create a progressive female image, among them the actress Pelegaia Strepetova and the composer Valentina Serova, who wrote ideological operas based on events from the populist movement of the 1870s and 1880s.

In the visual arts, women received their training mainly as auditors rather than fully matriculated students. Like serfs in earlier generations, they were excluded from examinations and other steps toward official

FIG 14.2. Ekaterina Khilkova, *Interior View of the Women's Section of the St. Petersburg Drawing School for Auditors* (1855). St. Petersburg, Russian Museum.

academic rank and professional careers. The conditions were no worse than in England and France, however. A Government School of Art for Females opened in England in 1859, and a few women were allowed to attend the Royal Academy in the 1860s, but without the chance to study nude models essential to mastery of prestigious classical and historical subjects. In the 1890s, after years of petitioning, English women were allowed to work only from "nudes" who were strategically draped, and mixed classes were nonexistent until 1903. In France, where several professional studios were open to women by the 1830s, nude models were available only at the Academie Julien in the late 1870s. Moreover, according to Marie Bashkirtseff, a Russian artist who spent most of her short life in France, the level of instruction in the women's class was inferior to that for men.[3]

Until 1890, the St. Petersburg Academy stood fast as a bulwark of self-protective tradition. Its authority was challenged in the 1870s by the independent Association for Traveling Art Exhibitions (known as the Peredvizhniki or Itinerants), some of whose members painted the positive images of women mentioned earlier. By the mid-1880s, the group had become so successful that its annual traveling exhibitions were the main venue for artists to show their works and become known to the public. Ironically, this prestige encouraged complacent and conservative attitudes among some of the veteran members. They introduced a strong jury system to control submissions for exhibition by nonmembers and refused full membership to Elena Polenova, Emiliia Shanks, and other qualified young artists, both female and male.

By the end of the decade, the tension between senior Peredvizhniki and young artists was extreme. Polenova, born in 1850, chronologically midway between the two groups, played a central role in discussions about the issues: Like the younger Moscow artists Sergei Ivanov and Avram Arkhipov, she found it impossible to produce "worthwhile" work while waiting in an "agony of suspense" for acceptance or rejection.[4] Some of these artists petitioned for a more equitable system of submitting works for exhibition, but without success. A few proposed forming a "*salon des refusés* or even a separate exhibiting society," but Polenova decided that the idea was premature and would have taken too much time from "creative work."[5] Fortunately, the Moscow Society of Lovers of Art (a group similar to the St. Petersburg Society for encouragement of the Arts, founded in 1858 to hold exhibitions and award cash prizes) alleviated the immediate problem by sponsoring several exhibitions of studies and drawings in the period from 1889 to 1893. Some members of the Peredvizhniki participated, but younger, unestablished artists benefited most, and women were relatively well represented. Exhibitions of these years averaged about seventy to one hundred exponents, of which about ten or fifteen were women.[6] The growing visibility of women coincided with the younger generation's growing disenchantment with the Peredvizhniki. Increased efforts to create more varied and liberal exhibiting opportunities resulted in new groups such as the World of Art, the Moscow Association of Artists, the 36 Artists, and the Union of Russian Artists, which in turn paved the way for the burgeoning of avant-garde groups in the next decade. The critical issues of self-determination and artistic freedom, on both practical and idealistic levels, appeared with special clarity to Polenova. She recognized the potential strength in adversity; because artists of her generation would never have the "collective security" of the Peredvizhniki, they would have to develop independence: "We have left the well-beaten path. Conscience does not allow us to pretend that we believe in the way pointed out by our predecessors, but a new way has not yet been found, and much energy and time must be spent in seeking it. We grope in all directions. . . . This is difficult . . . but we shouldn't complain, for it's the truest, if the most burdensome, way to search."[7]

Repin was one of few senior members of the Peredvizhniki who supported women artists and unestablished artists in general (Hilton 1988, 677–98). When he began teaching at the academy in 1894, he welcomed women students, and the proportion of women to men in his classes, as seen in the group portrait, was greater than that in other studios or even in the exhibitions mentions earlier. On the eve of his retirement from the academy in 1907, Repin compiled a list of the "outstanding female artists associated with the academy." His valedictory speech began with the statement, "In recent years, women artist have begun to prove their right to count themselves artists in the professional sense."[8] Repin's attentiveness to female students was not entirely professional: He fell in love with several of them, flaunting his artistic impulsiveness. But his infatuations sometimes gave way to more serious intellectual discourse: His correspondence with former students, such as Tat'iana Tolstaia, Mariamna Verevkina, and Elizaveta Zvantseva, was not merely flirtatious but covered a range of aesthetic and moral questions.

Zvantseva played an important role in increasing women's access to art training. After leaving Repin to study in Paris in 1895, she returned to Moscow four years later to establish an independent art school. Another artist, Anna Khotiaintseva, was largely responsible for the curriculum, while Zvantseva ran the school, in Moscow until 1906 and then in St. Petersburg until 1916. Zvantseva hired as teachers some of the best artists of her own generation, among them Valentin Serov, Konstantin Korovin, and an outstanding group of younger artists, Konstantin Somov, Mstislav Dobuzhinskii, Lev Bakst, and Kuz'ma Petrov-Vodkin. Among the school's graduates was Ol'ga Rozanova, who studied there in 1912 and 1913, and then immediately plunged into the avant-garde maelstrom of Cubo-Futurist paintings and manifestos. Zvantseva's commitment to training for women made her schools the first in Russia at which men and women worked together from nude models.

The best-known artists among Repin's former pupils did not follow his stylistic or thematic interests, but acknowledged his help in achieving independence and finding their own artistic directions. Among them were the graphic artist Anna Ostroumova-Lebedeva, known for her brilliantly composed etchings and color woodcuts of urban vistas, and Zinaida Serebriakova, whose monumental paintings of peasants show her affinity for High Renaissance mural art.[9] These two artists were among the first women elected to the rank of Academician. In the nineteenth century, the highest designation given women was Artist of the Third Rank (awarded to Khilkova), but the academy finally in 1916 voted to break this precedent, and award the title of Academician to four women. Ironically, the session of the academic council at which the awards were to be made was canceled when the February Revolution broke out.

Preserving Traditional Crafts and Exploring Decorative Forms

Notwithstanding increased access to art education at the end of the century, women were still encouraged to study suitable "minor arts" such as embroidery, weaving, and porcelain painting, much as female medical students were channeled into the midwifery course. Such direction arose from patronizing attitudes about women and "handwork," and reinforced the notion that art was suitable for women when it was identified with domestic tasks, embellishment of the home, or refined accomplishments. This was certainly the case in France, judging from illustrations, articles, and exhibition reviews in journals such as *L'Art français* and *La Gazette des femmes*.[10] But Stasov's article suggested another consideration. Heralding the "hundreds of young men and women" who emerged from the schools' museums and classrooms to teach in towns and villages throughout Russia, Stasov envisioned the students sharing "their understanding of how fine art can serve in ordinary, daily life" and carrying everywhere they went "those little sparks of artistic thirst and inspiration, love and amazement at all that is talented and beautiful." These young artists, Stasov added, would show the public the best that Europe and Asia had created, but above all, "love and admiration for the 'minor,' practical, everyday arts at the ancient roots of our Russia" (Stasov 1889, 43). This equation of "minor" arts with Russian tradition was all the more emphatic because Stasov was known as the champion of "nationalist" arts: He had promoted the "mighty handful" composers and the Peredvizhniki, and had published an important study of Russian folk ornament (*Russkii narodnyi ornament*) in 1872. Moreover, as the brother of Nadezhda Stasova, a leader of the Russian feminist movement, he was alert to the accomplishments of women in all spheres.

The high level of support for the applied arts (serious criticism as well as substantial commissions from court and upper classes) gave impetus to women who might otherwise have had no training in the arts, and the applied arts schools opened doors to more ambitious careers. In the 1880s, Anna Golubkina, a granddaughter of serfs, and virtually uneducated until the age of twenty-five, moved to Moscow to learn the skill of painting on porcelain. She went on to study painting and sculpture, in Moscow and at the St. Petersburg Academy, and then traveled to Paris in 1895. She met Auguste Rodin during a second trip in 1897, and studied informally with him. In Russia she became known for a strongly textural, impressionistic approach to sculpting, using facets in wood, clay, or stone to suggest depth, motion, and changing light: she was interested in conveying the character of a subject through material.[11]

Although the applied arts offered careers for many women, an ambivalent attitude about the relative value of crafts and "high" arts persisted in Russia, as in other countries; indeed, the distinction between "high" and "low" (or popular) culture remains an issue today. Even Polenova, known for her central role in the revival of folk arts and crafts, and the integration of decorative and fine arts, expressed reservations about devoting too much of her time to collaborative handcraft projects. Polenova's career touched on many facets of the experience of women artists in Russia.[12] Early in life she evinced the intellectual and moral commitment to become independent and do something for the good of others that motivated many women of her generation. After studying drawing in her teens, and working at a school for peasants founded by her older sister, she volunteered as a nurse in the Turkish-Bulgarian War and studied medicine, hoping to open a hospital for peasants near her childhood home. She met Nadezhda Stasova and began teaching in Stasova's elementary school for poor girls, first drawing and then sewing and tailoring. The teaching experience encouraged her to become a professional artist, and she enrolled in the St. Petersburg School of the Society for Encouragement of the Arts. She moved to Moscow to forge her career independently, and to support herself she began exhibiting and selling her watercolors and ceramic pieces. When a friend worried that she might sacrifice her standing as a pure artist, Polenova responded:

> A reputation isn't what I need now, but money. It's important for me to live on my own, not on someone else's means. Here, in Moscow, I'm not dependent on anyone for anything. Moreover, the buying public likes my work; all but one of fourteen pieces sold. There are circumstances under which the material side of life affects the moral side. That's the case now. Right now I need money because it will make me independent.[13]

Polenova's belief that mastery of a craft was a means to economic independence connects her experience with those of women in philanthropic and self-help circles of the 1870s and 1880s. This conviction inspired her to work with Elizaveta Mamontova and other members of the Abramtsevo circle to preserve and develop local peasant crafts.

Witnessing the impoverishment of peasant life and the decline of rural crafts at first hand, several women from the aristocracy and landowning gentry established schools and workshops for peasant women, most successfully in flax-growing regions, such as Smolensk, Riazan', and Tambov provinces, with strong textile arts traditions.[14] In the mid-1890s, Princess Mariia Tenisheva established a broad array of training schools and workshops on her estate, Talashkino, near Smolensk. Stasov urged organizers of workshops to collect and study antique embroideries and laces and to use authentic examples as models to improve the artistic quality of handwork in addition to helping peasant women to earn money through the sale of their embroideries. The most important collection, that of Princess Natal'ia Shabel'skaia in Moscow, contained thousands of antique ecclesiastical embroideries, traditional women's headdresses, and costumes, and provided models for the embroidery workshop that Shabel'skaia and her daughters operated on their estate. The practice of copying or adapting designs not only from textiles but also from manuscripts and other historical sources was characteristic of many folk art revival projects in the 1880s and 1890s.

Polenova's involvement in the revival of traditional crafts began when she moved to Moscow and her older brother Vasilii Polenov, an artist already established there, introduced her to Savva Mamontov and Elizaveta Mamontova. The Mamontovs regularly invited Polenov, Repin, Viktor Vasnetsov, and other artists to spend summers on their estate Abramtsevo, a short train ride northeast of Moscow. Virtually an art colony, Abramtsevo nurtured two generations of Russian artists, stimulated innovations in painting, sculpture, theatrical decoration, woodworking, ceramics, and other arts, and served as the locus for a major change of emphasis in Russian applied arts—a shift away from copying or adapting historical models of ornament toward the creation of individual styles in various media. Although Elizaveta Mamontova initiated the crafts workshops in the mid-1870s as part of her educational and philanthropic commitment, Polenova was the artistic innovator. Polenova's original aim was to study and preserve folk art, to "harness the still-living creative art of the people, and give it the chance to develop."[15] But by the mid-1890s, Polenova and several younger followers were creating highly stylized designs more aptly described as Russian *art nouveau*.

Mamontova had started a joinery and carpentry workshop in 1876, as part of her elementary school for peasants, in order to give them skills so that they could earn money with crafts during the winter and not have to seek work in the city. Beginning in 1881, Mamontova, Polenova, her brother Vasilii, and his wife, Natal'ia Polenova, visited villages in the

Moscow district and farther afield, made notes, drawings, and photographs of architectural details, and collected all kinds of objects, ranging from carved lintels of gates to distaffs, saltcellars, and spoons; in 1885 they set up a small museum of folk arts as part of the craft workshop. Polenova guided the workshop students in making furniture based on authentic designs, in order to establish a "valid artistic direction" for applied arts.[16]

Mamontova and Polenova wanted to teach crafts to children in the village school, joinery for the boys and needlework for the girls. The region was known for its textile industry, in which Mamontova's family was prominent; Polenova and Mamontova collected samples of textile arts and used them as models in teaching the girls weaving of homespun linen, sewing, and embroidery. They had to abandon the classes after a year because they could not find trained teachers to help, but their attempt to revive women's traditional arts would later inspire more substantial projects.

The Abramtsevo workshops' most successful activity was the production of furniture and other wooden goods. While Polenova devised models and supervised the pupils in executing the pieces, Mamontova took responsibility for establishing a sound economic basis for the enterprise. She began advertising items form the "Carpentry Studio of Abramtsevo Village" in 1886 and four years later opened a "Shop of Russian Handwork" in Moscow.[17] The furniture had the value of "novelty, originality, and style," Polenova said, although a growing fashion for "Abramtsevo style" objects sometimes resulted in technically poor work.[18]

A more serious issue was the departure from "authenticity" in some designs. Polenova was thoroughly familiar with regional styles of architectural carving and household objects. Her records were accurate, and her earliest shelves and saltcellers were direct copies of the authentic folk pieces she had collected. But over the years Polenova began to combine motifs from several sources that, she believed, conveyed similar feelings for nature. Contradicting her initial decision to use only works of "living" folk art models, she subjected folk designs to her own more inclusive understanding of the principles of ornamentation.[19] When Stasov raised the question of authenticity, Polenova replied that all her designs for the workshop and for her illustrations of fairy tales were "taken directly from the soil," based on objects she had collected in villages and monasteries.[20] Her work, unlike commercial reproductions of antiques, did not duplicate what had already been made; rather, it was meant to continue the natural evolution of folk art.

Polenova's mission to keep a feeling for ornament active and fertile in both Russian art and daily life extended in a new direction, in illustrations of fairy tales. She reread stories familiar from her childhood and learned local variants of the tales from storytellers in villages near Abramtsevo. She planned a series of watercolors conveying "the Russian people's poetic attitude toward Russian nature . . . to express the connection between the soil and the works that grow up out of the soil."[21] Her first set of watercolors, for "The War of the Mushrooms," combined close-up depictions of woodland plants with images based on icons, *lubki* (popular prints), and embroidery.[22] In later series, she achieved a balance between description and decoration in the composition of each page. Polenova knew German and English children's books, the work of Walter Crane and William Morris. Her later watercolors show the influence of modern graphic art in France, which she saw during visits between 1895 and 1898, and Japanese color woodcuts that she may have seen in France and at an exhibition in St. Petersburg in 1896.[23] Like her contemporaries in Russia and Europe, Polenova absorbed new visual ideas from many sources, and experimented with unconventional techniques and compositions.

Determined to concentrate on her illustrations and paintings, and intensely occupied with the problems of exhibition discussed earlier, Polenova left the Abramtsevo joinery workshop in 1893. She continued to be involved in applied arts in another way, through the new embroidery workshop at Solomenko, Tambov Province, run by Mariia Fedorovna Iakunchikova, a niece of the Mamontovs who was related by marriage to Polenova's close friend, the painter and graphic artist Mariia Vasil'evna Iakunchikova (Salmond 1987, 128–43). Hoping to take Mamontova's idea of training peasant women in needlework beyond the modest scale of the original workshop for village girls, Iakunchikova engaged professional designers to supervise production of articles such as tablecloths and wall hangings based on traditional patterns and, in some cases, on original designs by Polenova and other artists.

Polenova accepted a commission from the Solomenko workshop to design a large *panneau* with a Russian fairy-tale motif for the 1896 All-Russian Exhibition in Nizhnii Novgorod. This exhibition proved to be a catalyst for the emergence of Russian *art nouveau* styles, noted for bold combinations of media and techniques belonging to applied arts and "high arts," but there was still considerable resistance to such experimentation on the part of art authorities. Controversy arose over Mikhail Vrubel"s two large ceramic murals made specifically for the exhibition: Rejected by the "expert commission" as too unconventional in technique for inclusion in the fine arts section, they were finally housed in a separate structure provided by Mamontov. The same official conservatism relegated Polenova's panel to the applied arts pavilion, but the work was striking enough to excite widespread admiration. Depicting the Firebird guarding the tree of golden apples (fig. 14.3), the panel measured twelve by seven feet, a scale unusual for handwork, and was appliquéd and embroidered in brilliant vermilion, yellow, gray-green, and indigo, with heavy, cloisonné-like outlines.[24] Polenova's late, ornamental designs inspired Aleksandr Golovin, Natal'ia Iakovlevna Davydova, and other young artists experimenting with applied art techniques. Abandoning the traditional forms and methods that the embroidery workshops had set out to preserve, these artists expressed their conceptions not only of a "Russian spirit" but of nature, music, and feeling through stylized and increasingly symbolic forms.

At this point it was evident that the relationship between applied arts and fine art had shifted, or even that the definitions of both fields had changed. The process paralleled the mingling of applied arts designs with architecture, painting, and sculpture in international *art nouveau.*[25] Inventive use of folk and applied arts techniques, such as embroidery, ceramic glazing, and pokerwork (also called woodburning), entered the rubric of stylistic experimentation, comparable in some ways to the exploratory role of the sketch in painting. A special exhibition organized by Repin with Polenova's help in 1896 was devoted to "sketches and creative experiments," and featured works by many younger artists in Polenova's circle, including decorative panels combining oil and pokerwork by Mariia V. Iakunchikova (Hilton 1988, 691, 694).

Iakunchikova, who lived in Paris for much of the decade, was conversant with the varied manifestations of Post-Impressionism and Symbolism, while remaining in close communication with Polenova. Her art exemplified the emergence of a Russian *style modèrne* in an international milieu. Concentrating first on landscape painting, she emphasized contrasts of scale, and juxtapositions of natural and architectural or constructed forms (views through windows, between the columns of a veranda, a path along the edge of a reservoir). Like the Symbolists, she was drawn to transitory states of nature and subjective moods, but she avoided the "foggy, strange, and melancholy" inner visions evoked by much of the Symbolist art she saw in France.[26] Instead, she shared Polenova's predilection for firm contour lines that both defined subjects and created expressive, decorative rhythms on the canvas or paper. Under Polenova's influence, she began to study Russian folk art in 1887; in 1894 she organized an exhibition of applied art by women artists in

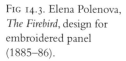

Fig 14.3. Elena Polenova,
The Firebird, design for
embroidered panel
(1885–86).

Paris; she designed large appliqué wall-hangings to be executed at
Solomenko for the Paris World's Fair of 1890.[27] Some of her graphic
works echoed designs of the appliqué work, with boldly simplified, flat
colored surfaces and stylized foliage motifs; like Polenova's second group
of fairy-tale illustrations, they also incorporated features of Japanese
woodblock prints.

Despite the short span of their careers—Polenova died in 1898 and
Iakunchikova in 1902—both artists had created a great range and variety
of works and were on the threshold of new styles. Posthumous evaluation of their works was equally varied, emphasizing both their roles in
the revival and development of Russian applied arts and their more pro-
phetic formal innovations. Stasov admired Polenova's early illustrations
for "War of the Mushrooms" and interpreted her work at Abramtsevo as
a continuation of his own generation's nationalist movements in architecture, painting, decorative arts, and music. But he was dismayed by the
growing stylization and "decadence" that he saw in her later work, for
which he blamed Iakunchikova and the even more cosmopolitan Sergei

Diaghilev and the World of Art group.[28] The leaders of the World of Art group, however, considered themselves modern, but not non-Russian. When Diaghilev and his friends began publishing the journal *World of Art* (Mir iskusstva, 1898), they included substantial sections on the Abramtsevo workshops and other craft enterprises. The beginning of each issue carried a statement of purpose emphasizing "the development of modern Russian Art in its purely aesthetic manifestations, as well as in its applications to applied art." Polenova was obviously an ideal choice to personify these qualities; she was interested in plans for the journal and agreed to give Diaghilev several ornamental designs for the first issue. After she died in 1898, Diaghilev gained the support of her family and friends, including Iakunchikova, to organize a special posthumous exhibition of her work and to publish a long article on Polenova in the journal. Iakunchikova also participated in the World of Art, designed several vignettes for the journal, and exhibited seven pieces in applied arts techniques (Kiselev 105). She accepted a commission to design a cover in 1899 (fig. 14.4), basing the work on one of her earlier pokerwork panels showing swans in a wood-fringed lake, but emphasizing the contrast between the strong, angular outlines of the trees and the sinuous but tense curves of the swan. This was one of Iakunchikova's most complex works, combining graphic design with decoration and a strong element of symbolism. The World of Art group and other young artists valued Polenova and Iakunchikova for their ability to integrate differing visual idioms or approaches to the creation of form, to bridge the barriers that had compartmentalized and restricted applied and fine arts. When Polenova stressed the need to "get rid of conventional prejudices and earlier standards" in order to understand new styles in painting,[29] she anticipated a goal that would motivate many artists in the following century.

During the period in which Polenova and her colleagues were bringing about a major change of outlook on the role of applied arts, other projects helped to bring applied arts and traditional techniques of women's handwork into the broader spheres of fine arts and an international art world. The last prerevolutionary private enterprise, Princess Tenisheva's arts and crafts workshops at her estate Talashkino, chronologically overlapped with several state-sponsored projects to study and preserve traditional crafts. Though largely conservative and nationalist, these projects laid the ground for the more experimental free state schools and workshops established in the early Communist years.

Tenisheva made her estate near Smolensk into an educational center and art colony.[30] In 1894 she hired Repin to direct her studio in St.

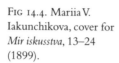

Fig 14.4. Mariia V. Iakunchikova, cover for *Mir iskusstva*, 13–24 (1899).

Petersburg as a preparatory school for young artists; she later established a drawing school in Smolensk, intended, like the Stroganov and Stieglitz schools, to improve the artistic level of applied arts. Because Smolensk was in a linen-producing area, she opened an embroidery studio in the city, giving training and employment to two thousand peasant women (Suprun 176–78). Talashkino housed a woodworking shop, a ceramics studio, and an embroidery and textile workshop. Like Mamontova, Tenisheva opened a sales outlet in Moscow. She founded a Museum of Russian Antiquities and Folk Art at Talashkino, and in 1905 built a museum in Smolensk to house a collection of nearly ten thousand pieces. She participated, along with members of the Abramtsevo and Solomenko workshops, in the Paris Exposition Universelle of 1900. During the political upheavals of 1905, Tenisheva closed Talashkino and moved to Paris, taking part of the collection. She exhibited a selection of historical and contemporary Russian arts at the Musée des Arts Decoratifs in 1907: This was one of the first steps in awakening international interest in Russian decorative arts (Suprun 150–53). Like Abramtsevo, Talashkino emphasized the collaboration of academy-trained artists and peasant artisans, and aimed for a unity of artistic and practical goals. The combined efforts of Polenova, Mamontova, and Tenisheva affirmed the conventional association of women with the applied arts in new and positive ways.

The Avant-Garde: Handwork and Abstract Form

The crucial change of direction—from preserving traditional forms to exploring and promoting applied arts techniques as part of a new creative vocabulary—opened the way for artists of the next generation to relate technical and aesthetic aspects of folk and applied arts to abstract concepts, new principles of form, or, in Ol'ga Rozanova's words, "new bases of artistic creation" (Rozanova 102). The most lasting achievements of the avant-garde stemmed form the artists' ability to apply these principles both to easel painting and to art in a more inclusive sense—designs for plays, films, and pageants, typography and posters, revolutionary "propaganda" porcelain, textiles, and clothing design—ultimately, to the task of restructuring the environment of daily life.

Turning to the well-known women artists of Russia's avant-garde, Natal'ia Goncharova, Ol'ga Rozanova, Aleksandra Ekster, Nadezhda Udal'tsova, Liubov' Popova, and Varara Stepanova, we can briefly examine aspects of their work connected with the idea of integrating art and real life, specifically that of women. Goncharova's work maintained ties with the national elements of folk art revival. Stimulated by Russian icons, folk and popular art, and modern French painting, Goncharova and her Neoprimitivist colleagues used these sources as starting points in a search for new formal systems. According to Kazimir Malevich, he and Goncharova not only were interested in the visual qualities of folk art, but felt a strong "social concern" for peasants (Gray 134). Having grown up on an estate in central Russia near a linen factory established by one of her ancestors, Goncharova enjoyed the rhythms of the repeated tasks of harvesting and preparing flax, spinning, weaving, and washing the linen, and sought to communicate them in paintings such as *Bleaching Linen* (1910, Russian Museum) (fig. 14.5) and *Grain Harvest* (1910, Russian Museum). She did not have to look far for stylistic sources, although she appreciated their value after studying at the Moscow School of Painting, Sculpture, and Architecture, meeting Mikhail Larionov, and becoming involved with modernist experimentation. By the time the main tendencies within the avant-garde had taken shape, Goncharova was ready to reject European-oriented theorizing in favor of a more down-to-earth attention to the elements and structures of art. She expressed almost missionary nationalism in her preface to the catalogue of

FIG 14.5. Natal'ia Goncharova, *Bleaching Linen* (c. 1910). St. Petersburg, Russian Museum.

her first solo exhibition in 1913: "The art of my country is incomparably more profound and important than anything that I know in the West" (Goncharova 55–56). Her examination of both folk art and elements of the urban setting (textile looms, railroad stations) led to increasingly abstract analyses of form. She began a series of decorative paintings based on patterns and textures of women's clothing and accessories, emphasizing varying aspects of line, texture, and color in works such as *Ostrich Feathers and Ribbons* (1912, private collection); she also made dress designs based on folk motifs for the well-known fashion designer Nadezhda Lamanova. Goncharova's interest in textile and clothing, both as media in their own right and as sources for motifs in paintings, was shared by many women artists, including Rozanova, Ekster, and Popova (Hilton 1980, 142–45; Chadwick 245–49). Goncharova's *Laundry* (1912, Tate Gallery) and Rozanova's *Workbox* (1915, Tret'iakov Gallery) (fig. 14.6) suggest the notion of caring for clothing as a metaphor for art. The formal properties of women's materials also intrigued Zinaida Serebriakova: Working in a wholly different, representational style in her *Self-Portrait at the Dressing-table* (1909, Tret'iakov Gallery), she emphasized the visual patterns of pincushions, bottles, lace, and other intimate paraphernalia. All these artists subjected the familiar domestic objects to synthetic interpretations of pattern and design.

FIG 14.6. Ol'ga Rozanova, *Workbox* (1915). Moscow, Tret'iakov Gallery.

In her 1913 essay "The Bases of the New Creation and the Reasons Why It Is Misunderstood," Rozanova defined some of the concepts of abstract art. She emphasized the interaction of the "Intuitive Principle" and the "Abstract Principle—Calculation" in building a work of art. The modern artist, Rozanova thought, must subordinate perceptions of reality to a constructive process based on the principles of dynamism and equilibrium, weight and weightlessness, linear and planar displacement, rhythm and color relations. These principles constituted the "the self-sufficient significance of the New Art" (Rozanova 103, 105, 108).

The connection between the discovery of abstract principles and their use for a variety of practical functions is exemplified in Ekster's work. One of the most authoritative personalities in the Russian avant-garde, she made major contributions in both stage design and abstract painting and theory. In 1918, Ekster taught a course on "Color and Space" and produced an album of gouaches called "Explosion, Movement, Weight," which demonstrate her approach to problems of combining abstract surface patterns with the modulation of color in space. A contemporary

writer, Ivan Aksenov, recognized the connection between this investigation of form and a potential for using "certain motifs [as] the bases of new
forms, of domestic, handicraft art"; he predicted that these studies would
lead to a "high level of pure painting unprecedented in our country"
(Aksenov 63, 69). This new emphasis on the universality of artistic form,
whether attached to "pure" or to applied art, became increasingly important after 1915, with the rise of Suprematism and Constructivism.

One process of deriving abstract forms from the designs of applied art
evolved through Cubo-Futurist collages and collage-like paintings by
Rozanova, Popova, Udal'tsova, and others, in which word fragments
were juxtaposed with commonplace objects belonging to trades and oc-
cupations: barbershops, laundries, seamstresses' work tables, a kitchen
counter, a dining-room sideboard, a knifegrinder's stand.[31] In contrast to
the material concreteness of these works, Malevich, in his Suprematist
work between 1915 and 1919, identified color and form as the primary
elements of all arts and the bases of pure abstraction. During this experimental period, Malevich, Ivan Puni, Rozanova, Udal'tsova, and Popova
designed abstract patterns to be embroidered by the peasant crafts-
women at a workshop in the village of Verbovka near Kiev (organized
by Natal'ia M. Davydova and Evgeniia Pribyl'skaia, it was modeled on
the Solomenko workshops directed by Mariia F. Iakunchikova and
Natal'ia Ia. Davydova two decades earlier). The finished pieces, some
four hundred handbags, scarves, and blotters, were exhibited and sold not
only at craft outlets, but at a special exhibition in the Museum of
Figurative Arts in Moscow in 1919 (Zhadova 33–34). This setting, identifying the works with their abstract, Suprematist style rather than their
handcraft technique, marked a turning point in the definitions of fine
and applied arts. The pieces were not mere novelties, but deliberately
conceived and executed works of art based on full integration of abstract
forms and craft techniques. They were the result of the professional
artists' genuine interest in needlework arts and their design possibilities.
The spirit of collaboration emerged as one legacy of the Abramtsevo,
Solomenko, and Talashkino colonies.

As Aksenov had predicted, after the Revolution, collaborations
between academy-trained artists and those in crafts and industrial arts
continued under the auspices of new art institutions. Soviet porcelain,
probably the most successful project, involved many women in both designing and painting plates with political slogans, images, and even
Suprematist forms.[32] The work of Ekster, Popova, Stepanova, and other
avant-garde leaders in stage and costume design exemplified the direct

connection between the discovery of abstract formal principles and their use in applied arts. Along with Aleksandr Rodchenko, Vladimir Tatlin, and the sculptor Vera Mukhina, Stepanova and Popova used ideas from stage costumes in designing garments for Soviet citizens; they sewed and modeled garments for the "New Way of Life," and published ideas and patterns in popular magazines.[33] In 1922, the director of the First State Textile Print Factory in Moscow invited Stepanova and Popova to join the design staff. Unlike Goncharova and Ekster, whose more fanciful designs often recalled folk motifs, Stepanova and Popova stripped away ornament and exploited simple geometrical forms that could interact with the motions of the body (fig. 14.7). Their textile designs integrated artistic principles and real-life functions, and their appreciation of domestic and commercial requirements was a positive quality of the newly significant field, part of a major cultural change. Formal principles based on new analyses of traditional applied arts were used to create new art forms for the new society.

The Constructivists' program of making concrete, utilitarian forms the basis of a new environment was utopian, but it echoed certain practical goals of the late-nineteenth-century projects in the applied arts. Mamontova and Polenova were motivated primarily by their awareness that peasants and their arts were suffering under the pressures of urbanization. They set up workshops not only to rescue the crafts, but also to give the peasants a livelihood: practical social concerns went hand in hand with aesthetics. On a more sophisticated level, both groups discovered synthetic principles of design and function and built their work on these principles. Just as Polenova tried to preserve an organic link between the "native creative spirit" and the decorative forms she invented, Stepanova and the other Constructivists tried to connect artists' designs with the functions of a given product in the lives of ordinary people. The avant-garde artists' respect for the functional was not just an aspect of "revolutionary conditions," but the historical result of increasing educational opportunities and the attention given to the applied arts at the end of the nineteenth century. The role of women in promoting and practicing the applied arts in both periods was decisive. Equally important was all of the artists' determination to go beyond the mere copying of sources (nature, traditional folk art, or industrial materials) so as to discover the underlying relationships of form to function. Rozanova's concept of the intuitive and the analytical approaches to constructing art extended Polenova's combination of the "creative spirit" with the practical functions of applied arts.

FIG 14.7. Liubov' Popova, textile designs
and dress model (1923–24).

Contemporary Revision of Women's Art

The end of the avant-garde era forced by the Soviet imposition of
Socialist Realism left generations of Russian artists isolated from the
evolution of modernism, the legacy of their teachers' innovations.
Women artists were especially bereft, because the conception of the
avant-garde (as preserved in the West and reintroduced into Russia in
the 1960s) was altered to minimize the aspects of collaboration and
handwork and to promote a more heroic image of the modernist innovator. At the same time, the all-powerful Socialist Realist system prescribed a narrow range of female images (the happy peasant, the
hero-mother) and honored few women with prestigious commissions,
publications, or admission into the Union of Artists. Nevertheless, some
women artists survived and kept working without basic art materials or
financial support.[34]

The so-called thaw under Khrushchev did little to liberate women
artists. Artists who assumed the most visible and risky positions in the
struggle against censorship were men, and their boldest works featured
violence, voyeurism, prostitution, and dislocated female body parts.[35]

Since pornography, like religious and political subjects, was forbidden, it seemed natural and even laudable that nonconformist artists flaunt it. Men and male viewpoints dominated the short-lived exhibitions and the manifestos of the 1960s and 1970s. Few women exhibited. Only Lidiia Masterkova earned an international reputation with bold, austere works welding the abstract forms of icons and Suprematism to the textures of fabric, lace, and thick paint—works that strikingly recalled features of avant-garde art. No one produced figurative art reflecting women's experience or sensibility.

For women artists it was even more difficult than for men to confront social, political, personal, or aesthetic issues. After a discussion about feminist art movements in the West, and in response to my questions about women artists in the unofficial art circles of the late 1970s and early 1980s, a male painter told me blandly: "There are many women artists in the schools and state-run salons, but not in the unofficial groups because that is too risky. Women need to hold secure jobs because they have to take care of their husbands and children."[36] Belying this dismal assessment, women continued to flourish in fields such as textile and clothing design, glassmaking, ceramics, metalwork, and other areas known as "decorative applied arts," areas considered important and given ample material support from the very beginning of the Soviet era.[37]

The situation has changed little. The assumption persists that women alone bear family responsibilities, and few can afford to emulate the nineteenth-century radical "going against her family" to devote herself to political action. In times of crisis, political women struggle not with "women's issues" but with presumably broader, more "universal" problems. In the art world, women's issues are ignored. Although women artists have been gaining exposure abroad since the mid-1980s, the Russian art establishment remains anti-feminist.[38]

In contrast to the West, a sense of female group identification has been lacking in Russia until very recently. The artists now emerging as feminists are working apart from any broadly supportive context. But a few have related their work to the avant-garde legacy in creative new ways. Larisa Zvezdochetova, for example, makes collages of mass-produced rugs and other decorator items, recalling the avant-garde artists' enthusiasm for "women's" materials.[39] Other women take verbal and cerebral concepts, usually assigned to the male sphere, and alter them to create ambiguity. Svetlana Kopystianskaia transcribes texts from the Russian literary canon onto canvas, then crumples and tints them, yielding soft, suggestive forms. Irina Nakhova makes environmental works that draw viewers into flexible, irrational spaces. Elena Elagina and Mariia Serebriakova use found materials (including familiar domestic objects) in cynical pieces questioning gender values. The theme of gender identification motivated exhibitions organized by Olesia Turkina and Viktor Mazin in 1989–91. In "Text-Veiled Art from Leningrad," all the pieces, made by both women and men, were signed with female pseudonyms. Another exhibition, "Femininity and Power," sought to break down stereotypical gender values connected with certain materials, spaces, and forms of presentation. The IdiomA collective in Moscow held exhibitions, sponsored the first Soviet symposium on feminism and culture in 1990, and collaborated with the New York feminist collective Heresies to jointly publish *Heresies—IdiomA* in 1992. These confident first steps promise advances for Russian feminist art, criticism, and research in Russia and abroad.

Russian artists who reject the masculine conformism of much Soviet official and nonofficial art, as well as the blatant commercialism of many Western cultural enterprises in Russia, cannot simply borrow Western feminist art forms and ideas. They must mine their own culture for materials, visual idioms, and new directions. The marginalization and distortion of women's experience and artistic expression were so extreme during much of the Soviet era that attempts to find artistic foremothers may seem tentative or even artificial. But the examples of Polenova, Iakunchikova, Goncharova, Rozanova, and other women artists who strenuously searched for meaningful artistic roots may encourage today's artists to reexamine and revalidate their heritage. Several artists, both women and men, are already exploring a range of subjects and themes related to the social, political, and domestic concerns of women, and are finding ways of using traditional "women's" materials and tools in new contexts that not only question received values but invent forms and concepts. Stimulated by a spirit of revisionism, and aided by the breakdown of the official art establishment, the emerging women's art movement can try to achieve self-determination and creative freedom.

Notes

1. See Suprun (passim) and Hilton 1995, chaps. 15–18, on artists' participation in both private and state-sponsored applied arts projects.

2. G. Uspenskii, "Po povodu odnoi malen'koi kartinki," *Otechestvennye zapiski* 2 (1883): 557–58. See I. S. Zil'bershtein, "Obraz peredovoi russkoi zhenshchiny v maloizvestnykh proizvedeniiakh Repina (1880–e gody)," in *Repin. Khudozhestvennoe nasledstvo* (Moscow, Leningrad, 1948), vol. 1, 170, and Hilton 1978, 108–25, on revolutionary women in Russian art. For background on women's education and radicalism, see Daniel Brower, *Training the Nihilists:*

Education and Radicalism in Tsarist Russia (Ithaca, N.Y.: Cornell UP, 1975), 79–89; Richard Stites, *The Women's Liberation Movement in Russia* (Princeton: Princeton UP, 1978).

3. Linda Nochlin first raised the issue in 1971 of educational and other institutional barriers to women artists (Nochlin 22–39) and examined it further in Harris and Nochlin 50–53.

4. Polenova, letters to S. Ivanov, March 19, 1890, and to M.V. Iakunchikova, June 1890; and S. Ivanov, letter to E. Polenova, December 8, 1891 (Sakharova 1964, 450, 455, 474).

5. Polenova, letters to Ivanov, March 19, 1890; to Iakunchikova, June 1890 (Sakharova 1964, 450, 450–51, 455). The proposal was recorded in the minutes of a meeting of the Peredvizhniki, February 22, 1889 (Tret'iakov Gallery Archive, fond 69, ed. khr. 10, 1. 44). On the debates over access to exhibitions, see M. Astaf'eva, "Iz istorii tovarishchestva peredvizhnykh khudozhestvennykh vystavok," in *Gosudarstvennaia Tret'iakovskaia Galereia. Voprosy russkogo i sovetskogo iskusstva* (Moscow, 1974), 302–40.

6. Indicated in catalogues of the exhibitions, averaging about 300 to 370 oil painting, studies, watercolors, and drawings. *Obshchestvo Liubitelei Khudozhestv. Katalog vystavki etiudov i risunkov russkikh khudozhnikov* (Moscow, 1889, 1891, 1891, 1892). For background on the society see N. Galkina, "Materialy k istorii moskovskogo obshchestva liubitelei khudozhestv," from *Gos. Tret' iakovskaia Galereia: Materialy* (Moscow, 1958), vol. 2, 125–36.

7. Polenova, letter to S. Ivanov, December 15, 1891 (Sakharova 1964, 476).

8. Repin's notes for the speech, and the list of women he ranked as the best students in his classes and at the academy overall, in the Archives of the Academy of Arts, St. Petersburg (A-3, op. 54/II).

9. On these artists see Ostroumova-Lebedeva; Kniazeva; Hilton 1982/83.

10. Garb analyzes these journals in relation to state policies encouraging traditional values (home, family, and patriotism) against the growing challenges of modernist and feminist ideas.

11. Ardentova; Yablonskaya 29–36. Golubkina, like many more highly educated women, worked for social causes, and in 1907 was arrested and imprisoned for distributing illegal documents.

12. On Polenova's life, art, and role in the revival of folk art, see Sakharova 1952; Stasov 1898; Vasilenko 1974, 140–44; Hilton 1983; Salmond 1989, 11–35, 62–79.

13. Polenova, letter to Pelegaia Antipova, May 5, 1887, Sakharova 1964, 382.

14. Among others, S. P. Kaznacheva founded a workshop for drawn-thread work in Riazan' Province in 1878; Princess N. N. Shakhovskaia and Princess S. P. Dolgorukaia opened a school and workshop in the same province in 1880; Princess Urusova set up a spinning and weaving workshop in Smolensk province in 1885, and Princess A. N. Naryshkina founded an embroidery workshop in Tambov Province the same year. On the workshops' role in the Russian craft revival, see Salmond 1989, 50–55; on collections see Vasilenko 1965, 354–56.

15. Polenova, letter to Antipova, April 26, 1885, Sakharova 1964, 362.

16. Suprun 114, citing a statement by Mariia F. Iakunchikova and Aleksandra S. Mamontova (January 6, 1910); Polenova, letters to Stasov (1894), in Sakharova 1952, 17–18, and Sakharova 1964, 513.

17. On the commercial enterprise, see D. Kogan, *Mamontovskii kruzhok* (Moscow, 1970), 164, 168; Suprun 125–32, 136–44; Salmond 1989, 24–30; Vasilenko 1965, 355–56.

18. Polenova, letters to Antipova, March 3, 1886, and to Mamontova, December 15, 1885, Sakharova 1964, 366, 403.

19. Polenova's sketchbooks (V. D. Polenov Museum, Polenovo) illustrate her wide-ranging sources from reference books, journals, museums, and exhibitions as well as nature. See D. V. Polenov, ed., *Muzei-Usad'ba V. D. Polenova. Katalog* (Leningrad, 1964), 151–52, 156–60.

20. Polenova, letter to Stasov, October 1894, Sakharova 1964, 505–508.

21. Polenova, letters to Antipova, October 25, 1886, and to Stasov, April 2, September 30, 1894, Sakharova 1964, 373, 497, 504. Polenova used the collection of fairy tales by A. N. Afanas'ev, *Russkaia detskaia skazka* (Moscow, 1883).

22. Polenova's manuscript with the original watercolors (1886) is in the Museum of Books, Russian State Library, Moscow. This was the only story published in Polenova's lifetime: *Voina gribov. Narodnaia skazka* (Moscow, 1889). Natal'ia Polenova edited a posthumous edition of all Polenova's fairy tales, in three volumes with illustrations in color, *Russkie narodnye skazki i pribautki, pereskazannye dlia detei i illiustrirovannye E. D. Polenovoi* (Moscow, 1906).

23. Polenova, letters to Stasov, 1894 (Sakharova 1952, 20) and May 19, 1897 (Sakharova 1964, 568). Crane's children's books first appeared in 1865; Morris's Kelmscott Press, founded in 1891, attracted the attention of the Abramtsevo artists. The English magazine *Studio* planned an issue with Polenova, but illness kept her from participating. See Sakharova 1964, 780–82. On contacts in France, Polenova's correspondence from summer 1895, Sakharova 1964, 532–35. On the Japanese art exhibition, which included many woodcuts, see G. Iu. Sternin, *Khudozhestvennaia zhizn' Rossii na rubezhe XIX–XX vekov* (Moscow, 1970, 119, 232–33.

24. On the *panneau* design, see Polenova, letter to Stasov, January 29, 1896, Sakharova 1964, 543–44; Salmond 1987, 132–34. Several accounts of the Nizhnii Novgorod exhibition emphasize controversies about media and style, especially the "scandal" over Vrubel's panels *Mikula Selianinovich* and *The Dream Princess*; see Sternin, *Khudozhestvennaia zhizn' Rossii*, 20–23; Sakharova 1964, 550–52.

25. S. Tschudi Madsen, *Art Nouveau* (New York, Toronto, 1967); Dmitrii V. Sarabianov, *Stil' Modern* (Moscow, 1989).

26. Iakunchikova, letters to Polenova, January 11, March 30, May 28, 1893, May 15, 1894, Sakharova 1964, 478, 483, 483, 500. On Iakunchikova, see Kiselev; Yablonskaya 14–20.

27. Iakunchikova, letter to Polenova, December 4, 1894, Sakharova 1964, 512–13.

28. Salmond 1989, 68–70, summarizes the conflict between Stasov and Diaghilev. On the World of Art see Janet Kennedy, *The "Mir iskusstva" Group and Russian Art, 1898–1912* (New York, 1977).

29. Polenova, letter to F. A. Polenova, May 10, 1895, Sakharova 1964, 535.

30. See Zhuravleva; Salmond 1989, 151–83; Tenisheva 125–32, 140–42, 203–205; Bowlt 1973.

31. E. G. Rozanova's *Workbox* (1915), *Hairdresser's* (1915), and *Sideboard with Dishes* (1915), Tret' iakov Gallery; Malevich's *Knife Grinder* (ca. 1913), Yale University Art Gallery; Goncharova's *Laundry* (1912), Tate Gallery; Udal'tsova's *Barbershop* (ca. 1914), location unknown, and *Kitchen* (1915), Ekaterinburg Regional Art Museum.

32. See Lobanov-Rostovsky; Wardropper et al. Among the women porcelain designers were Liubov' Gaush, Alisa Golenkina, Zinaida Kobyletskaia, Elizaveta Rozendorf, and Aleksandra Shchekotikhina-Pototskaia; Natal'ia Dan'ko was famed for "revolutionary" porcelain figurines.

33. See Bowlt 1970; Strizhenova 1972; Strizhenova 1987; Adaskina; Zaletova et al. for essays and reproductions.

34. For the range of Soviet female imagery, see Hilton 1993. On Beatrisa Sandomirskaia, Mariia Syniakova, Efrosiniia Platova, Antonia Sofronova, and Tat'iana Glebova, see Tupitsyn 1983; on Sonfronova see Yablonskaya 174–80 and the Tret'iakov Gallery catalogue *Antonina Sofronova* (Moscow, 1993).

35. Some of the nonconformist artists intended the violated figures to express a universal condition; Dodge 44.

36. I owe this opinion, shared by many women and men, to a conversation with Vladimir Naumets in 1982. A similar sense of futility was expressed by a young woman in 1983. Divorced, with a small child, she remarried a fellow student at the Academy of Art, and then, when he finished, she had to follow him to a job in Kalinin. After five years, she began studying again: "When I started to do well, he got jealous and said that a woman should stay at home and take care of the house." See Hansson and Liden 140–41.

37. The official "All-Union Art Exhibition—USSR, Our Homeland," held in Moscow in 1982, included approximately 20 to 25 percent women artists, a higher number in the categories of theater and cinema design and "decorative-applied arts." Ministry of Culture and Union of Artists of the USSR, *SSSR— Nasha Rodina. Vsesoiuznaia khudozhestvennaia vystavka* (Moscow, 1982).

38. Women artists have been well represented in international loan exhibitions, such as the Barbican Gallery's *100 Years of Russian Art from Private Collections in the USSR* (London, 1989); *The Quest for Self-Expression: Painting in Moscow and Leningrad, 1965–1990* (Columbus, 1990); *Keepers of the Flame: Unofficial Artists of Leningrad* at the University of Southern California (Los Angeles, 1990); and *Between Spring and Summer: Soviet Conceptual Art in the Era of Late Communism* at the Tacoma Art Museum and the Institute of Contemporary Art, Boston (Cambridge, Mass., and London, 1990). Women were also present in the 1988 television film documenting the Sotheby's Auction in Moscow, *USSR-ART.* In contrast, see Eleonora Yakovleva, "Women Artists United," *Soviet*

Life, March 1991, 59–62, on the group "Irida," which advocates humane goals, education, a women's art museum, and international cultural exchange—but no feminist agenda.

39. Zvezdochetova also creates highly stylized environments, as she did at an exhibition in the "L Gallery," Moscow, in 1993. On Zvezdochetova and other female conceptualist artists, see Tupitsyn 1990; Tupitsyn 1991; Boym.

Works Cited

Adaskina, Natal'ia. 1987. "Constructivist Fabrics and Dress Design." *Journal of Decorative and Propaganda Arts*, Summer, 144–59.

Aksenov, Ivan. 1913. "Concerning the Problem of the Present State of Russian Painting" (Moscow). Translated in Bowlt 1976, 60–69.

Ardentova, K.V. 1976. *Anna Golubkina.* Moscow.

Bowlt, John E. 1970. "From Pictures to Textile Prints." *Print Collector's News-letter* 7 (March–April): 16–20.

———. 1973. "Two Russian Maecenases: Savva Mamontov and Princess Tenisheva." *Apollo*, December, 450–53.

———. 1976. *Russian Art of the Avant-Garde: Theory and Criticism, 1902–1924.* New York: Viking.

Boym, Svetlana. 1993. "The Poetics of Banality: Tat'iana Tolstaia, Lana Gogoberidze, and Larisa Zvezdochetova." In Helena Goscilo, ed., *Fruits of Her Plume: Essays on Contemporary Russian Woman's Culture*, 59–83. Armonk, N.Y.: M. E. Sharpe.

Chadwick, Whitney. 1990. *Women, Art, and Society.* London: Thames and Hudson.

Dodge, Norton. 1978. "Conceptual and Pop Art." In Norton Dodge and Alison Hilton, *New Art from the Soviet Union: The Known and the Unknown.* Washington, D.C.: Acropolis.

Garb, Tamar. 1989. " '*L'Art Feminin*' : The Formation of a Critical Category in late Nineteenth-Century France." *Art History*, March. Reprinted in Norma Broude and Mary D. Garrard, eds., *The Expanding Discourse: Feminism and Art History*, 107–29. New York: Harper Collins, 1992.

Goncharova, Natal'ia. 1913. "Predislovie k katalogu vystavki" (Moscow). Translated in Bowlt 55–56.

Gray, Camilla. 1986. *The Russian Experiment in Art, 1863–1922.* London, 1962. Revised ed., New York: Thames and Hudson.

Hansson, Carola, and Karin Liden. 1983. *Moscow Women: Thirteen Interviews.* New York: Pantheon.

Harris, Ann, and Linda Nochlin. 1976. *Women Artists, 1550–1950.* New York: Knopf.

Heresies: A Feminist Publication on Art and Politics—IdiomA: Zhurnal Feministskoi Post-totalitarnoi kritiki. 1992. New York: Heresies Collective.

Hilton, Alison. 1978. "The Revolutionary Theme in Russian Realism." In H. Millon and L. Nochlin, eds., *Art and Architecture in the Service of Politics*, 108–25. Cambridge: MIT Press.

———. 1980. "'Bases of the New Creation': Women Artists and Constructivism." *Arts Magazine*, October, 142–45.

———. 1982/83. "Zinaida Serebriakova." *Woman's Art Journal*, Fall–Winter, 32–35.

———. 1983. "Russian Folk Art and 'High Art' in the Nineteenth Century." In T. Stavrou, ed., *Art and Culture in Nineteenth Century Russia*, 237–54. Bloomington: Indiana UP.

———. 1988. "The Exhibition of Experiments in St. Petersburg and the Independent Sketch." *The Art Bulletin*, December, 677–98.

———. 1993. "Feminism and Gender Values in Soviet Art." In M. Liljeström, E. Mäntysaari, and Arja Rosenholm, eds., *Gender Restructuring in Russian Studies: Slavica Tamperensia II*. Tampere.

———. 1995. *Russian Folk Art*. Bloomington: Indiana UP.

Kiselev, Mikhail. 1979. *Mariia Vasil'evna Iakunchikova 1870–1902* Moscow: Iskusstvo.

Kniazeva, V. P. 1979. *Zinaida Evgen'evna Serebriakova*. Moscow: Iskusstvo.

Lobanov-Rostovsky, Nina. 1990. *Revolutionary Ceramics: Soviet Porcelain, 1917–1927*. New York: Rizzoli.

Moleva, Nina, and E. Beliutin. 1967. *Russkaia khudozhestvennaia shkola vtoroi poloviny XIX–nachala XX veka*. Moscow: Iskusstvo, 1967.

Nochlin, Linda. 1971. "Why Have There Been No Great Women Artists?" *Art News* 69: 22–39, 67–71.

Ostroumova-Lebedeva, Anna P. 1974. *Avtobiograficheskie zapiski*. Edited by G. Priimak. Moscow: Izobrazitel'noe iskusstvo.

Rozanova, Ol'ga. 1913. "The Bases of the New Creation and the Reasons Why It Is Misunderstood" (St. Petersburg). In Bowlt 102–10.

Rybchenkov, Boris, and Aleksandr Chaplin. 1973. *Talashkino*. Moscow: Izobrazitel'noe iskusstvo.

Sakharova, Elena. 1952. *Elena Dmitrievna Polenova, 1850–1898*. Moscow: Iskusstvo.

Sakharova, Elena, ed. 1964. *V. D. Polenov—E. D. Polenova: Khronika sem'i khudozhnikov*. Moscow: Iskusstvo.

Salmond, Wendy. 1987. "The Solomenko Embroidery Workshops." *Journal of Decorative and Propaganda Arts*, Summer, 128–43.

———. "The Modernization of Folk Art in Russia: The Revival of the Kustar Art Industries, 1885–1917." 1989. Dissertation, University of Texas at Austin.

Stasov, Vladimir. 1889. "Vystavki dvukh khudozhestvenno-promyshlennykh shkol." *Khudozhestvennye novosti* 2, no. 7: columns 25–35. Reprinted in V. Stasov, Stat'i i zametki, ne voshedshie v sobrannye sochineniia, Vol. 1, 42–51. Moscow: Iskusstvo, 1952.

————. 1898. "E. D. Polenova." Reprinted in V. Stasov, *Stat'i i zametki, ne voshedshie v sobrannye* sochineniia, vol. 2. 221–68. Moscow: Iskusstvo, 1952.

Strizhenova, Tat'iana. 1972. *Iz istorii sovetskogo kostiuma.* Moscow Sovetskii khudozhnik.

————. 1987. "The Soviet Garment Industry in the 1930s." *Journal of Decorative and Propaganda Arts*, Summer, 160–75.

Suprun, L. 1971. "Professional'nye khudozhniki i narodnoe iskusstvo v Rossii kontsa XIX–nachala XX veka." Dissertation, Research Institute of Artistic Industries, Moscow.

Tenisheva, Mariia K. 1933. *Vpechatleniia moei zhizni.* Paris. Reprint, Moscow: Iskusstvo, 1991.

Tupitsyn, Margarita. 1983. "What Happened to the Art of the 'Russian Amazons.'" In Norton Dodge, ed., *Lydia Masterkova: Striving Upward to the Real.* Mechanicsville, Md.: Cremona Foundation.

————. 1990. "Unveiling Feminism: Women's Art in the Soviet Union." *Arts Magazine*, December, 63–67.

————. 1991. "U-turn of the U-topian." In D. Ross, ed., *Between Spring and Summer: Soviet Conceptual Art in the Era of Late Communism,* 42–47. Cambridge: MIT Press.

Vasilenko, Viktor. 1974. "Narodnoe iskusstvo." In I. Grabar', V. Kemenov, and V. Lazarev, eds., *Istoriia russkogo iskusstva*, vol. 9, book 2, 352–88. Moscow, 1965.

————. 1974. *Narodnoe iskusstvo.* Moscow.

Wardropper, Ian; Karen Kettering; John E. Bowlt; and Alison Hilton. 1992. *News from a Radiant Future: Soviet Porcelain from the Collection of Craig H. And K. A. Tuber.* Chicago: Art Institute of Chicago.

Yablonskaya, Miuda. 1990. *Women Artists of Russia's New Age.* New York: Rizzoli.

Zaletova, Lidiia; Fabio Ciofi degli Atti; and Franco Panzini. 1989. *Revolutionary Costume: Soviet Clothing and Textiles of the 1920s.* New York: Rizzoli.

Zhadova, Larissa. 1982. *Malevich, Suprematism and Revolution in Russian Art, 1910–1930.* London: Thames and Hudson.

Zhuravleva, L. 1974. *Teremok.* Moscow: Moskovskii rabochii.

CONTRIBUTORS

Nadezhda Azhgikhina is an editor at the weekly *Ogonek* who teaches journalism at the Russian State Humanities University (RGGU). She has published widely in Russia on literary, cultural, and social problems, as well as contributed articles on women's issues for the *Women's Review of Books*. As a fellow at the Kennan Institute during 1995, she examined the politico-philosophical framework within which Russian and American mass media have formulated the image of Russian womanhood.

Lina Bernstein is Assistant Professor of Russian at Franklin and Marshall College. Her monograph *Gogol's Last Book: The Architectonics of "Selected Passages from a Correspondence with Friends"* was published in August 1994. Her current research focuses on Elagina's letters.

Nancy Condee is Associate Professor of Slavic Languages and Literatures at the University of Pittsburgh. Her edited volume *Soviet Hieroglyphics: Visual Culture in Late Twentieth-Century Russia* appeared in 1995. Her current work examines the cultural politics of the Khrushchev era.

Darra Goldstein is Associate Professor of Russian at Williams College. Her publications include *Nikolai Zabolotsky, Play for Mortal Stakes, Russian Houses, A Taste of Russia, The Georgian Feast*, and numerous articles on Russian poetry, art, culture, and cuisine. She is currently working on the poetry of Tikhon Churlin and organizing an exhibition of twentieth-century graphic art.

Helena Goscilo chairs the Slavic Department at the University of Pittsburgh. Her most recent publications include *Skirted Issues: The Discreteness and Indiscretions of Russian Women's Prose, Fruits of Her Plume: Essays on Contemporary Russian Women's Culture, Lives in Transit*, and *Dehexing Sex: Russian Womanhood during and after Glasnost*. She is currently completing a monograph on Tatyana Tolstaya and writing a study of Liudmila Petrushevskaia.

Gitta Hammarberg, Associate Professor in the Department of German and Russian at Macalester College, is author of *From the Idyll to the Novel: Karamzin's Sentimentalist Prose*. She is currently working on minor genres and gender in late-eighteenth- and early-nineteenth-century Russia.

Alison Hilton, Associate Professor in the Fine Arts Department at Georgetown University, writes on may aspects of Russian and Soviet art. Her books include *New Art in the Soviet Union: The Known and the Unknown* (with Norton Dodge),

Kazimir Malevich, and *Russian Folk Art.* She is now working on a book devoted to Russian impressionism.

Beth Holmgren, Associate Professor of Slavic Literatures at the University of North Carolina–Chapel Hill, has authored *Women's Works in Stalin's Time: On Lidiia Chukovskaia and Nadezhda Mandelstam,* as well as essays on Russian women's studies and contemporary Russian and Polish literature. Her current research examines the commodification of the writer in fin-de-siècle Poland and Russia.

Mary B. Kelly is Professor of Art at Tompkins Cortland Community College. Her publications on folk art include articles in *Threads, Fiberarts, New York Folklore,* and *Women's Art Journal,* and her monograph *Goddess Embroideries of Eastern Europe.* Kelly's photographs of women folk artists were featured in "The Changeless Carpathians," a spring 1995 exhibit at the Ukrainian Museum in New York.

Louise McReynolds is Associate Professor of History at the University of Hawaii and specializes in the history of popular culture. Her major publications include *The News under Russia's Old Regime: The Development of the Mass-Circulation Press* and the coedited *Popular Urban Culture in Nineteenth-Century Russia: An Anthology.* Her current project is a book-length monograph titled *Russia at Play: Leisure Time Activities and Social Change at the End of the Tsarist Era.*

Nadya L. Peterson is Assistant Professor of Russian Language and Literature at the University of Connecticut. She is the author of articles on Chekhov, Russian women writers, and recent Russian literature: her monograph on the last decades of Soviet literature is slated for publication in 1996. She is currently working on a book dealing with various aspects of postrevolutionary Soviet culture.

Stephanie Sandler, Professor of Women's and Gender Studies and Russian at Amherst College, has authored *Distant Pleasures: Alexander Pushkin and the Writing of Exile* and coedited *Sexuality and the Body in Russian Culture.* She currently is finishing a study titled *Alexander Pushkin: The Myth of a National Poet in Russia.*

Ol'ga Vainshtein teaches theory, culture, gender, and literature at the Russian State Humanities University. She recently spent half a year at the National Center of Scholarly Research in Paris investigating the role of psychology and feminism in contemporary theoretical currents. Her many publications include books on Matthew Arnold and Victorian criticism, as well as on the philosophical style of Novalis and Schlegel, plus articles on postmodernism, American fashion, and Russian and American culture.

INDEX